6G $4.00 N

D1535452

THE ECONOMICS OF
SUCCESS

THE ECONOMICS
OF SUCCESS

LUDWIG ERHARD

Vice-Chancellor and
Minister for Economic Affairs of the
German Federal Republic

D. VAN NOSTRAND COMPANY, INC.

Princeton   New Jersey
Toronto   London
New York

TRANSLATED FROM THE GERMAN BY
J. A. ARENGO-JONES AND D. J. S. THOMSON

© THAMES AND HUDSON LONDON 1963
PRINTED IN GREAT BRITAIN BY
BILLING AND SONS LTD, GUILDFORD AND LONDON

Library
I.U.P.
Indiana, Pa.

338.943 Er39

c. 1

CONTENTS

FOREWORD

This book is published in the English-speaking countries at a time when Atlantic co-operation is facing grave difficulties. It is our task to deal with these difficulties. Publication of my speeches and articles at this moment may perhaps bring home to the reader the fact that German economic policy has, since the end of the war, sought consistently and unswervingly, to establish an ever closer link with the entire free world. The German revival was, to a significant extent, only possible because we formed close political and economic ties in Europe and across the Atlantic, and awareness of this will continue to shape my political thought and actions in the future. We shall not be deterred by anyone or anything from contributing to a wide European unity, and to the strengthening of Europe's transatlantic ties.

In the political, military and economic spheres, three decades have made the world shrink; it is now too small for us to indulge in the luxury of repudiating our alliances and our close co-operation with all the countries of the free Atlantic world, in favour of a narrow and exclusive independence. A prosperous future cannot be built upon a policy of isolation; the need is for active unity and close collaboration.

Freedom is too precious a thing to be jeopardized; and yet the perils are too great and the threats to freedom too powerful for a single people or a small group of peoples to attempt to withstand them alone. As we have begun, so we shall continue.

Bonn, March 1963

I

AT THE TURN OF THE YEAR 1945-46

(Article in *Die Neue Zeitung* of December 31, 1945)

When Hitler's war ended in 1945 it left untold misery in its wake.
Large areas of Europe had been devastated. Many millions of
people had no country they could call their own; millions more
had no roof over their heads. And in the shattered towns and
villages of Germany people eked out a hopeless existence, without
food and without warmth. Ludwig Erhard, who in 1944 had
drafted a memorandum on the rebuilding of Germany for Carl-
Friedrich Goerdeler and his followers of the German resistance
movement, was appointed by the US Military Government to the
post of Minister of Economics in Bavaria. Realizing as he did that
any political consolidation of post-war Germany could only be
achieved on the basis of economic recovery, he addressed the fol-
lowing New Year's message to the German people:

The value of human labour grows with the size of the economic
field to which it is applied. All our efforts must be bent on working
our way out of a state of isolation. Admittedly the very fact that
Germany as a whole is no longer a political entity has enabled the
Länder to acquire independent status, but at the same time we are
only too well aware that this delimitation must on no account
prevent us from striving for a more comprehensive solution,
starting with the economy. I would go further to say that we
must aim to build bridges to the rest of the world and participate
in the benefits of the peaceful exchange of goods between all
peoples.

If we are ever to rebuild our productive capacity, make good
the ravages of war, and above all relieve our people's distress, it
can only be by dint of rationalizing the use of our labour to the
utmost possible extent. And I am afraid there is so far little sign
of this happening.

I do indeed hope that before the end of 1946 we shall have succeeded in putting our at present artificially stabilized currency once more on a sound footing and getting it as far as possible into fixed relationship with foreign exchange. The present high level of employment is unreal and deceptive; from the point of view of the national economy we shall only be in a position to do useful work when the purchasing power represented by our income is honoured in the market by an assured supply of goods.

2

TWO ZONES INTO ONE ECONOMIC UNIT

(Article in *Die Neue Zeitung* of September 23, 1946)

*In Germany people began to debate the country's economic policy
and the future structure of the economy—often with some heat—
as soon as the war was over. Only a small number of long-sighted
politicians, scientists and economists, foremost among them Ludwig Erhard, pleaded from the very start for a free but at the same
time socially committed economic system. Facing them were
socialists of diverse camps, communists, laissez-faire liberals, and
the great mass of unthinking people whose only idea for the future
was how to live as well as they could from one day to the next.
The struggle for the* soziale Marktwirtschaft *(socially committed
free economy, a covenanted as opposed to either a completely un-
fettered economy on the one hand or a steered or planned economy
on the other hand) began as a struggle for men's minds.*

Shortly before the following article appeared in Die Neue Zeitung, *US Secretary of State Byrnes had announced in Stuttgart
that the United States did not intend to discriminate against Germany indefinitely. General Clay ordered the discontinuance of
reparations deliveries to the Soviet Union. General Draper, then
Head of the Economics Division of the US Military Government,
declared that the economic independence of Germany was a necessary precondition for the establishment of German democracy.
The US and British governments resolved to set up bizonal
administrations.*

What everyone with insight saw to be a necessity and consequently worked for unremittingly has now become reality through
the economic fusion of the American and British zones of occupation. Having freed ourselves from the threat of extreme provin-
cialism by overcoming the constricting influence of the all too
narrow *Länder* boundaries, we shall now be able to extend this

3

process beyond the zonal limits and thus make correspondingly better use of our productive potential. The merging of the zones does not entitle us to expect miracles or a cure for all our economic ills, since the prevailing shortage of raw materials and resources of all kinds in the two zones cannot be more than partially alleviated by even the best of organizational measures. The only ultimate solution lies in developing close trade relations with world markets. But still, this form of complementary economy will have an immediate beneficial effect on many industries and will lead to an easing of the supply position. Neither the economic nor the political success of this step need be questioned, even though the advantages of the larger economic area will not be fully felt until better management is made possible by greater over-all efficiency in the use of our industrial capacity, while the present concern for the lame ducks of industry and still more the desire to meet the exigencies of the social situation tend to produce action which is not always wholly sound from the point of view of the economy as a whole.

In view of the still unsettled state of our currency and the consequent lack of strict accountability in the economy as a whole the fact that economic policy should have been dictated by external circumstances may so far have caused but little harm; under the new dispensation, however, maximum efficiency will prove only just sufficient to enable the country's most pressing economic problems to be solved. By increasing the potential capacity of the economy, the zonal merger will at the same time provide a sounder basis for the solution of inescapable monetary and fiscal problems. Nothing that has occurred since the collapse of Germany has been so welcome or so encouraging as the decision on the part of the United States, announced in the Secretary of State's recent speech, to give the German people the chance to shape their country's destiny. This change of attitude is still more striking in the British Zone where the German administrations have been kept on a very tight rein by comparison with the degree of freedom and latitude prevailing for some time past in the American Zone.

The negotiations leading up to the merging of the zones showed quite clearly that the dangers of divergent development resulting from different ways of thinking engendered by separate administrations are real and considerable. It is betraying no secret for instance to point out that, in spite of identity of aims, the German representatives in the American Zone thought predominantly on federalist and those in the British Zone mainly on centralist lines. Opinions were equally divergent on the subject of the basic principles on which the economic structure should be built. Here again it was in the Southern German provinces that opposition to any too rigid and bureaucratic planned economy was strongest. At the same time, the intermediate gradations and shades of opinion holding positions somewhere between the generally accepted notion of a socially responsible economic order and a planned economy in the fullest sense of the term are so numerous as to defy detailed analysis in the present framework. But the very presence of such a problem of differentiation clearly shows how necessary it is for the German economy to acquire a sufficiently unified and purposeful sense of direction to provide even the basis for organizational coalescence.

This attempt to ensure that the federal economy should once more become viable by winning back lost ground was based on economic and social considerations, but has nothing whatever to do with any expansionist, acquisitive aspirations. These, as we know full well, can cause, and have in the past caused, the proper and permanent task of the state—namely to serve the good of its people—to be denied, and the economy to be made merely an instrument for the pursuit of selfish nationalistic aims.

Economic and administrative areas are in many ways closely inter-related and inter-linked, for instance where commercial law, the administrative structure, and policy relating to currency, trade and taxation are concerned; but such functional correlation is by no means so essential that the act of forgoing a definitive political settlement need, or should, prevent us from trying hard in the meantime to solve the economic problem.

If our German economy is to be restored to health and to fit organically into the wider framework of world economy, its structure must first be reorganized and this cannot be achieved satisfactorily as long as the zones are isolated from each other. Thus both for political and for economic reasons it is essential to bring together people and human institutions that belong together, and so may we be permitted to hope that as good a compromise as possible be achieved. As long as we strive for economic unification we shall be reminded of the fact that, whatever our political limitations may be, we neither desire nor are able to evade the responsibility of establishing the closest possible links with the rest of the world. The better the national markets are organized in themselves, and the more closely and frictionlessly they combine for the exchange of goods, the more evident will become the advantages of a flexible economic area over a rigid and politically delimited one. At the same time, to realize this is to understand why the question of a larger German economic area is for us today a matter of life and death.

3

FREE ECONOMY VERSUS PLANNED ECONOMY

(Article in *Die Neue Zeitung* of October 14, 1946)

Local government elections in the Länder *demonstrated the German people's will to live, to turn away from despair, and to shun both nationalism and communism, and this in spite of the fact that food rations still fell short of 1,500 calories a day per head of the population. All attempts at mending matters were frustrated, not only by the prevailing conditions of devastation, exhaustion and disruption, but also by the supposed experts, in and outside Germany, clinging tenaciously to their reliance on controls. The people worked on doggedly, tormented by hunger and exasperated by zonal restrictions, corruption and the black market. The outlines of a new approach emerge in the following article, the title of which at once indicates the dividing line along which the intellectual and political arguments of those days were ranged.*

In the work of threshing out the *Länder* constitutions, discussion of what shape the future economic order should take naturally occupied an important place. I shall attempt in this article to disentangle the specific problems of the moment from the web of polemics and to make a sober assessment of our position by formulating what is common to all the proposals that have so far emerged. It is typical of our present situation that these conflicting views should invariably be pushed to extremes terminating on opposite sides of a supposedly unbridgeable gulf—on one side free economy, on the other planned economy, here socialism, there capitalism—although the economic developments actually taking place should rather make us ask ourselves whether influences are not in fact emanating from both fronts and tending to bridge the gap between conflicting viewpoints. To imagine, for instance, that any free economy must exhibit symptoms of the uninhibited exploitation associated with the early days of capitalism is to mis-

7

understand the dynamism of the advanced economies of today as completely as does the detached individualist for whom any kind of economic planning is tantamount to the life-destroying levelling of a soulless bureaucracy. And the same applies in regard to the concepts of capitalism and socialism. Today it is just as hopelessly biased to think that capitalism means exploitation of the workers as it is to think that socialism means the ruthless denial of the last trace of freedom. If, for example, the main characteristic of a capitalist economy is taken to be merely the capitalist mode of production involving the large-scale investment of capital formed within the national economy, then there is no difference between it and a socialist economy. Conversely, a free economy, which simply because it is free is commonly dubbed 'capitalist', need not preclude full regard for the social needs of the day. And whereas in capitalist countries with a free market economy the accumulation of capital is often violently criticized, the formation and use of capital in socialist countries is often not subjected to such effective public scrutiny and criticism. In other words, catch-phrase criteria are no longer applicable in appraising an economic system, least of all its social aspects. When it is remembered that a capitalist and a socialist economy are equally compelled to make provision for the building up of capital resources, and at the same time it is agreed that this can only be done, whatever the shape of the economic structure may be, by saving and consumer restraint, then it looks very much as if the systems are not so irreconcilable after all.

It is indeed true that a socialist economy cannot do without planning on an extensive scale, but this does not mean that a free economy—or, to be more precise, a market economy—can be written off as aimless or anarchical. The fact is that it uses the highly developed methods of market research so extensively for the systematic recording of economic data and the evaluation of trends, that with this type of economic order there is a very strong and growing tendency to put plans first. In an earlier article I pointed out that between an economy which embraces many plans and a fully planned economy there are any number of possible systems, varying according to the particular kind or degree of influence or guidance brought to bear on the functions of the economy, and that it is therefore wrong and dishonest in this connection to play around with absolutes.

The real contradistinction is not between free and planned economic systems, nor between capitalist and socialist economic systems, but between a market economy with free price-level adjustment on the one hand and an authoritarian economy with state controls extending into the sphere of distribution on the other. In the last analysis it is simply a question of whether the market as the voice of the economic society as a whole or, alternatively, the state or some other collective entity is better able to decide what is conducive to the common good or the well-being of all. It is still a widely held fallacy that the outcome of free competition is to arrest movement and change within the social structure or at least to set up economic strains and stresses. In actual fact, all liberal-minded experts with a sound knowledge of the social organisms are agreed that it is precisely the other way round, that it is the limiting of freedom of movement that throws the economy out of balance and produces crisis after crisis, each more unmanageable than the last. Provided in future the state sees to it that neither social privileges nor artificial monopolies impede the natural process by which economic forces reach and maintain a state of equilibrium, and that the operation of supply and demand is allowed free play, the market will adjust the total input of economic forces so as to create optimum running conditions and to compensate any mistakes made at the controls. Anyone who wishes is welcome to believe that a planning and regulating economic authority might be a better judge of the economic intentions and wishes of society; but just let him try to prove it. What can be said is that in a free market economy mistakes of judgment in the management of affairs automatically produce price changes with all their attendant repercussions, whereas in a state-directed economy there is always the danger that equally serious mistakes can be covered up and left to fester until they ultimately erupt with elemental force. We have had experience in recent years of how easily a state-directed economy can deteriorate, by imperceptible stages, into a travesty of what an economy should be.

Our criticism is thus not directed against the planned economy *per se,* whose manifold forms can be variously interpreted, but

B

most definitely against the state-controlled authoritarian economy, which if carried to its logical conclusion wipes out the market and robs the consumer of all freedom of choice. On the other hand, a collectively managed economy responsive to market reactions is a contradiction in terms and therefore unthinkable; disregard for the wishes of the consumer as reflected in market reactions is bound to destroy freedom of action and stems from the fallacy that human happiness can be secured by maximum satisfaction of statistically measurable needs. So, even assuming that the authority wielding economic control had no other motive than to serve the good of the community—and this not even the socialist state guarantees—it is still open to doubt whether the people as a whole would prefer any form of collective economy to the free market economy.

As things are today, the state must provide the economy with the principles and broad lines of a policy and with objectives designed to guide and regulate its functioning. In this respect the state indisputably has and should have the initiative. But to go further and reduce the independent businessman to the status of a mere puppet or servant of the authority's will would be to destroy all the values derived from personality and to rob the economy of its most precious source of inspiration and strength. Now, if ever, is the time to realize that the economy is not opposed to social progress but, on the contrary, treats it as a yardstick. All steps capable of contributing to a fair distribution of the national product, and with it of the national income, deserve our most careful consideration. But then we have the chance to do this through the very act of honouring the obligations arising from our country's distress, if only we put actuality before dogma.

I am convinced that the tasks of today call for the full participation of the individual. We shall be doing our country a real and lasting service if we establish an economic order which is purged of the theorizing and bureaucratic spirit that everyone hates and which enables people to act freely in response to a sense of their social responsibilities.

4

CONFUSION OF TONGUES ON THE QUESTION OF THE ECONOMIC ORDER

(Article in *Die Neue Zeitung* of June 23, 1947)

On June 5, 1947, the US Secretary of State, George Marshall, outlined his far-reaching plan for aid to stricken Europe and its vanquished peoples, and for European co-operation. While controversy was still raging behind the scenes in Germany as well as in Allied circles, Ludwig Erhard—then Honorary Professor in the Department of Political Science of Munich University—threw himself into the general discussion of what had to be done and of what could be done towards reconstruction and recovery.

The purpose of all economic activity is to meet consumer needs and thus to contribute to the well-being of the community. Since this purpose is inalienable and independent of passing phenomena and theories, it is only the means and methods to be used to this end that should really be discussed. Yet it is extremely difficult today to conduct a sober discussion of any one specific problem. The reason for this is that the political parties insist on making acceptance or rejection of particular economic systems a matter of policy, even of dogma. Another reason is that a low standard of living tends to magnify the importance of economic as compared with all other considerations both social and political.

Any attempt to lift the discussion of economic affairs out of the turmoil of party strife comes up against the blind credulity with which large bodies of the electorate or significant social groups cling to political beliefs put out by individual prophets as if they were immutable and absolute truths, making it utterly impossible for them to appreciate the complexity of most economic and sociological problems. It is widely held, for instance, that anyone who has socialist leanings must be in favour of a planned economy, and anyone in favour of the market economy must be a capitalist at heart—a completely mistaken view. Another mistake is to try to bring moral judgments to bear. Or, again, to identify any totalitarian system, whether fascist or bolshevist, with a planned economy in order to disparage planning *per se*. Equally, opponents of capitalism ought not to use the admitted faults of this system as an excuse for condemning the market economy. From the point of view of economic development, fascism and bolshevism on the one hand and capitalism on the other are in reality merely historically delimited phases in the fluctuating development of the two basic or generic types of economy, namely the planned economy and the market economy.

The present author, who has never made any secret of his liberal outlook, is at any rate very far removed from the slightest intention of supporting one-sided capitalist interests, and is indeed far rather inclined to charge capitalism with progressively betraying the basic principles of the market economy, namely competition and price freedom, and becoming itself *dirigiste* by assuming one collectivist attribute after another. Looking back, it was surely a tragic aberration on the part of the socialists to deprecate competition, thereby playing into the hands of the cartels and other economic monsters, instead of realizing that competition was the very giant-killer they were looking for. It is sheer economic muddle-headedness to go on imagining, as people now commonly do, that capitalism can be fought by obstinately trying to arrest competition, for if they succeed they would paralyze the mainspring of the market economy.

If the idea behind this form of attack is by any chance the marxist idea of 'expropriating the expropriators', to compel strongholds of private power to give way to strongholds of public or state power and to set up a centralized, in place of a ramified and more or less privately controlled, type of planned economy, then it is indeed time to point out to those who think on these lines that in any decently run state there are, after all, limits to the power of private institutions, and that, furthermore, the various group interests tend to counterbalance each other, whereas the power of the state must of necessity be absolute, so that (as indeed history proves) the danger of arbitrary and wrongful use of power is then immeasurably increased.

May I therefore say to non-doctrinaire socialists, who are prepared to draw lessons from experience, that the accepted tenets of
socialism do not tie them down in this way. Liberal socialism, for
example, is unequivocally in favour of the free market economy
and of freedom of action for the individual and recognizes in
legalistic and artificial monopolies the real evils of capitalism. It
is not the market as an institution, but the misuse of power, invariably preceded by suppression of the free market, that is responsible for robbing the economy of its capacity to respond to the will
of the public, so that it goes further and further downhill and
finishes up by clamouring for one piece of planning after another.

What we are up against here is a plain case of confusing cause
and effect, with disastrous results. The social strains and stresses
generated by capitalism in the early stages were concomitants of a
technological revolution and of misinterpreting the so-called liberal
freedoms, and not effects of the market economy principle as such.
What posterity will blame us for is that the state was so rooted in
class prejudice that it failed to apply the force of law to deal with
the evils that had grown up. Yet the functioning of the market
economy did not become vitiated—one has but to remember the
delicate and finely poised mechanism of the world economy in
those days—until the capitalist system itself began to break the
rules and to assume more and more of the attributes of a planned
economy by allowing the individual to be replaced by collective
agencies or entities in the performance of economic functions. One
is surely entitled to speak of a Babel of voices, a confusion of
tongues, when in certain quarters capitalism in its most advanced
and orthodox form is condemned because by eliminating competition it has become in effect a planned system, while elsewhere
people attack it because they regard the market economy itself as
a bad thing and merely want a different kind of planned economy.
Economic mismanagement and malfunctioning cannot be ruled
out by replacing a privately controlled planned economy by one
operated by the state or any other collective agency. It is not
between the thinking of the advocates of a planned economy as
against that of the advocates of a collectivist version of it that
the gulf is fixed, for, however much they may differ in their social
and economic aims and ideals, they are at one in believing in the

complete accountability of all economic phenomena; no, the real cleavage is between reliance on planning of any kind and belief in the truly free market economy kept in rein by the rule of law, or in other words between collectivist and individualist-libertarian modes of thinking and living.

The preconditions for the successful application of the planning principle simply do not exist in the world as it is, however much one may delude oneself into imagining that they could be artificially established by some systematic authoritarian limitation of man's freedom of action in the decisive areas of economic life and by instituting some form of regimentation. In modern times planned intervention has invariably upset the economy. The planners are in a logically weak but tactically strong position. Except for the fact that a disrupted fiscal system makes a free market economy unworkable without overt inflation, it has to be admitted that the transition from a market economy to a planned economy is easily effected whereas the converse process is immensely difficult. This is because it is easy to act freely, and therefore foolishly as well as wisely, on the basis of an economy having an inherent tendency to maintain itself in a state of equilibrium, but difficult to restore at one stroke the workings of a free market in an economy that has been thrown out of a naturally balanced state. The great opportunity that will undoubtedly accrue to us in the foreseeable future as a result of the currency reform will be of regaining, through this operation on the living organism of our economy, the ability to decide, freely and in full awareness of what we are doing, which road we shall take.

And there is one other point to bear in mind: at a time of dire stringency it is not possible to say anything conclusive about the quality and workability of a planned economy. When the consumer will accept anything and everything the market has to offer there is no risk of off-target production, and there is nothing to prevent the planners from cherishing the illusion that they are on the right lines. But if the planned economy is to be accepted as the pattern of the future, it must stand the test under very different conditions, that is to say when the producer has to work hard to sell and cannot rely on coercing the consumer. Its inferiority to the market economy will then be shown up clearly enough. Here again the confusion of tongues is reflected in the attitudes of the political parties, although there is in fact no point on which it is more important that there should be clarity and full understanding of the implications. The advocates of economic planning elevate it to the status of a dogma yet remain unaware of the inconsistency involved in going on to promise that it can provide full scope for freedom of action and initiative. Others again put the accent on these very freedoms yet feel obliged to make a half-hearted semi-confession of belief in a planned economy. Of course all the parties would like to see the economy so constituted that it was no danger to peace at home or abroad, yet they apparently do not realize that the strains and stresses involved in getting collective economies to deal with national economies can be far greater than those engendered when individuals everywhere are allowed to conduct international trade; and in my opinion they will make a better job of it, by looking after their own interests in their own limited spheres without regard for the balance of trade and payments between the countries.

It is not a case of deciding between socialism and capitalism, both of which have undergone change under the stress of social and economic development. And, above all, there is no kind of correspondence between the two commonly 'bracketed' pairs of concepts: socialism and capitalism on the one hand, and planned economy and market economy on the other. If it is true that socialists work for fair distribution of the social product, then it is equally true that supporters of the market economy can whole-heartedly subscribe to the same aim, since this is implicit in the principle of order to which they are committed. When capitalism misguidedly calls for still more privately controlled collective agencies, determined liberal opposition is certain to be aroused. Modern liberalism does not seek freedom to exploit, but combats intolerance and the denial of freedom in any sphere of life. True liberalism fights the dragooning of the spirit—begetter of every political tyranny—wherever it may appear.

5

DETERMINANTS OF THE GERMAN LIVING STANDARD

(Article in *Die Neue Zeitung* of December 1, 1947)

A people cannot consume more than its entire economy can produce in the shape of goods and services. Not money, but the volume of goods and services are the yard-stick by which its standard of living is measured. The Germans, like other peoples whose currency was destroyed by the war, had this fact driven home to them in no uncertain manner. They learned that there was no miracle cure, that nothing but hard work could produce the goods needed to meet human and national needs and to keep the machinery of production running. At the time Ludwig Erhard wrote the following article, the supplying of the German population with the bare necessities of life was on the point of breaking down, in spite of the great efforts made by the Allies to help.

In the violent controversy over dismantling, which now lies behind us, people concentrated their attention on the political aspects to such an extent that they tended to overlook the inescapable fact that a nation's living standard depends strictly on its economic performance. The plain fact is that both the incurable optimists, with their faith in concealed inflation, and the inveterate pessimists, with baseless prognostications, were equally blind to the realities of Germany's economic plight. Now, it is not the purpose of the present article to assess to what extent Germany's economic future is likely to be encumbered by measures such as the dismantling of plant or benefited by the part of loans and other forms of assistance. However important it may be to give these matters their due weight in calculations relating to the national economy, the fact must never be lost sight of that the factors which are going to decide the standard of living of the German people in the future are factors shaped and determined from within the country. In essence, Germany's economic future depends on the best possible disposition of the factors relating to production. Only if this task is tackled with vigour and foresight can we create the atmosphere in which the world will be prepared to give German pleas a fair hearing and to provide such help as may be needed.

True, the loss of financial standing due to the chaotic state of our currency prevented us from providing statistical or budgetary proof of any contention relating to the country's external burdens or even to most of its non-economic burdens. In any case it has now become abundantly clear, in view of the diminished social product and the rapidly shrinking working capacity, that our economy is no longer able to meet the people's day-to-day needs, let alone to do anything towards reconstruction and still less to fulfil any external commitments, until such time as the whole of our remaining production capacity can be used to better effect.

It remains for us to look into the reasons for the lack of any upswing in productivity. As long as claims on the social product earned by honest work are repeatedly elbowed out by established non-productive purchasing power, and as long as, in the absence of a genuine building up of capital, a large proportion of the work still being done is directed to ends outside the production of consumer goods, there is no hope of the worsening deficiency being compensated by the tightening of existing controls. It may be that enforced austerity has meanwhile enabled some economically valuable jobs to be done, but on the other hand it must be remembered that there are limits to both the willingness and the capacity of working people to make sacrifices.

No artificial measures for arousing the economy from its present state of torpor can succeed, unless it can be set in motion on a steadily growing scale or at least effectively safeguarded against internal wastage. The flow of goods can only be restarted provided an increasing social product ensures material rewards for work done, and provided the use of real capital does not carry the risk of material wastage. In view of the fact that as things are the loss through wear and tear of producer and consumer goods exceeds the power of the economy to replace them, which creates a threat of exhaustion, the ban on clearing transactions (*Compensationsverbot*) will not have the effect expected of it.

Much as one may regret the reactions of individuals to prevailing economic conditions, and however much one appeals to people's sense of responsibility, the fact remains—and it is no good shutting one's eyes to it—that this approach will never get the economy to do more than just drag along. All the experts are agreed of course that a currency clean-up is the only real solution, but meanwhile, more food and an adequate supply of raw materials would work wonders in present circumstances. In conditions of constriction and shrinkage, bad instincts and negative influences abound and the downward trend gathers way until complete paralysis sets in; conversely, any increase in the supply of goods and in total working power would be effective in raising output to an appreciable extent.

It may indeed be argued that diminution of the social product is invariably accompanied by growth of public administration, more bureaucratic methods and greater inefficiency, while conversely, any stimulation of the economy leads automatically to less and simpler administration and lends more weight to what the authorities do. If only the German people were given more opportunity to do productive work, that is to say work that produces goods, the immediate result would prove that the German national economy is perfectly capable of higher output and even of producing surplus yields. Attempts in any other direction are a waste of time, and lack of perception cannot be covered up by the search for scapegoats. From whatever angle one looks at the present-day economy, one finds in fact practically nothing but elements which impede or obstruct productivity: unused capacity in workshops and businesses which for social reasons ought to be utilized as fully as possible, raw materials in short supply being worked up into the highest priced goods so as to get as much as possible out of the manufacturing process for private interests, uneconomic employment of highly skilled work for unproductive purposes, and complete lack of co-ordination between the various sectors of the national economy; all these things are typical of an economy in which prices have broken loose from costs and costs are no longer a measure of performance.

No people can consume more than the economy provides in the shape of consumable goods, and it is only insofar as the supply of such goods is sufficient for the needs not only of those directly engaged in their production but also of those engaged in the production of capital goods, in reconstruction and in the work of distribution and administration, that these activities can be taken into account and recognized with due regard for their size, the prevailing economic trends, and the aims of economic policy. However, considerations of this kind also reveal that generalized experience and the lessons of history are of very little help where the need is for an economy which can only fulfil its social task even passably well provided working efficiency is pushed to the highest possible level—a level at which it is able to offset the additional burdens imposed by the continuing necessity to improve the capital position, by contributions to the reconstruction programme, and by the pressing demands of the social services.

In the immediate future what will be needed is to carve up the work of the national economy in such a way as to limit temporarily or to spread over a longer period of time the capital investment still regarded as essential, so that the available resources can be more fully devoted to the production of consumer goods. The maintenance of the social order will largely depend, particularly in conjunction with a currency reform, on ensuring that the income—which in spite of all demands on it is still available—is backed as soon as possible by a commensurate supply of goods. In trying to reach a settlement between the rival claims—economic and national on the one hand and social on the other—to strike a balance between future economic gain and immediate alleviation of distress, priority must of course, within reason, be given to the social needs of the present.

Even if everything goes well, it will be as much as Germany can possibly do to ensure that her people as a whole attain a living standard in any way related to the efforts demanded of them. Our population structure with its great preponderance of female labour and disproportionately high percentage of old people and people unfit for work, the loss of material resources through the war coupled with our present undeniable technological backwardness, the urge to rebuild our cities, and the burden of reparations all combine to put our national economy at so serious a disadvantage as compared with other national economies that we can only compete by dint of sacrifices in the matter of our living standard. Only by achieving the most rational combination of all production factors through maximum competitive effort can the German people hope to survive in the struggle for existence and to have any real chance of economic and social recovery.

6

THE ROAD TO THE FUTURE

(Speech at the 14th plenary session of the Economic Council
in Frankfurt-am-Main on April 21, 1948)

*The year 1948 had opened with attempts by the Western Powers
to bring order into the German chaos and to meet the increasing
Sovietization of the Eastern Zone by promoting democratic life in
the Western Zones. The Six-Power Conference in London from
February 23 to March 6, 1948, envisaged the amalgamation of the
three Western Zones, in spite of protests from the East, and the
eventual formation of an all-German Federal Government. On
February 27 the Communist* coup d'état *in Prague administered
a rude shock to those who were still under the illusion that a combination of communist-totalitarian and liberal forms of government was feasible. On April 1 the Russians began the blockade of
Berlin, which for a full year subjected the population of Germany,
and in particular of West Berlin, who were determined to live in
freedom, as well as the Western Powers to a very severe test.*

*The Marshall Plan marked the beginning of a new epoch in
international relations on both sides of the Atlantic. On April 3,
President Truman put his signature to the Bill for the European
Reconstruction Programme. Between April 10 and 17 the Charter
of European Economic Co-operation was signed in Paris by delegates of the 16 ERP countries and representatives of the three
Western Zones of Germany. In the Western Zones themselves the
revival of economic life after the war had been a slow process. By
the beginning of 1948 industrial production was only 40% of the
1936 level and was furthermore confined to certain sectors of basic
industry. The flow of goods, meagre as it was, went largely into
stockpiling; a mere trickle reached the normal markets. Due
mainly to the irresponsible wartime methods of finance, there was
a fantastic abundance of money which made it impossible even to
attempt to introduce a reasonable monetary and financial policy.*

21

By imposing economic controls together with a price and wage freeze, some semblance of order could be maintained, though with difficulty, but all attempts to stop inflation were futile, and the economy had reverted to the primitive state of trade by barter.

It was in this apparently hopeless situation that Ludwig Erhard was appointed Director of the Bizonal Economic Administration. Following his appointment he submitted his economic programme, which embodied his conception of an economic policy based on freedom and responsibility:

The desire of this distinguished assembly for the formulation of an economic programme is one that I comply with all the more readily as it comes at what, in my view, is a decisive moment for our nation and our economy, when entirely new avenues of development are opening up before us and when the Economic Council will soon be faced with such vital and far-reaching decisions, that only a clearly-defined and forward-looking economic policy can offer any real prospect of success.

Ever since the collapse of Germany our frequent hopes of making a fresh start in our social and economic life have come to nothing, yet they have never been so justified as they are at present, when on sober and realistic reflection we can feel confident that, given the salutary effect of the carefully calculated currency reform on our economy, the help made available through the Marshall Plan will enable us to increase the buoyancy of our economy.

Today, and for some time to come, Germany's economic policy will clearly be influenced by two important factors, the currency reform and the implementation of the Marshall Plan. In spite of the tragic division of Germany's economy into zones, and in spite of the lamentable sociological and political effects of such a division, I use the phrase 'German economic policy', because we can surely administer the Economic Bizone as the heart and core of a German economy. We can, therefore, look upon ourselves as trustees for the German people, if we are prepared to devote all our energies to building up an economy, even within the limits imposed on us, which, in close co-operation with the rest of the world and, indeed, by virtue of that co-operation, will be in a position to pursue its real and ultimate aim of promoting the welfare of a peace-loving people.

But I also employ the phase 'German economic policy' because I would like to correct the fairly widespread and complacent impression that the limitations on our freedom of action in certain spheres relieve us of all responsibility for our own future. The opposite is the case, for the more obstacles we encounter in our struggle to build secure foundations for our national life, the greater must be our efforts, the more courage and power of conviction we must muster, the more insight and experience we must gain, if we are to create an atmosphere of unshakable confidence in the clarity of our aims and the genuineness of our will to achieve what will merit the description of a German economic policy.

When I accepted this post, I realized that in our position neither normal experience nor administrative routine would be enough to master the problems facing us, but that we must acquire from practical experience and technical knowledge a deeper insight into the highly complex social and economic implications, if, in the far-reaching structural changes that are taking place, we are to bring order and purpose into events that seem to be unconnected and arbitrary, perhaps even chaotic.

The material decline of our industry and the social distress arising from it are so obvious that it would be pious self-deception to regard the slight improvements in production since 1945 as marking the beginning of a genuine recovery. By deliberately concentrating our energies on specific sectors we have developed certain basic industries and reduced bottlenecks, but by working on one side of our national economy the imbalance in the economic structure has become more and more apparent and disturbing. However sensible it may appear to be from a purely rational viewpoint to start our reconstruction programme by restoring and building up the production of capital goods, in order to gain the maximum yield from human labour, this policy is also quite unrealistic, if it regards human labour—or more exactly the working man—as merely one of the factors of production, which can be completely neglected in any long-term planning.

We are, however, increasingly in danger of falling into this error and it is high time, in my view, that we altered course and planned an expansion of our consumer goods production, in order to stimulate our human labour force to greater efforts. Supplying our working population with consumer goods and adequate foodstuffs is, in our present situation, merely a form of productive investment; for this reason I felt it was justifiable to look upon credits for the importation of foodstuffs not as consumer- but as producer-credits. When we have reached the point where, for example, 90% of the 1936 employment figure is producing only 40% of the 1936 output figure; when, in short, almost the entire labour force at our disposal is producing only a fraction of normal output, then the national economy will benefit much more from an increase in the productivity of labour than from a one-sided improvement in capital production. From a sober commercial viewpoint alone this is clearly the more economic and, I would even go so far as to say, the cheaper way.

How much greater and more urgent is our commitment, however, when we remember that our national economy cannot be looked upon as a soulless mechanism but that it revolves round living people with highly individual wishes and ideas and that, precisely because our needs are so great, we would inevitably invite the most serious social and political repercussions if we continued to overlook the fact that the ultimate aim of economic planning must be consumption. So, while I am anxious not to go to the opposite extreme and am aware that our recovery would be seriously retarded if our production of capital goods were not maintained, it is nevertheless essential that we make a radical change in our order of priorities in order to regain a natural equilibrium with all the organic benefits it will bring.

There are also sound monetary reasons why we should rethink our economic policy, because up to the currency reform the formation or renewal of capital, especially where liquid capital is mobilized from the past, implies a considerable degree of expropriation of all nominal incomes from current production; for, in view of the limited economic resources at our disposal and of a taxation policy that makes it impossible to form new capital, any capital expenditure involves an invisible but inevitable loss of consumption. If this process were to continue, it would have disastrous

Library
I.U.P.
Indiana, Pa.

338.943 Er39
c. 1

social and moral consequences and private industry might well be accused of acquiring an unfair share of the nation's wealth, even although no individual could be faulted or blamed. But this policy is also untenable as far as the national economy is concerned, because today, in the absence of any visible and reliable barometer of the soundness of an investment and its future value to the nation's economy, such a policy leads nowhere and will all too easily arouse the suspicion that the search for new capital is not based on economic considerations but merely reflects a deliberate move to amass capital goods. The important thing is that you cannot expect a nation which is going through hard times, which is spiritually on the brink of despair and which has suffered disappointment after disappointment, to go on working without some return, to go on earning nominal wages without any real value, and politically we cannot afford to expect any such thing. But also with an eye to the future and in particular to the period after the currency reform, it would be foolish and short-sighted to leave the replanning of our industrial production until such time as it is unmistakably apparent that private supplies of liquid capital for investment purposes are not available for a transition period. I shall have more to say about that later.

For all the reasons I have given I would like to be sure that I have your support in pursuing the general aims I have outlined in what is, after all, a crucial question of industrial policy; more particularly as I realize that not merely economic but also social considerations compel us to pursue this course. The strong position of the Rhine and Ruhr industry in the more limited sphere of the combined zones must not lead us into overrating their industrial sectors and giving an increasingly one-sided bias to these branches of heavy industry. They carry sufficient weight in themselves to be able to maintain their position in the economy, but to give them preferential treatment at the expense of our finished and manufactured goods would be contrary to our finest German tradition; it would allow that very German quality to degenerate which gave German finished products their reputation for good taste and quality in peacetime international trade and made them so much sought after throughout the civilized world, and on which, in the long term, our future export markets will undoubtedly depend. If

c

my policy is approved I will also be asked, and rightly so, whether the stimulus I propose to give to the consumer goods industry will eventually lead to an appreciable increase in supplies and whether, at the same time, provision can be made for fair over-all distribution, which will rule out the evil of compensation and the abuses of hoarding. It is impossible to answer this without taking into consideration our monetary situation and the conditions arising from it. It would be quite wrong to paint a too rosy picture and to create the unrealistic impression that the present economic controls can guarantee a smooth flow of goods from the raw material to the finished product, from the first stage of production to the ultimate consumer; but, in my view, it would be equally wrong to blame everything on any omissions or defects in these controls, and it would also be extremely unwise to look round for guilty persons or groups. Not that I am saying there are no faults, no people who act irresponsibly—such handicaps do undoubtedly exist, but they do not go to the heart of the matter. This is not where the real root of the evil lies. We must, in fact, recognize that a price-control inflation can have just as damaging repercussions as open inflation; indeed it can, in many respects, be even more serious, because it obscures causes and effects, and because the connections are not apparent to the mass of the people. To the working man it makes no difference whether, due to inflationary price levels, his purchasing power is insufficient to enable him to buy what he wants or whether he has sufficient purchasing power but finds that the national product is quite inadequate to meet the demand. It is almost a miracle, and it certainly points to a high degree of discipline amongst the people, that economic restrictions and price controls should have kept our economic structure together and have preserved order for so long. But to expect a faultless economic machine and an equitable distribution system to emerge from this would presuppose that we are dealing not with human beings but with gods and angels.

These observations of mine are not intended as ready-made excuses for failure; but if you bear in mind that, as a result of our chaotic currency conditions, our economy has been deprived of any standards of value and comparison, that in every purchase and sales transaction we are operating with quite unpredictable monetary values and are living in a world of fiction, if you bear in mind what it means to have to reduce a highly-developed, modern monetary system to the level of primitive barter, then what we really need is not scapegoats but—and the need is urgent—the restoration of sound monetary conditions.

I regard it as my bounden duty to make this point here and to press it home, and I would also like to stress that, apart from the material considerations, which can never be fully satisfied in present conditions, the need to re-establish a sound currency is particularly acute because without it we cannot hope to make the best use of our labour, capital and material resources for economic and social purposes. I said at the beginning that our economic policy should be seen to resolve round the currency reform and Marshall Plan aid; let me now add that both these contributory factors of economic recovery are simultaneous and must operate simultaneously, if they are to be fully effective.

The German people have been made aware from a number of official sources that a currency reform is to be expected before very long, and it is, therefore, not always for moral motives but often rather from simple anxiety about an uncertain future that people commit actions which weaken still further an economy that is already weak and open social and political divisions even wider. So it seems to me all the more important that I should speak in some detail on this much discussed theme of 'currency reform' from the viewpoint of economic policy as a whole.

To begin with: it is not a scourge which fills our cup to overflowing. This reform will undoubtedly shatter any illusions people may still have and expose the stark realities of our social and economic life clearly and, if you like, brutally. But this process also has its own healing qualities and lays the foundation of a new system which will enable us to make the best use of our labour and will once again give it meaning and substance. That a currency reform must be more than just a financial operation, that it also has to take account of economic and social requirements is something that has been frequently and unmistakably emphasized by the Economic Council. I take the view—no, I am convinced—that these three elements can and must be reconciled and that they form an organic whole, the preservation of which is of vital concern to anyone who wants to see our national economic life restored to full health and the future of our people assured.

A financial operation by itself, seen as a purely technical measure, would be a relatively simple affair, but any such numerical calculation which did not take into consideration the social requirements and economic possibilities would not add up. They are inextricably bound up together; but precisely because of that, precisely because the cleaning-up of our currency, unlike other partial reforms, affects and embraces all sectors of the nation's life, it is essential that Germany should play a responsible part not only in solving the technical problems but also in laying the foundations. It is my firm conviction—one that I have tried to put into practice as Chairman of the Special Bureau for Money and Credit and will also continue to press home in my present office— that the inevitable sacrifices implicit in the currency reform will undermine our whole social system unless they are fairly distributed and unless there is an honest readiness to share the burdens of the reform.

I assure you that I will do everything in my power to scotch any attempt within my own sphere of influence to evade this responsibility.

How exactly this equalization of burdens will work out in practice, particularly as regards the time factor, must naturally depend to a large extent on the technical procedure adopted and on the practical implications of the currency reform. One thing, however, is certain: that the solution lies in a distribution of the total national product based on the idea of equal shares. Without in any way prejudicing the possibility of equality of ownership, the equalization of burdens brings about in principle a redistribution of the national income or social product. But for that very reason we are much more likely to achieve speedy and lasting results if we succeed in shaking our economy out of its lethargy and re-establishing economic foundations on which we can build an expanding production. We must seek and find the remedy not in spreading shortage and want evenly but in the fair distribution of a gradually increasing prosperity.

Anyone who realizes the importance of the currency reform and has recognized how completely our future depends on its success can only hope that it will be backed by the courage to follow it through to the end; in other words, that it will not burden the economic and social future of our people with the sins of the past but will eradicate any elements that might hinder our recovery and thus ensure that the income accruing from new and honest labour will once more be fully covered by the goods on the market. This solution, which people tend to look upon as a hard one, is, I am firmly convinced, also the best for our society, if it only provides the necessary social assistance for those who cannot work. It is no longer merely mistaken but deliberately misleading to try to make people believe, with the most blatantly inflammatory intentions, that it is in the power, or only requires the goodwill, of certain individuals or groups to wipe out the consequences of our heritage and to relegate the crimes of the Nazi totalitarian system to the dead past. It is equally misleading to create the impression that the currency reform will make the poor still poorer and the rich still richer. The German people can rest assured that such crimes will not be committed.

However positive a part the currency reform will play in restoring our economy and once more giving human labour a purpose, it will also—and I am all too aware of this—bring serious hardship and structural changes of far-reaching significance. Only then will we be able to judge the full extent of the injury done to our economy by the brutal exploitation and anti-social objectives of a totalitarian government.

For this reason I believe it is essential that the Economic Council should take stock as soon as possible of the economic and social consequences we must expect to follow; and, as far as my administration is concerned, I regard it as my main task to plan ahead in such a way that ways and means can be found to meet and overcome these consequences.

Let me describe in broad outline the probable developments that lie ahead, for it is only in this way that we can work out effectively tomorrow's economic policy. You will gather from what I say that I am far from being a starry-eyed optimist but am all too conscious of the difficulties confronting us.

By contrast with the generosity that has so far prevailed in all financial matters, the first effect of the currency reform will be one of considerable shock, which may even lead to near-panic. Aspects of management which have become almost obsolete will once more play a decisive part in trade and people will again start making careful calculations. Only those forces immediately engaged in production can reckon that their work will continue undisturbed, whereas all those outside this sphere will gradually suffer a recession. Moreover, we must expect a substantial addition to the labour market from sources that have so far remained hidden, principally women, though at present it is impossible to make any precise estimates. The number of people seeking employment will be swollen by redundancy in trade and public administration, whereas the pattern of the manual workers may change but the over-all position will probably remain substantially the same.

If we also take into account that, in view of the at least temporary shortage of capital for the capital goods sector of industry, there is the danger of an appreciable shrinkage with a consequent freeing of manpower, then such a development implies not merely structural changes but also latent unemployment, which, in view of the limited public funds at our disposal, must be absorbed at all costs. Our aim must be the employment of all available manpower in industry and particularly in the production of commodities, but whether we can achieve complete absorption must depend on the magnitude of the problem and the capacity of our industrial production to expand. In any case forward-looking plans must be worked out in co-operation with the existing labour organization, which take into account the present material, social and financial state of the national economy. If the requisite improvement in Germany's labour output is accompanied by a downward trend in the number of employed, this may be even more than compensated for by increased imports of raw materials and the expansion of production which should follow, so that the Marshall Plan would produce the twofold benefit of increasing both individual and national output. If we are to achieve the maximum of steady and full employment, then our economic policy must aim to strike a balance between the volume of production that results from our imports of raw materials, the available labour resources and the output capacity of labour. As any discrepancy here could have serious social repercussions, these factors must be taken into account especially with regard to our imports and to the formulation of our industrial policy.

The shift of emphasis in industry from the means of production to consumer goods will also have to be applied on the monetary and credit side. It is understandable that people should be worried about obtaining adequate credit for the maintenance of current production, but their fears are unjustified insofar as there is nothing in our monetary policy to prevent the granting of short-term turnover credits, which can be arranged for the most part in the form of trade-bills. On the other hand, the scope for consumer or investment credits, and indeed of long-term credits as a whole, is very limited, because, although both play very different parts in the economy, the first effect they have is to create an additional demand for consumer goods, which the market cannot meet. In spite of the unavoidable tax-reform, one also cannot expect German industry to be capable of producing further substantial supplies of capital. On the contrary, it will require a considerable effort to prevent the capital resources of our national economy from dwindling still further; for, although people should be offered inducements to increase their savings, material conditions during the transition period will not be particularly favourable. So if, on this showing, there would seem to be very little scope for large-scale capital investment, those industries requiring small-scale capital expenditure will benefit. Thus we must see to it that they have enough building and repair materials to enable them, both in the production sector and in the domestic economy, to check any further decline in living accommodation as well as in capital and utility goods.

If we have been able to show that, as regards both money and credit on the one hand and demand on the other, special attention will be given to the production of consumer goods, then it follows that the smaller industries will also have an important part to play in this development. On the one hand, the urgency and volume of the as yet unsatisfied demand will lead to the mass-production of certain types of standardized utility and consumer goods; on the other hand, the role of the artisan seems to be to counteract a tendency towards collectivised consumption by introducing a note of individualism and by introducing some of the colour of life into consumption. The shortage of raw materials alone will force German industry to develop both forms of production side by side.

But a currency reform will also have a decisive influence on commerce. There can be no doubt that this sector of our economy, which has the extraordinarily difficult task of sorting out highly specialized manufacture into consumption categories and seeing that the consumer market is completely covered, has been particularly adversely affected by the decline of our economy. In certain circles the entirely false impression was prevalent, that this function did not call for any specialized skill and, given the availability of the goods, provided a safe livelihood. So there was a movement towards commerce at the expense of the skilled traders which, I am convinced, will be very quickly corrected by the currency reform. Those elements which thought to find a comfortable source of income will undoubtedly be weeded out. In view of the limited turnover and variety of our social product, commerce will have to fight hard to maintain its key position in the national economy and will have to undergo considerable rationalization and internal reorganization. The currency reform will put a stop to the unhealthy trend towards increased commercial activity at a time when the social product is dwindling. But let us not forget that the complexity of a country's trading machinery is a striking reflection of its prosperity and that, as the over-all position of our economy improves, commerce will recover its former importance.

That public administration, and in particular, if I may say so, our economic administration, must undergo a sharp reduction as a result of the currency reforms does not call for any explanation. Here we have a crass anomaly in the way economic efficiency threatens to drop as the machinery increases. Although this adverse trend will soon be arrested, I have already arranged for a commission of experts from three *Länder* to be set up, which will investigate our economic administration with a view to reducing it.

To sum up, therefore, it is safe to say that the currency reform will effect far-reaching changes both in the structure of our industry and in the state of the labour market, which, in view of the prevailing material and social conditions, must be brought in to some kind of new and organic equilibrium as soon as possible. A successful currency reform—and any other is unthinkable—will close all the easy escape routes, leaving openings only for work and effort that are of value to the nation's economy. This is a difficult road but it is the only one that will lead to recovery and, in following it, we must strain every nerve not to imperil our chances of success.

It was with this goal in mind that I believed it my duty as the person responsible for our monetary affairs to make known my opposition to any reduction of our stocks that might endanger the economy and to sacrificing our last reserves of goods. I am determined not to invite even the semblance of a suspicion that I might approve or even excuse hoarding, and anyone who quotes remarks I have made to justify private profiteering is guilty of gross slander. I have therefore issued instructions in my office that regulations are to be followed particularly carefully and, above all, that commodities from current production should be made available to the ordinary consumer.

As regards the success or failure of the currency reform—something that will be decided in a matter of months—this vital issue should on no account degenerate into mere party political slogans. Again I am not speaking of hoarding when I say that a wholesale disposal of stocks before the reform would be as serious a step as any one could imagine; for, judging by previous experience, not only would there be no guarantee that those most in need would get their fair share, but the available purchasing power, even with the Marshall Plan, would find no outlet at least for the time required to switch over production. The gravity of this problem will depend upon the actual material implications of the currency reform, but it will in any case be a major one. I have personally made it known quite clearly that I think it desirable to pass legislation against hoarding, and yet I hope I can persuade you that it is no contradiction to say that any encroachment on our national reserves beyond a given point would have consequences which, I am convinced, you cannot contemplate if you wish our recovery to be effective. Ask the man in the street what he expects from the currency reform—it is precisely what I have laid down as its essential prerequisite. Let anyone who takes the opposite view explain to me how he proposes to supply the goods to meet the demand without drawing on reserve stocks!

Whatever measures are agreed upon and adopted after hoarding has been stopped, the fact remains that, in the view of those immediately concerned, the success of these measures will be limited and that the really interesting problem lies in preventing these people from becoming currency profiteers. Although I have no patent recipe for the total abolition of such profits, one thing is quite certain: that after the currency reform, when money and credit are short, it will be much easier to trace supplies of hoarded goods than it is today, when money is circulating freely. That will be the time when I hope to be able to show by strict anti-hoarding measures that my sole concern is not to protect amoral interests but to safeguard our currency. I sincerely hope that events will not force me to exonerate myself by quoting what I have said here today, for, after all our nation has suffered, the disaster of an unsuccessful currency reform would completely undermine its will to live.

All my remarks are naturally based on a conception that does not confine itself to a quantitative and positive improvement in the relationship between the supply of goods and an active demand but goes to the roots of the problem. Any solution that maintained the present discrepancy, though in a milder form, and compelled us to preserve the existing form of economy, including the price-freeze, as the economic system of the future, any solution, that did not banish the spectre of price-frozen inflation but revived the process of building up excess purchasing power, would either make it necessary to impose further currency controls or might even perpetuate the evil. One certainly could not talk of a forward-looking economic policy, if the outlook were so grim. There would be the same problems to contend with as today and the means would be equally ineffective. In rejecting this economic principle outright, I am not by any means advocating a return to the liberalist economic forms and an irresponsible free-for-all, as in the past.

The perpetual tension between the individual and the community cannot be removed by the negation or denial of one or the other, so that the question is always one of principles and means which the individual, without sacrificing his own identity, has to observe in order to fit in with, though not subject himself to, the higher forms of society. That the principle of today must lead either to more liberal forms of market economy or to complete totalitarianism is a fact that everyone will accept who is aware of the strong element of coercion in our economy as a result of the chaotic monetary policy. If we are not entirely unanimous as to our aims, at least we are clear as to the course we must adopt: to break away from a state-controlled economy, which subjects everyone to the yoke of a stifling bureaucracy, which must kill all sense of responsibility and duty and all ambition and must, therefore, eventually turn even the most loyal citizen into a rebel.

But neither anarchy nor the ant-hill is an appropriate form of human life. Only where freedom and obligation are binding upon us, can the state find the moral justification to speak and act in the name of the people.

In concrete terms this means that, after the currency reform, we must again provide more scope for the human will and human activity both in production and in consumption and then automatically allow the competitive spirit to develop. Wherever in such a development society is afraid of being misled or of running into danger, it can introduce social, economic or financial measures to impose certain limits or restraints—in fact, in times of emergency this will have to be done—but it cannot suppress and kill the most elemental of human urges without injuring the whole community. Traditional phrases such as 'free economy' and 'planned economy' became so devalued and watered down in party-political strife that they are now unusable in serious discussion. The idea that government policy in the sense I have just mentioned did not permit of coherent economic planning but that much more far-reaching forms of intervention were necessary to give the average citizen direct guidance is one of the tragic fallacies of world history; there are enough examples in history to show that this kind of guidance soon leads to controls, to orders and to ruthless suppression. Any system that does not at least allow the individual to choose his profession and his consumer goods violates basic human rights and, as experience shows, eventually turns against those very sections of society for whose protection the artificial controls were introduced. Who, for example, would still deny that under the present system of economic coercion—which everyone certainly resents but which, after all, is the curse of evildoing—it is the weak and the poor who in the spheres both of production and consumption have suffered most, and that this system, which has oppressed and humiliated them, nowhere arouses such bitter hatred as amongst this section of the population.

In order to dispel any doubts or misgivings, I may say that I regard the total abolition of controls either with the introduction of, or immediately after, the currency reform as neither possible nor practicable. Indeed, we shall have to proceed very circumspectly when deciding into which markets, and in which sequence, free competition and decontrolled prices are reintroduced. The dogmatic view that this market-economy principle would result in a trend towards a proportional reduction in wages is not borne out by practical experience and is, in fact, disproved by it. One could quote many instances to prove that the proportional capital and the degree of internal investment financing are on the average higher in enterprises in a controlled economy than in those in a competitive economy, and that capital, whatever form it may take, is a more decisive factor in a state-controlled economy.

Another fact that is all too easily overlooked is that the competitive idea does not impinge upon certain classes of society only, while others have to bear the consequences. There are varying degrees of output on every level and to reflect these in the form of income is always justifiable. In our difficult situation an over-all increase in output is imperative; otherwise, even with the aid we are receiving and any other efforts that are made, the German standard of living will remain at an intolerably low level and every exchange of essential commodities across our frontiers will demand tremendous sacrifices. The material losses we have suffered in fixed capital of all kinds and the consequent necessity for its renewal, the wear-and-tear on technical apparatus that is also out-of-date, the heavy drain on our labour force as a result of years of privation, the influx of millions of refugees and the overriding need to care for them, the economically unfavourable composition of the German population in terms of age and sex, the unduly long isolation from world markets—all these are examples of the kind of negative factors that explain—and indeed prove conclusively—why only a supreme effort of will can produce from such material, spiritual and mental resources as we still have enough in the way of economic yield to guarantee for our people at least a basic livelihood. In this difficult situation it will become apparent, if we can get back to honest accounting, that there is little room for any differentiation of incomes or living standards and that the binding obligation of which I spoke earlier—quite independent of economic systems—makes the social adjustment of economic policy not only necessary but imperative. But whereas we are striving with all our might to solve these problems, an egalitarianism that kills individual character would be a false social ethos, which would help no one, harm the entire nation and block the way to a better future.

An economy which has to measure and compare output and, in fact, to attain the maximum increase of output cannot do without the instrument of price policy. I am using the phrase here in its widest sense, which theoretically includes tax and tariff policy, wages policy as well as monetary and credit policy. Here too there is bound to be a link with the currency reform, for the technical process of cleaning up our monetary situation could only be carried out piecemeal were we not able to start by laying a new and sound foundation upon which to base an over-all stabilization, thereby closing the gaps which are a symptom of misguided private or state planning. The price freeze provided a cover for a state policy that was deliberately creating chaos. The price freeze allowed mismanagement and the exploitation of the workers, the price freeze was the logical forerunner of a state-controlled economy, which poisons the political atmosphere and which we must not water down but remove if we are to return to sound moral standards. Here too we may avoid a certain amount of social hardship during a period of transition by retaining certain ties, but in principle there can be no compromise if the currency reform is to be carried through as a dynamic process to a logical and successful conclusion. Free price-fixing would not be at variance with a planned economy if the planning authority were only wise enough to abide by the vote of the market, which means the voice of the people. But free price-fixing is absolutely essential if there is to be a free exchange of goods with the rest of the world on a firm currency-exchange basis.

From this viewpoint it would also seem advisable to make price adjustments from now on until the completion of the currency reform, so that subsidies that become intolerable after the reform can be dispensed with but at the same time enterprises can cover their costs. In making this price adjustment one would try in principle to keep fairly close to the relevant market-prices, but one cannot use a slide-rule to find a price level that is economically sound and socially tolerable. To fix prices too high on a cost-basis, where a concern is not working to full capacity, is just as unrealistic as to fix them too low and find that no amount of effort can bring costs into line. Between these two extremes there is a happy medium which revolves round wage costs and wages policy. Because I know for certain that, after twelve years of price freeze, all prices must be artificial, there can be no question, now that the new prices for basic commodities have been fixed, of any price assimilation and wage adjustment being anything but approximate, whereas a radical solution of this problem, perhaps the most vital to our economy, seems out of the question until after the currency reform. The relationship of prices to wages will reveal the true picture of our economic and social situation, but it will also bring it home to us that we must husband our resources and that our straitened circumstances can only be overcome by working harder and more productively.

It is at this level of economic, social and financial policy that the share of the individual and social groups in the social product is decided; any subsequent controls or correctives by subordinate officials can only disturb the economic system. Where possible alternatives in economic policy are concerned, it is abundantly clear that mutually antagonistic elements cannot be allowed to operate side by side. One cannot influence living conditions by, on the one hand, applying a wage- and income-policy, or, on the other, the state agreeing to withhold licences, any more than, after the currency reform, production can be controlled through commodities on the one hand, and money and credit on the other. This leads inevitably to discrepancies, as a result of which the contradictions in the system eventually reach the point of absurdity or new, artificial forms of intervention become necessary with inevitable consequences. This makes it all the more essential that, after the reform, there should be a genuine co-ordination of the various responsible economic bodies and that the methods to be adopted should be kept constantly under review. The establishment of a special co-ordinating authority, perhaps in the form of a currency office, should be carefully studied.

I come back to what I said earlier about the inextricable links between the currency reform and Marshall Plan aid and about the particularly fortunate fact that, when the desperate nature of our situation became apparent, we were not left almost helpless but, thanks to the aid we received, could take the safe road of systematic reconstruction and recovery. Systematic reconstruction should not be taken to mean, as a perusal of the German Marshall Plan proposals might suggest, that we are being forced to adopt a narrow and rigid system. On the contrary, it is generally accepted that there should be considerable freedom of action and that only the goal—Germany's economic rehabilitation within the framework of European recovery—is predetermined. That there is no question of isolationism, of setting up a self-sufficient 'sphere of influence' is implicit not only in the absence of political hysteria, but also in the realization that any artificial or conscious limitation in space would also limit the chances of material success and cannot therefore be in keeping with Marshall Plan policy. German history in its good and in its bad periods proves that our destiny depends on world peace and that our prosperity can only be built on this foundation. So we are happy to accept the responsibility and obligation to think of ourselves as merely part of a greater whole and to act accordingly. On the other hand, it is understandable that we should for once at least want to be rid of our most pressing anxieties and that it is only as we recover economically that we shall be in a position to take less and give more. One should remember that Marshall Plan aid must mean something completely different, not only quantitatively but qualitatively, to a country that is working to only 40% of its capacity from what it does to the other European nations, whose national economies were disturbed and in some respects even disorganized by enforced isolation and the effects of war but whose productive power has remained on a very much higher level.

It is not my intention in making such remarks to support in any way the eternal grousers and grumblers, who are already calculating whether Germany received an adequate share of the total funds; on the contrary, I would like to appeal to my fellow-citizens to forget the 'ifs' and 'buts', and to bring it home to every man and woman that it is their work, their physical, mental and spiritual energies that will decide whether we succeed in multiplying the material resources given to us. To make ten out of one is not sorcery but the natural object of any economic action. If we regard aid merely as a sort of consumers' bonus, then even substantially larger amounts would not help us, for nothing would help us. But if we look upon it as a basis on which we can rebuild our exhausted and emaciated economy, then the way back will still be steep and arduous but we shall at least have firm ground under our feet.

The acknowledgment of our determination and belief in our future have nothing in common with optimistic speculation. I would even like to issue a stern warning against harbouring any illusions that immediately after the currency reform, with the help of the Marshall Plan, abundant supplies will be guaranteed. The increased effort and the additional imports of raw materials can only be converted into consumer goods very gradually, and it may take on an average six to nine months before the fruits of these efforts become apparent. Before then, however, it should be easy, following the reform, to enforce a reduction in domestic stockpiles, which, together with the steady flow of goods from allied military stocks, should bring an appreciable increase in supplies. This prediction, which is based on a factual assessment, has nothing to do with prophesy and can therefore be made in all seriousness. The success of our policy will come all the sooner and will be all the more lasting if currency reform and Marshall Plan aid can be made to coincide; therefore, as far as I can, I shall give this question my special attention.

To try to determine the mechanical course of events in advance would be pointless, because we are dealing here not only with material factors but also and essentially with imponderables of a psychological and sociological nature. In the first place, there is the firm and not entirely rational conviction of the German people that they are not only to be given unlimited scope to develop their own resources with a view to securing a good livelihood, but that this constructive effort will even be given active support. In so far as regulations still exist which are at variance with this, we can only hope that, in the period that lies ahead, an adjustment will be made in keeping with the spirit of the Marshall Plan.

This Plan is so constituted—and this is an advantage that is all too easily overlooked—that it not only provides for a flow of imports into Germany, but also prepares the ground for new capital to be raised. The whole of the supplementary imports worth about $1\frac{1}{4}$ milliard dollars are sold to German producers or consumers and so find their way into a fund of several milliards of German currency, which, as far as credits are concerned, in view of their long-term nature does not have to be immediately transferred. Although no final decision has yet been reached as to how and where this money should be spent, it must of necessity be done within the German economy and it is in accordance merely with the character of this fund if the money is used for productive purposes.

Here, indeed, is a possible way out of a dilemma. If you remember what I said, on the one hand, about our economy's urgent need for capital after the currency reform and, on the other, about the need to maintain and improve our capital production, if you think of the structural changes that are envisaged and realize that the large sector of the capital goods and investment industry with its millions of workpeople requires more capital if it is to continue, then I think you will agree that this particular aspect of Marshall Plan aid cannot be rated too highly. In one respect it closes the gap which holds up the work of reconstruction. It not only promotes, but has a cumulative effect on, the conversion of material aid into productive power. It must, therefore, be the aim of our economic policy to see to it that these funds are not spent exclusively on a few ambitious, public programmes but that the private capital requirements of industry, and above all of small and medium-sized concerns, are satisfied. This is the only way we can build up our economy organically, without sociological upheavals and without any further anomalies. Theoretically there are, of course, other possible uses for this stock of capital, such as to balance official budgets, but these would reduce the Plan's chances of success and would place a not inconsiderable burden on our economy for the future. It is precisely because this question is of

D

major importance to our economic policy that I felt in duty bound
to discuss it more fully.

The balance of imports and exports for our economic area in the
first Marshall Plan year stands at two milliard dollars, of which
some 700 millions should be covered by our exports. About half of
these are basic products such as coal, timber, scrap-iron and the
like, while roughly the same amount again represents exports of
manufactured goods and services. We shall have to devote all our
efforts in the coming years to increasing our exports of German
finished products, although it is already clear today that the difficulties facing us will be insuperable if the German proposals for
facilitating our import and export trade are not considered and put
into effect very soon.

Finally, as regards the rate of conversion, which has been so
widely discussed lately, I would like to say that the rate of RM 1
to 30 cents should not be regarded as more than a temporary
solution. I concede it an advance that a uniform rate has been fixed,
but I am certain that it will be revised as our domestic price index
changes and that, so long as the over-all price situation not only
here but on the world market remains obscure, we cannot hope,
in stabilizing the German currency, to proceed at once to make the
new conversion rate an official exchange rate. This is another
sphere in which German's recovery can only go forward by stages,
but each stage will bring with it a greater measure of clarity and
security.

It is interesting that the suggestions for a German exchange rate
show marked divergences, although it is understandable that actual
figures should vary according to the particular interests they reflect.
But in most cases the fact is overlooked that we are interested not
only in exports but also in imports and that some balance must be
struck between them. But above all we must disabuse people of the
idea that the conversion or exchange rate is an instrument of trade
policy and is designed to modify or even eradicate the effects of
economic developments by means of mathematical sleight-of-hand.
I am convinced that, difficult though it is to fix, there is only one
correct rate of exchange, which depends upon the price level of
two countries and, as far as possible, provides for and promotes an
organic assimilation of genuine equivalents. Any other principle

debases the idea of fair exchange and can only introduce a disruptive element into foreign trade and into international relations as a whole.

Let me sum up. I realize that I have presented you with a programme in broad outline and may have left unsaid many things which you would like to have heard. You may rest assured that this was not my intention and that I am ready to give frank answers to your questions. Although from a purely administrative viewpoint I am responsible for industry, commerce and the trades, I regard it as my function to cover a much wider field, particularly in relation to economic policy, and therefore feel it my responsibility that the aims I am pursuing should not benefit certain interests or sections of society but should contribute to the welfare of the whole people. For this reason I am anxious to co-operate as closely as possible with the representatives of both employers and workers, and I lose no opportunity of consulting them before reaching a decision. The sooner circumstances permit me to hand over economic responsibilities to these autonomous bodies and the more we can restrict the administration of our economy to its original sphere of economic policy, the happier I shall be and the happier we shall all feel.

The duality of a centralized and a federally-constituted economy cannot be overcome so long as circumstances compel us to apply the present economic system. Despite all opposing trends, the principle of centralization must always, in the nature of things, triumph, because a decentralized planned economy is self-contradictory. Those who want to see a federal system created as a political instrument—and I am one—cannot be in favour of a planned economy as an instrument of economic policy, without becoming involved in a contradiction. As far as economic policy is concerned, however, the problem of 'federalism or centralism' need no longer occupy our minds, if, with the currency reform, the influence of the state on the economy is confined within the limits I have suggested.

Today our economy threatens once again to become a matter of life or death. This thesis always reflects a state of emergency, but it must not become an established principle. Just as the human being needs his physical body in order to be able to develop his

mental and spiritual powers, so a nation and its economy need
material security, but they too need it only as a basis from which to
reach out for higher things, to aim at targets above and beyond
economics, which it is the state's function to set. That they take
precedence is not open to dispute.

To show you, as the chosen representatives of our people, a road
to a new future, to reawaken in our people the belief that it cannot
just hope fatalistically but can believe confidently that a turning-
point lies ahead if we combine all our efforts to achieve a new
prosperity, that was my task as I saw it when faced with the decisive events of this year 1948. We do not believe in miracles and
must not expect them to happen. But it is none the less certain that
the entirely peaceful aims of an industrious nation and the labour
it expends on improving social welfare, in close communion with
the rest of the world, must bear fruit and deliver it from its misery.
Harsh as the present may be, we can look ahead to a future that
will bring our people happiness again.

7

THE NEW RATE

(Broadcast on June 21, 1948)

On June 2, 1948, the Western Allies at a conference in London resolved 'to give the German people the opportunity to achieve, on the basis of a free and democratic form of government, the eventual re-establishment of German unity at present disrupted'. For this purpose the Minister Presidents of the West German Länder were to summon a Parliamentary Council.

The same day Ludwig Erhard declared at a press conference in Frankfurt that the nation's economy had completely collapsed. A currency reform must provide real wages for real work. Finally on June 16: proclamation by the three Western Military Governments on the introduction of a currency reform in the three Western Zones. June 20: in the three Western Zones the first German Marks were issued and were received partly with hope, partly with scepticism. Everything depended upon creating confidence amongst the German people in the new currency and on restoring money to its proper place in the economy. The German Director of Economic Administration made a special appeal to the Germans in the Western Zones:

After several days of mental and spiritual anxiety we have relapsed into the routine of everyday life. Today the German people went to work calmly and quietly, and I believe that most of them must have felt a sense of relief when it dawned on them that the dreadful threat of mass hysteria had gone and with it the shocking financial swindle of a price-frozen inflation. Only now that this fever has passed do we fully realize how close we came to the edge of the abyss and how urgent it had become to introduce our new currency and so return to the path of honesty and sincerity.

During the past few days leading statesmen and politicians have commented on recent events and I too, as an expert, which is all I

would wish to be in my position, would like to explain to you why
I am convinced that we can have confidence in the new currency
and why the decision to abandon the principle of a state-controlled
economy was essential to the success of the currency reform and to
our economic recovery in general. In order to ensure that this aim
was achieved, the Economic Council gave me full powers in the
sphere of economic planning and price policy, powers which were
circumscribed only by guiding principles set out in the relevant
legislation and were granted until the end of the year. These full
powers have been interpreted by a section of the press as a kind of
Enabling Act; they certainly raise, by their very nature, very important considerations of national policy. No single party has disputed the need for granting such full powers, so that the only
question open to discussion is that of parliamentary control and
responsibility. I myself have readily agreed to the setting-up of a
committee to carry out these functions and I have also agreed to
co-operate closely and frankly with representatives of all Parties.
I did so all the more willingly as experience has confirmed time
and again that serious men sharing a burden of direct personal
responsibility in technical matters can always reach agreement. But
if this full power was to have any real meaning, if it was to serve
its true purpose, it had to enable the holder to act as swiftly as possible in any given economic emergency and could not therefore be
tied to majority decisions or even minority votes, which would
have a delaying effect. We cannot afford any arrangement whereby
a parliamentary board of directors might prevent the director of an
administrative body from exercizing his responsibility and thereby
hold up the work. This does not mean that the parliamentary committee which has now been set up must accept my decisions unreservedly and cannot in the last resort call upon the Economic
Council to introduce amendments, the consequences of which I
would have to bear. But I am convinced that it will not come to
this, for at this grave moment I am only too conscious of my
responsibility to our people, and this sense of involvement in a
common destiny impels me to speak to you all and to keep you
constantly informed, from now on, of how things are going, of
my anxieties and expectations. In this way I believe I can best
uphold the democratic rights of our people and, at the same time,

put every issue, good or bad, to the vote. It is not to curry popular favour, not for myself but only to gain your confidence for what has to be done, that I feel bound to make it clear that I have no private vested interests of any kind to defend and therefore, despite suspicions voiced in certain quarters, in championing the market economy principle I do not have the so-called property-owning middle class in mind but am solely concerned to promote the welfare of our economy—which means the broad mass of the people.

I am not appealing to some vague, obscure faith nor to an irrational belief in miracles, when I try to strengthen the confidence of our people in our new currency; on the contrary, I am appealing to the sound common-sense, the insight and the intelligence of all of you, when I tell you that the stability of the new money can never be threatened so long as we settle down to systematic public budgeting and, by means of an equally systematic monetary and credit policy, see to it that our commodity production and our purchasing power remain in harmony. But this cannot be left to chance; this is not a question of luck but depends entirely on the firm determination to act in accordance with the principles of a sound currency. As national income and social product are, in effect, merely different ways of looking at the same economic process, but have in fact the same material content, it is a complete illusion to believe that a general price increase is possible. Where, however, there is a danger of partial price increases as a result of a disproportionate demand for certain commodities, for example, clothing or footwear, there are ways and means, such as regulating consumption, of dealing with this. And if preventive measures or controls should also prevent the fixing of prices on a cartel or monopoly basis, then we can look ahead calmly and with confidence to future developments in the sphere of price policy.

I am, in fact, convinced that as our economy becomes stabilized the tendency will be for prices to drop, and this also can be shown to be a logical development. If, as should soon become apparent, the currency reform gives rise to an increased effort everywhere and businesses are compelled by the restricted purchasing power and the growing competition for customers to rationalize and cut down costs; if, finally, as a result of rising imports of raw materials, businesses work to full capacity, then it would be nothing short of miraculous should prices not yield to this downward pressure. But I personally do not believe in miracles, particularly in the economic field, so I regard it as imperative that we should in principle abandon price controls of every kind and make way for competition and the drop in prices that will follow. This pattern is so clear that anyone can understand it who does not view the world through dogmatic spectacles. Equally clear is the fact that to maintain the price freeze in such a situation could only benefit those entrepreneurs whose overheads, for whatever reason, are too high —in other words uneconomic—and whose survival, thanks to state support, depends entirely on sacrifices by the working population which could be avoided. But this is the sort of luxury that a poor and hard-pressed national economy really cannot afford. So I am definitely not speaking for the entrepreneurs as a whole, many of whom have been living on state support in our planned economy and have done tolerably well, but only for those of them who are hard-working and conscientious and, in particular, for the broad mass of the people, when I defend the principle—and I do so consciously—that the weeding-out process, which is so essential, cannot be carried through according to any fixed rules but only on the basis of efficiency. Higher efficiency in all fields of economic activity is imperative if we are not to vegetate in poverty, destroy one another in a sheer struggle for existence and become increasingly embittered. But higher efficiency is also imperative, because an economy that is expanding on sound foundations is much less vulnerable to disturbances and therefore has the biggest contribution to make towards stabilizing the currency.

Characteristically, the question of so-called cover for our new currency has not featured at all in the recent discussions and I believe that there is more to this than simply the absence of any material backing. I would like to explain my view; for, however valuable a gold reserve can be, when it comes to manipulating exchange rates between one currency and another the stability and intrinsic value of either currency is not seriously affected by whatever cover it has. In the Nazi period we were told that the stability of money depended upon the work of the nation, but that was only a half-truth and therefore a lie. What is absolutely true, as my previous remarks about the connection between national income and commodity production imply, is that the current purchasing power of our people can only be satisfied by the current labour or the product of labour, and that, in consequence, a nation can only afford labour that is economically useful and socially acceptable. I can think of no economic system which better meets this requirement than the market economy, in which the individual, for better or for worse, is dependent on the consumer and which, therefore, in contrast to all forms of state-controlled economy, offers the best protection against the abuse of a nation's honest labour. So the surest guarantee of the stability of our new currency lies in our determination to use our labour to further the national economy. If we act on this principle, then we have nothing to fear.

If you sum up all I have said, you may come to the conclusion that in your own best interest there is no need to avail yourself immediately of the newly-acquired purchasing power, but I do beg of you to believe me when I say that this advice is not given with any mysterious ulterior motives. If you have considered whether it might not be to your advantage to buy more cheaply, and perhaps even better, tomorrow, then you must be free to decide for yourself, and, even bearing in mind the need for capital savings for our national economy, I do not wish to restrict the freedom of any individual however marginally. For the same reason I am opposed to the idea of compulsory saving, and here too I prefer to leave it entirely to our people themselves to decide, in the light of the tax concessions offered, what use they choose to make of their income.

But they should and must know that the transition to a new economic system will be easier, the risk of unemployment less, if by building up an adequate reserve of savings and capital we can avoid a drain on labour in the capital goods industries and in the investment sector of the economy. If I say further that the increased efficiency of our national economy depends largely on the continued development of our capital goods production, and that, if we are to achieve the same standard of efficiency as in other countries, we cannot afford to neglect our fixed capital, then, despite the urgent need to meet demand, a need which I in particular have stressed time and again, let us nevertheless express the hope that every individual will conduct himself with due regard to our economic interests.

I frankly admit that, in spite of the short-term aid we are receiving, our credit situation worries me. Nevertheless, I believe that a mild deflationary purge is essential in order not merely to discourage further hoarding but also to force business to rationalize as much as possible. Everything will depend on whether we can exploit this trend in time, that is, before the economy begins to shrink, by providing adequate supplies of credit, but I would like to feel certain that this will happen. In my talks with Military Government economists they expressed the same view, so this problem, perhaps the most difficult of all, stands a good chance of success. From the German side no effort will be spared to make the capital funds in new German marks which accrue from Marshall Plan imports available for production purposes in the form of medium-term and long-term credits and to set up the necessary machinery without delay. There is admittedly still much to be done, but the German people can rest assured that the problems weighing on their minds are receiving our full attention and that, within the limits of Germany's responsibility, everything will be done to keep pace with future developments. Inevitably the traditional instrument of the bill of exchange will have to become once more the primary means of financing short-term credits. Although, with an apparent superfluity of money, we have almost lost the habit of using this particular financial expedient and must handle it cautiously, the reintroduction of the bill of accommodation marks an important step towards sound financial management and I hope that any reluctance to make use of it will soon be overcome in the interest of our national economy.

The Economic Administration announced yesterday that controls on certain utility and consumer goods had been lifted, and preparations have been made to release other commodities. The reaction of the people to this move towards a freer economy shows how unpopular this system of state patronage has become and how relieved people are at being given the responsibility once again to shape their own destiny. We were well on the way to regimenting democracy to death and reducing the fundamental democratic rights of our people to a mere shadow. Only when these rights find expression again in a free choice of occupation, in the freedom to change jobs and, above all, in freedom for the consumer, can we expect the German people to play the same active part in political affairs as before. In the same context I have submitted legislation to the Economic Council, which will lighten and eventually remove the restrictions on tradespeople and which is intended to enable those, particularly refugees, who cannot be given sufficient immediate material aid, at least to find a new source of livelihood, undisturbed by petty and egoistic local interests. The German citizen will only regain his sense of dignity and be able to feel himself personally committed to a democratic way of life when he is no longer obliged to go cap in hand to any public official. I regard it as my main task to help him achieve this.

When, in the next few days, my office issues instructions for the removal of certain price controls, I do not think I need fear the accusation that such measures are designed to further the interests of the entrepreneur at the expense of the working people. Although I am certain that the drop in prices which I expect to follow will in fact take place, I shall nevertheless keep a watchful eye on our economic development. I shall avail myself of the services of any organization which can keep me informed about what is happening throughout the country, so that I can where necessary take swift action.

I would like to remind all those engaged in free enterprise that we are passing through a grave period and to appeal to them not to exploit what, at any given moment, may appear to be rosy opportunities, if by so doing they are not contributing to the general good. This short-sighted outlook can only breed bitterness, and I therefore appeal also to the autonomous bodies in industry, to the Chambers of Commerce and the Unions, to bring it home to their members that the testing-time has come and that, if the economy is unequal to the test and cannot command confidence, we will almost certainly revert to some kind of state-regimented economy. I am optimistic about our chances of success, but I am conscious not only of the heavy responsibility I carry but also of the difficulties that lie ahead. Every step we take will be calmly and carefully considered, but, as long as I can feel sure that I enjoy the confidence of the Economic Council and the German people, I will follow with courage and resolution this road that leads to the removal of the controlled economy.

I have no political ambition, unless it be for my own party. When I hand back to the Economic Council the full powers vested in me, I shall be happy and thankful if I have succeeded in overcoming all the hazards and have been partly instrumental in ensuring that our people has a sound economic basis on which to work and can once more have its share of enjoyment in life without the need to encroach upon, or suppress, the rights of others.

8

A GENERAL STRIKE TO SAVE A DOGMA
FROM OBLIVION

(Broadcast on November 11, 1948)

The first signs of an upswing become visible. The air-lift to Berlin and United States aid for Europe raise the German people's hopes for co-operation with the Allies and for the success of their own efforts at self-help. On September 1, 1948, the Parliamentary Council met in Bonn under the chairmanship of Dr Adenauer. But there was unrest among the workers caused by the dispute over prices and 'hoarding'. On November 8, the National Executive and the Advisory Council of the Bizonal Trade Unions Confederation called a general strike for November 12. The demands included the official declaration of an 'economic state of emergency', the appointment of a price controller, and sequestration of material assets. On November 10, a vote of no-confidence directed against Professor Erhard by the Socialists was defeated in the Economic Council by 52 votes to 43. On the eve of the strike Erhard made the following appeal to reason in a broadcast address:

The German Trade Unions Confederation has called a 24-hour general strike for Friday, November 12. This decision was taken before the Administrative Council's reply to the Trade Union demands had been made known, and before the agreed final talks between Administrative Council and Trade Unions Council had taken place. Strike action is being taken at the very time when not only is a more stable price trend observable but far-reaching economic measures have been taken or initiated to overcome the existing discrepancies between wage rates and prices as completely and rapidly as possible. It is nothing less than a piece of deception on the part of the trade unions to say not a word about the incontrovertible economic fact that prices have been rising as an inevitable consequence of the currency reform and because there has

53

been too much money in the hands of the consumers, and to try to make out that only mistakes of policy are to blame. We have got to establish an economic balance between the volume of money in circulation and the volume of goods available, for without this no healthy and efficient working economy can be created. If we fail to reach this balance we should have to remain in a state of price-controlled inflation and continue to be saddled with the black market, barter trading and all other evils of a controlled economy that bear so heavily on everyone who works for a nominal wage. The trade unions cannot deny the existence of these dangers, but want to ward them off by appointing a price controller invested with extraordinary powers, by state control of raw material supplies, credit expansion and foreign trade, measures to supervise and control the flow of goods and so on. Planning on lines such as these amounts to nothing short of a completely and compulsorily controlled economy, and there is no need for me to remind you of what this means in terms of its effects on the lives of ordinary people. As long as I am in a position of responsibility, it is incompatible with my convictions and conscience to lend myself to a policy which would leave the wealthy unscathed but hit everyone else, and I am thinking once more of the ordinary consumer. All responsible circles, German and Allied, hold, as I do, that the rise in prices has been due to the necessary process of adapting the price level to the volume of money in circulation. Let me quote from a relevant report: 'It would be a grave mistake to try to combat the present excessive rise in prices by the obsolete methods of state control, that is to say by going back to a system of enforced prices. Experience in recent years proves that such action would immediately bring back all the undesirable manifestations which have been successfully banished by allowing prices to find their own level. Goods and commodities would disappear from the market, the grey market and the black market would spring up once more, barter dealings would again be commonplace, and the payment of wages in kind and inducements of one sort or another would have to be resorted to. The net result would be the collapse of all that has been achieved by the new economic policy, and the currency would be gravely endangered. If abuses occur in the market economy they must be combated with means appropriate to the market economy.' That is the end of the passage I wished to quote to you.

If it is the purpose of the strike to bring home to responsible quarters the seriousness of the situation, then this action is, to say the least of it, utterly superfluous. The administration, and my department in particular, was well aware, without the help of the trade unions and before they started their present action, that the way prices were going threatened to undermine the workers' real income and also enabled unscrupulous elements to make excessive profits. Among serious-minded and responsible people there can be no two opinions about the need to deal with these abuses as quickly as possible and to aim at establishing the most favourable relationship possible between wage rates and prices, bearing in mind our limited economic powers. All the interlinked and co-ordinated measures envisaged in the fields of economic policy, monetary and credit policy, and also tax policy are designed to subserve this one aim. In particular, the proposed vigorous taxation of goods held in stock—proposed by me, mark you, not by the Socialists—in the framework of the emergency measures for the equalization of burdens, is designed to exert pressure in the direction of bringing goods out of hoarded stock and bringing prices down. What is in dispute, however, is not aims but methods, and here I will state openly that in my opinion the material losses and political dangers of a strike dictated for the sake of saving the doomed dogma of the collectivist economy are not in the national interest and cannot be justified.

For weeks past my office has been working all out, in collaboration with the economic bodies concerned, on the intensification and expansion of the 'Everyman Programme', and every effort will be made to ensure that by the end of the year more and more 'Everyman' goods of all kinds covered by the definition of 'utility' are brought on the market at fixed consumer prices. The process of liquidating the STEG (Staattiche Einkauf Gesellschaft, army surplus trade organization) stockpiles will be speeded up and current consumer goods production stimulated to the utmost by ensuring adequate raw material supplies. By negotiation we have obtained Military Government sanction for the reintroduction of retail price fixing, which will allow industrial undertakings, subject to my department's permission, to fix the retail prices of their products and to check compliance therewith. At the present moment I am conducting negotiations with no less than five European and non-European countries for the immediate supply of consumer goods to supplement the German market, particularly with reasonably priced textile goods and footwear. All these transactions involve credit operations which constitute the first steps in the direction of opening up channels to the international credit and capital markets. There is renewed confidence abroad in Germany's recovery, in our goodwill and in our strength, and I am very well aware that the German worker's reputation for hard work and skill is an important factor in this connection. Do the trade unions really believe that calling a strike is a valid means of remedying our need? Is this a fitting step to take in a situation in which anyone who looks facts in the face must realize that the difficulties we encounter have not only to be recognized but also mastered? Why do the trade unions deliberately shut their eyes to the truth? Why does no one tell our German workers that rising prices, however objectionable and undesirable, at least have one desirable effect in helping to prevent the spread of unemployment? Does it not occur to the unions that the sympathy expressed by the SED in the East Zone for the strike is dangerously and highly suspect? Let me then repeat to you what I said yesterday at the meeting of the Economic Council. If our German workers only realized where the unions' demands are leading them, namely back to bureaucratic thraldom and the whip-hand of state controls, they would stand up and repudiate these demands.

At the same time I wish to make it clear, in the name of the Administrative Council, that the firm stand taken against the trade union demands does not imply an negative attitude to this institution as such, nor disparagement of its economically and socially important role in the life of the community. But an economic policy resting on the will of a parliamentary majority must not be subordinated to the arbitrary dictates of social, industrial or political groups, or democracy becomes a farce. On this basis of the rule of law, not only is it open to the trade unions to play their part and to carry their share of responsibility, but their co-operation will be welcomed, gratefully. The Administrative

Council refuses to recognize the strike on the grounds that it is calculated not to relieve but to aggravate the German people's distress. Here, by way of example, are a few figures: the strike will cost us 300,000 tons of coal, enough for 2 weeks' domestic firing for the whole country, 20,000 tons of steel, 165,000 pairs of shoes, 3,000 bicycles with 55,000 tyres, some 150,000 electric light bulbs and other badly needed consumer goods. Let every man be mindful of his democratic freedom and act according to his own conscience.

E

9

THE END OF THE MAKESHIFT PERIOD

(Article in *Tagesspiegel* of April 23, 1949)

The boom conditions created by the currency reform and the re-organization of the economy gave way after 1949, at first to a period of quiet consolidation. While the stimulating forces still made their presence felt, there were restraining factors which gradually slowed down and stopped the upward price trend and produced in combination with rising wage rates a perceptible improvement in the real income level. The words 'depression' and 'deflation' crept into the conversations and public discussions on the economic situation at that time.

Ludwig Erhard analyzed the situation thus:

The currency reform which came into effect in June, 1949, brought the period of makeshift measures to an end. The transition from an essentially inflationary planned economy to a balanced market economy could not be effected without producing some strains and stresses, particularly since the supply of new currency was not related to productive output and consequently soon gave rise to a considerable discrepancy between the volume of money and the volume of goods available. The first phase of economic recovery, which was successfully completed by the end of 1948, was characterized by the effort to convert the excess of consumer money into producer money or, in other words, by rigorous economic expansion to tie up the purchasing power created as a result of the currency reform in the form of working capital, thereby neutralizing it in the interests of the market economy. Insofar as nominal price increases—to be accounted for not only by the cessation of home and foreign trade subsidies—were inevitably incurred in the course of this development, it became necessary to ensure that the price increases on which recovery of economic equilibrium depended should not be suppressed by

58

artificial expedients typical of a planned economy, even where they did not appear justified because of the cost involved. Had the economic administration given way to the inducements and threats to which it was exposed during this outwardly hectic period, and taken the undeniable social strains and stresses as an excuse for reintroducing economic planning and state control of prices, the German economy would have relapsed once more into a state of frozen inflation and the German people would have been thrust back into the tread-mill of rigid economic planning. The political pressure operating in this direction was in the event relieved by a safety-valve created by the economic administration in the form of what came to be known as the 'Everyman Programme'. This measure provided, for all those in receipt of fixed nominal incomes, particularly wage and salary earners, a socially shielded market zone which was largely immune to the dynamic workings of un-fettered supply and demand. In this way it became increasingly possible to check the hysteria manifested by producers and con-sumers alike, and to gain recognition for economic reasoning and principles. Today my critics are loath to admit that they treated me with contempt and scorn when I predicted in the autumn and winter of last year, with increasing confidence, that the climax in the struggle for the achievement of a sound price structure, and with it the attainment of a new point of departure in the develop-ment of the economy, was in the offing. This prediction was based on a perfectly sober evaluation of the economic situation, and the fact that history proved me right in no uncertain manner was evidence, not of any prophetic gift on my part, but of lack of per-ception on the part of my critics.

Although the volume of money and credit is today not less than in October and November 1948, the economy has an entirely dif-ferent look. At that time it was typified by an apparently extreme degree of liquidity coupled with practically unlimited purchasing power; today the general complaint is of stagnation, a dearth of credit and empty order-books. Then, prices were going up all along the line; today the opposite tendency is equally widespread. In the first phase after the currency reform, the capital goods in-dustry could be financed out of the profits and excess profits gained in the consumer goods industry; today this dangerous surplus capital has disappeared and there is a shortage of capital; and this, although a source of complaint and worry, is nevertheless one of the indications of recovery. The change thus brought about in so short a time is indeed a measure of the success of the policy which set out to establish a market economy, and in particular of those elements of this policy which are concerned with steadily expanding production and simultaneous credit restriction.

This complete reversal of the economic picture gave rise to a good deal of undesirable and factually mistaken speculation. Just as it was wrong to take the expansion of output and the price increases that occurred in the second half of 1948 as signs of a boom, so it is equally wide of the mark to look upon what has been happening since the beginning of this year as a depression or, to use the term now generally applied, deflation. These developments have nothing to do with trade cycles in the classical sense but are in fact merely processes of adaptation. In the first phase after the currency reform it was a case of establishing equilibrium between the volume of money and the volume of goods available, by arriving at a new scale of prices; whereas now, after that problem has been solved, it is a case of bringing prices into line with costs by giving a new impetus to competition in the field of output.

Output per man-hour having gone up by 20-30%, and the utilization of industry capacity on the average by 100%, since the currency reform, the law of decreasing costs will have become so effective as to allow room, since the beginning of the year, for a considerable lowering of prices. In spite of all that we have been through, we can today regard it as a stroke of luck that, owing to the faults inherent in the currency reform, the inescapable cleaning-up process did not start immediately afterwards when the employment index stood at 40% of that in 1936, but has only now started when the index has reached 85%. While it is true that our economy today is still highly sensitive to external influences with their psychological overtones, yet it is equally true to say that the social hazards bound up with the process of putting the economy on a sound footing have become appreciably less marked. It was, of course, inevitable that the dogmatic opponents of the market economy should put forward the rise in the unemployment figures as evidence of the sinfulness of the freer economic system, although in fact the way things have gone in the labour market constitutes the most striking justification of the transition to the market economy. Since the currency reform not only have all non-binding terms of employment had to be replaced by genuine contracts, but some 800,000 new wage-earners have swelled the employment figures, thus providing concrete proof of the fact that the market economy has succeeded in eliminating numerous economically useless pursuits. Wiping out black-market activities and superfluous trade channels constitutes a solid achievement, even though the economy has so far only been able to absorb an additional 500,000 production workers. The fact that in the course of reorganizing the structure of the economy it has been necessary to shift workers from place to place and to incur temporary increases in the total unemployment figures does not invalidate our economic policy. I ask you—what sort of miracle would be needed to avoid an economy undermined by, or geared to, non-economic purposes for fifteen successive years requiring reorganization if it is to become fit to fulfil its due functions in the service of peace and social improvement?

Only the free play of competition in the field of industrial output is capable of solving this problem in a manner fair to all, and at the same time only competition fulfils the social function of bringing prices and incomes, more particularly prices and wages, into the optimum relationship which will both raise the standard of living and ensure distribution of the national product. A planned economy is bound to fail in this task, since either it tolerates the inherent faults that enable an entrepreneur class to batten on the working population, or it has to conduct a weeding-out process by authoritarian methods. If one thinks what this would involve when pushed to its logical conclusion, when one contemplates the petty tyranny, corruption and error that would almost inevitably occur, one recoils in horror.

The conserving and driving force at work in the market economy is and always will be competition, but what is still needed, and needed most urgently, is that the workers themselves should come to recognize in competition a force for good and not for evil. They have yet to realize that the fruits of more intensive and better organized work benefit not the tycoons but the people as a whole. In other words, the socially committed free economy disavows both the entrepreneur type and the state-controlled type of planned economy, because both aim to suppress competition and establish socially unjust positions of power.

As long as it remains true that the economic cleaning-up process cannot be dispensed with, and that the policy of credit restriction, however burdensome, must be adhered to, the present course deserves to be accepted and supported by all who wish for a healthy and stress-free economic order of society and feel strong enough to play their part in it. Those, on the other hand, who cling to the existing unhealthy state of things have no claim to protection because they can only be maintained in their artificial existence at the expense of the productive elements in the economy as a whole. Let no one on any account imagine that the road to a healthy economic state is bound to lead through some direful crisis or out-and-out deflation. On the contrary—and this is the pointer to the way economic policy should be directed—everything will depend on so adjusting the pressure to which the economy is subjected, and so determining the length of time taken to complete the cleaning-up process, that the objectives of increasing and improving output and raising the standard of living are attained without sapping energy to such an extent that output suffers and employment is reduced. I am firmly convinced that by carefully adjusting and combining the numerous economic factors involved it is possible to steer a successful 'middle course' between the dangers and the blandishments of an over-rigorous cure for our ills. As you know, my view is that, contrary to all orthodox trade-cycle theory, we should aim at expanding production while maintaining a slight downward price trend. And I firmly believe we can do it. After all, expanding production does not only bring down costs; intensified competition in the field of industrial output will sweep away quite a few warped notions about profit and price margins which may be part of current thinking in a rigidly controlled economy, but which are alien to that in a market economy. The sooner the industrial economy frees itself from unhealthy traditional notions like these, the sooner the way will be clear for real recovery and renewed progress. The more this positive way of thinking is adopted by active, go-ahead men of business, the less stupid talk we shall hear of impending or actual deflation. When it ceases to be possible to sell any goods one likes at any price one chooses to ask, and the buyer no longer goes cap-in-hand begging for the goods he wishes to buy, but instead, the seller has to go in search of the buyer and it becomes hard work to hold one's own in the market, then it is time to say these are not the signs of approaching deflation but very much the reverse. They are positive indications of economic recovery and consolidation. Seeing how hard put to it I was not to give way to social pressures during the past year, in order to stave off the reintroduction of controls, no one can rightly expect me to start having second thoughts now that the situation is changing in such a way as to shift the burden more on to the shoulders of the entrepreneur. The socially committed market economy is impervious to the wishes of any sectional interest or pressure group; it aims at building a healthy economy, providing an assured existence for the entire population, and enabling each member of it to enjoy a fair share of the national product commensurate with the share contributed towards its achievement.

10

POLICY ON CARTELS

(Article in *Der Volkswirt* of December 16, 1949)

If the economy was to be based, and remain based on the principle of constructive competition, it was going to be necessary not only to eliminate state-held positions of power in the economy, but also to legislate effectively against restrictive practices of any kind. Early in 1948 the Allied Powers had laid down certain governing principles under this head, and after currency reform the Economic Council had adopted a resolution in favour of the competitive principle. Soon after the formation of the first Federal Cabinet in 1949, work was begun on the drafting of a German cartel law. In the following article Ludwig Erhard explained the issue as he saw it.

In setting out to explain my views on the proposed Cartel Law I am not prompted by any desire to join in the chorus of speculation or to comment on draft provisions, but feel it to be my duty to do what I can to clarify the issue and bring it into proper perspective. My belief in the development of competition as the best means of ensuring steadily increasing productivity and a just distribution of the national income, as an indispensable motive force for healthy economic development, and as the one sure key to a truly 'social' market economy is sufficiently well known as to require no further stressing. All that I should like to add in the present connection is that I am equally convinced that interference with the free workings of competition, through planning and controls, is no less deplorable and harmful when it is exercised on the part of the entrepreneurs than when it is exercised by the state. It is thus not simply a case of being for or against cartels. Market arrangements are not to be judged on form but on how they work and the spirit behind them. In spite of all the subtleties involved in cartel policy, there is no getting away from the fact that all market agreements, and especially those concerned with prices, are in the last analysis directed towards imposing a limitation of some kind on the free operation of competition. Not that this is the primary or declared objective, of course. The curbing of competition is not practised for its own sake but as the chosen instrument for ensuring a given sales volume, stabilizing production or even maintaining an established or predetermined price level. There has never been any lack of arguments that could be adduced in support of such procedures, and I am perfectly prepared to believe that many of the protagonists of the cartel scheme are convinced in their own minds of the usefulness and value to the national economy of these market agreements. They are at liberty to do so, only they should then realize that they are in fact operating in response to the same mode of thought as the economic planners, since like them they are in fact proceeding from the illusion that it is possible to take a process which is based on and shaped by human action, and force it into conformity with a preconceived scheme or compel it to follow a predetermined course.

In my opinion all attempts in this direction constitute a sin against the spirit of life, since this spirit calls for flexibility, mobility and the capacity for spontaneous development. That is why the heavy-handed measures of planning, controlling and stabilizing are bound to fail. Life—and economic processes form part of life— cannot be lived without risk, yet people are always clamouring for security; and this does not apply only to those in a weak economic position, in whom hankering for security would at least be humanly understandable, but also to business people who are in the best position to judge how far removed any mere wishing for security is from the truly business-like approach. I would almost go so far as to say that were it possible to ensure stability and security in market operations, then no serious objection could be raised to state economic planning. But if the purpose of a smoothly running and steadily developing economy is to ensure complete exchange of the social product by according freedom of choice to the consumer and putting up with whatever adjustments may have to be made in the process, then no cartel arrangements must be allowed to interfere with the function of free market prices as a working principle. Rigid or fixed price levels are just as incompat-

ible with the essence of the market as they are with that of free
enterprise. Any entrepreneur therefore who rejects the trade union
demand for full employment as an economic principle and rightly
refuses to accept this as a measure of the soundness of economic
policy, is thinking and acting illogically in imagining that the
unattainable, namely constancy of economic data, can be achieved
coercively by a cartel policy. Have we not learned through bitter
experience what happens when human institutions are empowered
to trade human freedom for security, to offer stability at the price
of rigidity and compulsion? There is indeed no other way to attain
this objective, but then the objective itself involves the negation of
the true nature of human society and social behaviour.

I have given so much space to this line of thought because it is
only from this angle that the dangers of the old German cartel
policy can be recognized and assessed. The objection will be raised
that cartels here or there have had useful results and in a wide
variety of branches of industry have in fact, and contrary to my
fears, brought about a thoroughly harmonious ordering of production and sales; that agreements of this kind have in fact
eliminated certain abuses in the competitive system, thus enabling
sound businesses to remain in being, providing small and medium-
sized businesses with a chance to succeed and having a stabilizing
effect on the level of employment. What more, these people will
say, can one reasonably expect of any cartel policy? I am afraid
these claims do not allay my scepticism but if anything increase it.
If, I say, cartels have in fact functioned so smoothly, then it is
reasonable to assume that real positions of power have been established, and this arouses the suspicion of exploitation. The resulting
harm may not become apparent at the source of this power but
will certainly have broken out at some other point in the economy;
and since we are here concerned with investigating this problem
from the point of view of the national economy, the problem has
to be subjected to more thorough scrutiny.

If we start from the postulate (which in itself is a conscious sim-
plification but which need not for this reason be in any sense misleading) that the level of the national income in any given unit of
time must correspond to the value of the social product—since
every income is derived exclusively from work actually done and

resulting in the production of goods—then the quantitative exchange, so considered, should never be in danger, if it were not for the fact that the qualitative exchange in a free society, reflected in the constantly fluctuating level of demand and changing composition of the social product, constitutes the basic equation of the market economy. If we insert in this equation the quantity 100 to represent in each case the national income and the social product, and assume for the sake of argument that one half of production be allotted to industries tied by cartel agreements and the other half to branches of the economy in which free competition operates without limitation, then the effect of the cartels could only be regarded as neutral, provided the further assumption were made—a quite unrealistic one—that these cartels do not exploit their more powerful position, that they exercise self-restraint in the face of all temptation and act in perfect conformity with the operations of the free market. But in this case what sense would there be in having any such agreements? It is much more probable and realistic to assume that those who dispose of the cartel-controlled half of the social product are out to get more than half, say 60%, of the national income, and are in fact able to do this through the extra power they wield. The net result is beyond dispute : the other half, namely the freely mobile half of the social product represented by 50 units is matched against 40 units of purchasing power, and consequently the market can only get rid of its stock by making substantial sacrifices in the shape of price cuts or even actual losses.

Let no one contend that this argument is tantamount to toying with theoretical abstractions; it is, on the contrary, a matter of stern reality and explains the dramatic course of events that took place in the early 1930's. Let us carry the investigation a step further and consider what happens in the second phase of this development. The cartel-protected industries may very well continue to turn out goods at the former rate, thanks to their smoothly-running sales machinery, and seek to keep their price policy operating as before. The industries operating under open market conditions, on the other hand, will adjust themselves to the market situation, either by closing down undertakings that can no longer pay their way or by reducing output generally, and will only bring 40 units of production on to the market. Of this new total of 90 units of social product a proportion corresponding to 60 units of purchasing power would be absorbed by the cartelized industries, while the remaining 30 units of purchasing power would have to take up a free social product amounting to 40 units. In other words, the ratio would inevitably become progressively loaded to the disadvantage of the free sectors of industry outside the cartelized sectors, until in the end we should reach a state of affairs in which the threatened sectors of free industry would become insolvent and unable to continue in production. It goes without saying that the actual course of events would not follow exactly the lines indicated by the solution of this hypothetical equation. It is even safe to assume that the resulting price pressure would bring about, within certain limits and according to the relative strength of the power factors involved, a reduction of the cartel prices; but broadly the equation remains valid. The objection that excess profits accruing to the cartelized industries become ultimately converted into purchasing power, e.g. to investment, may be valid in individual instances; but this is offset, broadly speaking, by the braking effect exerted by any cartel policy geared to obtaining stability and security, on the dynamic forces at work in the national economy, or on the other hand by errors in capital investment due to a misguided assessment of the actual market conditions. Meanwhile the market itself, being impeded in the proper exercise of its faculties, does not react as it should, and it is absolutely safe to assume that the limitation of competition in the area under the influence of the cartel, coupled with the unfavourable state of the market in the free sector would restrict the utilization of the available capital for productive ends either by direct action or by discouragement on the grounds of risk.

This kind of entrepreneur-planned economy certainly set its seal on the crisis in the 1930's. Those were the years in which the market economy went off the rails and which faced us with the problem of whether to return to freedom, thereby restoring the capacity of the market to function properly, or to make it a matter of economic principle to tread the path leading to a progressive curtailment of freedom and increasing reliance on constraint. The German economy of those days took, under short-sighted leadership, the wrong path. Instead of granting freedom of action, freedom of movement all along the line, getting rid of the cartels, and providing for the exchange of the social product on the broad basis of a national economy freed from constraining forces, what was done was to multiply the cartels in order that they should take in hard-pressed industries for their supposed protection; with the result that in those hapless years Germany had some 2,500 cartels and we became hopelessly bogged down in a crisis from which there was no escape and in which the unemployed were numbered in millions. The fact of the matter is that if, all available or willing purchasing power having been spent as a result of this inordinate price fixing, unsaleable residual portions of the social product were to be left on the market, it is inevitable that any increment of production would be encumbered with this growing mortgage and consequently become steadily smaller. In the end the cartels themselves would of course no longer be viable, and nobody's interests will have been served by this mistaken policy.

I trust that my critics when they consider these arguments will understand that if anyone tries to point out to me the benefits that have been bestowed by cartels, this will not convince me that they are harmless but will rather make me still more distrustful of them. We made the mistake, when the signs were bad, of failing to put our trust in freedom, and instead opened the door to planning and control. It was no mere matter of chance that the process was carried through to a disastrous conclusion not by the business world but by the planning authority of the state.

For the sake of completeness, I had better say something about a further argument used by those in favour of cartels, namely, that responsible cartels have shown a high degree of discipline in boom periods with the result that cartelized branches of industry have often tended to keep prices steadier than they would otherwise have been. This may be so, but to put a dynamic economy into this kind of a strait-jacket is quite unsuitable, and may very possibly impede, in the private interest, developments which are desirable from the point of view of the economy as a whole. In theory, it is just as unhealthy to keep prices down artificially as to raise them artificially; the only price scale which is satisfactory from the point of view of the national economy is that which remains responsive to market conditions and brings about a complete exchange of the social product. But the main reason for discontinuing the moderating influence under boom conditions of which the cartels boast is that it is bound to give rise to excess of demand over supply; this in its turn creates a problem of distribution, or properly speaking in such conditions a problem of allocation, and the end of the story is bound to be some kind of scheme or arbitrary action which cannot be brought into line with the standards laid down for the conduct of the economy.

I am confirmed in my opposition to restrictive arrangements made by cartels by knowing as I do that every move in that direction invariably awakens the demand for protection against outside influences, so that its limiting effect on competition is two-fold. This limitation of competition in its turn reduces the freedom of action and the real purchasing power of the great mass of the population, and for precisely this reason a largely cartelized economy can never adequately fulfil its social obligations. Cartelization is thus inimical to a liberal foreign trade policy, although it is not possible to discuss this further point within the limits of this article.

I am quite aware that I may have been dealing too much in absolutes and general terms, but I believe that in this way it is possible to bring out most clearly the actual nature of the problem. Excessively strict orthodoxy is surely always harmful, but at the same time readiness to arrive at a fair assessment of individual phenomena and states of affairs must not be allowed to water down, still less to deny, the validity of a principle recognized to be true. Recent trade union pronouncements indicating a pliant and indeed almost indulgent attitude towards cartels should really make the business world suspicious. Far be it from me to wish to exacerbate opposing views, but there is surely no denying that the trade unions are trying to be circumspect in their assessment of concentrations of power in the hands of cartels for fear that, by condemning cartels out of hand, they might make nonsense of the principle of allowing the state to attain to positions of power in the economy. To those who are acquainted with marxist theory the attitude of the trade unions on this subject will only too readily bring to mind the thesis of the expropriation of the expropriators. In my view, both institutions, that is to say, private cartels and state monopolies, are on one and the same level, and I should therefore like to put one last question to those who are searching for the right solution to this problem. Do they believe, in view of the fact that both systems are based on the same mode of thinking, that they would be able to offer any effective resistance once the demand for a change-over from planning by the entrepreneurs to state planning arose, as is bound to arise for political reasons when the functioning of the market is thrown out of gear? The freedom and happiness of the German people stand and fall with the freedom of the market economy, and only an economy which is free from concentrations of power can fulfil or even remain aware of its social obligations.

II

KOREA

(Broadcast on September 15, 1950)

The Petersburg Agreement of November 22, 1949, between the Allied High Commissioners and the Federal Government brought a further easing of the restrictions on production and assurances that dismantling would cease. On May 9, 1950, Robert Schuman put forward his plan to merge the coal and steel industries of France, Italy, Belgium, Luxemburg, Holland and the Federal Republic in the Iron and Steel Community. The Western Powers at their conference in London in May, 1950, confirmed their readiness to take Germany into the community of free European peoples and promised that the peaceful reunification of Germany would remain the final objective of Allied policy.

But on June 25, 1950, Communist troops crossed the 38th Parallel and the Korean war broke out. It brought the world to the brink of a world conflict, held up the work of reconstruction in Western Europe and jeopardized the unmistakable and uninterrupted upwards trend in the Federal Republic.

One result of the heavy fighting in Korea and of the fear that the conflict might spread was a world-wide shortage of goods and price increases which many countries tried to offset by imposing government controls. West Germany's foreign exchange position became appreciably worse. In many sectors there were signs of nervousness. The entrepreneurs, who had kept their stocks of raw materials low on the assumption that prices would fall again, were taken unawares by the sudden rise in world market prices and there was a mad rush to buy. The consumers were also caught up in a wave of speculative buying; they drew on their savings and released considerable quantities of ready money. The liberal economic system which Ludwig Erhard had set up only two years before ran into serious difficulties. It was not merely the 'pragmatists' who wanted a return to economic planning and price

72

controls; there were also growing doubts in Erhard's own camp and he had to throw the whole weight of his authority into the scales:

The Korean conflict with all its economic, social and psychological repercussions hit the German economy at a time when it was clearly on the road to recovery and expansion. Since February the unemployment figures have been dropping sharply, the average monthly increase in production was 3 to 4%, German exports rose from 300 or 350 million marks a month at the beginning of the year to 730 million marks in July, and with the changes in the world situation they will go up still further. So these changes arising from the Korean conflict were by no means 'lucky' from Germany's point of view, for they interfered with her organic development. This does not mean that the boom conditions could not be turned to advantage, although they carry just as many risks as opportunities. These risks pertain, on the one hand to price policy and on the other to the widely held view that, as the economic situation has changed, the system must also be changed; in other words, that the market economy should give way to a planned economy.

The attitude we adopt towards economic policy must, to begin with, take into account the fact that the supplies of raw materials from abroad for German industry and also our food supplies no longer depend, or at least only to a minor extent, on Marshall Plan aid but on our own exports. To set against Marshall Plan aid funds of 350 million dollars (which are rapidly being reduced) we have today foreign exchange from exports to the value of some two milliard dollars, so that only one-sixth of our import requirements is covered by Marshall Plan aid. If, therefore, we are to make our life-lines secure, we must increase German exports still further. Here again we must bear in mind that our export chances were better served by working to shorter terms of delivery than by higher prices or quality. This latter advantage we have almost entirely lost, and we must be prepared to measure up to our competitors both as regards prices and quality. Nine months ago this would have been out of the question, for, as we saw when the first moves towards liberalization brought a sudden drop in the volume

F

of our imports, we were not yet able to compete on the world market. Today, thanks to the liberalization policy, we have every right to assume that we have achieved the same over-all standard of efficiency as other countries.

In the same connection it should also be noted that, apropos of the facts I have just mentioned, the exchange rate of the D-Mark was undoubtedly fixed too high in autumn last year at 4.20 to the dollar, and that in the meantime we have succeeded in bringing the rate down to a more practicable level. But, as the free valuation of the Mark abroad clearly shows, much still remains to be done; in other words, the Mark must be strengthened at home, if it is to achieve genuine, free market-economy parity with the dollar. To realize this aim is all the more necessary in the long run, as we can only enjoy full economic recovery if we do away with foreign exchange controls and make the D-Mark freely convertible.

The ideal solution would, of course, be to keep Germany's price index more stable than that of other countries. That would certainly improve the value of our currency and our export prospects, and we could then expect not merely to maintain the existing level of employment and guarantee our food supplies but even expand them. This again is essential, for if we cannot meet any demand that arises it will be impossible, for psychological reasons alone, to keep prices steady. The whole situation is complicated by the fact that, in view of the price increases on the raw material markets, we must increase the value of our exports by 30% in order to be able to import the same quantities of raw materials and foodstuffs; which means that we must make it our aim to step up German exports in as short a time as possible by about 50%.

This is the background to my attitude towards the trades union demands for general wage increases of 15 to 20%. In my considered opinion we have a good chance of keeping the prices of finished goods at about their present level, in spite of higher raw material prices, if, by keener competition—which results quite spontaneously from growing liberalization—by increasing the volume of our output and by more efficient production, we can make corresponding reductions in costs and, wherever possible, reduce prices. In other words, the higher raw material prices will gradually become dissipated in the course of production and could finally be completely absorbed. At the same time, I realize that immovable prices are no more possible than immutable wages.

We must also remember that we are no longer living in an age of economic isolationism but are part of a world economy and that, in consequence, our economic policy must take account of developments in other countries. If they, for example, do not experience wage demands similar to those in Germany, we cannot afford to give away. If, on the other hand, there is a general wage increase in other countries, particularly in America, we can afford to be more flexible. In the first place we must realize that we cannot permit any reduction in our exports, otherwise employment and supplies in Germany will dry up. The German worker must be made to see then he risks his social security and his job if he expects social benefits from the action of the trade unions. If any such benefits did result, they would be short-lived and would lead eventually to even greater misery. The worker should bear in mind that, in September of last year when the D-Mark was devalued, we succeeded, in spite of a $22\frac{1}{2}\%$ rise in the cost of raw materials, in not merely keeping the prices of consumer goods stable but even in bringing them down still further. If, despite a number of hectic price fluctuations, he still feels inclined today to exercise self-discipline we will not merely be offering him vague consolation when we hold out the prospect of an improvement in his position. After all, the increased employment as a result of the boom and greater rationalization in production will also benefit him, and it is nothing short of grotesque to create the impression today that the boom in world trade will have an adverse effect on our social conditions.

Looking at our economic policy as a whole, we must take account of the fact that in Germany strong forces are again attempting to undermine the market economy system. There may be many amongst them who have not given the matter much thought but who believe, out of sheer habit or for historical reasons, that a government's objectives, as, for example, the financing of some kind of armaments programme, can only be achieved by a planned economy; there are also others in the ranks of my opponents who are working quite deliberately and systematically for a planned economy, without any consideration for the social and economic consequences. If, for example, the trade unions were to succeed with their demand and Germany's exports, instead of rising, were to drop appreciably; if, as a result, our economy and social product were to shrink and regular supplies could no longer be guaranteed, then the demand for rationing and government control of prices would be more or less a foregone conclusion. Although this demand might not in itself be taken too seriously, in fact the entire market economy would come under attack and its very existence would be threatened.

Our policy can therefore pursue only one course, which is to maintain our competitive capacity and secure a leading place in the world market, thereby ensuring, and if possible improving, our supplies of raw materials and foodstuffs to such an extent that any demand can be satisfied without restricting the free choice of the consumer. The present situation on the world market suggests that it is beginning to stabilize itself again, so that the expansion of our exports will make it possible for us to buy all the raw materials we need.

There is, of course, always the danger that supplies of certain raw materials may temporarily run short even on the world market and that this may result in speculative dealing on the German market. In such a case I would not hesitate to arrange, at government level, for certain imports of raw materials and foodstuffs, with a view not merely to supplementing our stocks but to putting supplies on the market at short notice, thereby forestalling irresponsible attempts to throw it off balance. That our market economy is not based on any rigid dogmatism is apparent from the fact, for example, that we decided at a very early stage to cut down exports of scrap-metal and later to stop them more or less completely; or, to take another case, that we reduced our disproportionate exports of pig-iron and crude steel and shifted the emphasis to exports of manufactured goods.

The situation will change again should the Foreign Ministers' Conference make it possible for us to play some part in the defence of Europe. If this happens, we will have to reckon once again with large-scale state orders and we shall then have to consider, whether the raw material for production of this kind should not also be acquired by the state. Everything will depend on the condition of the market at the time, on the volume of production required and on the behaviour of the economy itself.

All I am trying to say is that, while a certain amount of direction may become necessary, it should not be allowed to interfere in any way with the market economy system, much less threaten it. The great danger here, which I can almost certainly foresee, will come from another quarter. If the state has to spend substantial sums of money for such purposes, not a few people and also certain parties will maintain that this expenditure could not be met out of the budget but that some form of credit would have to be raised with the issuing bank. While precisely the same procedure as in the case of the 'Mefo' bills or the endless renewal of treasury bills will not be adopted, basically every device of this kind amounts to the same thing, namely, the beginning of an inflationary process. But once the economy is subject to inflationary pressure, then, in a market economy, price increases must inevitably follow. These, however, must on no account be allowed to appear at the political level, so a further consequence is the introduction of a price freeze, the restoration of the black market, and the reintroduction of rationing; in short, we are back precisely where we were before. I regard this policy as dishonest and dishonourable, because it must create the false impression in people's minds that these government responsibilities could be carried out without affecting the purchasing power of our people. This method is simply cold-blooded, invisible expropriation, steadily reducing purchasing power, depriving the people of their rights and finally of their moral integrity.

If we take the honest course, we have to ensure and to demonstrate that expenditure of this kind can be met out of taxation. It must be made clear what sacrifices the various strata of the German population have to make in order to carry out this responsibility, and they must be in no doubt that their living standards can only be maintained if there is a corresponding increase in output. By choosing this honest method of financing, we preserve the balance between national income and social product, and if, in addition, we manage to expand production sufficiently to avoid short supplies, there is not the slightest need, even with partial rearmament, for any departure from the market economy system. On the contrary, I would even say that it is all the more necessary to stand firm in such a situation, because only the market economy can stimulate higher output and guarantee a rise in productivity, whereas an unnatural and irresponsible change of course would produce not only the results I have described but also a decline in our output. There is no knowing where we in Germany would end up if, with the reintroduction of a planned economy, our price system became completely artificial, and if the situation so deteriorated that all national economies had to erect protective barriers instead of pursuing the path of liberalization towards even higher and more functional units. A planned or controlled economy is only feasible as an economic principle in the context of a fortress under siege, in which a monetary system is superfluous and all that is required is a system of distribution in kind. But we are living in an age which is pointing in exactly the opposite direction. The democratic world is drawing closer together and striving to increase its economic potentialities by forming larger units. Anyone who seriously believes that this is an aim worth achieving must see to it, above all, that the various currencies remain stable and that the international traffic in goods and services functions as smoothly as possible.

To sum up—as I see it, the problems involved in implementing our economic policy are not so much material as political in character, and I regard the misguided views on financial policy which have become so widespread as particularly dangerous. I am convinced that we have a very good chance of turning this dangerous political development to considerable advantage for our economic recovery, but run a grave risk of losing the economic advantages we have gained by adopting a misguided and cowardly policy.

12

LET US FACE THE FUTURE WITH COURAGE AND VIGOUR

(Speech at the opening of the German Industrial Exhibition
in Berlin on October 1, 1950)

*The Korean war and the world economic crisis continue. In the
USA there is a growing trend towards economic controls and
other forms of state intervention. At Erhard's insistence, the
Federal Government continues to pursue its policy of liberalization.
But there are unmistakable signs of crisis: coal supplies running
down, shortage of sugar, price increases at home and abroad,
danger of a price-war spiral, adverse trade balance. On September
29 in Paris Erhard discusses the possibility of closer Franco-
German economic co-operation. At the opening of the first German Industrial Exhibition in West Berlin Erhard voices his optimism in public:*

This festive occasion for Berlin is also an occasion that gives me
great personal pleasure, for I have regarded Berlin's development
into an 'exhibition city' as an essential ingredient in the improvement and consolidation of conditions in Berlin and West Germany.
If I was in a position at the opening of the Motor Show to express
the hope that a large German Industrial Exhibition might be
organized here in October, I am particularly happy today that this
hope has been realized. This exhibition is being held at a time of
considerable historical importance, when we are proving to the
democratic and peace-loving countries of the world that this
democratic system has not merely succeeded in producing additional social benefits and promoting human happiness but can
generate the power within itself to protect the system against destructive and subversive forces anywhere in the world.

The target we have set ourselves is to incorporate Germany more
and more fully in the democratic world system, and the decisions

reached at the Foreign Ministers' Conference in New York have laid the foundations which will enable us to fell ourselves an integral part of the peace-loving democratic world. I, for my part, would like to take this opportunity of expressing my gratitude, in particular to the American people for the Marshall Aid, and I am especially pleased that I can thank Mr Hoffmann in person. At the opening of the Frankfurt Fair I said that, in my view, we had made good use of the Marshall Aid. We know now, in retrospect, that it is thanks to this aid that our country has become viable again and our nation has survived. If, on the other hand, the position today is such that, as against 350 million dollars a year of Marshall Aid, which will continue until 1952, we are earning from our exports foreign exchange worth two milliard dollars; if, in other words, we can already pay for five-sixths of our imports from our own resources and only need to cover one-sixth—though a characteristic sixth—with free dollars from the Marshall Plan, then I believe this is the best and most dignified way in which the German people and the German economy can thank the American people.

This exhibition will provide still further proof that the vitality of the German people, its spiritual vitality and its will to create and develop, are unimpaired, and that a free nation of free consumers can, with the current output of our industry in the Federal Republic, demand that a social product amounting to 115% of the volume in 1936 should be employed for its own ends, for the ends of human and social welfare. The recent upheavals in the arena of world politics have naturally affected the German economy in common with that of all other countries, and the main effect of these upheavals, which had not merely economic but also psychological repercussions, was to create a feeling of uncertainty about our prospects of keeping our economic affairs in good order. I think that today we tend once more to see things rather more calmly. It is my firm personal conviction that, if the forces of the democratic, peace-loving, non-Communist countries of the world are united, the defence of this world of ours is assured, without any need to abandon our other aim, namely, to work for the happiness and welfare of mankind.

We are in the happy position today of witnessing not only the recovery of our economy but also, arising directly from it, the re-integration of our country's foreign trade in the whole world complex. There is hardly a country on the globe, hardly a state or continent, with which we do not have close economic relations of some kind. So I believe that the present turn of events in the political sphere will also prove a blessing for us. We have become conscious of the fact that, in moments of danger, in periods of grave political tension, we are no longer alone, no longer a beleaguered fortress shut off from the democratic world, but have become an integral part of it. We want to play our part, to throw our weight into the balance, in order to defend that world.

Earlier in my speech I quoted certain figures to illustrate the advance made by German production and pointed out that our present volume of production stands at 115% of the 1936 level; an equally positive development has taken place in our foreign trade, which has reached the equivalent of two milliard dollars annually. Let me remind you—for it seems to me a significant pointer to the future of Berlin and to our confidence in the growing prosperity of this city—that our exports stand today at two milliard dollars. Who could have imagined, when the Marshall Plan started and when Germany's 1947 export figures were between 600 and 700 million marks, that it would be possible to come even within striking distance of the targets we had set ourselves for the termination of the Marshall Plan; targets which entailed exporting to the value of some $2\frac{1}{2}$ milliard dollars, if we were to keep our economy on a sound basis and guarantee our people a reasonable standard of living? I am convinced that Germany's exports will continue to develop, and if we do not lose sight of the aims, the peaceful aims, of our economy, whatever else it may be called upon to do, then I feel sure—and here I am speaking to the Berliners and I am again making a favourable forecast—that Berlin's economy can be stimulated still further and, above all, that it will make an important contribution to the expansion of Germany's exports. I had the pleasure today of meeting the British President of the Board of Trade and exchanging the documents of the Anglo-German Trade Agreement. It is yet another sign of the progress we have made that both parties to this agreement have provided for a total import and export figure of 1.1 milliard dollars.

I would like, on this occasion, to thank West German industry for the active part it has played and the initiative it has shown in arranging this exhibition. I promised the Berliners that for every exhibition hall they could build in Berlin the demand from West German industry would be so great that all the available space would be used. I am grateful to West German industry for enabling me to keep my word. But I would also like to take this opportunity of appealing once again to all sectors of industry in West Germany to establish even stronger and closer ties with industry in Berlin. This gap must be bridged, for only if we are united in mind and spirit can we lay the necessary foundations on which our political aims, on which the future of Germany as we all see it, can be realized. In order to achieve this, in order to be strong enough, we must put our hearts into it and let the devil take the hindmost. This is the only way to get on in life, and particularly in Germany today. If life were all cut and dried, if our daily problems could be reduced to a materialistic, rationalistic formula, then this city of Berlin would have no present and still less of a future. But these things have their roots in another and superior part of our being. That is why I believe we must summon all our courage, all our energy and all our confidence to the task of making our destiny—and at the very heart of it lies the destiny of Berlin—a happy one and one of building a happy future for our people in a free and peace-loving world.

13

THE DANGERS ON THE ROAD TO
UNRESTRICTED FOREIGN TRADE

(Address given at the opening of the International Trade Fair,
Frankfurt on March 11, 1951)

*Mounting hostilities in Korea, the continuing upward trend of
prices for raw materials on the material markets, and a continuing
boom in demand at home and abroad, all contributed towards
increasing the demand for imports to such an extent that early in
1951 the balance-of-payments position of the Federal Republic
began to deteriorate rapidly. The gap, which amounted to over
500 million marks in the second half of the year, seemed likely to
go on widening, especially since liberalization of imports from
OEEC countries had been raised to 60% in the autumn of 1950.
Four months after the European Payments Union was formed,
Germany had exhausted her credit quota. Intensified monetary
restrictions (raising of the minimum reserve rate by 50%, raising
of the discount rate to 7%, and instructions to the commercial
banks to reduce the volume of short-term credit to one billion
marks) failed to check the deterioration in the balance-of-payments
position. It became necessary to tighten up foreign exchange regulations, to introduce a system of special cash deposits amounting to
50% of the counterpart in marks of all foreign exchange applied
for on import account, and finally, in February, 1951, to discon-
tinue the liberalization of imports from the EPU countries. In
addition, it became necessary to apply to the EPU for additional
credit.*

*The Frankfurt International Trade Fair, which Erhard opened
on March 11, 1951, thus started under poor auspices, in spite of
the encouragement expected from the first-stage revision of the
Occupation Statute announced on March 6. The Minister for
Economic Affairs was faced with the task of pleading for inter-*

*national confidence in Germany's reliability as a debtor and for
greater exertions on the part of exporters.*

Walking round the Industrial Fair today took my mind back to
October, 1945, when, as the Bavarian Minister for Economic
Affairs, I made the first attempt to get an exports exhibition started
in Bavaria. Looking back over the five years that have gone by
since then, I am confirmed in the optimism for which I have so
often been criticized. What has been achieved in Germany in these
five years is indeed something to be proud of. By 'we' I mean not
only those in charge of economic affairs, but the whole German
people. We managed to create out of despair and hopelessness the
basis for economic health and social well-being, in spite of all that
still remains to be done, and in spite of the political cares that still
weigh heavily upon us.

I had really intended to visit this exhibition today masquerading,
so to speak, as a buyer or in the role of Harun-al-Rashid. But I seem
to have certain attributes which are difficult to disguise, and so my
attempt failed. Nevertheless I was very much impressed by what I
saw, and when I left I said with conviction that here was proof that
Frankfurt had made tremendous strides in the fields of organization, technology and industrial know-how.

But I was also conscious of a certain wistfulness as I toured this
exhibition, as well as of pride in what had been achieved in the
short span of five years, for I could not help feeling that these two
events—the holding of the International Trade Fair on the one
hand and the slowing down of the process of liberalization on the
other—were in fact mutually contradictory. Was this feeling
justified? You know that in recent weeks discussions in the press
and radio have been turning on the anxious question of whether
Germany could find a way out of the adverse balance-of-payments
position which would yet enable her to remain within the association of the European Payments Union. Would not financial
pressure, it was being said, lead inevitably to a limitation of our
liberty and of our freedom of action in the longer term? Might not
the public declaration of our willingness be in fact no more than a
formality, merely an apology for what was forced upon us by the
tide of economic circumstance?

But first let me say something about the principle of liberalization, because this, I would say, is the main point on which opinions are divided, or is at least the main talking point. I was perfectly aware that as soon as we were compelled to revert to the problem of Germany's balance of payments we should be laying ourselves open to the criticism of having acted irresponsibly. This criticism comes not only from economic and political circles inside Germany, but is levelled mainly from sources outside our country; I must therefore say something about it. I doubt whether foreign critics, who are once again inclined to dismiss us as irresponsible debtors, realize the problems that faced Germany in 1945. Not only had we lost the war and suffered all the consequences of the collapse of our country; the entire economic structure, and with it the social and political structure, had been shaken to the foundations and changed beyond recognition.

This meant that at the outset, in 1945, I had to adopt economic measures that could only show very little in the way of results. The will to throw ourselves open to the world was there, but this led inevitably to Germany having to adopt a policy destined to turn it into something like a larger Belgium.

The situation in which we then found ourselves, and still find ourselves, is one of slavish—or, if you will, fatal—dependence on world markets, since we could only succeed in assuring our food supplies, let alone an adequate supply of raw materials for a population of 50 million (ten million more than before the war), provided we succeeded in getting German goods and services accepted in the outside world. Anyone who tries to think clearly will appreciate that a process of this kind, constantly interrupted and hindered by political counter-currents, could not possibly be carried out without creating friction. But this in its turn also makes it clear why Germany and the authors of her economic policy welcomed all the measures involved and were prepared to go ahead with them as long as there was any hope of breaking the bonds of isolation, self-sufficiency and protectionism.

It is beyond dispute that these evils were not peculiar to Germany. Isolation and protectionism characterized European trade policy for many years. And it was precisely because we recognized that the only chance for the German economy was to head in the opposite direction, and that the only hope of solving our own urgent social problems was to tackle the problem of the larger European market successfully—it was precisely for these reasons that we had to act. There may be those who say, and I am not disposed to quarrel with them, that we may have shown a good deal of courage in going ahead with the system of liberalization. But let me say this: what inspired us was not megalomania, let alone presumption or irresponsibility, but something entirely different, namely anxiety as to whether we could ever succeed in solving our urgent social problems in a politically tolerable length of time. One has only to remember the ten million refugees and the appalling number of unemployed to realize that it would have been no use saying to them: we shall not forget you, we shall do our best to work our way step by step out of isolation into a wider community. Other countries not labouring under the same degree of social pressure were not apparently ready to respond with the same openness of heart. Powerful forces had to be generated if the barriers were to be broken down.

On looking back I feel sure I can take credit for this achievement; but when you think of the German balance-of-payments position you may equally well say I was at fault. In this connection I can at least kill some recent reports of an impending ban on imports. You can take it from me that there is no truth in them. We import what we can, that is to say, we import what we can afford to pay for with the foreign exchange we earn by our exports; no more and no less. You may say if you wish that we have overdone things and earned too much in advance. As you know, we were granted an EPU credit of up to 320 million dollars. This figure was based, as in the case of all the other member states, on 15% of the volume of foreign trade as shown in the returns for 1949. But no other country has expanded its foreign trade since 1949 to the same extent as Germany has. Consequently our allocation of 'working capital' amounting to 320 million dollars soon proved inadequate, just as it would in the case of any commercial undertaking that was expanding rapidly.

We were therefore granted an additional credit of 180 million dollars, or to be more accurate 120 million, since to reach the supplementary limit of 180 million we were required to contribute 60 million dollars out of our own resources. Thus the position today is that we have taken up approximately 460 million out of a total available credit of 500 million dollars, but this has involved paying in some 175 million, so that our actual indebtedness under the EPU arrangement amounts in all to between 280 and 290 million dollars. I am pointing this out not by way of apology for my own actions, nor in order to make light of the problem. Nothing could be further from my mind; I know very well how serious the position is and I realize that we shall very soon have reached our credit limit. I realize too that we cannot count on any further extension of credit under the EPU arrangement. We have therefore got to cut our coat according to our cloth, that is to say that we have got to manage with the credit already granted us in order to cope with our foreign trade commitments.

Germany will fulfil her obligations to EPU, come what may. Even if the worst comes to the worst, that is to say, if the means to repay cannot be provided out of export earnings, there is still the sum of 120 million dollars at our disposal on a special account; whatever happens we shall therefore remain honest debtors in our dealings with foreign creditors.

Let me go further and give you some account of the measure of the tasks we are faced with in this connection. Consider for a moment that Germany has to pay promptly in hard cash, or even in advance by letter of credit, and in full, for imports of essential foodstuffs and equally important raw materials, while on the other hand German export business has to be conducted in accordance with established international practice involving payment terms of up to three months and in the case of capital goods far longer than this; you will then realize that this discrepancy in terms of payment alone is sufficient to explain why we were bound to get into payment difficulties as long as we lacked foreign credit of any kind. I would even go so far as to say that our danger of getting into fresh difficulty will increase for the time being with every increase in the total volume of our foreign trade.

This does not mean to say that it is the aim of German economic policy to seek a solution by restrictive measures, although we are bound at present to ensure that we do not incur more payment obligations than we can meet out of the foreign exchange we earn by our exports. This is scarcely the course we should have adopted, had we been free to choose, in order to get out of the present impasse. Every limitation and every restriction on the import side is, on the contrary, an emergency measure and can never as I see it be more than a temporary expedient. All our efforts must be bent on building up exports so as to recover greater freedom of action in regard to imports. We shall therefore take active measures to promote exports, for instance, by refunding turnover tax and by allowances on income tax and corporation tax.

I am happy to say that the efforts that I have been making for the past year in this direction are at last beginning to bear fruit.

At the same time we shall endeavour—shall, indeed, be compelled—to shape the structure of the home market in such a fashion that the operation of supply and demand will of itself tend actively to stimulate exports.

Whatever measures are adopted to deal with the situation, the economic experts, or rather the politicians, are not yet of one mind in this matter. Politicians and economists do not invariably agree. So a method will simply have to be found to put a brake on consumption and to prevent price inflation on the home market where conditions have already in part become too comfortable. The visible drop in savings is a further pointer to the need for this kind of action. I am not blaming the consumer; the consumer is prompted by uncertainty and anxiety, from which there are no ready means of escape. At the same time, reluctance to save has the undesirable and unfortunate effect of impeding the bloodstream of the economy, as a whole, so that all purchasing power throws its whole weight, increased as it is by high social pressure on to the consumer goods markets, while for lack of capital accumulation through savings—and in future, it must be added, for lack of the all too easy method of financing by tax manipulation—a vacuum is created in the capital market which has somehow to be filled.

Clearly what is needed is to coax the economy in the direction of the export markets by reducing the attractiveness of selling on the home consumer goods market. This would at the same time have the effect of cutting out those imports which constitute a harmful drain on foreign exchange and doubling the improvement achieved in the balance-of-payments situation.

I have been referring to these lines of thought in order to make it clear to our foreign friends that there is no question whatever of a change of direction in German trade policy. Nor need they fear that we might be considering disassociating ourselves from the European Payments Union. Very much the reverse. We shall in fact fulfil all import licences so far issued both under the liberalization programme and also as far as quotas based on trade agreements are concerned. If at the moment we are drawing up a kind of general balance-sheet and are compelled to adopt certain measures of a compensatory nature involving a certain degree of delay in meeting particular claims, these are merely matters of technical procedure and are destined to be superseded as quickly as possible by the effects of an intensified export drive.

When you look at the display of German products exhibited at this Frankfurt Trade Fair, you will have the impression that you are living in a peace-time economy. High quality goods are certainly calculated to make life better and more enjoyable. I am well aware that such a state of affairs can be regarded from another, more critical, point of view by those who are disposed to ask whether this is really in keeping with the present situation, whether it is right that an economy should be turning out consumer goods of higher and higher quality at a time when the democratic world is faced with the hard necessity of devoting a substantial part of its national product to the defence of liberty and democracy.

As I walked through the exhibition buildings I could not altogether escape these thoughts. That I was nevertheless able to enjoy the over-all picture of this Fair was due to the fact that I am firmly convinced that we can best play our part in the defence of freedom in Europe by continuing to foster peaceful development based on social justice and well-being. And we in Germany, of all peoples, situated as we are at this junction between West and East, cannot afford, either politically or socially, to alter the structure of our economy in any way or to an extent that would involve departure from our policy of concentrating on high quality processing work. This enables us to employ large numbers of workpeople, whereas if we devoted ourselves exclusively to the immediate needs of defence, we would incur the social consequences

G

of growing unemployment. Yet I am fully aware of the obligation resting on the German economy to do its utmost to contribute its share towards the defence of our world. But I believe that this must be done on lines different from those hitherto generally accepted.

We must get away from the piecemeal method by which contracts are at present placed whether for government work, work for the occupation authorities, or work on foreign account so far as it clearly serves this same purpose. As long as the method adopted by the American, British and French authorities persists, demand will tend to fasten on typical and specific bottlenecks in German industry. This tendency has its dangers, first from the point of view of the German economy, because extensive sectors of the processing industry are apt to become blocked, giving rise to unemployment. Secondly, those who place the contracts get the entirely mistaken and harmful impression that the German economy is unwilling to devote any proportion of its energies to the defence of democracy.

This will be one of the chief purposes of my projected visit to Washington, to come to a better understanding, and to gain recognition for the fact—which will have to be borne out in action —that we are very well prepared to play our part to the full, provided we are allowed to decide on the type of work and the system employed, so as to enable our economic resources to be used to best advantage.

We must approach these issues in all seriousness. Everything that happens today in the political field has a direct bearing on our affairs. I am very much afraid, for instance, that the Russians, in view of the tension prevailing in their own camp and of the uncertainty of the outcome of the cold war, may achieve more than they could ever have achieved in a hot war. We therefore have a duty not only to play our part in defence but also to maintain a social standard of living which, though it may have to be lowered slightly in certain respects, is high enough to save us from being forced to think on totalitarian lines or adopt collectivist institutions; or from having our living standard whittled away by a gradual lowering of the level of employment and shrinking of the social product.

I shall have been badly misunderstood if the press takes note only of my optimism; it would be truer to speak of me as an extremely sober realist. In this capacity I do not deny that the German people may have to put up with a lower standard of living, directly or indirectly. As yet, however, it is impossible to assess how far the claims made upon us are going to affect our living standard. One thing is certain: we must not relapse into lethargy, become fatalists, and say that if demands are made on the German economy and people for defence, we shall have no alternative but to make the sacrifices demanded, put up with restrictions, tighten our belts, do without. I should like to warn the German people against this kind of attitude, against allowing their thinking to become lifeless and petrified. As a politician, I dare not prophesy whether it will prove possible to counter-balance any sacrifice that may have to be made, by raising the quality and quantity of our industrial output, by a greater expenditure of effort; but I do know for certain that we must make the attempt come what may, because otherwise the situation will become unbearable for a country with social burdens as enormous as ours.

There must be no going back; we must not tread the path that leads to restriction. A rich country might be able to afford it, but we can only meet the growing demands made on us if we induce the German people to become united in the will to achieve more, to keep its head, to become more self-reliant. We must never let go of the conviction that if only we keep at it and maintain the sound foundation of our national life by making greater efforts and by providing our readiness to shoulder increasing social responsibilities, we not only avoid the risk of losing all but on the contrary stand to gain all.

As the man responsible for conducting our economic policy, I can assure you that I shall continue along this road with all the determination at my command. The road back into fatalism would inevitably lead Germany into a position in which she would have lost the close links which she has so far managed to forge with other countries, and in particular with the European economies. If we lack the energy and the will to overcome present difficulties, for instance, by intensifying our export drive (even if this has to be for a time at the expense of our home consumption), then we should have no alternative but to import less foodstuffs and less raw materials and submit to the evils of a lower level of employment and all that this would entail, including a lower standard of living.

Were we to consider following this dangerous road we should also have to realize that a country cannot unilaterally restrict its imports without in the long run risking that foreign countries mete out the same treatment in return and cease to accept German goods without reserve. In speaking to you here I can therefore only express the hope, and indeed the conviction, that if Germany ever had to invoke Article 3 of the European Payments Union and the bodies concerned recognized that Germany was justified in doing so, our partners—the seventeen member states of EPU—would not take steps under the terms of the Convention to check the flow of German exports to countries in question.

These European countries will be the more ready to show understanding because they can rest assured that the measures we adopt under the EPU arrangement not only do not herald a change of direction in our economic policy but are regarded by us as a burden which we shall do our best to rid ourselves of as quickly as possible.

I do not deny for a moment that the situation looks confusing. Some circles here at home accuse me of carrying love of truth too far in my approach to the problem of liberalization. My reply to this would be, either we want liberalization or we reject it. What we cannot do, in honesty, is to give the impression of adhering to the liberalization policy while at the same time using any and every kind of device to ensure that it is only half-heartedly put into practice. Our dealings have been open and above board, and I stand by them even though they may have resulted in things not having gone favourably for us. I wish to cast no aspersion on any other member state, but I am surely entitled to say that if the principle of liberalization had been followed in all the countries of Europe as wholeheartedly and seriously as in ours, events would probably have taken a very different course. After all, the EPU was intended to provide as satisfactory a substitute as possible for good international currency relations.

The plan was not, however, so conceived as to make this possible. And yet the aim of establishing a payments clearing system on an international basis was commendable. But how much of it is there left? Residual protectionism is basically responsible for the fact that each individual country tried to reach as full a settlement as possible with each partner bilaterally, thereby dealing a blow at the very concept of EPU. Let us nevertheless go on hoping that EPU can be developed into a more effective instrument and one capable at the same time of fostering a spirit of community across the national divisions of this age-old continent.

The most promising means to this end consist in paving the way for greater freedom and mobility in foreign trade. It is futile to coin political slogans about unity and international collaboration as long as national egotism is given full rein in economic matters.

In these last five years we have admittedly achieved a good deal. And yet in many respects our trade relations are still in a backward state more reminiscent of the age of the mail-coach than befitting the atomic age. Fear of technical development seems very often to put a brake on progress. And when national egotism joins forces with this fear, the result can hardly be encouraging. And so, although the programme of liberalization has had its setbacks, and in spite of the fact that it may appear as if Germany wanted to, or would, or had to, change course, I should like here, before you, to make this unequivocal declaration of faith.

We wish and intend in any event to continue on the course of cultivating free and unrestricted relations with all countries and particularly with our partners in Europe. To my mind, Europe is not an ultimate concept but simply a mould in which economic and political integration can take shape. We must look still further ahead, for if we are to defend our democratic world we must learn in the process. We must never again relapse into isolation. Heaven knows, the need for progressively closer association and collaboration between us is inescapable. There can be no kind of doubt about this: the efficiency of human labour and man's achievement in the world will reach their highest pitch when there is division of labour on a very wide international scale, through the confluence of the wealth of all nations in as free an exchange of goods as possible. If, in our present democratic world, we have got to be prepared to defend ourselves, and are willing to make the necessary sacrifice to this end, then we should also be prepared, from the same attitude of mind and spirit, to overcome as quickly as possible whatever may still be artificially blocking our path and keeping us divided, and to forget as quickly as possible whatever mistrust may still be smouldering beneath the surface. We shall become more prosperous, more productive, better fitted for the battle of life, if we unite to defend our right to live in freedom.

14

DISCUSSION WITH PROFESSOR NÖLTING

(Organized jointly by the CDU and SPD
in Düsseldorf, on December 8, 1951

Equality of status for Germany is nearing fulfilment: at the Washington Conference from September 9-14, 1951, the Western Powers agree to establish long-term relations with the Federal Government, until such time as a Peace Treaty is signed with a united Germany. At the Paris Conference the terms of a Treaty with the Federal Republic are discussed. In the second half of 1951 the balance of payments improves, largely due to increasing exports. But the SPD continues not merely to criticize the Constitution but also to attack Erhard's economic policy.

Erhard takes up the challenge and confronts his critics in public on several occasions. On December 8, 1951, in Düsseldorf he comes face to face with his main opponent, the SPD member of Parliament and former Minister of Economics in North-Rhine Westphalia, Professor Erich Nölting. The two men have their second encounter—the first had already taken place in Frankfurt in 1948—in the vast Rheinhalle, before an audience of 5,000 people. The discussion is frequently interrupted by bursts of applause or heckling.

Nölting contends that Erhard's economic policy will bring national disaster. It has undermined confidence in democratic government. Economic policy, he claims, had become bogged down in a jungle of conflicting interests and had degenerated into 'economic chaos'. Erhard handed out promises 'like a Father Christmas'. The SPD was against a controlled economy but was in favour of 'a planned economy'. 'Their economic policy,' Nölting continues, 'is confused, contradictory and chaotic. They come up against problem after problem but never make any headway. All words, no deeds!' Germany had become 'Paradise for the rich and Hell for the poor' . . . Erhard replies:

I expected just such a fireworks display. It consisted mostly of squibs, which depend for their effect on darkness and weak nerves! These statements will not bear examination in the cold light of truth. The best proof of this is the success of our economic policy.

My colleague Nölting maintained that he should have spoken after me. I entirely disagree. Throughout all this time I have been subjected to the most violent attacks by the Social Democrat opposition, by their spokesmen and their press. I wanted to hear them expound their views here, so that I could then give the relevant replies. This is only just!

People may say anything they like about me; I am accustomed to that. But no one has yet dared accuse me of lacking civic courage! I have not come here today with an escort or with pistols but, like all of you, as a simple citizen.

Herr Nölting has suggested that we should stop talking about controlled economy and market economy. Agreed! But he himself has just done it. And to think that I might have posed as a liberator! Grand gestures of that kind don't come naturally to me. But one thing I would like to say with all clarity, and this is an undeniable fact which just cannot be talked away: at a truly historic moment, the only possible moment to break away from a controlled economy—on June 20, 1948, to be precise—the Social Democrats—and this is recorded in the official minutes of the Economic Council—did everything in their power to prevent me from taking this step. Professor Nölting has now said that a new brand of controlled economy is looming up. Don't be alarmed; as long as I stand here, no such disaster will afflict you again.

I have never made any secret of the fact, and indeed I have said not once but a dozen times, that there is nothing in my conception of a free economy which precludes intervention in the national economy, if it is necessary to introduce an element of planning and guidance. At the same time, everything depends on the methods and aims of any such intervention. But to one specific charge against me, namely, that I was not slow to intervene on the state's behalf in the field of coal, iron, steel and power investments, the answer is simple. Yes, it was necessary, because it was precisely here that a free economy had so far failed to operate. If we had been able to convert coal, iron and steel to a free economy in the year 1948, then there too—and this is my firm conviction—as in all other branches of the economy, a natural and organic equilibrium would have been created. That is why our most urgent need today is not for legislation to remove this cancer but for an all-out effort to get beyond a production surplus to a reasonable balance of supply and demand, and so finally to lift controls also from the coal industry and allow this market once again to operate freely.

Professor Nölting claims that his party has a list of all the statements I have made and that, if I were to read it, I would have something to laugh at. As we all know, a sensible man should always be able to laugh at himself! But if I were to compile a similar list of statements made by the SPD, I think it would make one cry rather than laugh.

Prices and wages—in other words, real incomes—have been mentioned here, and in this context a 'wise' phrase has been coined: It's not the production but the standard of living that matters.

May I just ask you all where the standard of living comes from, if not from production? Anyone who can suppose that it is possible to raise the standard of living without the necessary production must be living in a world of fantasy or cloud-cuckoo land. We cannot consume more as a community than we have produced by our communal labour! On the other hand, we cannot and must not even consume all we produce. Some of our labour and our national production must be ploughed back to maintain, expand and improve our productive capital. It remains a fact, however, that the standard of living can only be raised by expanding our national output by increased production. Let me give you a few figures. In July, 1948, our production was 57% of the 1936 figure, by the middle of 1949 it had reached 85%, by mid-1950 it was 107%, and in July, 1951, it had risen to 127%. Since then it has increased further to 134%, which means that in the German economy, in the area of the Federal Republic today, in spite of the severe damage suffered during and after the war and of Germany's tragic history, 34% more is being produced than in 1936, a year in which, as you know, rearmament was already under way.

Reference has also been made to developments in wages and prices, another subject I shall be only too happy to discuss in detail. In so doing, I propose to quote official statistics, so that Professor Nölting will hardly be able to say they have been deliberately faked.

If one takes the figure for the first six months of 1950, when we and the rest of Europe had not yet felt the political repercussions of the Korean war, as 100, Germany's present wage index stands at 123, Britain's at 109, Italy's at 113, Belgium's at 109, the Netherlands' at 111 and Switzerland's at 101. If you compare the cost of living on the same basis, then the figure for Germany is 108, France 121, Britain 111, Italy 113, Belgium 112, the Netherlands 113 and the United States 110. I gave these figures personally to the German Trades Union Congress at the end of July and asked them to have them checked by their Scientific Institute. If there was any mistake, I would be glad to discuss it. At all events I wanted an authoritative statement by the Congress. I received the figures back—without comment; since then I have quoted them in roughly twenty public speeches. I cannot imagine that the Trades Union Congress would have shown such discreet silence, if it had been in a position to disprove these figures!

And now our expenditure on the social services! I believe that the figures I am about to quote will carry more conviction than the flowery phrases of the previous speaker. So let us see what the situation is as regards the social services that have been provided in the Federal Republic. The total expenditure on social services amounted in 1949 to 10.9, in 1950 to 14.5 and in 1951 to 17.8 milliard marks. So, in two years, from 1949 to 1951, it increased from 10 to 17 milliard marks. These indisputable statistics should be proof enough that our policy is not so unsocial as Professor Nölting would have us believe. In fact, we have every right to speak of 'social market economy'!

A few more details. In the Federal Republic, expenditure on social services represents 51.8% of tax revenue, in Belgium 26%, in Sweden 29.6%, in Denmark 31.3%, in Britain 39.3%. I repeat: in Germany 51.8%! That too may serve as an indication of the Federal Government's efforts to solve our social problems.

Answer this question honestly. Would anyone of you have thought in the middle of 1948 that the living standard of the

German people might reach its present level three years later? And yet no country in the world started on its reconstruction programme in such unfavourable circumstances as Germany. Torn in two by the tragedy of our own history, we had lost half our agrarian wealth. Our federal territory was in ruins and essential parts of our technical equipment had been destroyed. Into this area streamed 9 to 10 million refugees and expellees, without personal belonging and without tools. They had to find work, and we made work for them. Proof: in 1936 there were 11·2 million employed in the Federal Republic, in 1948 13·5, in 1950 14·3, and in 1951 the number of employed had risen to 14·9 million. There is, therefore, a steady increase. In the last year alone the number rose by 600,000, while the number of unemployed dropped by 100,000. This may serve to prove that we also feel competent to solve the employment problem.

On the other hand, this is not something that can be taken for granted! We began in 1945—or, more precisely, in 1948—at the lowest level from which any national economy could be rebuilt. Our output had dropped so far that only a superhuman effort could make us competitive again. But this was exactly what we had to achieve, if we were to lay new and stable foundations for life in Germany. For this reason we had to pursue a liberal course. We could not simply sit and wait behind protective walls till German industry had been gradually restored by artificial and state measures to the international output level; no, we had to take the risk of exposing it to competition, of putting it to the test.

I certainly do not underrate the unemployment problem. On the contrary, I have repeatedly pointed out that it is the most urgent of our problems. At the same time, I am not prepared to accept the present official unemployment figure as a measure of real unemployment, for we know from experience that in many places where unemployed were registered it was also impossible to recruit labour. A close check of the number of genuinely unemployed would probably present a somewhat different picture.

It has been stated that, as a result of German economic policy, 90% of the German people have suffered a lowering of their living standard, through my fault, and have tasted hardship, in order that 10% of the people could live better. This is a complete figment of the imagination, a mischievous and misleading fabrication. I would like to meet those who are worse off than before the currency reform. I can only describe such statements as political swindling or downright stupidity. Furthermore, the Social Democrats were fairly divided on the question of unemployment and possible methods of overcoming it; for, after all, it was Socialists who prophesied gloomily that after the currency reform we would have five million unemployed.

But now I come to the prize chapter, to our foreign trade or foreign trade policy, which, it appears, has been a complete failure. Professor Nölting made a statement to this effect as long ago as March of this year, and in September his parliamentary party was talking of our foreign trade balance collapsing. What has become of this collapse? Professor Nölting said we were no longer creditworthy and had lost our reputation throughout the world. This, he claimed, was the result of lack of planning in our foreign trade policy. England was out of the wood, she had starved herself back to health, while we had eaten ourselves into bankruptcy.

After the outbreak of the Korean war there were disturbances in the world market, the adverse effects of which were not confined to Germany. As one of the poorest countries in the world in terms of raw materials, we had to buy, had to make sure that enough raw materials and foodstuffs were imported. The shortage became more and more acute, for world-market prices rose in some instances by several hundred per cent. But we had no choice, we could not wait, because we were responsible for maintaining a high level of employment and, at the same time, the food supplies of the German people.

So we bought because we had to buy, although we knew that this high tide of imports would create balance-of-payments difficulties. You can take it from me that I had enough sense to foresee these difficulties quite clearly. We were faced by the following alternative. Should we concentrate like some subordinate book-keeper on the foreign currency figures, or assume more responsibility and see to it that German industry had enough raw materials to maintain production, while at the same time guaranteeing Germany's food supplies? Faced with this alternative, we chose the latter course. I did not find the decision at all an easy one, but we were prisoners of our own destiny. Subsequent events proved that this was the right policy. When you consider that in the so-called 'Korean Year' the average increase in raw material prices on the world market was 67% and in food prices 40%, because there was a world-wide demand for them, then it is obvious what a tremendous burden was imposed on Germany's economy. In order to acquire the necessary imports, we had to increase our exports correspondingly, and one must bear in mind that we have almost returned to peace-time conditions when more than 75% of our exports consist of manufactured goods. But on an average the price increases for our exports worked out at only about 17%. If you compare the rise in imports with the much smaller price increases on the export side, you will realize that burdens were imposed on Germany's economy which were far in excess of what we received in Marshall Plan aid.

I have expressed my gratitude so often for the generous support given to us through the Marshall Plan, that I do not think there is any danger of my being misunderstood if I deny the imputation of the Opposition, that virtually all that had been achieved in the past years can be attributed to Marshall Plan aid. The Marshall Plan undoubtedly provided very valuable assistance at the beginning, but the real work was done by the German people as a whole, in all classes of society.

An inevitable result of the political disturbances was that in March of this year the credit of 320 million dollars granted to us in the EPU was exhausted. This figure was based automatically on a 15% quota of our 1949 foreign trade. But, as I shall demonstrate, Germany's foreign trade has increased so rapidly, that this credit was too small. In view of this, it was agreed to grant the Federal Republic a further credit which allowed us to draw up to 480 million dollars, of which we have in fact used 475 million. We have also admittedly had to impose certain import restrictions. In the meantime the world market has settled down again, but in particular the German people have settled down. Immediately following the Korean crisis it was understandable that the German people, having barely found its feet again, should be especially sensitive to a world-political event of this magnitude. So every effort was made by industry to buy raw materials at any price. But the

German consumer was also prepared to buy at any price! Fear that supplies might run short was the predominant influence on the market last autumn and winter. This fear had to be overcome and it was overcome, not by reintroducing rationing and reviving state controls but by the simple and proven method of meeting all demands on the market. This we succeeded in doing. As long as I am here, you will not have the curse of rationed consumption. In the meantime we have also been able to make certain provisions, as a result of which the continuing restrictions on imports will not be felt by the consumer. In the past six months the situation has, in fact, changed for the better.

By May of this year we had again worked off the whole of the supplementary credit down to the official figure of 320 million dollars, and today we have even repaid the remaining 320 million dollars, which means that our position in the European Payments Union has changed from that of a debtor to a creditor nation! At the same time the reserves of the 'Bank deutscher Länder' have substantially increased. We do not owe a cent of foreign currency for imports, whereas for exports we have dollar credits or foreign currency claims totalling 500 million dollars. English economic journals are now suggesting that it would be interesting to know how and with what means Germany achieved this transformation; from Germany one might learn what a government must do.

Statistics always provide the most convincing evidence: in autumn 1948 we exported on an average goods to the value of 206 million marks per month, in 1949 335 million, in 1950 697 million and in 1951 1,368 million—these it should be noted, are monthly figures. So I can dispense with Professor Nölting's first suggestions; he must find another market for his wise advice.

To continue: Last year—1950—we still had an import of 2·5 milliard marks. This surplus was reduced in the first ten months of 1951 to 182 million marks. In the past month we have even become solvent. As against this I would like to quote the British figures arising from the policy of a Labour government. In the first ten months of 1950 Britain had an excess of imports over exports amounting to 300 million pounds sterling, about 3·12 milliard marks. This deficit increased in the first ten months of 1951 to around one milliard pounds sterling, about $11\frac{1}{2}$ milliard marks. It makes an interesting comparison. Far from gloating, however, I regard this as an unhappy situation, which is bound to affect the whole of Europe. But to those who claimed that Britain had starved herself back to health, while we had eaten ourselves into bankruptcy, I can only reply that the German recipe appears to have been better than Britain's starvation diet. The drive to achieve higher output by improved production is clearly more salutary than a policy of austerity. That is the whole secret.

When we speak of balances of payments, the stability of the currency plays an important part. When we started on this 'disastrous' market economy policy, the German Mark stood at 17 Rappen; today, without gold or foreign currency reserves, it is almost at par. Whereas Britain is finding it difficult to keep down inflation, we have achieved, by comparison, a much greater degree of internal stability. I would like to advise those who are constantly abusing Germany's economic policy to pay more attention to what is happening abroad and to stick their noses over the frontier occasionally! It is a well-known fact that prominent foreign visitors, economists and bankers, are coming to Germany to find out how we have done it, how we have emerged so skilfully and so quickly from such a precarious position and have mastered what looked like a severe crisis!

I have always proved to be a realist in my optimism! We live in fast-moving times and it is therefore a good thing that the German people can forget quickly. How could it otherwise have drawn the strength from desperation to rebuild Germany. I consider it my duty to inspire courage and confidence in the German people. For there are all too many persons intent upon plunging the German people into despair and anxiety. My critics are constantly at my heels like a pack of hounds, trying to persuade the hard-working German people that it cannot afford a single day of happiness.

The only positive concession Professor Nölting has made is that I am not 'in partnership' with industry. The word has, in fact, got around that I have been engaged in a hard struggle and tough exchanges with important bodies, particularly with the German consumer goods industry. No holds were barred in these exchanges of views, but I always managed to retain my own freedom of action. On the other hand, it is worth pointing out that no industrial enterprise or representative body has ever tried to bring the same pressure to bear on government policy as the trade unions.

Professor Nölting's account of my views on our defence contribution was completely false. According to him, I have said in my speeches that Germany is not in a position to make a defence contribution. On the contrary, I have pointed out that it is all a question of size and proportion. We are making a major contribution to the defence of the West by keeping our country with its acute social problems free from the bolshevist poison of eastern ideology. And I have always said that if we wish to become a part of the Western world, we must be prepared to make our contribution to its defence.

The Federal Government will do anything in its power to maintain the defence contribution—and that, as a free partner—at such a level that we are able to meet it. The difference is that, while some believe they can only make their defence contribution through a policy of austerity, we know that in our position such a sacrifice would be intolerable; it would inevitably plunge us back into social misery. Our production would shrink and the German national income would be reduced. For this reason we are against any such policy; on the other hand, we shall do everything possible to meet our defence contribution out of the products of an expanding economy.

One may take the view—and many undoubtedly do—that it is socially wrong to satisfy so-called peak demands, that there are too many splendid cars and other valuable things around. From a very limited viewpoint, this complaint is understandable. But doing without commodities of this kind also means doing without their production and the national income they earn. There is no revenue in the national economy that is not derived from some form of positive production. But there is such a thing as a policy of social hardship; it is a cheerless policy, which I rejected in favour of one that brought increased human welfare. I cannot, for example, feel any resentment that so many people can afford to spend freely but only that there are still too few who can. We will certainly not choose the road of austerity in preference to economic expansion. We have proved since 1948 that our efforts to make German industry more productive and to increase the productivity of labour have been successful.

I have rated the German worker's achievement every bit as highly as Professor Nölting. It was left to me to clear away a great deal of confused thinking; everything else was achieved by the German people and especially the German worker. That is why I cannot allow all that has been accomplished with so much effort in the past three and a half years to be dragged in the mud!

On the question of co-determination I would like to say that I for one cannot except a syndicalism that would lead to the breakdown of the parliamentary system. The right of co-determination should be applied where it is appropriate.

Reference has also been made to investment, and I would like to see this fulfilling its original purpose of stimulating the unrestricted flow of capital into the backward basic industries, iron, coal and steel, and giving them a material boost. One milliard marks will not be enough. But the objective must be to avoid bottlenecks wherever possible, to create further employment and to lay the basis for a further expansion of industry as a whole.

We can estimate the investments in capital goods production over a foreseeable period at between six and seven milliard marks. The sooner we can raise this amount the more successful will be the economic and social development. If these sectors of industry have not so far entered the capital market, there are various explanations: Germany's capacity in this respect has been limited; at the same time, the question of ownership was unresolved and with it the question of responsibility. Finally, despite all our efforts, we did not succeed in diverting enough Marshall Plan funds into these channels. No one need be surprised, therefore, that output lagged behind. But I will do everything in my power to remove bottlenecks in the coal, iron and steel sectors. Professor Nölting believes I am over-optimistic. I am convinced, however, that we are well on the way to solving this problem, though not overnight but gradually and over periods that are relevant to our political and economic circumstances.

There, then, you have the present picture of our economic policy! We began in conditions which could not have been worse. On the one hand, we had lost our productive capacity, while on the other we had critical social problems on our hands. Cut off from the world market and hampered by dismantling, bans and restrictions, we nevertheless continued on our course of liberalization undeterred.

That is how it will remain: I have no intention of deviating from this course. Behind me I have the parliamentary majority of the Bundestag! I am also not going to allow myself to be shaken by abuse and threats. At trade union demonstrations placards were carried bearing the slogan: 'Erhard and Adenauer to the gallows.' I would rather be strung up on the gallows than yield one inch to the forces that threaten our democracy!

We stand firm by the Market Economy!

15

GERMANY'S ECONOMIC POLICY IN THE LIGHT OF EUROPEAN POLICY

(Speech to the Swiss 'Institut für Auslandsforschung' in
Zürich, February 6, 1952

*With her entry into the Council of Europe and with the growing
trend towards equality of status, the Federal Republic had begun
to co-operate in many international spheres. In February, 1952,
Germany accepted the Schuman Plan. The Bundestag was about
to start its first major debate on Germany's defence contribution.
At this point Ludwig Erhard appeared before a distinguished
foreign audience to defend his conception of close international
economic co-operation:*

Europe is searching for fresh approaches and, while I confidently
hope that the solution to Europe's problem will be freely arrived
at, I am convinced that this solution is dependent upon all freedom-
loving countries standing firmly together. I use the word 'freedom'
here firstly in the economic sense, but we know that political
freedom also presupposes economic liberalism. Now, it is not easy
to deal with such a subject in so short a time, without improvisa-
tion or aphorisms. But, as I once before, in 1949, had an opportunity of speaking in Zürich, I can be rather more concise. My
basic views are already sufficiently well known.

I do not propose to indulge in historical reminiscence any more
than is necessary to clarify the situation and to explain how it
has developed. We embarked on the new German economic
policy in the middle of 1948 because the currency reform, despite
the many problems it gave rise to, nevertheless provided us with
a unique opportunity to break away from the pernicious trend
towards absolute central control and adopt a more liberal form of
economic policy. I believe that as much has been done in this

107

direction as seemed possible in the economic and political circumstances. But, in making that statement, I also feel bound to confess
to many shortcomings in our economic policy, which are a constant reminder to us to remove the last vestiges of state control. In
my view, Germany's only chance of rebuilding the foundations of
a sound national life and of mastering her economic and social
problems lay in following the path of freedom. So tragic or chaotic,
depending upon one's particular view of things, was the starting-
point that great courage was needed to regain control of German
industry and Germany's economic policy. For a wave of destruction had swept over our country, our production machine was
either in ruins or largely worn out. As we were completely cut
off from the world, we had no idea of the production standards of
the civilized countries we had to compete with. In addition, we
had to accept the division of our country into two parts, leaving
us, the Federal Republic, with only half our agricultural resources
and with an area, already over-populated and industrially lop-
sided, into which nine to ten million refugees were squeezed, without any personal belongings, without means of production. These
people could not be settled where employment could be offered
them but only where they could have a roof over their heads. We
realized from the beginning that the only chance of offering them
work, incomes and a new life lay in the industrial sector. But we
were cut off from the world, we had lost our foreign trade bases,
we had neither the machinery for international credit nor foreign
connections; in other words, we had become blind. And we were
faced with the task of launching an economic policy which would
enable us not merely to provide the 40 millions normally resident
in the Federal Republic with a decent standard of living again
but also to give 10 million homeless refugees new homes in West
Germany. So we could not afford to wait 10, 15 or 20 years till
normal development and organic progress created fresh opportunities; on the contrary, the depressed condition of these people
compelled us to move forward very quickly. We did this in the
first instance—and this is relevant in a speech which is predominantly outward-looking—by becoming one of the first countries in Europe, in close co-operation with Switzerland—a partnership which I am happy to acknowledge—to liberalize our foreign

trade relations. We applied the so-called principle of liberalization in a practical way. This simply means that we tried to free the national economies from the rigid grip in which they were being held, and were prepared to open up frontiers and to free the exchange of goods from the all too many barriers that bedevilled it. Circumstances compelled us to act in this way. In 1948 the Marshall Plan aid gave us a chance to overcome our balance-of-payments difficulties for a time, in other words, with generous help from outside the German people survived its worst crisis. But from the beginning a feature of the Marshall Plan was that the aid provided became smaller from one year to the next, so that we had to assume that it would end in 1953.

It must be remembered that in 1948 our output had dropped to 40% of the 1936 figure; what is more, the German people had also lost its freedom, in so far as an honest day's work did not earn it the freedom of choice in consumer goods to which it is entitled. No, the German citizen was compelled to produce evidence of his needs when he received at the hands of a bureaucracy a very dubious claim to a share in the social product. This, in my view, is the most humiliating state that a people can live in. It was, therefore, my aim—and I succeeded in realizing it—to free the German people, the consumer, from such servitude and to make money once again the only medium of exchange as in any well-ordered national economy.

If I tell you now that today our production, which reached its peak in November, 1951, stands at 140% of the 1936 output, that, in other words, the German social product has trebled in three years, then it would seem reasonable to assume that such an economic policy must have the unanimous support of the entire population. That would be a false assumption. I am reminded every day that it is not so. So I naturally wonder how one can explain this remarkable phenomenon, that a policy which saved the German people not merely from want but also from the clutches of an overbearing bureaucracy does not meet with the universal approval one might expect. Leaving on one side the party-political tactics, which are all too apparent, of deliberate distortion and negative assessment, I believe there is another factor to be taken into consideration. The German people has acquired the ability to forget very quickly. This gift of forgetfulness was in some respects a godsend, for it enabled the Germans to face up to a desperate situation, to tackle the problems confronting them, to believe in the future and the possibility of social rehabilitation. I like to think that this positive side is, in the last resort, much more important than the negative tendency of the German people to take for granted what has been achieved and to dwell upon everything that is not yet in order or even to condemn it as a failure. Well—I am not by nature a pessimist and above all I do not allow malicious criticism to shake me in my belief that we are on the right road. Nevertheless, this is a phenomenon which has to be taken into account, for economic policy is not pursued in a vacuum but in a political atmosphere. I would be the last to maintain that everything in our German garden is lovely, for not only am I conscious of the defects and shortcomings of the market economy system as it is at present, but, still more important, I am fully aware of the social tensions that still exist, and are bound to continue for some time, in Germany. It is literally impossible to solve the problem of ten million refugees more rapidly than we have done, particularly as the initial situation could not have been more unfavourable and more difficult. I do not think it can, or should, be regarded as presumption on my part, if I say that few if any countries have ever had to create order out of such complete chaos. The magnitude of Germany's problem becomes even more apparent when one considers that she is again being confronted today with fresh problems, not all of which are purely economic, although the political problems have grave economic implications. I am thinking of the European Defence Community and of Germany's defence contribution.

The only road that Germany could take was the one offering the maximum of freedom. And, as I have already said, the obvious starting-point was liberalization. I fully realize that liberalization is incompatible with a supranational system, so long as there are international currency restrictions. Free economic interchange is not possible with inflexible rates of exchange, and you cannot tinker with liberalization without destroying the basic principle. So liberalization as a catch-word will have to be severely trimmed if we want to make it fit into the present international currency system. On the other hand, no politician can be a perfectionist all the time and hope to achieve with one leap forward something that can only be achieved step by step. So let us not assume that the present stage is the final one or that, even in our methods, we have found the answer to all our problems; we are still employing expedients.

It is when we come to consider the problem of a European system that we find ourselves in a sort of Tower of Babel. The present situation in Europe is such that everyone is talking about Europe, everyone is prepared to embrace the idea, but, on the whole, very few have any clear conception what form this Europe of the future should assume and what steps must be taken to turn this honest endeavour into a reality.

First, however, let me deal in a little more detail with the situation in Germany and try to make it rather clearer, for I do not think it is very different from the situation in Switzerland. In pursuing a policy of liberalization, I came in for a considerable amount of criticism, especially in my own country. It was said, for example, that we were advancing much too quickly and that in consequence I was to blame for all our production and foreign exchange difficulties. I am prepared to take this blame, for, despite the difficulties, that first step was undoubtedly a success. Until then the European national economies had led their own separate existences and, leaving aside the worst symptoms of purely autarchic ambitions, there is no doubt that merchants found it impossible to develop their trade links as they wanted to and, instead of private industry acquiring more cohesion as circumstances clearly demanded, the state was exercising more and more control over foreign trade. The result was that foreign trade was frequently being conducted in an atmosphere that was not conductive to peaceful coexistence among the nations.

When two businessmen carry on trade beyond their own national frontiers, quite prosaic considerations come into play—questions of expediency, of utility, of price and quality—and it is only when both parties see some prospect of gain in an exchange of goods that a deal is made to everyone's satisfaction.

The situation is quite different, however, when states take the initiative and intervene in trade. Then political principles are of overriding importance; national honour, national interest and so on are at stake, although, in the final analysis, the real motive force is the honest and peaceful endeavour of people and nations to make their lives easier and more varied. For that, after all, is the real purpose of any international division of labour, to achieve the maximum of social well-being for all peoples. To assume, as some people did, that because the initial effect of our liberalization policy was to involve us in certain liabilities, it was an irresponsible policy was, in my view, both false and dangerous. Apart from purely economic considerations, it was also my intention to show the rest of the world that we have been cured of our madness and have only one desire, namely, to become once again peaceable members of the democratic world. Other countries may feel all the more inclined to believe us if we combine ideological virtue with economic and material self-interest. I really believe that there can be few countries in Europe who have a more immediate and more vital interest in pursuing a European policy than Germany, although I would like to add that a European policy must not be taken to mean economic expansion as an end in itself. A European policy implies taking a further step forward towards the ultimate economic objective of a free world economy. But here too we must move gradually, and it would therefore be a great advance if the concept of 'Europe' or a 'European economy' were to become a concrete reality.

The risks which liberalization is said to involve did not unduly worry me, if only because I realized that the productive capacity of Germany's economy could not be so high at the beginning as to enable us to keep pace with modern industrial countries which had suffered so much less. But there was also the fact that we had to show German industry how high production standards were in other countries, and we had to compel it—almost from one day to the next—to use every ounce of imagination and energy to reach that standard. For we knew that, in spite of the Marshall Plan, we could not rely on foreign aid indefinitely. The world was not prepared to trade with us because of the colour of our eyes, so that everything depended upon our ability to produce, from our own resources, goods which in quality and price would stand comparison with the best industrial products of other countries.

I believe that Germany has achieved this. If, in the first phase of liberalization, we incurred debts abroad, then this was only because other countries were prepared to supply Germany with goods and to use the credits to purchase goods in Germany. After all, Germany's imports can only be paid for by a corresponding volume of exports. And if, in order to meet our big demand for imports, we made every effort to increase the volume of our export trade, this was not because we had any imperialist ambitions. It was simply that, as honest debtors, we had to restore the basic living conditions of the German people as soon as possible. This is true not only of the present but also of the more distant future, in so far as one can rationally plan that far ahead. Today one can say that this policy has proved itself, but it was also the right policy in that it forced German industry to compete with the rest of the world and to make an all-out effort from which we were able to derive considerable benefit. Where Switzerland is concerned, I am particularly grateful, in the context of our trade balance and the balance of payments, for the help and support we have received from her.

The original purpose of the European Payments Union was to give more flexibility to existing bilateral trade agreements and to encourage unilateral clearing facilities. The German currency reform together with the change in economic policy paved the way for solutions of this kind. Whatever the shortcomings of the EPU system, one must recognize that it was the first step towards removing trade barriers. For it is clear that the bilateral system can never produce satisfactory results. It is inconceivable that the export requirements of two countries could be so completely and organically complementary as to give rise to a trade balance that would satisfy both sides. Either there will be dissatisfied customers or the total volume of trade will be so small that the economic aim of a maximum or optimum of co-operation between two economies simply cannot be achieved. Now, the European Payments Union undoubtedly has its defects, and I believe that what has been happening over the past year in Germany, Britain or France proves conclusively that there is urgent need for reform.

But this brings us to the problems which arose from the Korean war. Until then the German economy had developed very soundly.

Between 1948 and the middle of 1950—a period of exactly two years—we had not only made substantial progress in production and in expanding our foreign trade, but had also done much to solve our internal social problems. More and more labour had been absorbed into production, and, with rising wages and with prices tending to fall, the German worker's real income was steadily increasing. If I have chosen the middle of 1950 as a significant date, this is because at that particular time the critics had been virtually silenced. Our market economy had been so obviously justified by events, that its opponents were completely subdued. But then they sensed a change in the wind and were back in the race again. I do not know what happened in other countries, but in Germany all the price increases that were registered so dramatically on the world market were attributed to German economic policy. From one day to the next I was blamed for everything that disturbed national economics throughout the world. It is clear that price increases of 50, 100% and more—no matter what raw materials are concerned—must inevitably have an effect on national economies and that it is a fallacy and a dangerous illusion to assume that any state can possibly protect its own markets against such influences. Yet that is precisely the sort of wish, demand and threat that was directed at me. The year 1951—and this I can say in all earnestness—was the most difficult in terms of economic policy that I have ever experienced, certainly much more difficult than the currency reform year 1948. For my task was a much more thankless one. In 1948, it was a question of pushing forward and simply brushing aside opposition, whereas in 1951 the problem, and its eventual solution, lay in stubbornly defending the market economy principle at all costs. It gives me, therefore, particular satisfaction to be able to say that, of all the countries in Europe, Switzerland and Germany weathered the storm best. Price increases in these two countries have been lower than elsewhere, and the relative movements of wages and prices have been particularly satisfactory from a social viewpoint. I can give the German figures very briefly: industrial prices rose, on an average, by 12%, nominal wages by 24%. This means, in fact, that during this difficult and alarming period from the middle of 1950 up to the present the real wages of the German worker actually increased by a further 12%. Naturally, this is a source of great satisfaction to me, for Germany's social problems are particularly acute. The position today is such that labour problems are no longer predominant. After the Korean crisis, for example, when the stability of our currency might have been threatened by a continuing wage-price spiral, both employers and workers enjoyed considerable freedom to demand and negotiate higher wages. The incomes of employers and workers are, after all, extremely flexible; they adapt themselves to economic and political conditions. One had the impression that the employers were saying to themselves: 'All right, if the workers want high wages, we will let them have them, for the trade unions know perfectly well that higher wages must mean higher prices. If that is so, why should we put up so much resistance; why should we take the political rap?' At the time I pointed out repeatedly that not only the reasoning was false but such an attitude was extremely harmful to the country's economy. If, for example, wage demands were based on the argument that in Germany so-and-so many million poor people had an income of no more than 100 or 200 marks, then these same wage increases merely served to worsen the lot of the people (pensioners and those living on relief) whose poverty was the ostensible reason for the increases.

It was to be expected that an event such as the Korean war would have far-reaching repercussions in a country like Germany with all its experience of inflation. In other words, everyone, from the entrepreneur to the consumer, was caught off balance and lost his head. Some wanted raw materials at any price, which, in a country as short of raw materials as Germany, is understandable. On the other hand, we had to reckon with consumers who, from bitter past experience, wondered whether there would still be enough supplies available the next morning, whether we would not have to revert to economic controls and a rationing system, and, above all, whether freedom of consumption could possibly be maintained. So the average German, as consumer, preferred to buy inferior but expensive goods today rather than risk finding nothing at all tomorrow. And all this happened when we were going through a particularly difficult period in terms of currency and foreign exchange. We had a credit margin of 320 million dollars

with the European Payments Union, based on a 15% quota of our
1949 foreign trade, but this amount was particularly inadequate for
Germany's needs, because there had been a steep rise in her foreign
trade since 1948 and any quota based on previous years was bound
to be insufficient.

Let me quote two figures to illustrate this. When I first took
office in the Anglo-American zone in 1948, the average monthly
export figure was around 200 million marks, most of which consisted of compulsory exports of coal, timber and so on. Manufactured goods formed only a small proportion. Today the average
monthly figure for exports is 1.4 milliard marks, which reached
a peak of 1.5 milliard in December 1951, of which more than 75%
are manufactured goods, bringing us up almost to the normal peace-
time level. The situation before was precarious because we had to
solve our more acute problems very quickly. I rejected the price
freeze, which I have repeatedly put forward as an essential pre-
condition of wage stability, because it was clear that the higher raw
material prices and dearer foodstuffs must be reflected in the
German market, at least to the extent that raw materials were
used in manufacture. Another common illusion was that the
woollen goods in the shops after Korea had been purchased long
before the Korean crisis, so that the price increases were unnecessary. Such complaints may appear to have some substance, but
where would our industry have been, if it had organized an
enormous post-Korea sale and had not been in a position thereafter
to maintain the same level of production as before, in other words,
to employ the same number of people as before? In practice most
countries adopted a system of mixed prices, but rising raw material
prices always meant higher prices for manufactured goods. Everyone said to himself quite rightly: 'What will this commodity cost
tomorrow?' And, in fact, the main function of a national economy
is to guarantee reproduction. This basic principle had a sound influence on our society, for heaven help an economy that tried to
base its daily prices on the pre-Korea price of raw materials. On
the other hand, that would have been a typical planned-economy
manoeuvre. But as in Germany I obeyed the rules of economic
reason and plain commonsense, I was told: 'Freeze prices or
resign!' Well, I neither resigned nor introduced a price freeze.

For what would that have meant? I cannot blame my Socialist opponents for seeing things from a party-political viewpoint. What was worse was that even good friends lost their heads and said in effect: 'Your economic policy is taking all the (political) gilt off the gingerbread'. I believed, on the other hand, that we had to keep our heads, and, as indeed happened, everything would turn out all right. So I put the question again. What would a price freeze have achieved? It would only have served a purpose if I had been prepared to fix prices by force at an artificially lower level in order to bring about a completely fair distribution of the social product. But, in the context of a national economy, the national income and with it every individual income is closely and inextricably bound up with production, with a productive output of goods, so it is not at all surprising that national income and social product balance one another up and that, as a rule, the system works smoothly. It is a great fallacy of the planners that this allegedly so mysterious process must be controlled by the state if it is to function properly. It is the function of the market and of prices to establish a direct link between the volume of the social product and the value of the national income by means of price formation. So planning cannot take the place of the market. What would there be left for the entrepreneur to do, if it were not up to him to keep track of changes in consumption and in the mood of the consumer by exercising initiative, ability and the enterprise that goes with it, in order to produce of his best in open competition and to win favour in the eyes of His Majesty the Consumer. If the entrepreneur ceases to perform this function, then I can certainly replace him by state officials or functionaries, for in the last resort their arithmetic is better.

Anyone who wants a free enterprise economy and who sees something worthwhile in free enterprise can—and indeed must—support the market economy with all its risks. I have had ample opportunity of trying out these ideas on German employers. Here is one example. We all remember the symptoms of the world trade cycle after Korea. In February, 1951, when I first felt impelled to warn the German entrepreneurs and said in a public speech that, in my view, prices were no more likely than trees to reach the sky but that, on the contrary, there seemed to be clear indications that the democratic world was conscious of its natural wealth, its strength, and its potential industrial power and was gradually returning to a more settled state of mind—that in a free market economy the opportunities for increased industrial and agricultural production were almost inexhaustible and that this hysteria would presumably not last much longer, this statement was condemned everywhere as disruptive. And yet this is precisely what happened; my prediction was correct almost to the month. But what did people say? This chap Erhard has completely ruined the fine trade cycle with his price predictions. This was, of course, quite wrong, because the German Minister for Economic Affairs is hardly in a position to influence the world trade cycle. I merely looked at things fairly soberly, just as I believe in general that in economic policy calm is not only the duty of every citizen but the finest quality one can display.

Later things took a very different turn. In January, 1951, there was the famous slump on the industrial market, and then I argued that the economy must be prepared to take account of falling prices on the world market when fixing the prices of its own manufactured goods. But the same people who, in the autumn of 1950, had taken it for granted that rising world-market prices must affect manufactured products on the home market came to me and maintained that the drop in raw material prices could only be passed on the consumer when the commodity made from new raw materials had passed through all stages of production. The inconvenient aspect of a consistent policy is that it sees both sides! The manufacturer who is prepared to make profits must naturally also have the courage to carry losses. On this point I will not argue, but I believe that this attitude is eventually in the interest of the entrepreneur. The man who expects to reap the benefits of a boom cannot expect state support when the market turns against him.

In the meantime the situation had once more stabilized itself. But my problem was to make people see reason again. I only succeeded by saying after Korea: 'The most important thing now is to see to it that any and every demand is satisfied at all costs.' We could not afford to have a shortage of any kind, for, if this had happened, the situation would have become virtually unmanageable. But this again had far-reaching consequences. I had to be prepared to buy raw materials not just with an eye to our foreign exchange situation but still more perhaps with our political and social requirements in mind. I behaved like a banker who has to face a run on his bank. There is a golden rule for this kind of situation: 'Pay, pay, to the last halfpenny.' This is the only possible way out. The comparison can be carried a great deal further. For what does the purchasing power of the private consumer mean if not a 'receipt' for the contribution he has made as a wage-earner to the social product, which rightly entitles him to claim a share of the nation's production. I felt that we had to deal honourably with people whose purchasing power had been honourably acquired, and that we must on no account cheat them of the fruits of their labour. The difficulty was that not only current earnings but also savings were being offloaded on to the market. I do not know how many piggy-banks were emptied! And all this accumulated demand was invested with an urgency that you here in Switzerland would find it hard to believe.

This development and the conscious determination to operate in this way resulted in difficulties with the European Payments Union. The 320 million dollars at our disposal were fully spent and we had to ask for a further credit enabling us to draw up to 480 million dollars. In the end we drew 457 million. This all happened prior to May of last year. We had to make certain adjustments on the import side, as you in Switzerland well know, but we left no doubt in people's minds that we did not regard these measures as basic policy but as emergency measures which were forced upon us. Britain and France are now in process of recovering. In Germany itself the crisis soon passed. By the end of last year, in a period of seven months, we had not only paid off the deficit of 457 million dollars but had built up a balance, had moved into a creditor position, which was undoubtedly completely out of keeping with our structural economic situation. But this is another of the defects of this system. I gladly recognize that, if we surmounted this crisis so quickly, it was partly due to the fact that our European partners were prepared not to slow down imports from Germany; in other words, they were prepared to accept certain import restrictions on Germany's part without imposing any corresponding restrictions on German exports. I believe, however, that from the international standpoint this policy has been vindicated, for, as a result of this preferential treatment, we were able to revert in January to something like 60% liberalization. We are pressing forward as quickly as we can, and I would be only too happy if we could reach the point where we no longer think in terms of quotas and licences but achieve the only possible and reasonable solution of a breakthrough to a free exchange economy.

We have already seen for ourselves how time and again the principle of liberalization within the European Payments Union lands member countries in trouble. If we could avail ourselves of free exchange rates, then stresses would not build up to such an extent that one emergency regulation after another is required. The whole process would become much more organic. To lay down the principle of freedom and at the same time to try to restrain natural, spontaneous reactions by means of a fixed, rigid and even arbitrary exchange rate is an obvious contradiction. Certainly negation is not a satisfactory solution, but the only logical conclusion is that we must summon up the courage to attain the goal that is beckoning us on. Our aim is to create a free world, in which free men can move freely.

I do not propose to discuss here whether the establishment of an International Investment Bank is the final answer. It will overcome structural differences and to that extent make for smoother working, but it cannot be a substitute for free exchange rates. Perhaps, on the other hand, this is another phase we must pass through before we reach our goal. The reaction is always the same: there is approval in principle but the time is thought to be not yet ripe. The time will never be ripe, unless we so determine and make the most of it. Others, again, are afraid that national economies may collapse. They are certainly mistaken, for free exchange rates will make it much easier for the individual economies to adjust themselves, and the countries concerned will also be compelled to adopt sensible economic policies. In 1948 when I took over a completely rigid controlled economy which had become quite unworkable, and swept aside all the state controls, there were very few people in Germany who believed this was the right policy. They thought it was bound to lead to chaos and social disorder. In fact, it took us only six months to restore order and to get the market working efficiently. The same thing would happen if we had the courage to clear away the undergrowth that is hampering inter-state trade. We could save ourselves many a headache and solve many a problem. When I think, for example, of the most recent trade agreements, including one with Switzerland, and remember the questions that passed through our minds: 'Can we give way on this point or that?', or 'Does Switzerland want this or that?', I can only say that I find it all rather discreditable.

But let us return to Germany's economic development. The situation had barely stabilized itself in the middle of 1950, when new problems arose. European defence loomed up on the horizon. It had become the main subject of conversation. Reactions to it were not long in coming, and wishes and claims of all kinds started pouring in on us. It was interesting in this connection to see how opposing views were expressed not merely between one country and the next but also amongst individuals. Some said that if European defence demanded fresh sacrifices, then we had no option but to adopt a policy of austerity, accept further sacrifices and make the appropriate arrangements. In my view, this reaction is as false as it is dangerous. We must pursue exactly the opposite course.

I resisted this policy in Germany with all the means at my disposal, because I am convinced that the only solution to the problem is by way of expansion. No one can persuade me that an improved performance can only be achieved by increased sacrifice and self-denial. This is a policy that I completely reject as far as Germany is concerned, for we have proved beyond all doubt that there is another way, a way that comes much more naturally to us. We propose, by increasing our output, to provide the surplus required. From a purely fiscal point of view it is, of course, true that a defence contribution of x milliards must be found by the Finance Minister. The Federal Government is firmly resolved to maintain a balanced budget at all costs. The German people's experience of the tragedy of inflation was such that no one is likely to deviate from the straight and narrow path and risk a recurrence of such a

I

dangerous development. But I see things from a national economic viewpoint and arrive at realistic conclusions. Every national economy has certain duties to fulfil. It must, for example, safeguard the economic life of the people by seeing to it that consumer goods are available to meet the demand and provide a free choice. It also has the responsibility of keeping the machinery of production running smoothly and providing for its improvement and expansion as the national economy develops. This also presupposes that economic means are available. And a third task is to allocate parts of the nation's economic output, parts of our industrial capacity and potential economic production not only to consumption and to the maintenance and expansion of the machinery of production, but also to defence.

It seems to me a very fair question, whether a material defence contribution should be made by restricting consumption and cutting investment or by gearing the national economy to an all-out effort. I support the latter view; it is one I have advocated very strongly in Paris. There is, in my opinion, nothing more praiseworthy than to be prepared to make an all-out effort to defend what is, in fact, a matter of life or death to us, namely, freedom! We give our unreserved support to the idea of a European defence community, the function, and indeed the duty, of which is to generate sufficient strength to enable us to live in security and freedom. And we most of all, who live on the very borders of Bolshevism, exposed day in day out to the poison of totalitarianism and to the constant threat of infiltration and subversion—we must preserve our mental and spiritual powers of resistance. We must see to it that the gulf between this side of the Iron Curtain and the other in terms of human freedom and material living conditions is so much in the forefront of people's minds, that everyone is immune against any dangers that may threaten us. This, I believe, is something we can do to atone for much that happened in the past. No free people in this Continent can gainsay the fact that Germany, in her perilous forward position, has found this inner strength and has built a wall that protects Europe.

Apart from that, however, we are also prepared, like any other European country, to make further material sacrifices. But we do not want to relapse into a state of social need that would imperil our reconstruction; we do not want to make the sacrifice of renunciation and restriction; we prefer to draw on our own resources and try to mobilize Germany's productive capacity to the full. This is the recipe that I consider best suited to German industry. And I must say here that I am glad to have behind me a people—workers and employers—who are undoubtedly at one with me on this.

I am convinced that this is the policy which offers us all the most effective protection. If we retreat backwards, if we are prepared to resign ourselves, then we are already lost. For, with all the progress we have made in Germany so far, we must not forget that there is still widespread hardship, that we still have the problem of absorbing $9\frac{1}{2}$ million refugees, and that we cannot afford to neglect housing and other essential investments. What we now have to do is to combine our efforts and, having decided on priorities, to aim at a maximum production that will help to solve our economic, social and political problems simultaneously.

I believe that a better and a freer Europe is on the way. The steps we have so far taken have led to visible progress. If one takes the Marshall Plan with its aim to bring the national economies of Europe together and strengthen them, if one thinks of the European Payments Union, which with all its shortcomings nevertheless stimulated multilateral trade, if one considers an International Investment Bank or the settlement of debts as steps towards an efficient international credit system—all these are symptoms of an urge and a desire for positive solutions. Principles were laid down in the General Agreement on Tariffs and Trade (GATT), and to a lesser extent at the Torquay Conference, which are designed to free foreign trade from over-rigidity. In the GATT I particularly welcomed the provision made for a periodic reduction of tariffs as a means of achieving by stages a wider market, a common market. But I said jokingly: 'The slogan of the Tariff Conference in Torquay was obviously "Protectionists of all lands unite!"' I was disappointed with the results of this conference, but it too can mark a beginning, if all the countries taking part are prepared to reduce their high tariff walls slowly but surely. In the past few years there has certainly been no shortage of categorical imperatives, recommendations and moral appeals to break down national protectionism and egoism. But as is invariably the case with categorical imperatives, they sound so impressive but it is so easy to get round them.

Finally there was the Schuman Plan. I know that it is open to criticism. It all came out again in a private discussion I had here in Zürich, but I am still in favour of the idea as such. I defended the Plan and helped to realize it for the following reason: I feel more and more strongly that it is not enough to keep on talking about Europe and creating new institutions. What is probably necessary and perhaps even practical is to set up models and to tackle one specific problem quite modestly from the very beginning, in other words, to demonstrate in the case of coal, iron and steel, that big speeches are not enough to build a new Europe but that one must be prepared to do some practical work.

The Schuman Plan has two noteworthy features: one embodies the principle of supranational control by the High Authority; the other implies, as we see it, the pre-eminence of free competition in the Common Market. Whichever of these two principles eventually prevails in practice will determine whether the Schuman Plan is positive or negative. Here again, as in all man-made institutions, everything depends on the people who control the machine. We in Germany will certainly try to assign to the Schuman Plan Organization people who will throw their weight on the side of freedom, of the Common Market, and who have more confidence in competition than planning. Anyone who rejects the High Authority, however, should bear in mind that national coal and iron production has not been subject to the laws of free competition for thirty to fifty years. We had our Coal Syndicate and I do not think that competition in the iron and steel industry has been so keen as to cause anybody to get hurt.

So, if the worst comes to the worst, we will be in for nothing new; all we would achieve would be to apply the same principle on a supranational plane. But the Schuman Plan can have a very positive effect if the basic idea of freedom in the form of competitive production extends beyond national boundaries. Everything turns on this. No one can make any predictions—we can only hope that sound ideas will prevail, and we must do everything in our power to create the necessary safeguards by making the right people available.

I do not want to discuss the problem of freedom in industry in further detail. My views, for example on the question of cartels, are well known. If not, then I may perhaps describe myself as not precisely a friend of such institutions—to avoid stating my positive opinion too bluntly. As a champion of the market economy and free enterprise I take the view that this principle of freedom stands or falls with the principle of competition. I cannot in all conscience reject government price controls and at the same time grant private industry in the form of cartels the right to exercize similar powers. I admit, on the other hand, that the cartel problem in Germany is not quite the same as in Switzerland. In a smaller area things are very much clearer and much more subject to public democratic control. At the same time I must say that I see nothing positive in cartels. Time and again in the past three years people have come to me—one branch of industry after the other—and said: 'If we are not given a chance now to reach price agreements, we shall be ruined'. I did not give them the chance, yet no one was ruined!

It is always the same. The air in my office is thick with 'disaster' from morning to night, but I am still waiting for the disaster to happen! To pursue this light-hearted vein, I might say that over the last three and a half years German·industry has developed remarkably successfully from one crisis to another! We live in such a fast-moving age that we hardly have the patience to let events develop organically. Barely has a problem presented itself, than we talk of applying special state measures. I take the view that in a really free and efficient market economy immediate state intervention is not necessary to deal with every problem. I am in the somewhat comical situation that, as Minister for Economic Affairs, I must guard against state intervention even when most people in industry are demanding it, and I regard it as my prime task to saw off the branch on which I am sitting! And that, I assure you, is no joke.

I spoke of Europe and mentioned the methods and institutions which can only be understood in this context. This is really a serious subject. But in my opinion it is not so important to keep setting up new institutions as it is for these institutions to function properly in the European area. This is the fundamental difference, which becomes almost a question of faith, between those who always seek the solution in the institution, in the form, and those who want to see Europe performing a higher function. I do not think Europe was a bad place when one could travel freely with a hundred-mark or a hundred-franc note across frontiers without a passport and when merchants carried on their trade from country to country without enquiring if the state approved or not. Autarchy was unknown and protectionism taboo. In so far as structural differences were overcome by the legitimate means of tariff policy—means which in the meantime have been abused—in other words, where climatic hazards could be offset by means of customs duties, the procedure could hardly be faulted. But the barriers have grown to intolerable proportions. The struggle for Europe is being waged between national economies which are politically tied to the Socialist ideology (such as Labour, and in Germany the Social Democrats) and are centrally controlled on the one hand, and the other countries which see their salvation in enabling people to move freely across national frontiers on the other. The mere thought of Europe as a centralized super-state makes me shudder. This is a road which, I am convinced, we cannot follow without destroying everything of value that the countries and peoples of Europe have in common.

I regard Switzerland as a wonderful example of the way in which a happy Europe should be built up. I think it would be impossible and, moreover, tragic to allow a centralized super-state to crush everything that goes to make up our national life, all our historical, traditional and cultural ties. That would be a crime against the nations of Europe. But, in my view, any such solution is also quite unnecessary. It fills me with dismay when I think how such a centralized super-state would destroy all our values and would—indeed must—by its very nature ride roughshod over national characteristics and geographical necessities. We would become mere puppets in the hands of powers we know nothing of. What will this super-state be? Who is to constitute it? Is our fate to be decided by a quorum of equal votes? No, Europe can only be built if we are prepared to tear down the barriers between the various countries and nations. The prerequisite and at the same time the culmination of such a policy is the abolition of foreign exchange controls, which would do more for Europe than all the institutions, parliaments and governments put together.

It is essential that we should all be agreed on this. We must recognize the danger. We must take a close look at the countries with planned economies, whose very survival depends upon sheltering as much as possible behind their national boundaries. The experiments they conduct against all economic good sense are only feasible in isolation. Freedom for them means ruin. Far be it from me to criticize the economy or the government of any individual nation, but we know from everyday experience what happens when competition is deliberately stifled. I am not yet certain what the eventual solution will be—nor do I know who will find it—I only know that we need all our strength and all our efforts to defend our freedom. We want Europe, but we want a federally-constructed Europe, in which every single individual can enjoy the greatest possible freedom and the widest possible scope for the development of his own personality beyond the frontiers of his own country and yet without impairing the bonds between him and his own people. If we are agreed on this, it will give me particular pleasure, as it has done in the past, to work together with Switzerland. May this attitude and conviction bring us even closer. We know what is at stake! We are defending the freedom of the world but above all we are defending ourselves.

16

TEN THESES IN DEFENCE OF THE ANTI-CARTEL LEGISLATION

(An open letter to Fritz Berg, President of the Federation of German Industries, dated July 10, 1952)

In the summer of 1952—the 'year of normalization'—economic recovery in the Federal Republic seems to be coming to a standstill. The prevailing uncertainty on questions of national security may have been partly responsible for this. The 'German Treaty' (EDC or lifting of Occupation Statute?) had indeed been ratified by the United States. But France was holding back, and the German Socialist Party (SPD) was opposed to the plans for a German contribution to Western defence. The Federation of German Industries (BDI) continued with its opposition to a Bill designed to supress restrictive practices and to ban cartels in general while permitting their formation only in exceptional cases. Public concern with the question of cartels, which never abated from 1948 onwards, now increased. Ludwig Erhard held that the free and socially committed economic order could only be maintained provided competition was protected against becoming vitiated by the growth of cartels and large concerns capable of dominating the market, and on this he had the weight of the greater part of public opinion, both lay and expert, behind him. Draft anti-cartel legislation based on these principles and thrown open to public discussion was however rejected by the Federation of German Industries 'for economic, juridical and administrative reasons'. It was at this point in the continuing public discussion of the cartel issue that Ludwig Erhard entered the lists with his Ten Theses:

I understand perfectly well that you in your capacity as President of the Federation of German Industries have a positive duty to formulate the Federation's attitude on the vexed and important question of the cartels and to uphold what you regard as the interests of the Federation. That is why I am so particularly anxious to do the same on my part; that is to say, to gain your understanding for my attitude and for the fact that I cannot do otherwise if I am not to repudiate my economic policy, deny my own convictions, and risk the ruin of all that we have so far worked to achieve.

I also beg you from the outset to bear in mind that the Federal Government and the coalition parties have all along consistently stood out for the principle of a free and therefore 'social' market economy and defended this order, which has restored private initiative to a position of freedom and dignity and real opportunity, against any attack from wherever it may have come. I have received encouraging support, particularly from within German industry, in my efforts to get rid of state interference in the operations of the economy, to put a stop to the actions of a planning bureaucracy, and to allow prices to find their own level instead of being subject to state controls of one sort and another. Ever since 1948 I have been trying to make it clear that, having my face against state controls and interference, I could not concede to any entrepreneur organization the right to fix prices.

I cannot think that I was not taken seriously over this, for I believe that precisely in matters of economic policy I have at all times been completely honest with myself. In these circumstances I find it extremely hard to understand the surprise, annoyance and disappointment expressed in industrial circles. Not that this in itself matters, because what is at stake is something very much more important, namely no more and no less than the fate of the entire policy of the market economy, and that means the fate of free enterprise. I must say that the arguments adduced on the other side, in favour of cartels, seem to me extraordinarily weak, and that they deliberately evade the decisive issues with which the proposed legislation is designed to deal. Instead, the cheap line is taken that 'theory is remote from reality' and that 'professors are dreamy ideologists'. In reply to this kind of criticism I may at least lay claim to being no unpractical professorial type but to knowing as much about the facts of economic life and its laws as anyone. And I therefore beg leave to place before you once more my most carefully considered thoughts and conclusions on this matter :

1. It is beyond dispute and has been abundantly proved that a free market cannot continue to exist without free competition of effort, nor the latter without free movement of prices. A free economic order is out of the question where competition is suppressed and the price function eliminated. This is precisely the key to the market economy and the reason why it is superior to any type of planned economy; namely, that day by day and hour by hour the processes of adaptation take place, which bring supply and demand, social product and national income into their proper relationship and into a state of equilibrium. If you drop competition and free price movement you lose every argument at your disposal against the planned economy.

2. Any attempt to use cartel arrangements as a means of avoiding the fluctuations and changes of the market, and more particularly any attempt to prevent the market from attaining its own equilibrium by means of collective price fixing, must lead inevitably to a worsening of any existing disturbances and tensions and in the end to a planned economy. An entrepreneur who ceases to believe in the workability of a free market economy has I believe lost faith in himself. From the point of view of the functioning of the market it makes no difference whether the interference with the natural processes is conducted by the state or by some organization within the economy.

Not that I am in the slightest degree inclined to attribute any and every economic crisis to the spread of cartels; to do so would be sheer stupidity. But I am wholly convinced that to try to overcome a crisis by a cartel drive is futile, since the total volume of goods in supply at any one time is matched by a given volume of purchasing power and it is in the nature of things impossible for everyone to acquire more purchasing power at the same time. Price control by cartels brings with it the grave danger of enabling those branches of the economy which have to meet inescapable demand to skim off more purchasing power than would flow to them in a free market, but their gain would be the others' loss, since the latter would then find their product matched against reduced purchasing power. This brings us to the subject of economic power.

3. The advocates of cartels are perpetually harping on the need to stave off economic breakdowns and claiming that price fixing through the medium of cartels offers the one and only cure-all for this trouble. What they forget is that when a particular product at a particular price can only be sold in a certain quantity, and that quantity is insufficient from the point of view of the industry in question, or when, say, for reasons of consumption trends, the demand for the product in question falls, no amount of price fixing will help matters. If falling prices attract new customers, while rising prices repel customers (and this can scarcely be disputed), then a cartel, by dint of price fixing, can just manage to ensure that each member remains afloat in the sense of avoiding insolvency, but this in itself will do nothing to relieve the crisis and make the market more receptive for the product concerned. If the habit were to spread, the market would freeze up, a state of crisis would prevail, and no amount of cartel agreements would be able to revive the economy and pave the way for the creation of fresh means of production.

4. In a free market, on the other hand, there will in the first place be far less likelihood of violent distortions arising at all, since price freedom serves as a sensitive indicator of market fluctuations and changes and competition at once releases energies directed towards counter-balancing such movements and restoring equilibrium. Moreover, such tensions as may nevertheless occur in a free market economy will be eased organically by the operation of this dynamic process of quantity adjustment. Only on these lines can the economy as a whole and each individual business comprised in it operate successfully and to the satisfaction of all concerned. If it then ever becomes necessary to forego profits or to incur losses, the inherent and proven adaptability and resilience of a free enterprise economy can be relied on to meet the strain. It is precisely this requirement of having to stand the test imposed by the market that ensures economic progress and allows the gains achieved by improved efficiency and greater effort to benefit mainly the consumer, that is to say the nation as a whole. It is because of this organic relationship that we call our economic policy a policy for the achievement of a 'social market economy'.

5. Free enterprise stands and falls with the system of the market economy. In any other type of economic order the entrepreneur becomes steadily degraded to the status of a mere pawn, or a cog in a wheel of some planned piece of machinery. Where the man of business loses the will to shoulder the economic task of proving himself under competition, where an economic system becomes established which makes no call upon the energy, imagination, wit, capacity, and creative urge of the individual; where the more capable is no longer able or allowed to overtake the less capable in the race for achievement; where people seek to shed rather than carry responsibility, and a longing for security and stability creates a mentality that undermines the spirit of enterprise, there indeed no economic system based on free enterprise can thrive. I am perfectly aware that the attack aimed by collectivists of all shades against the market economy is designed to undermine the function of the entrepreneur, and if therefore the trend towards collective grouping is revived and spreads in the business world, the time will come, much sooner probably than these people realize, when the question will be raised on the political level as to what reasons can be adduced for allowing private ownership of the means of production and the right of the entrepreneur to take any economic decisions whatever on his own account to continue in existence.

6. As I have been able to show, price fixing as seen in the context of the national economy means that quantities are also fixed. But if, given a certain amount of purchasing power, and a fixed price, the quantity of a specific commodity for sale is also fixed, then the social effects on the living standard of a people would be so far-reaching that, in certain political circumstances, one could not expect the cartels to have complete freedom in making their decisions. On the contrary, one would certainly assume that, where the market is manipulated in this way, there will be a demand for co-determination on a parity basis, and it will be difficult in such circumstances to accede to this logical demand. Free enterprise and co-determination do not go together; collective agreements between entrepreneurs, however, which can lower the nation's living standard, cannot be regarded as genuine industrial activities and

should, in fact, as the entrepreneurs admit, be officially supervised. So it is not a purely academic question to ask whether the entrepreneurs themselves wish to embark on this dangerous course.

7. The argument over the relative merits of restrictive legislation and anti-cartel legislation does not go to the heart of the problem. I repeat yet again that my opposition to cartels is not based on any charge of dishonest intentions or practices on their part, which would amount to discrimination, but simply on the view that collective price agreements as such, however defensible they may be both on moral and on statistical grounds, damage the national economy. I would like to refer back at this point to the remarks I made earlier on the function of free prices. There is no room in such a system for restrictive practices legislation. I would even go so far as to say that a price agreement at too low a level can be just as harmful to the national economy as one at too high a level. The market price, which is the only right one for the national economy, simply cannot be defined; it is the natural result of the equilibrium created by prices in a free market. Any other interpretations of the price phenomenon leads to distortions, as in the case of the LSE calculation, and gives rise to the assumption that the entrepreneur can in every instance expect to cover his costs. Here too free enterprise is in grave danger.

8. Anti-cartel legislation is consistent to the extent that it draws the only practical conclusion from the negative results so far achieved by any kind of restrictive practices legislation and yet leaves room for any exceptions that may prove essential to the national economy. The supporters of cartels make the great mistake of judging the cartel system solely by the effect it has on the private economics of the firms involved and studiously avoiding any reference to the effects on the national economy. It is precisely the highly organized and highly successful cartels that must often be regarded as most harmful to the national economy. The Cartel Law, which will undoubtedly be modified in the course of debate, must on no account be altered where the principle of banning cartels is concerned, otherwise the whole Cartel Law becomes a farce, which will merely make the Federal Goverment's policy a

laughing-stock in the eyes of the general public. Political attacks on the free enterprise economy are bound to be silenced once free competition is shown to be the inevitable outcome of free enterprise, in other words, when, by virtue of free competition and the resultant economic progress, a price emerges which offers the consumer optimum living standards. The reaction of the consumer to this economic system will cease to be negative once the average citizen can feel sure that the free market gives him an opportunity to shape his own destiny and that he is not at the mercy of unknown economic forces.

9. Finally, as regards the principle of freedom itself, there is something almost grotesque in the way those who favour cartels try to base their support for such amalgamations on grounds of freedom. Freedom is a civic right which is inalienable. The freedom claimed by the pro-cartel school to limit or suppress freedom is certainly not the freedom I have in mind, which is designed to safeguard the continuance of free enterprise. If you talk about freedom, you must know what you are talking about. Freedom is indivisible and cannot be defended or rejected for reasons of expediency. The Cartel Authority is not designed to suppress freedom but has, on the contrary, as almost its sole function, to see that freedom is secure. Anyone who considers that this new Cartel Law heralds the appearance of a new planned economy is either guilty of deliberate distortion or has not the remotest idea what this law sets out to do.

10. A further objection, which is constantly being raised, is that the Cartel Law may give birth to a new mammoth bureaucracy. The first thing to be said in reply is that it will be up to industry itself to appeal only in exceptional cases where a Rationalization, Crisis or Export Cartel can be shown to be necessary and practicable within the meaning of the law. I, for my part, visualize the Cartel Authority as a relatively small body, which in terms of size could certainly not compete with the machinery of former cartels and would not even try. Nor should the Cartel Authroity become an end in itself but should ensure that free competition can flourish and that abuses are spotlighted.

The fear that this Cartel Authority might be overburdened with controls and interfere too much in private business affairs seems to me equally unjustified. And one thing is certain, namely, that, given restrictive practices legislation, the social consequences of amalgamations of the cartel variety will be so widespread that controls will have to be much more extensive, much stricter and much more numerous than would be the case with anti-cartel legislation.

Dear Herr Berg, there is no doubt in my mind that these ten theses cannot adequately cover the whole problem, but they may serve as a starting-point or basis for a further and, I hope, fruitful discussion. The entrepreneur cannot go on indefinitely evading the question as to whether he can visualize a free market without free competition and without the function of free prices, and, if he should answer this question in the affirmative, what sort of basis and effect he imagines such a deformed and artificial market economy system would have. I sometimes feel a certain bitterness when attacks on the Cartel Law force me, by their very nature, to the conclusion that I am obviously suspected of being prepared to gamble lightheartedly with the German economy and even with the future of the smaller concerns, to say nothing of the even more sordid suspicion that I am acting on American orders. Who in Germany has proved more conclusively how deeply, how completely he is committed to breathing new life and new vitality into German industry by means of a free market economy! That should surely make even the opponents of anti-cartel legislation pause to reflect and help to convince them that in the really important and compelling cases they will get justice and protection.

I must tell you frankly, dear Herr Berg, that I take the cartel problem much more seriously and am certainly a great deal more concerned about it than those who support cartels appear to be. When, for example, an industrial combine has this to say in a telegram of protest: 'It is hard to understand why the Federal Minister of Economics wishes to lead and force industry into economic freedom against its will,' then aberration and confusion have reached a pitch where, I think you will agree, one cannot feel much confidence. I console myself with the thought that this is a particularly grotesque, almost comic instance, but the unanimity in industry with regard to its desire for cartellization goes much too far for my liking.

I would welcome it if, in further negotiations, we could agree that the Federation of German Industries should, so to speak, allow freedom of conscience and, instead of being merely the mouthpiece of the pro-cartel majority, should also give expression to the profound anxieties and doubts felt in the other camp. There is no question now of the law being pushed through, and I myself have supported proposals that the subject should be discussed in more detail. On the other hand, I do not attach any value to official enquiries, because, as I have already said, the activities of cartels cannot be gauged and understood in isolation. They must be seen as a national economic phenomenon in a national economic context.

I would like, in conclusion, to bring forward one more idea, which is closely related to the cartel question: European integration. Not the least of the factors that will contribute to a fruitful development of German industry is the practical efficiency of larger and freer markets, such as are inherent in all European plans. The eradication of protectionism, the abolition of tariff barriers, the removal of currency regulations are all aims which breathe a spirit of greater and wider freedom, which, above all, provide scope at last for the untrammelled development of the individual and prevent the arbitrary use of state power. The phenomenon of cartels is not, as I see it at least, compatible with this trend of economic events, for a happy Europe cannot be a centrally controlled economic body, but it is just as unthinkable that the economic unity of Europe could be achieved by co-ordinating international cartel agreements. For freedom, I repeat, is indivisible. This principle is either true or false, either a blessing or a curse, and this is the final choice that confronts each one of us.

This letter may seem to you rather too solemn, but I am conscious of the gravity of the historical situation, and if I feel confident that the German entrepreneur, with all his skill and efficiency, has no reason to fear freedom either in national or in international competition and can, must and will prove his worth only in a free enterprise and market economy; in other words, if I believe that our liberal economic system must be maintained, then this letter will serve to document our responsibilities to the German people and before history. There is more at stake here than interests; the very foundations of our economic freedom are in question. If the dam that holds back complete mass-production and collectivism is breached, there will be no stemming the flood.

K

17

SELF-RELIANCE

(Speech at the opening of the Technical Trade Fair at Hanover
on April 26, 1953)

*The year 1952 saw a rise in production, employment and incomes,
while price levels remained stable or fell slightly. Everything
pointed to a 'quantity boom' and the only problem was how to get
the tide flowing in the direction of the consumer goods industry.
Ludwig Erhard's call for 'courage to consume' represented at that
time not merely a prosperity slogan but also a socio-political demand of the hour. Quality goods such as refrigerators, washing-
machines and motor-cars were coming on to the market in increasing quantities. The aim was to see that these goods did not become
reserved for a small over-privileged class but were made available
to a wide section of the consumers through low prices ensured by
mass-production methods. The inclination to invest was at a low
ebb, and 1953 became indeed a 'consumers' year', which prevented any downswing in the general level of economic activity.
The parliamentary election campaign began fairly early in 1953,
with sharp controversy over national security as the keynote.
Ludwig Erhard, who, on the occasion of the CDU Party Congress
in Hamburg, had again come forward as a protagonist of free
currency convertibility and individual property ownership, had
nothing to fear from the discussion of economic policy in this
election campaign.*

I am firmly convinced that this year of 1953 will be a year of considerable progress, particularly in international trade relations. I
dared to hope that last year would see a return of free currency
convertibility. This hope has not been fulfilled. Nevertheless,
things have progressed in this direction, inasmuch as no international discussion can take place and no international trade negotiations be conducted without this problem forming the central

theme. If we look for instance at the draft constitution for a European Political Community, we find it set down as a basic pre-condition of any genuine co-ordination, of any effective collaboration, and still more of any further development towards integration. And this is the urgent need of the hour. I almost hesitate to repeat yet again what I have so often said before; namely, that the present rules of the game in international trade have outlived their usefulness, and we are in danger of losing ground if we do not now at long last break down the barriers. In the press and wherever the problem of exports is discussed, people are at pains to point out how tough the export market is, how rigorous the competition, and how difficult to sell abroad. Why? It is not that there is any real lack of demand. No, the trouble lies in the questionable and indeed reprehensible techniques that have come to be more and more slavishly practised in the pursuit of our foreign trade policy. I am delighted that I shall now be able to take part in international discussions at which among other things the question of foreign trade promotion and state aids to this end will undoubtedly be brought up. Now, I am against all state action designed to promote foreign trade. I am convinced that it is just as senseless for individual nation states to set about trying to give their own industries a leg up as it would be for a club full of grown men to set about trying to lift themselves off the ground by tugging at their own hair. We shall make no real headway until we discard these practices completely, for they amount to no more than an attempt to get inter-state rivalry to do what genuine competitive effort within the sphere of private enterprise ought to be doing for itself. Hardly a principle to be proud of, nor one that can be expected to bring anyone happiness or prosperity.

It is of course an open question whether political or economic considerations should be paramount in the shaping of larger communities. The fact that economic co-operation is less effective today than forty years ago is due to external disasters including two world wars. Today economic forces are trying to break through, and link up across, the frontiers. And so are people. Dividing lines are an indignity. Customs barriers at the frontiers are antediluvian. Economic areas have shrunk to the narrow confines of state boundaries because in a disordered world bereft of political and social stability coercive systems can only be laboriously maintained in carefully sealed compartments. In an era born of 'total war' all the natural functions and reactions of a national economy have been systematically suppressed; co-operation is stifled under a blanket of currency restrictions; and we have sunk into a primitive state of barter, for what is the difference between exchanging bricks for pots and exchanging one quota of commodities for another? This is what we have come to, and this is where we must start to put things right.

Here at this Trade Fair, with so many of our foreign guests and friends present, I should like to take what I feel is a fitting opportunity to give the lie to the notion that competition is an aggressive, exclusive, embittered thing, as so many people seem to think. The very opposite is true. Competition, the idea of striving to do a better job, is something that brings people closer together, reconciles differences. I rejoice over any country, and be it our keenest rival in the world market, if I find that it is economically sound, financially stable, and socially equable, and am unhappy over any that has to struggle and is unable to hold its own; for there is room in the world for all.

Competition does not mean trying to get the better of each other, but trying to make as big a contribution as possible to the well-being of humanity as a whole. If you consider for a moment how many people in the world are still cut off from the benefits of civilization, and how much remains to be done before everyone in the world can have a fair share of what the world has to offer, you will realize that the scope for further economic development is incalculably great. And I need not remind you that an advanced industrial country like ours has undeniably a vital part to play in such development.

At the same time, I would remind our industrialists not to be content to take the line of least resistance by exporting to soft-currency countries with the help of state subsidies, but to take up the challenge where competition is harder. The desire to participate in the internal development of, say, the countries of South America, the Near and Middle East, and wherever there is the urge to establish new industries, exploit sources of natural wealth, and modernize agriculture is very understandable. Indeed, as I have already said, we cannot deny ourselves this chance, since those who help to make the riches of this world available can naturally expect to have a hand in tomorrow's task of carrying development a step further. If difficulties arise in this connection, we shall cope with them.

The splitting-up of the world economy into various areas—dollar area, sterling area and so forth, and the existence of numerous bilateral arrangements impeding the direct clearing of accumulated surpluses and deficits have created a very odd situation: on the one hand we are anxious to attract foreign capital to enable us to develop, equip and modernize our own economy, while on the other hand we are compelled to invest German capital in foreign countries in order to secure markets for our exports. There are people who say we should not export more than is necessary to pay for our imports of food and raw materials, but this means looking at only one side of the question. The other side is concerned with the fact that we cannot afford to stand aside and take no part in what is to my mind undoubtedly a completely new phase in the development of the world economic situation; because if we did, we should write ourselves off as second-class, and this is certainly not our intention.

Then again, there are people who take a gloomy view of scientific and technical progress, as if it were bound to lead to some immeasurable disaster. With them I do not agree either. Technical progress does not frighten me, and I do not share the fear that we may not be able to master the forces it puts at our disposal. Advances made in this direction may indeed profoundly alter the pattern of our economic and social structure, but this does not mean that the process of change need get out of hand. Our technologists need have no fear of ever being called upon to blow up the world. What we must do, though, is to get technology and economics, and—yes, if you like—politics, into proper alignment, into harmony, with each other.

I mean, provided technical energy is converted into economic power, we can achieve what is so urgently needed, namely, well-being and prosperity for all. There is no room for fear in the pursuit of this aim.

I say this quite deliberately, because I am constantly being told that the aim of affording ever wider sections of the community a higher standard of living is one that can never in practice be realized. As for the talk about the leeway having already been made up or consumption being already at saturation point, I prefer to turn a deaf ear. But there is one line of thought that I have been made very much aware of in recent months and that I should like to refute. When I have been pleading for an expansion of consumption beyond what is needed to satisfy basic material requirements, and saying that it was our aim to enable every household, and particularly every worker's household, to have durable goods such as a refrigerator, a washing-machine, a vacuum cleaner and whatever else modern industries can provide, I have been told to reckon out what a pensioner receives or can earn and to reveal the secret of how these goods can be brought within his reach. My answer is that of course pensioners cannot be among the first to benefit from the growth of consumption. In America it was not the poorest people who first had motor-cars. But we have seen over and over again how today's luxuries become tomorrow's utilities. We must have the courage to cast out social resentment and petty jealousy. Some people may benefit more than they deserve, others go short through no fault of their own. These things cannot be avoided, and if we are not prepared to put up with them we shall find ourselves in a permanent state of artificial impoverishment.

If no one is to be allowed to be the first to enjoy a higher standard of living, then we cannot even start to produce the better classes of goods; the volume of available purchasing power will then be cut down, and the economy robbed of the ability to expand at all. Our course must surely be set in the opposite direction. The only obstacles are a handful of fixed ideas or phobias that it is essential we in Germany should get out of our system, otherwise we shall soon reach the end of our tether in applying our technical ability and equipment. Technology, after all, is not an end in itself. However impressive the production plants of the future may be, their ultimate value will depend on the service they render to the life of the people, and on nothing else. Unless our aim, from the outset, is to bring about a continuous improvement in our people's standard of living, we shall make a mockery of technological progress itself and cut ourselves off from the rest of the civilized world. We can share in the further growth of happiness and prosperity in the world, but only if we have the courage to consume and at the same time rid ourselves of inhibitions rooted in envy and narrow-mindedness.

Another dangerous fallacy, born this time of the hysteria generated by the war in Korea, is that continued economic progress depends on boosting the armaments industry, as if there were some magical life-giving power in producing the instruments of death. Let us make no mistake about it: this way of thinking is sheer wickedness. In America, I was immensely impressed by the answer I used to receive when I asked what they would do about their annual steel output of 100 million tons once they no longer needed to think about arms production. Everyone, including quite ordinary people, immediately replied that when that time came they would be needing not 100 million but 110 or 120 million tons of steel a year. When this belief in the possibility of lasting peace becomes a reality, the opportunities for development, for increasing prosperity and achieving social progress will indeed be limitless.

The size of our contribution to European defence is here quite beside the point. I myself never look upon this as in any sense a trend-determining factor, but as a much more serious matter of national duty. It is my conviction that peace will be assured to Europe as long as we in Europe demonstrate unequivocally that we have the combined will and the strength to put the defence of our freedom before everything else. And I do not say this lightly or as a mere figure of speech. Recent political events have caused people in other countries to raise their eyebrows and wonder whether Germany may not be having second thoughts about its wholehearted adherence to the terms of the defence agreements. They have no cause for such misgivings, even on the most cursory view, and I give you a categorical assurance that the Federal Government will make every effort in its power to ensure not only adherence to, but also fulfilment of, the terms of the defence agreements. And there is an economic aspect as well. It is a sign of the times that all over the world countries are striving to establish their own industries, to exploit their own natural resources, and to make the utmost use of the possibilities afforded by new techniques. We are directly affected by this trend, for the following reasons.

Germany cannot survive in isolation, but only as an integral part of the free Western world. This means being one of a large number of partners. And if we go out into the world market and offer to sell things like manufacturing plant and equipment, our partners may be willing to start doing business with us, but they will first want to be certain that later on they will be able to get supplies of spares, replacements and supplementary deliveries. They will ask themselves whether Germany can be relied on to remain true to the West through thick and thin, to continue as a reliable supplier irrespective of political fluctuations. Unless we can give these assurances, all our chances will be jeopardized.

Economic realignment is taking place throughout the world. Our own supply position will depend on our becoming involved in the world-wide process of raw material distribution. In this connection, too, we should lose not only prestige but also security were we not able to state unreservedly that we shall remain faithful partners for all time, both in respect of what we provide and of what we take. On this issue there is no room for the slightest shadow of doubt, for on it depends the security and stability of our economic future.

18

A REFRIGERATOR IN EVERY HOUSEHOLD

(Article in *Welt der Arbeit* of June 16, 1953)

At this juncture, the word 'refrigerator' became more than merely the designation of a household gadget. It became a symbolic term, used first as a controversial byword and later taken into the current vocabulary of serious economic discussion.

In the Woman's Column of *Welt der Arbeit*, No. 23, of June 5, 1953, under the above heading, the Federal Government was criticized for its policy of making quality goods available to an ever-growing proportion of our population. Although the article was not free from ideological and political bias, it was a sufficiently serious contribution to discussion of this subject to warrant attention, and I therefore present the following observations in reply.

The 'racy' headline 'A Refrigerator in Every Household', as used in reference to an official aim of government policy, could be put down to mere journalistic exaggeration or over-simplification, and as such ignored. But in fact there is more to it than that, because it also reveals a dangerous confusion of thought, inasmuch as it can be taken—or intended—as a reminder of the era of controls with its slogan of 'equal shares for all'. I have often pointed out that the consumption of quality goods can only be expanded provided we tolerate their use being confined initially to a relatively small number of people in the higher income brackets. If this is not accepted, and if the enjoyment of such goods is regarded as indulgence and made the subject of social obloquy and hostility, then the economy will be forced to abandon production in this sector, and there will be a corresponding loss of potential national income (and jobs) and the growth of the country's productive capacity will be forcibly curtailed. One section of the press actually challenged me to say how an old-age pensioner was to set about getting his refrigerator. To this puerile question I replied that the first motor-cars in America were presumably not run by pensioners but by millionaires, and I do not consider this reply unduly flippant. Does not the history of the world in the last hundred years afford abundant proof of the fact that every single improvement in the standard of living can only be effected step by step, spreading progressively over a gradually mounting proportion of the population?

I am glad to see that the article in question has no quarrel with the basic aim of raising the standard of living over a wide front, and confines its criticism to ways and means. Earlier this year I called for expanded consumption, but I would not dream of charging the German worker with indulging in luxuries. I deny that there is anything the least 'odd' about my attitude; ever since 1948 I have been propounding an economic policy which puts the consumer at the very centre of all economic processes, by ensuring freedom of choice to him and restoring him to a position of dignity and power. Nor can the author of the article deny that conditions today are those of a buyer's market, and that competition has led to a progressively improving and more priceworthy service to the consumer.

I agree with the author of the article that large-scale improvements in the standard of living cannot be achieved by excessive consumer credit, but I do not agree that wage and salary increases are better calculated to enable us to get on a par with more advanced countries. If this were true, there would be nothing to stop every country from at once achieving the highest possible standard of living. I prefer to assume that we are in fact agreed that the only sound economic development is based on increasing productivity free of inflationary price trends and designed to increase the real purchasing power of the broad mass of the population to the full extent allowed by the actual increase in production achieved.

My particular reason for wishing to reply to this article, however, is an utterly sober and almost scientific one. I am perfectly prepared to accept a good deal of what the article says about the financing of consumption. I, no more than its author, believe in consumer credit expansion as the *ultima ratio,* and there is undoubtedly a limit beyond which it would be dangerous to go without risking harm to the economy and indeed to the consumer.

When we consider that—in proportion to the national product— the financing of consumption in the United States is some six times as high as in our country, we must at the same time re- member that the real purchasing power there in the hands of such sections of the population as are concerned is undoubtedly very considerably higher than in Germany, giving far greater freedom of action. But this surely also means that there can be no question of consumer credit having been expanded to a dangerous extent here in Germany. We are told that the financing of consumption is a chimera, and that the consumer is bound to be taken in; that in actual fact consumer credit does not increase the volume of pur- chasing power but merely shifts its incidence, since only producer credit can lead to an increased production yield. Increased con- sumption in one direction is bound to reduce consumption in another direction.

At first sight, this argument seems reasonable enough, but in the balance-sheet of the economy as a whole the picture looks different. Consumer credit enables goods to be produced which could other- wise not find a market. Thus, although the consumer who buys on credit has to redistribute his purchasing power and revise his con- sumption to take account of instalment commitments, the net result from the point of view of the economy as a whole remains unaltered, since the consumer still brings all the available pur- chasing power to market. Now, consumer credit goes a step further and initiates an expansion of production (e.g. of refrigerators), and this expanded production creates new income which in its turn appears as additional purchasing power on the market. The volume of goods at the disposal of the economy has in other words been built up to a higher level, the national product and the national income have been extended. Whatever is done to stimulate production, provided it is successful in achieving this result, it will also, with certainty, increase the national income.

In this connection of course the question of magnitude is of vital importance. Consumer credit cannot carry, but can usefully sup- plement an upswing of the economy as a whole. The Government had no more than this in mind when it advocated the use of con- sumer credit as one of the means capable of subserving a general policy aimed at expanded consumption. I myself have repeatedly pointed out that it would be dangerous to let hire-purchase be used for day-to-day consumption, while conceding that it is a useful means of making durable goods available to a larger number of consumers.

I see all the less reason, incidentally, for attacking this suggestion, since the same procedure is already being followed in regard to motor-cycles, radio-sets, furniture and the like, with good results and to the complete satisfaction of all concerned. It is noteworthy that practically no losses are incurred over the entire field of hire-purchase business, and this again testifies to the care exercised by purchasers in regard to the choice of purchases and the disposition of their incomes.

In passing judgment, *Welt der Arbeit* should therefore not concentrate its attention on those consumers whose household budgets have to be readjusted to allow for such additional consumption, and instead should take into account the fact that consumer credit can be a means of increasing employment, creating additional returns, and thus enlarging the national product and the national income. The wider the choice of goods available to the consumer, the more active competition becomes, and the more prices will tend to come down, to the benefit of us all.

19

ECONOMIC PROBLEMS OF REUNIFICATION

(Article in *Bulletin* of September 12, 1953)

After the tragedy of the revolt in Central Germany in June, 1953, there was some hope that Soviet Russia would admit that the Ulbricht regime was a failure and would accede to the conference the Western Powers wanted. Up to September, 1953, more than 250,000 people had fled from the Eastern Zone. In West Berlin production figures were 17% higher in the first half of 1953 than in the previous year. Erhard called the Federal Parliamentary elections of September 6 an overwhelming expression of confidence in the 'Prosperity from Within' programme. In the Bulletin *he outlined the possibilities for solving the economic problems involved in reunification by means of the liberal policy that had proved so successful in West Germany:*

In spite of the general yearning for the reunification of a dismembered Germany, many people—including refugees—are afraid that reunification and the resulting economic struggle would mean an intolerable drop in the standard of living and threaten the economic existence of refugees in the Federal Republic as well as of people established in the East Zone. Laymen find it impossible to form a rational idea of the economic consequences of reunification, and as a result speculation is rife.

I should like to say at once that I am not in favour of trying to forecast the course of such developments with mathematical accuracy. This is the planner's way of going to work and would be dangerous, serving only to make the task of reunification still more difficult by inhibiting organic development and natural forces. On the other hand, there is no doubt that some such blue-print of a 'plan for reintegration' is what many people think is needed. These are the people who regard the economy of a country as essentially an 'organization'. They have neither a feeling for, nor any understanding of, the inherent balancing and compensating forces at work in a free market, and of the resultant dynamism. Instead, they think they must 'organize' as much as possible—although in this way distortions and discrepancies are not removed but, if anything, are multiplied and aggravated.

In judging the situation one's thoughts inevitably revert to problems that had to be met in 1948 in connection with the currency reform and the simultaneous change-over from a planned and controlled economy to a free economy. I well remember how at that time I was bombarded with statistics, graphs, figures relating to raw materials, production and consumption, foreign trade and goodness knows what else—all designed to prove to me rationally and logically that it was impossible to do away with controls, rationing and price fixing. From the planner's view-point these figures and the forecasts based on them were doubtless incontrovertible; what was contestable was the whole underlying philosophy, which made out that the economic process in human society was merely the result of adding economic figures and material facts together without any regard for the human forces at work beneath the surface of events.

Basically we are facing very similar problems over the reunification of Germany, and once again opinions are divided.

I myself stand squarely by the conviction that the reintegration of East Germany must take place in accordance with the principles of a free economy. I hope it will not be counted against me if I am sceptical towards the work of the various bodies that have been planning for reintegration. In some individual cases I have been reassured on matters of detail, but broadly, from the policy-making point of view, the practical value in these studies is nugatory.

Of course it is important to know, say, what the transport situation will be when the time comes, what public and non-public institutions will then be responsible for the various public, economic or social services, to what extent private property will have been tampered with, what new forms of co-operation within and between firms may have been developed, and to have as much factual information as possible concerning internal organization and administration. But of hardly any practical value or interest are data concerning production, capacity, employment, raw materials and foreign trade conditions. This is because after reunification productive capacity will be applied under entirely different market and environmental conditions, and inferences drawn from the present and applied to the future almost inevitably lead to false conclusions.

As a first measure it will be necessary to reorganize the Soviet Zone currency—that is, to bring it into line with our currency system. This will necessarily involve approximating the price and wage level to the conditions obtaining in the Federal Republic. The experience gained during the currency reform of 1948 can be drawn upon here and the method of initial currency allocation per head of the population and to each individual business could again be followed. To what extent, in a final settlement, the East German mark could be converted into the West German mark—thereafter to be the national currency—is a question that will have to be more closely studied. Owing to the totally entangled system of controls and of the 'economic terror' in the Soviet Zone, it is impossible at the moment to estimate the true purchasing power of the East German mark. Once the facts come to light, the economic situation of the Soviet Zone would be relentlessly exposed, and there can be no doubt that the picture will be a sobering, if not a shattering one. We shall have to reckon with a pronounced difference in levels of performance as between East and West and, as a result, with possible grave consequences for the population's living conditions. Yet we shall have to look facts clearly and courageously in the face, for only then can effective remedies be applied.

This is the crux of the problem—to raise productivity in the Soviet Zone so quickly and so energetically that the difference in performance is made up as soon as possible. It is over the manner of fulfilling this task that there are different opinions. Some are in favour of initially protecting the East Zone from outside competition, in order to give its economy a chance to catch up—according to a previously worked-out plan and in definite stages; while others —myself included—are of the opinion that this inescapable process of adaptation can run its course more quickly and effectively if from the start the two regions are as closely interlinked as possible and private enterprise is given every chance to develop. A protected East Zone economy would be too narrowly confined to develop its potential and would be deprived of fruitful free relations with the West. An economic union between East and West manipulated by the state would never be a substitute for full freedom of action in an interim period. Hence the danger of nurturing an economic entity which might indeed develop sinews, but which would lack direction and proportion, because the specific position and task of the Soviet Zone economy can only crystallize out of the general situation and the comprehensive relationships within the larger economy of a united Germany.

In 1948 too, we were faced with the question of whether in our need for protection we should open up links between Germany and the outside world in gradual stages, or whether we should adopt a more liberal trade policy from the outset and yet try to stand up to international competition. In coming to a decision we had on the one hand to examine whether there was a real chance of making the Germany economy competitive in a short space of time, and on the other hand to take into account that we could only set the German economy going again and ensure a satisfactory employment situation if we covered our imports of food and raw materials by exports. With 'liberalization' we opted for the bolder policy, and no one can deny that this step has proved in fact astonishingly successful.

There are no grounds for fearing that the Soviet Zone economy would be hampered by lack of raw materials after the link-up with the West. Our foreign currency situation and our favourable export balance make it possible for us today to enlarge our imports by three to four thousand million marks, excluding the fact that reunification will itself tend to reduce our foreign currency spending. Further, it must not be forgotten that after this liberating step people will be able to move freely again and that Central and Eastern Germany will not merely count as a new consumer market: indeed, producer industries of all kinds will spring up in these regions. It is not too much to say that the entire economy of the Federal Republic is ready with good counsel and practical help to smooth the way for the East Zone economy to adjust itself to that of the West. It should be possible to mobilize private and public capital in sufficient quantities, especially since the reunification of Germany is anyway only conceivable in the context of a settled international atmosphere, and it can be assumed without overmuch optimism that at such time the Federal Republic will be able to devote funds hitherto used for defence to the economic and social rehabilitation of the Eastern region. In other words, for an interim period the West would place its production resources at the disposal of the Soviet Zone population and there can be no doubt that the resources of the Federal Republic are equal to the task.

But what will be the employment situation in the Soviet Zone? Will there not have to be widespread unemployment until the lee-way is made up, and is there any real prospect of ever making up the leeway at all? Here too there will certainly be those who (just as before the currency reform) will come up with shattering fore-casts based on rigid calculations. Before we undertook this reform a German scientific institute prophesied an army of unemployed numbering five to six million. So we need not lose too much sleep over the gloomy forecasts of those who in their rational perfec-tionism will again overlook the human and sociological im-ponderabilia, the impulses and energies that cannot be reduced to mathematical formulae. The parlous situation of people living under a tyranny, their hunger and their lack of everything that makes life worth living—these very factors will become a great stimulating force and will bring undreamt-of energies into play.

Although I am fully convinced that a protectionist policy would ill serve the East Zone, would indeed jeopardize a swift and suc-cessful reintegration, I am nevertheless fully aware of the need to give Government help to the economy of the East Zone. But tax relief and exemptions are much more likely to stimulate produc-tion than protective measures—which would have the opposite effect. The tax burden of our economy is today so great that tax relief has every chance (in spite of the differences in productivity) of helping Soviet Zone industry to embark on competition on an equal footing. This latter is also one of the considerations that decided me in favour of adopting free economy principles in the reintegration of the Soviet Zone.

So all in all we come to the conclusion that the widespread gloomy fears of tragic repercussions on the individual material fate of countless Germans are unfounded. Reunification will not mean an extra tax burden for the present population of the Federal Re-

L

public, nor will it in any way endanger the existence of businesses. The increased capacity resulting from the Soviet Zone's entry into the economy will on an average not even correspond to the growing demand of the Soviet Zone population, so that there ought to be room for even greater economic expansion. The labour market in the present Federal Republic will remain untouched by the change—or if influenced at all, it will be in a positive sense. In the Soviet Zone itself an increase in unemployment is not to be reckoned with. Businesses in the East will not be crushed by competition, but on the contrary will be stimulated by competition to greater productivity, more quickly and surely than otherwise. From the political, economic and human point of view the reunification of Germany will liberate forces undreamed of by the planner's philosophy.

20

AFTER THE BREAKDOWN OF THE EUROPEAN
DEFENCE COMMUNITY

(Article in *Bulletin* of September 22, 1954)

*After the breakdown of the European Defence Community, which
in the summer of 1954 brought on a crisis respecting Western integration, talks were begun in September, 1954, on the Eden Plan
for replacing the EDC by the Brussels Pact, with German membership of NATO. In the September, 1954, issue of the* Bulletin *Ludwig Erhard gave his views on the situation.*

The European Defence Community has broken down in the face
of French opposition, the integration tide is no longer running
high, and we may well ask ourselves whether we shall have to put
away any thought of European collaboration and consider the
spirit of togetherness as dead. I myself have been one of the few
who in the midst of all the clamour for drawing political frontiers
have pointed out not once but dozens of times that political and
military integration are on a par with economic integration, but
that to try to press on too zealously would have dangerous consequences, and might well be doomed to failure or even lead to a
reign of *dirigisme*. I have repeatedly pointed out that European
states are so sensitive where their nationhood is concerned, and the
meaning of sovereignty is so widely misinterpreted, that any proposal whatever involving a limitation of national freedom of action
is held to be suspect, and that it is therefore essential to establish
principles which are embodied in an accepted order and which
exert so to speak an anonymous pressure on nation states.

I have always been of the opinion that European integration
must be based less on institutions than on functions. It is here that
the degree of economic co-operation already attained is an excellent
starting-point and one which deserves more attention by statesmen.
For these first steps towards European integration have come about

organically, are based on insight and understanding and have been so successful that no country can any longer hold out against this trend. I refer to the efforts of OEEC, EPU, GATT and the World Bank to do away with trade barriers and discriminatory practices; to the efforts to achieve progressive liberalization and especially free convertibility of currencies. Any progress in this direction must in the nature of things strengthen the feeling for political solidarity, and it is surprising that the connection between the two has been so little realized. The irresistible progress of economic integration gives hope to all those who are aware that peace and freedom can be preserved only if all free peoples stand together. In this, France is shoulder-to-shoulder with us and I am confident that the French Prime Minister, Mendès-France, has grasped this inter-relationship between the political and economic spheres.

All this is immediately related to our theme of convertibility. In recent weeks voices have here and there been raised in alarm at the alleged risks and dangers of convertibility and urging caution, if not postponement. Whatever may cause individual countries to have such reservations—whether tactical restraint or political considerations, whether group egoism or national egoism—is there any possible justification, bearing in mind the higher common political aspirations of the free peoples, for upholding the accursed system of currency controls? It is apposite here to cite Lenin who stated categorically that one had only to destroy the currency system of the capitalist (that is to say, free) world in order to deliver it into the hands of communism. But the currencies of the free world need no destroying—they are destroyed and remain destroyed as long as currency controls exist. This is why it would be criminal not to go on working with all energy for free convertibility, now that so promising a start has been made.

Currency controls mean protectionism and narrow nationalism, isolation and backwardness, the denial of progress and prosperity; it is the very way to split up the free world once more into separate blocs and zones. Countries that have not yet of their own initiative found the right road to financial and economic stability will, so long as currency controls, and therefore bilateralism, continue in being, be almost helplessly at the mercy of this rotten system, and even be encouraged to continue on this course by the countries that

are themselves on the right road. It would be well-nigh tragic if
Soviet Russia, after its undeniable political successes, were now to
celebrate an economic triumph as well—for a triumph for the
Soviets it would be if the free world refrained from making full
use of the tremendous advantage that stems from the ability to
achieve economic and social progress in freedom.

What has yet to happen, I sometimes feel inclined to ask, to convince the democratic peoples once and for all what a great blessing
freedom is, to make them realize that in economics the principle of
freedom has proved itself over and over again? The Federal Republic has furnished the classic inductive proof: out of indescrib-
able chaos and distress she has rebuilt—within the short span of
six years and by virtue of such principles—a sturdy economy based
on sound financial and monetary foundations. Further, the development of other European countries has unequivocally docu-
mented the fact that progress is the greater the more the liberal
principles are embodied in the economic, trade and currency
policies they adopt. Let me cite another instance from Germany's
experience. At the beginning of this year, as a preliminary step
towards convertibility, we tackled the problem of the blocked
mark accounts, by releasing them gradually and keeping a close
watch on the effects at each stage in the process. The result has
given the lie to the pessimists and has furnished incontestible proof
that only freedom creates trust, and it is only because we had the
courage to believe in freedom that the almost unimaginable is
today a fact and the blocked mark has gone. The result is hardly
noticed any more in Germany and this is perhaps the best reward
for all the efforts I have been making for years to break down the
solid wall of resistance. Once more I have been proved right in
what I have been contending since 1948, namely that today's
Utopia is tomorrow's reality.

I shall therefore not cease in my efforts to awaken the conscience
of the world and will not see my task completed before the free
world—for otherwise it is no free world—is indissolubly united by
a system of freely convertible currencies. Only then will envy,
distrust, strife and malice disappear, and then at last statesmen
will be able to set about developing lasting forms of political co-
operation and integration on this foundation of economic unity

and strength. On the other hand it is sheer economic dreaming to imagine that an isolated economy (and that is what currency controls lead to) can be made internationally competitive. No—in this way national economies only grow further apart and the consciousness of a common political destiny must needs become ever more blurred. Neither is anything gained if everyone waits until the other party has fulfilled all the demands he considers desirable and a mathematical balance has been achieved—in other words, if we in Europe wait for America to come round to our conception of what constitutes trade or, conversely, until we have abandoned all discrimination against the dollar area.

This way lies no progress, but only captivity, for the economic and political freedom and unity of the free world is not to be gained by playing a super-clever game with a mechanically calculable formula as the key. We must (and all our experience tells us that we can) confidently believe that the principle of freedom will tear down all the barriers that the economy engineers with their rational outlook appear to be erecting against a liberal system. If we accept the views of those who are for ever hesitating, we shall in the end believe that economic progress is achieved by artificially maintaining a bad system, and that a good and healthy economic, financial and monetary policy must have detrimental consequences. Good sense becomes nonsense, and balm poison!

We Germans, who have learned from tragic but also from fortunate experience, cannot and must not embark with eyes open upon a course that will hold us captive to ancient thraldoms and bar the way out into the open. We have declared our solidarity with all the democratic states of Europe because we have allowed ourselves to hope that they all yearn for economic and political unity. Even if this expectation remains unfulfilled, we shall have regained our freedom of action and committed ourselves to the cause of freedom.

21

WORLD BANK AND INTERNATIONAL MONETARY FUND

(Speech on the occasion of the 9th Annual Meeting of the International Monetary Fund and of the World Bank held in Washington on September 27, 1954)

On July 28, 1952, the Federal Republic was admitted to membership of the International Monetary Fund and of the International Bank for Reconstruction and Development (World Bank). Both these institutions were founded by the Bretton Woods Agreement concluded in July 1944 to assist post-war reconstruction and the re-establishment of sound currency systems throughout the world on a multilateral basis. Ludwig Erhard was appointed German representative on the governing body of the World Bank and attended in this capacity the Seventh Annual Meeting held on September 5, 1952. At the same time, the President of the then Bank deutscher Länder (now Bundesbank) was appointed a Governor of the International Monetary Fund. The work of these two institutions, as well as of the International Finance Corporation created in 1956 and of the International Development Association created in 1960, was at first mainly concerned with the rehabilitation of the older industrial countries of the West, and subsequently came to be directed more and more towards assisting the younger and economically more backward countries of Africa, Asia and Latin America. The World Bank was thus the first international body to take up the work of assisting development, at a time when Europe had not yet begun to think about this new problem as the world-wide task of the future.

Since I last had the opportunity—two years ago in Mexico City—of taking part in the deliberations of this distinguished gathering, far-reaching changes have taken place in the economies of many countries and in their relations with each other. Many countries have made substantial progress in the development of their production of goods, in the expansion of their international trade, and in the raising of the standard of living. Above all, in these two years a number of countries have managed to return to free forms of international and monetary dealings by adopting strict currency and fiscal policies. At the same time, these countries have been able to increase their capital and build up their investment markets to the accompaniment of a more or less marked reduction of interest rates. In one or two countries there are even signs of a trend towards private capital investment abroad, although this trend has not developed as fully as it might have done for various reasons not the least of which is the inadequacy of existing systems of payment.

I should like to express the keen pleasure I feel in the contemplation of these achievements, not only, or even chiefly, because the Federal Republic has had a share in them, but because my economic philosophy tells me that it is a good thing for every country when its near and distant neighbours prosper and live a a well-ordered life.

Development in some other countries whose representatives are at this meeting has been less favourable in recent years. The drop in raw material prices since 1951 has brought balance-of-payment difficulties for some producers and made it difficult for them to raise capital for investment purposes.

In this situation the need for effective collaboration becomes more urgent than ever and the prospects for co-operation are improved.

On reading the Bank's report I was particularly aware of the unique nature of this institution which gathers resources from many countries and directs them into all corners of the world to bear fruit in the shape of economic growth, thus setting an example of co-operation in economic freedom and international solidarity such as the world has never seen before.

We must concentrate on ways and means of improving on the results so far achieved. It has repeatedly been said that the loans granted by the Bank supplement but cannot replace the operations of private capital. The main task before us is to stimulate these, now that the pre-conditions have improved, at least in a number of countries.

The pre-conditions have to be established on both sides; that is to say, on the side of the lender and of the borrower. The movement of capital between countries can only be effected on the basis of confidence and a properly functioning system of international payments. A good deal has yet to be done before this basis can be claimed to exist. There are inadequacies on both counts. Inflationary methods of financing, unreal rates of exchange and currency restrictions are enticing instruments, but they are also the most effective means known of blocking the way to co-operation.

Not all the member countries no doubt are able to make their currencies convertible to a like extent or at like intervals of time, but there is equally no doubt that the material pre-conditions for doing so are fulfilled in the case of a large number of countries. I am absolutely convinced that the removal of currency restrictions is a vital prerequisite for enabling the free world to become truly free.

Only then shall we be able to achieve the degree of economic efficiency needed to banish the threat of collectivism finally and for good. As long as currency restrictions are maintained, the evils of bilateralism will remain with us and we shall continue to be deprived of the recuperative power inherent in a sound and well-ordered conduct of our affairs. If we let the return to convertibility wait until all conceivable pre-conditions reach an ideal level in all countries, we shall never get there. I have a strong feeling that the time to make this move was never so propitious as now.

Those countries which are already ripe for a return to convertibility are charged with the immense responsibility and task of taking this liberating step, for if they hold back they will be actively encouraging the continuance of practices that are progressively undermining the foundations of the economy in their own and other countries. Courageous belief in order and freedom never yet let anyone down, and on my journeyings I have seen, and taken courage from seeing, that people everywhere are yearning for order and free multilateral dealings, even in countries which lack the strength to stand on their own feet. If the countries which are now ripe for convertibility were to unite to form the nucleus of a world order, I am convinced that the magnetic force thus set up would in itself be strong enough to ensure the ultimate economic integration of the entire free world. A policy of this kind would also go far towards eliminating the errors and tensions that still beset international trade, would in fact positively bring about a general clean-up.

Discipline in the matter of finance and credit policy is an indispensable component of any system of free currency convertibility. It is also the only system that allows of free movement of capital between countries, and it is for this reason that it is no mere formality that the Annual Meetings of the World Bank and the Monetary Fund are held jointly.

In view of the growing capacity of some countries to export capital, we should look into the matter of how far the Bank may be in a position in the future, within the terms of its statutes, to stimulate private investment operations by means of guarantees.

Allow me, in conclusion, to say a few words on my own country's participation in the work of the Bank. This has not of course reached the level attained by other countries that have had the advantage of being members for a longer time. But we are doing our best to give all the co-operation of which we are capable. The Federal Republic will contribute to the Bank's loan activities by liberating some of its 18% quota, and has indeed already begun to do so. The fact that this contribution is not as large as we should like is due to the relative smallness of our capital market and our own internal needs in the matter of investment capital which are as yet unsatisfied. To make up for this, we shall strive to further the aims of the Bank in other directions as well.

22

EUROPEAN UNITY THROUGH FUNCTIONAL INTEGRATION

(Speech at a meeting of the Club 'Les Echos' in Paris on
December 7, 1954)

In a speech given before an international forum, the Club 'Les Echos' in Paris, Erhard dealt with topical problems of international co-operation. Erhard had on November 30 in Basel made a renewed appeal for free convertibility and had affirmed Germany's readiness to take part in the policy of giving aid to developing countries. He made use of his stay in Paris to visit Premier Mendès-France and the Finance Minister, Faure. In his address of December 7 he said:

I am grateful for the opportunity of being amongst you and speaking to you. The subject I have been asked to talk about is Franco-German co-operation in the framework of a greater Europe, and here the first question to examine is what possibilities exist for bilateral relations between our two countries without prejudice to the greater task of creating a united and free Europe, especially in the economic field. There is undoubtedly a good deal that could still be achieved bilaterally as between our two countries. From the German point of view I should say, indeed I am convinced, that we shall be ready to go beyond the short-term agreements of the past and conclude long-term treaties, particularly with a view to enabling your agriculture to look further ahead.

But above all I believe that bilateral talks between our two countries and people are necessary and desirable because we need first to awaken understanding of each other's social, economic and political milieux. The present time seems to me to be so opportune that we should be missing a great chance if we failed to make a special effort to bring about this understanding, to get to know each other better, to learn to respect and, if you like, to love each other more. I also think that the reaching of an understanding between France and Germany—governments and peoples—would give a powerful impetus to European co-operation. I should like to put this in another way and say that whatever links us together in a bilateral sense and whatever may be contemplated in the shape of bilateral solutions to common problems should not aim at anything like an isolation of Franco-German economic relations from the rest of Europe, and should most certainly not be interpreted as an attempt to set up a Paris-Bonn economic axis. Co-operation between us must not set up a hostile dividing element within Europe, but should on the contrary give European-wide co-operation new impetus and serve as a call to other peoples to seek a happier future only in a spirit of community and all-embracing freedom. If this be the ultimate aim, then it is clear what Franco-German co-operation ought not to be and must not be allowed to become. We welcome the fact that the industrial organizations of our two countries show a desire to come together, to become attuned to each other, to examine ways of complementing each other, to eliminate structural differences, and finally to work out common economic aims. But I believe it would be a mistake to foster French and German industrial co-operation by means of cartel-like arrangements, or to subscribe to the principle of mutual protection or shielding. It would be equally misguided to base Franco-German co-operation on any form of state *dirigisme*. We must reject any artificial interference by the German or French Government in the public or private sectors of the economy which aims at steering natural development from world-wide relationships into the narrower waters of bilateral relations. What we want and are trying to bring about is a free and untrammelled tie-up between our two countries and at the same time with all other countries. The aim must be to open the door to competitive effort under free and fair conditions—although of course each individual country will have to be free to adopt interim measures according to its circumstances and its internal structure. A freely established relationship between two countries which is at the same time the basis for a more comprehensive European, and even world-wide, community naturally presupposes that sound foundations for an ordered economic life be laid within the national economies. These sound foundations can be labelled 'stable currency', 'free competition' and 'balanced economy'. Where these pre-conditions exist, the way is open to the growth of a wider community. But whatever conditions obtain in the particular countries, it is the bounden duty of all of us to see that in our own sphere of responsibility we go beyond the confines of national boundaries and so develop our productive powers, so pool our common efforts, that we achieve maximum results from the division of labour, and thereby maximum benefit, social welfare and social security for our peoples. There is talk in the world today—and I do not like it at all— about a 'German miracle'. I do not accept this term because what has happened in Germany in the past six years is anything but a miracle. It is no more than the fruits of the honest efforts of a whole people, who were given the chance, under liberal principles, to apply human initiative, human freedom and human energies. But if this German example is to have significance abroad, then it can only be by demonstrating to the world at large the blessings of human freedom and economic freedom of action.

It will constitute part of Germany's contribution to the shaping of the Europe of the future that we succeeded, under the worst possible external conditions, in pulling ourselves out of an utterly desperate situation, discovering that by applying a liberal but socially committed economic policy we could wrest order out of chaos and put the economy and the life of our people on a sound and healthy footing. The inductive proof thus furnished can be of real value to Europe. The point is not whether the institutions of this or that country allow a greater or less degree of freedom of action to its citizens; what is important is that we jointly realize where our future lies and what we must do in order to shape our destiny in harmony with each other.

A free and happy Europe, which guarantees our peoples the fullest possible life, can only come into being provided there are settled liberal relations between our two countries and there is an active sense of community and friendship between our two peoples.

Let us acknowledge the fact that a yearning to share a common destiny and a common future has been awakened in our peoples. Solutions to our problems are being sought in a number of ex-

tremely diverse institutions. Think of OEEC, the Organization for
European Economic Co-operation, known as the European Economic Council, or of the European Payments Union, the International Currency Fund or GATT—in all of them forces are at
work to find the way out of disunity into unity. The concepts of
autarchy, protectionism, national egotism, and on to the excesses of
nationalism are things of the past; we must turn right away from
all such thinking if we are to see the paths that lead to unity.

The objection is often heard that the obstacles to integration are
too great and that complete freedom, full integration and the
elimination of national boundaries in the economic sphere are unattainable because the individual national economies work under
too widely different conditions. Objections of this kind must be
looked at in the right perspective. In agriculture there are of course
some differences in the nature of things, and in the industrial
sector too; wages and social services may also differ from one
country to another. And yet I can state that unbiased enquiries
have revealed that serious, obstacle-forming differences do not
exist or at least not to the extent alleged on the political plane. But
this way of thinking is a fallacy for the further reason that the productivity of a national economy can only be considered as a complex whole. If we in Europe and in the free world let integration
wait until there is mathematical equality in respect of all cost
factors, then we shall never come together, but remain caught for
ever in the toils of autarchy, condemned for ever to isolation and
therefore to a state of poverty and despair.

Today we are clearly engaged in a constant struggle to reach
workable forms of co-operation or integration. If you ask me for
the difference between co-operation and integration, I would say
that co-operation involves in the first instance working together
and its yard-sticks are quantitative, while integration involves a
change of form—here co-operation takes on another shape; something new is born. In this sense integration is definitely more than
co-operation. It has qualitative implications, is of a higher order,
shall we say, than co-operation. But if you ask further whether we
ought to aim at co-operation or integration, then as a *realpolitiker*
I tell you that we should always take what we can best get. By no
means all men's early dreams of European co-operation, or call it

integration if you like—which seemed a new ideal to so many—
have come to fruition. But as we have seen in recent times, as soon
as one form seemed to dissolve, the desire for new forms sprang up
at once. For however diverse our conceptions of Europe and of
how to live down, or at least reconcile, national sovereignty may
be, we have always been united in the realization that no state, no
people, can today find within itself the measure of welfare and
social security we need to feel safe from the dangers besetting the
free world as a whole.

Thus recent developments and the trend of the times indicate
that there are two kinds of integration, one institutional and the
other functional. The former aims at the delegation of sovereign
duties and rights by the creation of institutions and by the trans-
ference of power from the national level to international or supranational authorities. This is an institutional way of meeting common tasks. This form of integration has up to now been neither
wholly successful nor wholly unsuccessful. The Coal and Steel
Authority is one example of this form; other projected bodies such
as the European Political Community have as yet come to nothing.
With things being as they are in Europe, in view of national sen-
sibilities, feelings of national sovereignty and the jealousy with
which these rights are cherished, I am inclined to think that the
prospects for institutional integration in the near future are not
bright. Might it be possible to achieve more by functional integration?

You will naturally want to know what I mean by functional
integration. I mean a system which, by reason of its inherent
organic structure, to some extent induces a definite pattern of behaviour in individual countries and national economies given the
condition that each entity comprised in the system wishes to
achieve harmonious development with the others.

The best example is furnished by currency convertibility. You
only have to think back to the time of the gold standard with
regard to this example to see that the individual economies were
not made by any coercive force whatever within this system to
abide by a pattern of behaviour suitable to a balanced economy.
This result was achieved by the system itself, in other words
anonymously. I think the kind of functional integration which sets

down common rules of play, adherence to which brings about a desired end, is more likely to help us to overcome national sentiment and prejudice and lead us to unity.

I have broached this subject because, as you know, the question of convertibility, involving real functional integration of the free world's economies, is a major talking-point, and because it is my dearest wish that France should be among the countries that first show readiness to step out with us on the path of freedom, even if only in the field of exchange rates.

If you then ask me whether, in general, political co-operation (or integration) should come before or after economic integration, I would say 'I don't care, but let us make a start.' I would not be an economist if I did not believe that we might perhaps find our joint way more readily on the economic plane than on the political. Certainly we cannot separate the two spheres completely. The desire for economic co-operation naturally springs from the wish for a common political destiny. But whereas politically the forms of co-operation and integration must first be discovered and worked out, much of the spadework has already been done on the economic plane.

In this respect we in Europe have already amply demonstrated —for example through the European Payments Union and GATT, the General Agreement on Tariffs and Trade—the direction we wish to take and the nature of our ideals. All this is beyond dispute. As I see things, it will be through economic development that we shall find our way to political integration. It would be a triumph for those responsible if they succeeded in demonstrating the primacy of politics over economic co-operation. I too would be happy. It would be a blessing for the nations if politicians were to strive for the palm only in the political field, and economists only in theirs, and if both were prepared to go forward together to achieve what is needed to secure a happy future.

I say, not only here in Paris, but repeatedly to my own countrymen, any present-day economic policy, however well conceived, is bound to fail if it is inward-looking; if I thought my task was simply to help my own country through the medium of economic policy, I should feel it was no longer worth tackling. The advance of science and technology, and the broadening of our horizons make national economic frontiers too narrow for fruitful development to be even thinkable within these confines. Metaphorically speaking, we are stuck economically in the age of the horse-drawn carriage and it is high time we woke up, grew up, and read the signs of the times. If I declare here that it is not only for the sake of European solidarity but also for selfish reasons that I find it helpful and valuable to see France strong and healthy and her economy strong and healthy, then I am only saying what I genuinely mean and what I desire for Europe. If we realize that, in spite of any resentment which may still survive from the past, we shall only attain a common future and shared good fortune if we set ourselves a common aim, then, I believe, we shall not only be serving our own natural interests in bilateral dealings, but also carrying out our responsibilities towards a free Europe and the free world.

Present prospects for the relations between our two countries are as favourable as could possibly be wished for. Trade and the two-way flow of goods have reached a pitch that justifies even greater hopes. But all this need only be a beginning. The volume of world trade is not a fixed quantity. If we think of ourselves as united, if we create a common market, and pool our productive powers—why, then I believe that alongside a thriving Germany your richly endowed and structurally healthy country will have a future as fortunate and full of promise as you could wish. Believe me : I am standing here before you not as a German economist in the narrow, self-conscious sense, but as a friend of France, as one who strives to be a truly good European, aware that we shall all either flourish or go under together, that we shall all go forward and preserve our freedom or else sink into servitude. If we were able to realize this, and see the well-nigh limitless chances and possibilities that lay before us, and yet failed to recognize where our duty lay, then I fear we should be past praying for and we could rightly talk of a decline of the West. Because that is not my way of thinking, and because I feel the strength stirring in us to free ourselves, let my last word to you be an exhortation, a request : work with us to put that which unites above that which separates. Then will the future belong to our peoples in a united Europe, reformed and inspired by the spirit of freedom.

M

23

THE AIMS OF THE LAW AGAINST RESTRICTIONS ON COMPETITION

(Speech in the German Federal Parliament on March 24, 1955)

The 'bill to make restrictions on competition illegal' had not been passed in the first legislative period of the German Federal Parliament between 1949 and 1953. After considerable resistance had been overcome both inside and outside Parliament, it had its first reading in the Federal Parliament on March 24, 1955.

In its second term of office the Federal Government presented a bill to make restrictions on competition illegal. It was put forward in its original form of June, 1952, when the first Federal Parliament had discussed it in Committee. The version now before you was drawn up on January 22, 1955, and contains some of the revisions suggested by the Upper House. They are substantially the same as those put forward by the Economic Committee in the last Parliament. It is not my intention in the first reading to state my views either on the bill as a whole or on individual paragraphs. It seems to me much more important to outline once again the basic idea behind this bill and to explain its social and economic origins.

I see in the Social Market Economy system the economic basis for a democratic form of government, which regards human freedom as an inalienable right. It follows, therefore, almost as a matter of course, that a market economy system must centre round the principle of freedom and liberalism, and in consequence the state has a duty to see to it that this basic right is not made inoperative by private collective agreements and obligations.

The harmony of a market economy rests upon the free play of forces which cancel one another out and balance one another up. In this way a quantitative and qualitative harmony is achieved between demand and supply. Whereas in other systems collective

170

controls are introduced in an effort to achieve this, the market economy produces this effect by means of the free market. But the phrase 'free market' only has meaning as long as the economy is motivated and guided by free competition and free price formation. For competition is the most essential ingredient of a market economy system, and its elimination, limitation or prevention must inevitably lead to the collapse of the entire system.

The same is true of free prices, which alone make it possible to measure and compare output, and price development is the only barometer by which one can judge the performance of management. Only prices can show whether production plans have gone too far one way or the other. That is why production can only be adapted on a continuous basis to changes in consumption if there is a free price mechanism. That is also why all measures leading to control or fixing of prices must be rejected as incompatible with the market economy.

But, quite apart from these questions of basic principle, I consider that, after seven years of a market economic policy and the success it has achieved in our economic reconstruction, we have really no reason to abandon this economic system in favour of the apparently easier policy of economic controls. The vast majority of the German people today are undoubtedly in favour of the Social Market Economy and would not take it at all kindly if the German Federal Parliament were to pay undue attention to interests other than those of 50 million consumers. But this would, in fact, be the case, if this so-called Cartel Law were to be passed in a form that left the way open for the emergence of cartels and meant a complete reversal of present economic policy.

Cartels are alien to the very nature of a market economy. If you reject state controls in industry you cannot at the same time accept the collective control of industry by cartels or even regard it as useful and necessary. If you see political, social and economic dangers in collectivism, you cannot at the same time defend cartels, which are a special form of collectivism. Far be it from me to attribute any such nefarious intentions to those who support and favour cartels. All I am saying is that their judgment of the cartel problem is based on false premises and that they therefore fail to grasp its full significance as a social and economic phenomenon.

Seen in its historical context the cartel has been judged either from the purely legal angle or as an aspect of private industry, whereas the interests of publicly-owned industry were neglected. Yet it is precisely from this viewpoint that the real character of cartels can be fully appreciated.

Differing views about cartels and their effects lead to one of two conclusions: legislation that forbids cartels, or legislation that prevents their misuse. A stupid propaganda campaign has been launched in the form of pamphlets asserting that the supporters of anti-cartel legislation must expose themselves to a charge of dogmatism, while those who favour restrictive legislation are alleged, surprisingly enough, to be free from any such suspicion. But if it is dogmatism to pursue a problem to the end and not to be satisfied with so-called common experience, then I gladly confess myself guilty of it.

Quite apart from the fact, however, that the bill now before us does not envisage anything like the idea of complete competition, which has come in for so much criticism, but allows for the formation of general business, export and rationalization cartels and I would even go so far as to say that, as far as this bill is concerned, too many cooks have already somewhat spoiled the broth, apart from this, as I say, I am firmly convinced that a meaningful economic policy in any case must have a clear theoretical basis and should not be geared to vague, fleeting ideas that change from one moment to the next. What this means is that, if you accept competition as a stable factor in the economy, you cannot reject this principle at will for reasons of opportunism or expediency. You would accept it today and deny it tomorrow and at the same time proudly imagine that your lack of purpose is realistic. The fact that people in general are not pure angels, but are also not pure devils, does not entitle us to abandon ethical standards and turn lack of character into a moral imperative.

What is much more important, however, is that legislation merely to prevent abuses by cartels completely fails to reach the heart of the problem and provides no means of preventing cartels from becoming too powerful. If we leave aside any criminal or moral offences, which must be punished in some other way, I would like to ask where, in the view of those who support this principle, abuse is to begin and end and by what criteria we are to judge abuse. I can only go on repeating that I would not accuse any entrepreneur who chose to seek shelter in a cartel of intending any form of abuse. Even if I were to acknowledge that, as far as price agreements are concerned, cartels behave most correctly and responsibly and that, in consequence, legislation to prevent abuses could never have any effect, I would still, where the national economy is concerned, have to oppose cartels as harmful. Abuses lie not in the actions and behaviour of the cartels but in their very existence and derive from the fact that the establishment of a cartel limits and even kills competition and that, as soon as prices are fixed, they cease to perform their essential function as a sort of steering-wheel for the national economy. Industrialists who speak so readily of ruinous competition, cut-throat competition, and so on, merely damage their own reputation and cut the ground from under their own feet. We simply cannot afford to confuse the unexceptionable principle of competition, which is so essential to a market economy, with the amoral conduct of certain individuals in competition and to deduce from this that cartels are necessary.

Equally interesting and equally misleading have been the attempts to argue that cartels are necessary for the protection of light industry. It has been proved that the bigger concerns in heavy industry and in capital goods production are more or less ripe for cartellization, depending upon their particular product, and are correspondingly ready and willing to be cartellized, whereas the same conditions do not apply to the manufacturing industries with their increasing production of finished goods. But it is precisely in this sector, as in the retail trade or the handicrafts, that the professional middle class is most widely represented. As cartels do not add to the nation's purchasing power, over-cartellization would result in those industries which are ripe for cartellization concentrating too much purchasing power in their hands at the expense of the lesser concerns in the middle of the scale.

If these were then to take refuge in cartels, it would very soon become apparent that the divergent forces are, for the most part, impossible to control and that technical problems would arise which are extremely hard to solve. At the same time one would be forced to admit that, while one can perhaps preserve the cartel price,

one can never maintain the volume of sales. It is practically unthinkable that in an economy dominated by cartels there should
not be many of those organizations which, by virtue of a collective
price policy, absorb more purchasing power than they would
attract in free competition with free prices. But more at one point
means less at another and leads either to a fall in prices or a drop
in sales in the free sector. For this reason cartels must be condemned. But above all the 'middle class' is bound to have a vital
interest in keeping the national economy as a whole free from
cartels. For it is clear that the so-called good cartels, namely those
that work, are precisely the ones that have the most damaging
effects, because such effects are not always confined to the sector
immediately concerned but are invariably felt elsewhere in the
economy.

Now, any cartel legislation clearly requires a certain administrative machinery to implement it, and we are told that legislation
banning cartels would require a mammoth machine of this kind.
The logic of this is not immediately apparent, for it is undoubtedly
easier to prevent the spread of cartels than to track down abuses
inside cartels which cannot be pinpointed. But perhaps this fear
of a mammoth bureaucracy is the clearest indication of how widespread the desire for cartels is, if such a ponderous machinery is
thought necessary to cope with the problem. It is certain that the
size of the Cartel Authority will depend largely on the extent to
which German industry is cartel-prone.

As far as the dreaded state-control is concerned, the reasoning
is completely false. The critics of an anti-cartel law make no mention of the enormous private cartel bureaucracies that emerge with
any legislation to prevent restrictive practices. This centralization
in private industry must inevitably be much more far-reaching
than any similar trend in a cartel authority, which has only one
function, namely to prevent any undesirable expansion of cartels,
to maintain competition and to see that the market remains free.
And one cannot, in all conscience, speak of state intervention when
the state is merely safeguarding the basic principles of a free,
democratic social system.

In this connection I must say something about the responsibility
of the state and the responsibility of the entrepreneur. Amongst

the many pronouncements that have been made was the assertion that by making cartels subject to official approval one would be giving the state a unique position of authority in our economic life. This is, to say the least, far from clear. It is surely an accepted fact that one of the state's main responsibilities is—and must be—to establish and maintain the foundations on which the nation's economy can function. The state is also responsible for the social implications of economic policy, for ensuring the smooth functioning of our trade and a steady upwards movement in the economy. It is responsible for keeping the nation's industry competitive as an organic part of world industry. The Social Market Economy has helped the entrepreneur to regain full freedom of action. For that reason it is unthinkable that the same government which carried through this policy should ever fail to understand the economic needs of private industry, should do anything to limit the freedom of the entrepreneur or, least of all, should introduce a new form of state *dirigisme*.

The initiative of the private entrepreneur cannot, however, be allowed to develop beyond the point where the rights and vital interests of other sections of the population are adversely affected and where an economic position, or even a position of power, is likely to be built up not by individual enterprise in open competition but by collective agreements and artificial accretions of power. Free competition, I repeat, is a basic ingredient of our democratic and economic system and cannot, therefore, be brushed aside by private organizations. Only if this is assured, can the state carry the responsibility for the national economy, which it would not be in a position to do if it allowed complete freedom for the establishment of cartels and exposed the free market with its free prices to the whims of private cartels. As soon as the state allows price fixing by cartels, it can no longer pursue an active economic policy.

One must also remember how much our conception of responsibility and competence has changed in the last thirty years. If today a bottle-neck appears at any point in the economy, the public does not hold industrialists or industry responsible but the state, and the state is expected to take the necessary action. But you cannot apply economic policy effectively to the economic life of the nation unless you have a free market, otherwise any economic measure you may take can be stultified by collective decisions at board-room level.

Finally, as regards the social aspect of the problem, the Federal Government has made it abundantly clear by its actions and its general attitude that it believes the definition of our economic policy as a 'Social Market Economy' carries with it a grave responsibility. But an economic policy can only be called 'social' if it sees to it that economic progress and higher productivity largely benefit the consumer. This aim is achieved primarily by free competition, which keeps down profits or even unearned income and preserves the dynamism of our economy. Thanks to this policy the popular image of the entrepreneur is no longer one of a man who leads a comfortable, carefree and good life but of the first man in the factory, who carries the heaviest burden of responsibility. Every worker is prepared to recognize that, where the volume of trade and the market are concerned, the entrepreneur must be highly experienced and highly skilled if he is to hold his own against his competitors. If the entrepreneur were to give up his freedom of action of his own volition he would be undermining the political, social and moral reputation of his class and, indeed, opening the door to collectivism.

It is also wrong to try to justify cartels by arguing that their aim is to protect the employer and the employee. Cartels give artificial protection to jobs that are, for the most part, unproductive. As a result the entire national economy is frequently in danger of becoming bogged down in a production slump, which can have particularly serious consequences in the field of international competition. No policy can be called 'social' which holds up progress and deliberately prevents the creation of fresh, productive employment. If you want to create more and better opportunities for employment, if you want to achieve a dynamic expansion of trade, then you must oppose cartels. If you favour protection, then you will support them. But with our growing shortage of labour we simply cannot afford the luxury of cartels. And anyone who knows what cartels really are and how they function will understand why it is so important that as large a public as possible should be made to share in this decision.

The view expressed during the debate in the Upper House that the Cartel Authority should only intervene in a case of genuine public interest, even if a restrictive practices law were passed, is completely unacceptable. For in most cases where cartel measures interfere with a company's economic expansion or even threaten its very existence, the restrictive practices employed are not known to the victims, who are not in a position to gauge the effects of a cartel policy on them. They are confronted with market conditions which are too complex for them to understand. This applies to primary products in industry, it applies in trade, and it applies on an even bigger scale to the consumer, who cannot possibly know how a price is arrived at and whether he is being cheated. At best he can draw comparisons, but these become valueless if a branch in the cartel pursues the same price policy. Then, inevitably, the consumer gains the impression that he is at the mercy of invisible forces in the market. If this feeling spreads and hardens into political resistance, it is the end of economic and social peace. As I have already said, the broad mass of the people today has regained confidence in the entrepreneur, but they will never be prepared to place their confidence in cartels.

It is a symptom of our time that when group-interests of special wishes are at stake or when there is a demand for stronger protection of competition, reference is always made to the need for a system, although partial arrangements of this kind undermine order and lead to atomization and isolation. I declare, on the other hand, that in a well-ordered state there can only be one system: the social system as a whole. The disintegration of any society must become all the more apparent, the more it is split up as a system. State control and collectivism will prosper more and more as the need increases to bind the parts together by artificial means. Where market regulations and professional regulations become too common, they breed egoism. Where all groups want to have special protection and more security, people will enjoy less and less freedom and will lose more and more of genuine security. There can be no doubt that the advantages some people are out to acquire can only be acquired at the expense of others.

It would also be a remarkable contradiction if a country like the Federal Republic, which, on the one hand, is straining every nerve to become an organic part of the free world in conformity with its market economy principles, were, on the other hand, to erect protective barriers round certain branches of industry and certain groups at home and were to break up the national economy into parts. Just as the world economy was destroyed by the protectionism, egoism and nationalism of individual states, so a national economy must suffer the most severe damage if the same principles prevail. Just as the reconstruction of a viable world economy has only been possible during recent years by applying a liberal policy, so individual national economies can also prosper only if they remain true to these same principles.

It is surely not a sign of insight and wisdom to go on thinking in terms of the past and to model one's economic system on something that failed before. At a time when we are striving to realize new and higher forms of integration both on a European and a world scale, the idea of resuscitating a cartel policy from the past has something almost mediaeval about it. For this reason we would be betraying the progressive idea of integration if we regarded international cartel agreements as suitable instruments with which to create larger communities. I would even go so far as to say that, as concepts and as principles, integration and cartels are not only in contrast, they are mutually exclusive. But in reality the victory of the modern economic conception is now assured. Not only in Germany but also in all other European countries a perceptible change has set in and the demand is growing on all sides for control of cartellization, for an end to restrictive practices and even to monopolies as such.

In the last few days alone news from England, France and Holland has confirmed this. I would like to ask those who favour legislation against restrictive practices, when and where a country has ever achieved its ends by this means. Professor Welter is quite right when he says in the *Frankfurter Allgemeine Zeitung* that their policy suggests to him someone who is looking for a rare species of fish in the ocean and hopes to catch it with his bare hands. Without pointing a finger at anyone in particular, I find it difficult to believe that this conception is really sincere. At all events, it would be nothing short of a tragi-comedy, if we in Germany, in the Federal Republic of all places, were to abandon our present economic policy and pursue a retrograde course.

Legislation against restrictive practices seems to me to be merely a misuse of legislation, for it creates the impression, against our better judgment and against all historical experience, that such a law could prevent the defects and abuses which, it seems, should be prevented. But as Minister of Economics, I have to defend not the interests of certain business circles but the fundamental rights of 50 million consumers. That is what is at stake. These are the problems inherent in this bill before you and a satisfactory solution for them must be found. One does not have to be intransigent—and this I would like to state quite clearly—when one has a clear conception in one's head. So in introducing this bill I expect the German Bundestag to be aware of the implications of what is probably the most important domestic measure so far proposed, and to find a good and happy solution that will benefit our people and our economy.

24

VOLUNTARY INSURANCE AGAINST
SOCIAL RISKS

(Article in *Versicherungswirtschaft* of January 1956)

The reform of social Pensions and Old Age Insurance for workers in the Federal Republic in 1957 had been preceded by a year of public discussion on the basic requirements of social insurance. Many people took the view that the state compulsory insurance scheme should be extended to cover all employed as well as self-employed persons, regardless of income. Such a measure would have struck a fatal blow at the Social Market Economy, not only because it would have imposed an enormous additional burden but also because it would have represented a further step towards the complete Welfare State. Ludwig Erhard dealt with this subject on several occasions:

The Social Market Economy is the fundamental principle on which the economic life of the Federal Republic has been built up and which made possible the exceptional economic progress we have made so far, progress that is frequently described abroad, quite wrongly, as an 'economic miracle'. The essence of this market economy is that the economic process, namely production, the distribution of goods and incomes, is not controlled from above but is directed within the framework of a clearly-defined economic policy by free prices and free competition. The driving forces in the market economy which lead to maximum production and increased prosperity for the entire population are freedom, personal responsibility and initiative in choosing one's employment and consumption, thus giving each individual as a producer and a consumer an awareness of the economic opportunities open to him. So the market economy is the one economic system that combines the maximum of productivity, prosperity and personal freedom.

The success achieved by this economic system and the economic policy behind it in the Federal Republic during recent years is apparent to all and is generally recognized today. One has only to remember that the gross national product rose from 79·4 milliard marks in 1949 to 145·3 milliard in 1954 and will reach nearly 160 milliard in 1955, and that the real earnings of the average worker have risen by more than 20% since pre-war, those of the industrial worker by more than 30%. But the high productive capacity of the market economy is reflected still more clearly in the field of social policy. The unemployment problem created by the war and its after-effects was solved and full employment was achieved, while millions of refugees and displaced persons were also absorbed relatively painlessly into the economy. Last but not least, the increase in public expenditure on social welfare from 10 milliard marks in 1949 to more than 20 milliard in 1954 was only made possible by the sharp upwards trend of the Federal Republic's economy.

Facts such as these show how closely our economic and social policies are inter-related. On the one hand, the more successful our economic policy, the less need there is for intervention and emergency aid in the social field, although it must also be recognized that, in a modern industrial economy, even the best of economic policies has to be accompanied by certain social measures. On the other hand, it is equally true to say that effective social benefits are only feasible if there is a sufficiently large and increasing social product and, therefore, a productive economy to back them up. It is, therefore, of the most vital interest to social policy that an expanding but at the same time stable economy should be maintained. As the hidden earnings derived from social security benefits are no longer a 'quantité négligeable' but a factor of considerable importance in the economic process, economic policy and social security are closely interdependent. An autonomous social policy divorced from the national economy is a thing of the past and the social policy of today must be in tune with economic policy, in other words, it should not hamper the productivity of the national economy and should conform to the basic principles of the market economy system.

If we want to preserve a liberal economic and social system on a long-term basis a fundamental requirement is that, side by side with an economic policy which guarantees people their personal freedom, there should be a correspondingly liberal social policy. It is contrary to the market economy system, which leaves decisions on production and consumption to the individual, to rule out private initiative in making provisions for the emergencies of life if the individual is prepared and qualified to make such provisions on his own responsibility. Economic freedom and entirely compulsory insurance are not compatible. Hence the need to recognize the contribution principle as one of the most important principles in social security and to give priority, as far as possible, to self-help and personal responsibility. Automatic protection by the state should stop at a point where the individual and his family are in a position to make provision of their own. As far as employees are concerned this certainly applies to those in the higher income brackets who are holding responsible positions in industry or the civil service.

Apart from this, however, it would represent a move towards the Welfare State which would endanger our social and economic life, if a compulsory state insurance scheme covered citizens whose position in society and industry is such that it can only be maintained by personal initiative and energy. It is to some extent understandable that the war and the currency reform with their far-reaching effects on everyday life should have given rise, even amongst the more independent members of the community, to a demand for collective security. But it would be a grave mistake to tie down security against disability in the future to a catastrophe in the past, which we hope will never happen again, and particularly at a time when we have regained our economic security and prosperity and can look forward to further economic progress.

As regards social security for the self-employed, the decisive factor is that the readiness to meet any emergency on one's own responsibility is one of the prerequisites of independence in a free economic and social system. Independence in a market economy means pursuing some independent calling or profession of one's own volition and on one's own responsibility and thereby exercising organizational or spiritual initiative. The self-employed are, therefore, in a particularly favourable position to weigh up the opportunities in industry, but this carries with it the responsibility for taking economic risks. The holder of such a specialized position in our economic life cannot, in a market economy, be protected by the state but must, if he is to fulfil his real purpose, maintain this position day in day out by achieving results, by having the courage to take risks and by pursuing an individual and responsible way of life.

It follows from this that those occupying responsible positions in our economic and social system must also be required to make their own independent provision for social security. It would be a striking contradiction if, in our free economy, we were to give each citizen the chance to pursue his own independent vocation and formulated our economic policy with this in mind, and if, on the other hand, we were to introduce an element of state compulsion that deprived these same people of any responsibility for economic and social hazards or for leading their lives as they choose.

The right to make one's own security arrangements has this further justification, that, in the case of the self-employed as against the wage-earner, the element of economic dependence, which requires some form of protection, is lacking, and as a rule there is property involved—usually, in fact, in the form of industrial plant—which represents in itself a considerable reserve. There is also the fact that, in periods of labour shortage, tradesmen and peasant-farmers can usually rely upon members of the family or even outsiders to keep the business going, and old people invariably find a comfortable living in the bosom of the family, even after they have handed over their business or farm. Finally it should be borne in mind that in the trades and professions there are many heterogeneous groups for which social security provisions can only be made on a highly individual and selective basis. No compulsory scheme, which is rigid by nature, could allow for this, and besides in many cases the effect would be to impose unnecessary and frequently onerous contributions.

It is a mistake to believe—as many people do—that the only way to a complete Welfare State is by collective security wholly or partly provided by the state from general taxation, and to think that this can be avoided by introducing compulsory insurance, but at the same time taking contributions from output. Any form of national insurance based on compulsion—whether it is one over-all scheme or is worked out on a group basis—differs only in degree, not in principle, from general state welfare. So there is also a clear tendency towards the Welfare State if state compulsion extends beyond those in need of protection, and if people are subjected to it for whom, because of their position in the economy, compulsion and dependence are unnatural.

The drift towards a welfare and collective state with all its economic and social consequences would become irresistible if we began to include all gainfully employed people, regardless of whether they are wage-earners needing protection or whether they are self-employed, in one compulsory welfare scheme. The long-term effect on the German economy, to say nothing of our political and social system, would be disastrous. Total compulsory insurance and the Welfare State are, by their very nature, bound to discourage the enterprise, the interest in personal saving, the individual initiative and the sense of responsibility, without which a free economic and social system cannot exist. The consequences would be a growing socialization of personal expenditure and increasing collectivization of our everyday lives, a gradual suppression of individuality and a corresponding dependence on the collective or the state, with the result that the free and efficient capital market, on which the expansion and stability of the market economy depend, would shrink to nothing. At the end of this perilous road stands the 'social serf', whose material security is guaranteed by an almighty state, while economic progress in freedom becomes a thing of the past.

Although this may be a nightmare that will never materialize, there are certain trends even here in the direction of the Welfare State which make it necesssary to impose a check right at the beginning and to point out that personal freedom is indivisible. For a free economic system can only survive if the maximum of freedom, private initiative and self-reliance is guaranteed in the social sector.

25

ON THE SUEZ CRISIS

(Broadcast on November 30, 1956)

As a result of stern measures taken by the Government and the Issuing Bank in the autumn of 1956, the economic situation in the Federal Republic had begun to show signs of becoming stabilized. Then further international crises threatened to reintroduce the upward trend. The Suez crisis and the rising in Hungary had both started. Both conflicts seemed likely to spread; entrepreneurs and consumers, remembering Korea, were clearly afraid that there would be supply shortages. In particular, the fear that power production, which had become increasingly dependent on oil, would suffer, brought demands for controls. Undismayed by alarmist appeals for state controls, the Federal Minister of Economics refused categorically to introduce rationing:

The past few weeks have been anxious ones. We have been witnessing international events that have had a marked effect on the political and economic situation in the Federal Republic.

Only a few hundred miles away—in Hungary—the flames of rebellion blazed up out of bondage, hunger and poverty. Hour by hour fresh and exciting news reached us of the bitter struggle of a brave people for its most elementary human rights. With our own eyes we saw the cracks appear in the foundations of Soviet Socialism.

But in these past weeks we have witnessed something more than the first steps towards a more liberal trend in the countries of the Soviet sphere of influence; we have seen a profound spiritual revolt, inspired by a passionate desire to be liberated from a way of life that had become intolerably sterile and which threatened to imprison human beings in a soulless formula.

It is still too early to interpret these events objectively, but, as in the period following the Korean war, so too in these latest critical developments the economic policy of sober reflection and steady nerves which we have pursued has proved to be the most sensible and the most fitting.

Let me hasten to add that you also have, for the most part, kept cool heads in those critical days of the Hungarian and Suez conflicts, thereby ensuring that our economy could pursue its normal, steady course, unhampered by any outburst of panic.

Of course, I would be painting a false picture if I pretended that, during those anxious days, there were not some even amongst us who, recalling the period of controls and rationing, thought fit to hoard supplies. The German market met this demand without difficulty, and this is not the least of several reasons why the situation is normal again. There could be no more striking proof of this than the fact that not a few attempts are being made today to return hoarded supplies. But nothing I have just said can lessen the sense of gratification I felt at the sober and disciplined behaviour of the German people. They thereby did themselves a great service.

During the past few weeks, then, this country's economy has again shown the German consumer and the world at large that it is not to be panicked: it has remained stable in spite of unsettled conditions abroad. We have experienced difficulties in certain areas but our main trade links with the world market have remained unbroken, and the accumulation of reserve stocks of raw materials by private industry has proved the best method of guaranteeing adequate supplies. The Federal Government will continue to encourage entrepreneurs to increase these reserves.

The Federal Republic is undoubtedly one of the countries that have dealt most effectively with the economic repercussions of recent events. Thanks to the good work we have done over the past few years, we have succeeded in building up our exports and our foreign exchange reserves to such a point that the Federal Republic is in a better position to meet any shortages that may arise.

But let me say a word at this point about oil supplies in particular. Not surprisingly, I have had anxious enquiries recently from many people, some of whom were concerned about the supply of petrol for their cars, some about their central heating, some about factories which they had converted from coal to oil.

Throughout all these conversations or exchanges of correspondence the same general question kept cropping up, whether controls and even rationing might not be—indeed, might not have to be—reintroduced.

The mere fact that I am prepared to discuss this question quite openly and that I do so as dispassionately as I have dealt with other problems before should help to reassure you.

As you know, Western Europe is dependent for its oil supplies on imports. This is, of course, also true of the Federal Republic, whose home production only covers about one third—a by no means negligible proportion—of her demand. So the blocking of the Suez Canal and the disruption of one of the major pipelines affects all the countries of Western Europe, though in varying degrees. At the same time, those supplies which so far have reached us by way of the Suez Canal or the pipeline have not entirely ceased; tankers are compelled to make a detour round the Cape of Good Hope, which means that supplies are correspondingly delayed. But any reduction in oil deliveries or any delays can be made good, if alternative or even new sources of supply can be found. Technically, American oil production, for example, can easily be increased, and the question of tanker tonnage is also being examined. Negotiations on all these important questions are going on more or less continuously and, from the results which have already been achieved, I can assure you that any supply difficulties we encounter here in Germany—and this applies not merely to oil —will be purely temporary.

Every country in Western Europe has problems to face at this moment and not one can hope to solve them without reducing consumption. But each country must be responsible for taking such steps as it thinks fit.

You all know me and you know that I have never made any secret of my aversion to a state-controlled economy. Anyone who tries to overcome shortages by rationing merely creates and aggravates them. It is not, however, for dogmatic reasons or from any stubborn prejudice but because I have given this question the most careful consideration and examined all the facts that I now declare once more over the air : I have no intention of introducing any form of petrol rationing, nor do I believe it is necessary. With equal frankness I repeat that full supplies of diesel oil and fuel oil cannot be guaranteed for several months to come, so that consumption of both these commodities must inevitably be cut to some extent. These cuts will, however, be that much easier and simpler to implement if each individual is prepared to make allowances and to adapt himself to the situation. Here, too, there is no cause for alarm. It is simply a question of not living entirely from day to day but of looking and planning ahead. But even with regard to diesel oil and fuel oil you need have no fear of government control; on the contrary, our aim is to keep any cuts in consumption as flexible as possible, depending upon our supply position and the output of the oil companies, in other words, to give the German consumer maximum deliveries.

You yourselves are best able to judge how you can best tide over this transitional period by reducing your consumption of diesel or fuel oil a little here, a little there. You may then discover for yourselves that quite often you have become rather self-indulgent and all I would now ask you to do is to be a little less so. These modest contributions alone will be enough to ensure that each one of us has sufficient for his comfort, for his real needs. At this particular moment it would clearly be irresponsible and extremely short-sighted to try to lay in supplies of diesel and fuel oil for next year or for lengthy periods. You can rest assured that, in the course of next year, you will be able to obtain supplies without difficulty and perhaps even more cheaply. So all existing stocks and any other supplies of oil readily available should not be hoarded over the winter but should be used, as was originally intended, in the coming months.

You will, I hope, have gathered from what I have been saying that we in this country have no need whatsoever to be concerned about our basic necessities. If you will only show moderation, there is enough to give each of you what he really needs. And this you can have and continue to have, without anyone making an inventory of your stocks and deciding, by highly questionable standards, what you should or should not do. But you must be sensible. As I said before, there will be no petrol rationing in Germany, and, as far as oil itself is concerned, there will be no state controls.

Let me, in conclusion, pick out a few sentences from yesterday's debate in the Bundestag on domestic coal supplies. Supplies of coal for the present winter are guaranteed. In saying this, I realize that statements have been made to the contrary by people whose experience during the past few weeks has not been reassuring. I know that retail coal merchants are not having an easy time of it with old as well as new customers expecting special consideration, with some people anxious to lay in the whole of their winter supply, while others are not in a position to do so. This gives rise inevitably to certain inequalities in distribution and the few who suffer assume that what the Government says about adequate supplies of house coal is simply not true. But one must not generalize on isolated cases of this kind. The retailers have tackled this problem very responsibly. Nevertheless, I would like to make an urgent appeal to all who are connected with the distribution of domestic coal, to the marketing organizations, the wholesalers and the retailers, to make the distribution as fair as possible, so that the poorer members of the community are not neglected but preferably are given special consideration.

Let me emphasize once again that supplies of coal this winter for domestic consumption in particular but also for other consumers in Germany are adequate to cover all our real requirements; they are, in fact, appreciably larger than last year.

One final word about prices. The German public knows what efforts I have made to ensure stable prices. The result is that today the price level in the Federal Republic, compared with that of the other larger countries inside and outside Europe, is one of the most stable, despite the fact that a great many internal and international economic factors have been working against us. I make this observation particularly for the benefit of our critics in the Socialist camp, to whom I would recommend a study of price developments in those very countries with Socialist governments. Over the past few years the rise in prices in these countries has been four or five times more than in the Federal Republic. So in this field, too, the Social Market Economy has proved itself.

26

PROSPERITY FOR ALL!

(Speech at the 7th Parliamentary Party Congress of the CDU
in Hamburg on May 14, 1957)

*The CDU Party Congress in Hamburg in May, 1957 was held in
preparation for the Bundestag elections. Its major topics were
economic policy and opposition of state controls. In a world of increasing armaments the internal stability of the Federal Republic
was an essential factor in the economic and social struggle which
Krushchev had already launched. Ludwig Erhard's slogan 'Prosperity for all' rapidly gained significance as a statement of policy
which was by no means confined to the elections. This is the speech
he made:*

'Prosperity for all', merely as a policy directed to improve the
material living standards of our people, would be important
enough to become an article of faith for a party which embraces
all classes of the population. But we cannot be accused of being
materialists, if in our policy of 'Social Market Economy'—inspired
by the will to create a new society on and out of the ruins of the
war and the post-war period—we had to give top priority to providing our German people once more with the basic necessities of
life. How else could we have effectively overcome the want which
threatened us in every walk of life?

Our people would have had no political, no economic, no social
future, if we had not succeeded in removing the quite intolerable
burden of material hardship, in once again giving labour a purpose
by increasing the rewards, in restoring productive and competitive
capacity and so steering the Federal Republic back into the world
economy, and in regaining the confidence and friendship of the
world by honest work and equally honest intentions. The alternative would have been to condemn ourselves to a primitive way of
life, which would have marked the end of our nation's history.

But without this new Germany, for whose political regeneration in those historic years the CDU was largely responsible, the political situation in Europe would also have taken a very different turn. We are not making ourselves out to be strong and we are certainly not forgetting the help we received, particularly from America, in our greatest need, when we say that the success of Germany's reconstruction has contributed to the security of Europe and to closer and freer international co-operation. On such international links depend the peace and freedom of those nations in our continent, to whom these ideals are sacred. While we should, and must, always bear in mind that material values are relative, we cannot afford on the other hand to underestimate the political and social implications of a new and broadly based prosperity. It seems to me that it was a simple Christian act on our part to free our fellow-Germans from need and misery and give them back a sense of security and dignity.

Let me illustrate what we have achieved in this field by quoting a few figures. Our gross national product, which is a measure of our economic position, is double what it was in 1936. Compared with the same year, our industrial production is 220%. Over the past eight years the Federal Republic's foreign trade has shown a rise in exports at an average rate of 245 million marks a month to the present level of 3.2 milliard marks. This improvement has been reflected particularly in our gold and foreign currency reserves, which stand at nearly 19 milliard marks. The total of net wages and salaries has risen in the past five years alone from 34 to 68 milliards and the gross income figure rose in exactly the same proportion from 45 to 90 milliards; in other words, it has doubled. Another effect of our economic policy during the past eight years has been to increase the employment figure from 13.5 to 18.6 million.

In short—the economic and social achievements of our policy are now so patent and irrefutable that it is worth reminding the German people how bitterly and ruthlessly the Socialist Opposition fought against the whole conception of a Social Market Economy. Yet those same doctrinaire Socialists, who were constantly prophesying that our economic policy would lead to bankruptcy, have been dogged by the shadow of their party's political past, and they are offering the German people an economic policy today that brought disaster in every country in which it has been tried out. The countries which have failed to solve their balance-of-payments problems and have been compelled to bolster up their currencies by the most devious means are precisely those with blatantly Socialist governments. These are the states which are obliged to impose restrictions on internal and foreign trade and where the relative increase in the price level has been sharpest. One can well understand why our German Socialists never mention these facts, but the German people should not lose sight of them.

Apart from the occasional blinkered demagogue, the German people as a whole has enough mental and moral integrity to be able to distinguish good from evil and right from wrong. There must be very few people who do not recall in moments of sober reflection what things were like in Germany nine years ago and how hopeless the future appeared to all of us. No one painted a grimmer picture than the late Kurt Schumacher, then leader of the Opposition. Like him, no German then dared to hope that a clear-cut policy could be worked out which would rebuild the foundations of our national life in so short a time. Man's achievements will ever fall short of his endeavours, but this sort of insight and humility is on a very different moral plane from the petty criticisms which have become an inherent part of Opposition policy.

'Prosperity for all', if I may now expand a little, cannot and should not mean that a nation will lapse into a state of sated contentment, that the basic values of the individual and the nation will be sacrificed in a longing, and indeed obsession, for purely material things. But we must guard against false hypocrisy; we must not become so immersed in our good resolutions that we lose touch with the world and with the people. You cannot make an omelette without breaking eggs, and where prosperity comes quickly it produces repercussions in all classes of our society, which are disturbing, which are worrying and sometimes even alarming. But is this effervescence not simply a very understandable reaction to hardship, misery, and despair?

It is very much to our credit that we have managed to rid ourselves of the all too conservative and even reactionary idea that there is some economic law or even divine dispensation whereby

society must be divided into a thin layer of well-to-do and a great
mass of under-privileged. On this principle no modern, efficient
and competitive economy could possibly have been built up. The
alternative to lapsing into barbarism lay not in the Socialist proposal for an allegedly fair distribution of poverty but in eradicating
poverty itself. This meant, however, that we had to create mass
purchasing power, 'prosperity for all'.

The productive capacity of any country for peaceful purposes can
be developed only in a free society; only by stimulating the creative
initiative of the individual can one produce that dynamism which
is so characteristic of our German economy today and which has
benefited the community as a whole. How many more abortive
attempts at a socialist planned, guided and controlled economy
must we have, to convince the world, and particularly organized
labour, that this dogma is a mere delusion which, far from producing positive results, will make steady inroads on our freedom.
One can almost draw an exact parallel and say that, as Socialist
economy policy becomes more undiluted and more consistent in
practice, the threat to human and economic freedom is thereby
increased.

The Socialist Opposition in this country appears to be not entirely unaware of the connection, otherwise it would hardly offer
the German people the pathetic yet comic spectacle of one party
spokesman trying to interpret contradictory economic statements
made by his colleagues—with the sole result that the SPD economists are now in a state of such complete chaos that the entire
German public is aware of it.

If you accept the thesis 'Prosperity for all', then you must be in
favour of a market economy. But this economic system does not
admit of any number of variations or interpretations or the introduction of alien principles. This applies particularly to the reunit-
ing of Germany, which is the wish of all Germans and which we
can only achieve if we create a social order for the whole of Germany which, in accordance with the will of the German people, is
a free society. The spirit of freedom which we have kindled in the
Federal Republic is more likely to capture the hearts of all Germans if we ourselves are imbued by it and make it clear that there
can be no happy mean and no compromise between a free and

Social Market Economy on the one hand and a socialist economy with a more or less obvious collectivist flavour on the other—assuming, of course, that any compromise is possible between a free society and totalitarianism.

It is precisely on important questions of this kind that we must have the courage of our convictions, and the alternatives before the German people are clear. If they want to preserve the market economy with all the advantages it has brought us over the past years, then we must continue to bear the responsibility. But anyone who believes that German's destiny should be shaped by other hands must face up to the far-reaching consequences of his decision.

We can look ahead to the coming months with calm confidence. What we are aiming at and striving for has already, to a large extent, been achieved and has become history. We have not become bogged down in negative criticism but have acted and, although there is still much to be done, the worst is over. We had not merely to announce but also to implement a policy; our action was not taken in a void but could be measured by results. The fact that the Federal Republic has become a stabilizing factor in Europe's economic policy, that, although it met with almost insuperable problems to begin with, the German currency is now one of the hardest in the world, that we today occupy third place in world trade, that the enormous burdens left over from the war and post-war destruction could be carried without impairing the country's economic and financial stability, and, indeed, the fact that this programme of material reconstruction was crowned by a social development of the highest order, the great insurance reform, which guaranteed the whole German people not merely a steady increase in prosperity but also higher social security—all this and much more should make every single German citizen realize how frivolous and even absurd is the emotional slogan of the SPD: 'It is time to give others a chance.'

At this CDU Party Congress, however, we must make a special effort to give the concept 'Prosperity for all' a new and deeper meaning than one of mere material advancement. For we are moving so to speak into a new phase of the Social Market Economy, in which prosperity should bring to each individual something more than just freedom from material want and social security but should awaken a new awareness of life. Freedom from want should be accompanied by a sense of spiritual freedom. If we reject the Socialist form of Welfare State and a system of collectivization, it is not merely because this apparently well-intentioned tutelage creates a state of dependence, which must eventually breed subjection and stifle civilian freedom; it is also because this kind of self-deprivation by the abandonment of individual responsibility must in the end paralyze individual initiative and reduce the economic production of the nation. Then we would be back at the point where all classes of society feel they have been cheated and the distribution of our national income will be completely overshadowed by struggles for political power. If and where the operation of the market is ever controlled by a bureaucracy instead of by responsible officials and the laws of competition, there is no room for higher output and for progress; but, what is even worse, there is also no room for social welfare and material prosperity. The frequent attempts by the Socialists to introduce what they call a 'redistribution of the national product', in order to protect the workers against the ill-effects of a wrong policy while increasing the burdens on the employers, have lost any relevance they might have had to social justice, particularly with the growth of the middle-class element in our economy, and they can only be described as an anarchical policy, which would destroy our free institutions. You cannot seriously challenge a nation's economy with socialist tricks of this kind. But the damage done by such a 'street-corner policy' would be even more far-reaching. Short of trying to cover up its inherent defects by embarking upon a policy of inflation, in other words, by creating purchasing power over and above the national output, the price of economic mismanagement can only be paid by cutting down on essential investments, which means abandoning all prospect of an increase in production and productivity, on which every nation's future depends. The nation in question is condemned to live from hand to mouth, and any government which underwrites such folly is acting on the principle: 'Après moi, le déluge.'

It is an incontestable fact—and one on which we have therefore based our policy—that economic and technical progress and the investments essential to it have no real meaning in a nation's economy, unless the nation itself feels confident in its present and its future—for, without rising consumption, increases in productive power cannot find an outlet. But it is equally inescapable that if a people wishes to increase and improve its consumption it must improve the efficiency of its output, in other words, invest, and to do this it must save. If the principles underlying a responsible, forward-looking economic policy were to be summed up in one phrase, it would be not 'either . . . or' but 'both . . . and'. There must, of course, be changes of emphasis to fit in with changing political trends, but without affecting the basic pattern. It follows from this, however, that a pattern of human behaviour must emerge in keeping with the political-economic aims, behaviour which cannot be produced to order but must result from the correct application of economic policy and its influence on human actions.

This is not mere theory but proven fact, which we have all experienced. Over the past nine years, for example, since 1948 the prevailing economic trend has been one not of cycles with regular ups and downs but rather of steady and even very rapid growth. This is certainly no mere accident or gift of providence but the result of a deliberate policy. I suggest, therefore, that this same steady and assured process of economic development has done much to strengthen the feeling of security of all engaged in the economy, employers as well as labour. It has made it possible to plan ahead and has freed everyone from the fear of an uncertain future, to which they had previously seemed hopelessly exposed. Anyone who regards shifts of political emphasis or periodic changes in investment policy and the production of consumer goods as contradictory or inconsistent knows very little about modern economic machinery. Our motto here is : 'Judge them by their deeds, not (and this is intended for our critics) by their words.'

One would have to be both complacent and blind to fail to recognize the shortcomings and frustrations which still pursue us —and will always pursue us—at almost every turn. The Opposition's reply to such humility is to behave as if they alone had found the magic formula. One cannot take this seriously if for no other reason than that a party whose economic policy has become almost grotesquely threadbare since 1948 cannot command confidence, and when—as we have seen—it has proved impossible to conceal, much less make presentable, the frequent atavistic relapses into the marxist-collectivist ideology, then the German people can surely be in no doubt what they can expect if they entrust their economic and social future to Socialism.

We, meanwhile, will continue honestly and doggedly to increase the social welfare and the prosperity of the nation. The communal and individual incomes can only be raised by increasing the national product, in other words, by stepping up production, and only by increasing prosperity for all can we acquire the means, that is, the capital, which enables us, as a modern industrial country, to keep pace with technical progress and to compete in world markets. Capital does not drop from heaven but must first be earned by the sweat of our brows and then consolidated by cutting back on immediate consumer demands. This applies, moreover, to all economic or social systems. The crucial question is always how much capital is amassed and how it is spent. And the main problem which concerns us from a social and political view-point is into whose hands the capital goes and who should dispose of it.

This brings me very close to the position taken by my friend Karl Arnold in his speech, for, if the concepts of capital-ownership and the disposal of capital are not identical with that of 'Ownership for all', both reveal the direction and the aim that our party is pursuing in its efforts to mould German's social system. We do not accept the Socialist idea of 'redistribution' of productive capital or of the titles of ownership which represent this capital, because such terminology could encourage the dangerous illusion that some institution like the state should have the power to take over ownership of capital at will and to distribute it or even give it away, as it thinks fit. So long as capital ownership is synonymous with free and private property, it can only—and must only—be acquired by work and restricted consumption. Romantic ideas will not help us here; they will only lead to confusion and error.

Even a superficial study of German's post-war capital resources and capital investment policy is enough to show that our efforts to revive the productive capacity of our economy were successful and indeed had to be successful, if they were to create opportunities of

permanent employment for all workers, and particularly for the
refugees and expatriates. At the same time the raising of capital
was, to a considerable extent, in the hands of the state and private
employers, while the savings of the mass of the people—although
they increased over the past seven years from 3 to 24 milliard
marks—lagged somewhat behind. One might regard this as a
regrettable defect—possibly even as something more serious—but
one must also realize in all fairness that, during the period in
question, this was the only possible method of reconstruction. For
example, how could the state have solved all the pressing problems
before it without acquiring the necessary means through taxation?
And, having lost our former capital reserves, how could our
economy, with no capital market to draw on, have embarked upon
such a rapid programme of reconstruction without financing itself?
All the normal standards for a 'just' accumulation of capital simply
did not apply, nor were there any historical analogies to help us;
our course of action was dictated by the pressure and urgency of
external circumstances. Moreover, it seemed only natural that those
in employment and those seeking it, after the hardships they had
suffered, should feel like consuming and not saving, at least to
begin with.

In such a situation an ostensibly just but necessarily free distribution of fresh capital, both money and equipment, would have
led inevitably to a very substantial slowing-down of development
in the public and private sectors of the economy. Taking all the
circumstances into account, the price we would have had to pay
for a prolonged period of hardship would have been too high. In
the final analysis, all classes of the population have profited by the
rapid and expansive advance of Germany's reconstruction programme. Let me remind you, for example, that in two periods of
legislation the Federal Republic built $3\frac{1}{2}$ million new dwellings;
that in the past six years nominal wages have risen by more than
55%, real wages by more than 40%, that social expenditure from
the Federal Budget alone was doubled during the same period and
the great insurance reform brought annual insurance payments up
from 7·4 to 13 milliards. So, all things considered, my friends, no
one can have any further doubts that those amongst our political
opponents who always know better cannot succeed in their

childish, not to say childlike, efforts to belittle our achievement in the eyes of the German people.

We regard it as our duty and responsibility, however, not merely to improve over-all living standards but also to awaken a social consciousness which will produce a more mature and more intelligent awareness in the individual and at the same time lead us as a nation to a new way of life. This presupposes that we should cease to think in terms of classes or even groups, that we can look beyond our immediate group-interests, acquire a real sense of community life and feel responsible, as a community, for the future destiny of our country and our people. For this reason I am not addressing myself today to any professional or commercial groups, for, as a true People's Party and especially on the eve of such an important election, we cannot take the easy way of promising everyone everything. Either we prosper as a people, or we all suffer.

The consciousness of a common responsibility should make it impossible for us, for any one of us, to live thoughtlessly only for the day. But each citizen will be the better able to see things in this way as he gains confidence that he, his children and his children's children will share in the happy future of our people. The more pronounced this sense of individual responsibility becomes, the sooner will we be in a position to put the state and all other collectivist organs of power in their place; the greater the longing of every single person to gain independence and inner freedom by his own efforts and without any collectivist security, then the more confident we can be that increasing wealth will not enslave but liberate us.

The Socialists believe, and have, in fact, expressly said so, that the capital requirements resulting from the application of modern technical methods cannot be satisfied through the traditional channels of the so-called capitalist system and that the spectre of automation, which they invoke for reasons that are all too transparent, could become such a menace that once more the state, and only the state, should be empowered to shape the present and future of our national economy, or at least to control and direct it. For reasons that are not difficult to understand, the SPD no longer have the courage to preach a planned economy, but they lose no opportunity of smuggling their dogma into the German economic and social structure by the back door. So we shall have to be constantly on our guard never to lose sight of this threat to the prosperity and freedom of the German people.

As no power on earth can produce capital by waving a magic wand, the state can only raise capital if it is prepared and in a position to tax the people. That sounds relatively harmless but in practice it means that the citizen is expropriated, without compensation, in order to provide the state with an accumulation of capital and wealth. It means that, as a result of this specific form of national compulsory saving, the fruits of restricted consumption fall not to the saver or taxpayer but to an increasingly powerful state.

There is no more false ideology than that it would be in the interest of the people, that is of workers and traders, to hand over the nation's productive capital to state ownership and public control, because—it is cunningly argued—what belongs to the state also belongs to the people. There was a time when it was thought that the demand for socialization or nationalization might arouse the enthusiasm of the masses; today only the most diehard ideologists and cynical bureaucrats can derive any warmth from their lukewarm memories of that false social ideal. In the long run the concepts of prosperity and of property are inseparable; in fact, I will put it even more plainly: the CDU have made it their political aim that, with each stage of economic expansion, ownership of the means of production should spread more and more widely, in other words, regardless of whether and in what sectors technical progress leads to a concentration of the means of production, that there should be a steady process of deconcentration in the ownership of this national economic capital. This applies in the first instance to productive resources at present under public ownership, for the citizen's imaginary, anonymous claim to these capital goods is, to put it bluntly, not worth a straw, because pseudo-property of this kind is not freely negotiable by the individual. It only serves to reinforce the power, or indeed the omnipotence, of the state or any other collectivist authority to the point where the central power is deified, and at the same time it increases the dependence of the citizen to the point of slavery. And if the individual's scope for creative work and expansion is more and more restricted by the growing intervention of the state in the economy, the possibility of personal advancement is not strengthened but reduced.

A glance at the economic system and methods of totalitarian states—of the Soviet bloc, for example— is enough to show that state-ownership of the means of production does not lead to an increase of wealth for the people but, on the contrary, to their exploitation, whereas the reverse is true of the free countries and peoples, which are denounced for their so-called capitalism but which clearly illustrate how private ownership of the means of production is contributing more and more to the general welfare. So we decline with thanks to adopt as a model for the whole German people, when the long-awaited day of reunification finally comes, the kind of social system represented by the so-called 'social achievements' of the ostensible German Democratic Republic. I simply cannot imagine, and I would be sadly out of touch with the spirit of the German people and especially of the German worker if I believed, that he could derive happiness and satisfaction from knowing that so-called 'People's property' was being run by party officials. After all, what could he buy for it!

But, as I have already said, a wider distribution of ownership in the nation's productive capital should also extend to private enterprises. This certainly does not mean that the returns and profits which help firms to finance themselves would fall into disrepute; on the contrary, it must be the aim and object of every management to work along those lines. Even socialized concerns must make a profit, otherwise there is a deterioration in the living standards and way of life.

At this point, however, let us remember the principle that quantity has to give way to quality, in other words, that it is a question of proportion. The process of growing prosperity sets up a train of events and changes which are incalculable and can lead only gradually to the desired sociological regrouping. Furthermore, anyone who concluded from the desire for a wider distribution of ownership that the share of wages and salaries in the national product is basically inadequate today would find it hard to prove his assertion. At the same time, it is equally certain that such a change in our economic thinking as resulted in every man playing an active and responsible part in economic developments

o

would throw quite a new light, both sociologically and economically, on the problem of the distribution of the national income.

If we do not compensate fully, or even over-compensate, for an increase in productivity by a reduction in working hours, we can be sure that a growth of mass-income will create a real and increasingly sound basis for higher savings and for more active participation in share-purchases by relatively small income-groups. In this way growing prosperity will also lead to a change of outlook, as the horizon widens and values change. Then prosperity will no longer be reflected merely in the number or quantity of goods consumed, social status will no longer be expressed solely in a display of better material living standards, but, as people become interested in satisfying their mental and spiritual needs, they will look into the future and feel the urge to find peace, security, satisfaction and fulfilment by shaping and directing their own lives. Everything we can do to stimulate self-awareness in the individual is bound to free him from the disastrous influence of collectivism. A thinking man will always resist any threat to his spiritual freedom.

If this goal can be attained—and it undoubtedly can—then we need not fear for the security of the free world. On the other hand, it must be added—and this is not a sign of resignation—that no precise formula exists or can exist whereby one can forecast what stages or how many stages we must pass through to reach our goal. A nation that is strong enough to sweat the evil poison of collectivism out of its system has opened up the way not only to spiritual freedom and independence but also to prosperity and security.

To the undoubted relationship between industrial self-financing and the widespread raising of capital from savings must be added a third factor, namely, that of taxation. To an appreciable extent the burden of taxation reflects not merely the individual's attitude to the state but also his view of life in general. The more primitive a nation's way of life and the less inclined the average person is to carry personal responsibility, the more this self-deprivation will cost him. On the other hand, those human qualities which I have already mentioned, qualities that create and preserve personal prosperity, also free us from too much state interference and thereby become yet another source of individual well-being.

It might be argued that, however desirable such a goal might be, it is, for that very reason perhaps, an illusion. But who in the year 1948 would have believed, my friends, that we could surmount our apparently insuperable problems in so short a time? As was the case then, so the second phase of the Social Market Economy will lead through further prosperity and wealth to the topmost peak of human freedom and dignity. We need that faith again, and our opponents will be once more put to shame. There could be no better way of dealing a death-blow to collectivist and totalitarian ideologies and powers than by this policy, which seeks to create social equality and justice not by means of an inhuman bureaucratic machine but by making people realize that true standards of justice must be based on free human responsibility and cannot be realized without it.

Without human conscience there can be no free democracy. When, for example, Victor Agartz, who seems to be in a position to make the comparison, declared—and he was warmly applauded —that the Federal Republic has 'little in the way of democratic features', and even went on to argue that Parliament, as a freely elected body representing the people, should be safeguarded by other democratic institutions against failure to carry out the people's will, one cannot be too forthright in attacking such a view-point, which comes suspiciously close to the principles of the Socialist Unity Party. As we know from experience, democracies have never yet been safeguarded against decay by powerful organizations; they can and will only survive as long as they are upheld by people who know the value and the blessing of freedom. When democracies are threatened, they can only be maintained by the personal courage or, if you like, civil courage of their citizens. These are not exactly the qualities that are fostered in a collective state.

The social problems we have to face are also brought home to us when we seek new and certainly not definitive patterns for the integration of Europe and the free world. It will very soon become clear that uneven numbers cannot be reduced to a common denominator, and that the gulf between the Western type of socialist economic ideas and the principles of a free economy, such as we believe in, will not be easy to bridge within one economic community. But as long as this conflict of ideas continues, we can at least hope that the free system will triumph by virtue of its greater economic and social achievements. But, to put it in concrete terms, if Germany were to succumb to socialist dogmas, then there would be a serious danger of the scales tipping in favour of that doctrine even in Western Europe. Whether, in that case, a socialist system would be strong enough to hold out against collectivism and stand up to it is a question I merely put to you. European integration presupposes prosperity—for all the countries concerned—national discipline and a well-balanced society. In this respect the Federal Republic need fear no comparisons with other countries; precisely because 'Common Market' means common destiny, each partner must have the right to broach any problems that concern the whole.

You may now ask, quite rightly, what action the CDU/CSU proposes to take to realize the aims I have just outlined. If I were a *dirigiste* and a Socialist, then I would probably, indeed certainly, talk of a great many administrative controls and plans to be applied by the Government—in short, I would announce the imposition of new measures of compulsion on free men. But this is contrary not only to all my personal instincts but also to my conception of the basic ingredients of human society. So I address myself once more to the individual himself, to remind him that he is free to make his own decisions and to shape his own destiny but that he can also trust the state to guarantee him sufficient protection and security to enable him to carry the responsibility. Any forward-looking project implies confidence in the stability of the economic system, of the currency and the prices. While, it is true, no country can be completely immune against the ups and downs of international trade fluctuations, we have nevertheless proved beyond all doubt that it is our most earnest endeavour to protect the German people against constant monetary devaluation or currency crises. The record of the Federal Republic in safeguarding its stability and internal security will compare with that of any other country. But the realization that economic expansion does not admit of rigidity is no reason for pessimism or for basing one's policy on the possibility of disaster. When the Social Democrats criticize our price policy, they would be better advised, particularly in view of the much-vaunted international solidarity of their movement, to put forward their suggestions elsewhere, where the need seems greater. We ourselves know that to maintain a stable currency is one of the most important and most immediate duties of any responsible government.

I have also heard the Opposition argument that in pursuing our social-economic aims, I am again trying to employ psychological weapons. This is quite true, for I maintain that only a people which wants to free itself from too much domination by the state and other collectivist organs, which is familiar with the economic situation and is constantly mindful of its future, can turn growing prosperity to proper use. Increased prosperity must lead, in the long run, to degeneracy, if its sole object is increased consumption with no thought of freeing the individual from collectivist influences. In this the German people must and can rest assured that it is not merely possible to move in this direction but that the goal will certainly be reached, if the nation will only have confidence in itself and in a progressive policy.

It is important, however, to make a start, to provide some visible proof that we are determined not only to open up fresh vistas but also to give practical pointers. True, the Federal Republic, as I have already said, has nothing to give away but it is ready to abandon its claim to such property as it has and to see to it that as many people as possible have a chance to acquire and enjoy the productive capital of our national economy. An attempt has been made by party-political propagandists, who are opposed to private ownership, to condemn the participation of shareholders in industrial enterprises as capitalist exploitation of the workers. But the days of the speculator, whose least concern was the welfare of the people, are numbered. The conviction is growing and spreading, that, without adequate capital resources, employment can neither be created nor assured. The hypocrisy of certain party-political propagandists becomes fully apparent when the political reactionaries in the Opposition point, on the one hand, to alleged profit-making by shareholders but, on the other hand, do their utmost to prevent the worker from becoming a shareholder. Yet, they know what they are doing, for, if the general public becomes familiar with the workings of our economy and takes an active interest in the productivity and potential wealth of the national economy, then socialism will lose its hold over those who, although brought up by tradition in the marxist ideology, finally come to their senses.

I am, therefore, very happy to be able to announce, that the Parliamentary Party of the CDU/CSU intends to bring in an Initiative Law, by which probably the most efficient concern under national ownership, the Volkswagen works, will be transferred to private ownership on a broad basis.

It is a symbolic pointer to the direction in which we are moving, that our party should have decided to transfer the Volkswagen works to the ownership of the widest possible sections of the population by means of People's Shares. Without in any way anticipating the deliberations and resolutions of the Bundestag, I can say this much—that this law, together with whatever action is finally taken on the question of ownership as a whole, will also contain safeguards against the formation of large or majority share-holdings. Above all, it is those with small or medium savings who will and must be given priority and even a certain degree of material preference in the purchase of shares. The same law will also ensure that the exercise of voting rights cannot be concentrated in a few hands.

Although I myself have very definite views on the form this People's Share should take, the few remarks I have already made should suffice to make it clear that our party is firmly resolved to go on expanding and at the same time strengthening our free economic and social system by increasing over-all prosperity and individual wealth. And the transfer of the Volkswagen works to private ownership by the people will not be the end of the matter. According to the amount of savings available for investment and depending upon the free decision of the German people, still more publicly-owned enterprises will be considered for transfer. This is neither the time nor the place to decide how the proceeds of such transactions should be spent. We shall certainly not want for suggestions and wishes. But on one point we can surely be unanimous, that the state has and can have no intention of hoarding unproductive money.

The SPD, of course, will greet these plans with a storm of protest, but we are determined to fight this battle with them in public before the whole German people. They will say again that any 'People's property', which can only be mentioned in quotation marks, should not be squandered, that the state must not relinquish its ownership of industrial concerns and expose them to industrial and price fluctuations. My reply to that is that no one is thinking of squandering and that the people's property, which, we are told, should be protected, only acquires real social meaning and significance when the people itself comes into direct ownership by virtue of holding private title-deeds.

By remodelling our society on a modern and, in the true sense, socialist basis, the CDU/CSU are not only making way for progress and the growing extension of ownership throughout the country, without hampering creative human initiative and without stultifying the competitive capacity of free enterprises, but they are also keeping the spirit alive which will protect us against the threat of collectivism and totalitarianism.

That is why this year's decisive political victory and the future will belong not to marxist reactionaries, who live eternally in the past and cannot shake off their dogmatic traditions, but to us, who have pointed the way that will lead the German people out of misery and despair to a happier future, prosperity and social security, and who, moreover—and this is much more important— have proved that we can keep the promises we have made.

27

COMMERCE AND EDUCATION

(Article in *Der Volkswirt* of August 17, 1957)

Modern education must cover the economic side of our life if it is to perform its true function, namely, to build character. If it is the aim of all education to create a morally sound individual, then, for that reason alone, the economics of life cannot be ignored. But it is also true to say that the more complex and concentrated our industry becomes, the more it needs people with a high standard of general education who are capable of meeting the growing demands of the modern labour market.

Commerce and education, which are separate sectors of our social and national life, nevertheless are more closely linked both in essence and in aims than they might appear to be at a first glance or after a superficial study. It is true that those who take a professional interest in commerce have done so for reasons which are fundamentally different from those actively interested in education. Similarly, the functions and aims of each are dictated by their own particular guiding principles, organic laws and values. But in a well-ordered state the various fields of activity and culture, such as industry, education, government, home and church, are not mutually exclusive but, as we can see wherever we look, are closely interwoven and, by a sort of cross-fertilization, increase their yield to the benefit of the individual and the community. So the nation's commerce is a vital life-force which radiates energy and stimulates the expansion of education, both in its content and in its aims. Moreover, in creating and maintaining special facilities in factories and other organizations for the training and education of the skilled labour and management which it needs to remain efficient, industry is also playing an active part in the formation of character. At the same time, the results achieved in schools and other educational establishments open up possibilities of further industrial and

commercial expansion, for they bring out the forces and personalities with the moral and mental qualities best suited to meet
the economic, technical, social and cultural requirements of a constantly changing and advancing technology, economy and culture.

Although commerce and education are organic parts of the state
and society and therefore perform over-all functions and pursue
higher aims, which are those of the community as a whole, their
first task is to fulfil their own inherent purpose and to perform the
specific functions allotted to them. So it would be wrong to deduce
that education in the wider sense of character-formation is based on
economic necessity or the needs of industry. This would imply a
process of levelling and spiritual impoverishment; it would lead to
pragmatism and, in fact, to materialism. But it would be equally
wrong for the elementary and secondary schools, the training
colleges and universities, to ignore the growing demand for
workers and management personnel and to underrate the importance of sound social and ethical standards in industry and among
industrial workers. It is one of the aims of true education that the
individual should make proper use of the mental powers and moral
qualities he has developed through education for his own personal
satisfaction and for the benefit of the community. It is therefore
necessary to underline the importance of industry and commerce
as a not inconsiderable subdivision of culture, because there has
been a tendency to over-emphasize the humanities, as a result of
which it has frequently been impossible to provide effective education and training for industrial posts and in technical or commercial subjects. Equally, in the past the real meaning and purpose
of commerce was misrepresented and distorted both by former
theories of capitalism and by historical materialism. As a result the
functions and aims of commerce and industry were underrated
and misunderstood and the ill effects of this are still being felt
today.

There is yet another reason why it is of the utmost importance to
look at the problems confronting both commerce and education in
the widest perspective. If one understands by education not merely
the conscious and systematic process of education in schools and
public educational establishments but also the formative and educa-
tive influence of environment in the building of character, then

commerce represents an educational medium of considerable importance and with appreciable character-building potentialities and powers. For no one can deny that a large and very effective part of juvenile and adult education today is carried on not only in schools and other public institutions but also in industry and commerce, in the factories, and in the training schools set up and maintained by industrial and commercial organizations, where specialized subjects are taught. Hundreds of thousands of young people are being systematically trained at any given moment in trade, commerce and industry, and this vital period of instruction plays a decisive part in their subsequent development, in their choice of profession and in their way of life. There are a large number of these internal and extra-mural instruction courses, both general and technical, which are run by industrial and commercial firms and which are designed to carry on the training of skilled workers and to educate others for responsible posts in management. Schooling, training, instruction and education of the sort of people whom any efficient and expanding economy needs to maintain its existing standards and plan for the future are going on all the time in industry and commerce on a scale and with positive results which cannot be overrated. In this way, commerce and industry are making a cultural contribution of far-reaching importance to the nation's education.

The 'Social Market Economy', the basic aim of which is to combine the principle of a free market with that of social equality and the moral responsibility of the individual towards the community, can only fully succeed if it provides for the comprehensive training, instruction and education of the skilled workers and management, for whom their daily work and professional involvement in the economic field gives them a real sense of fulfilment. The sort of mature and morally sound character which revels in the cut and thrust of free competition can only be developed by a carefully and responsibly conducted education and training; in other words, by systematically promoting ability and knowledge, by awakening those mental gifts that enable a man to take the broad view, and by encouraging those qualities of will and character that equip him to carry responsibility because it satisfies his sense of duty. The success of a competitive economy depends to a considerable extent on the ability, initiative and competitive spirit of people in industry, on their technical, mental and moral qualifications. The more modern and progressive our economic and technical machinery, the broader and deeper must be the training and education of personnel; otherwise progress will master us instead of our mastering it to the advantage of all. The more complex the technical apparatus and the interplay of economic forces become, the more exacting are the demands made on manual and non-manual staff and on their moral resources, and there is a corresponding increase in the demands of industry for the type of person that only a comprehensive system of training and education can produce. This is true not only of the management class and the entrepreneur, but also, and no less so, of the man in the workshop and office, at the design-board and shop-counter.

A characteristic feature of the present situation is the growing importance of the natural sciences and the rapid advances that are being made in the technical field. Many people regard the development of atomic energy and the growth of automation in industry and administration as marking the beginning of a process whose economic and social consequences might arouse tragic memories of the social problems created by mechanization and industrialization in the last century. But it would be a mistake to believe that the dynamic evolution of our economy and the changes that are taking place in the technical world must lead to the destruction of our present way of life. Nor is there any reason to expect revolutionary upheavals in the near future in industry or in labour conditions, drastic changes in the present economic systems or a break-up of the social and cultural structure of human societies. What I have just outlined is not a revolutionary action the outcome of which cannot be controlled, but a timeless process, which, in our present social and political situation, should be regarded not as a threat but as a challenge. Furthermore, this process provides endless opportunities for positive sociological changes. Modern technical achievements free the individual from the monotony and the burden of heavy physical work, from the deadly dullness of purely mechanical activities. They are a means of making work easier and, in the long run, of shortening working-hours, raising the general standard of living and allowing more time for leisure in an atmosphere of freedom and social security. Of course, the question then arises, what should be done to harness this additional energy and to create the new society which the future has in store. People today are alive, as never before, to the continuous change that is taking place in their material and spiritual life, in the personal and social environment of an increasingly technical world, and this awareness will increase as time goes on. And here we come to the inescapable conclusion that the education of our people must have a decisive influence on the course and the consequences of this technical and economic development. For the people will only be masters of this development if they are prepared for it by training and education which are geared to this future evolution.

The demand for qualified, skilled labour is becoming more and more urgent. The shortage of technicians, engineers and research-workers is constantly being emphasized. People everywhere are coming to realize that, even in the future, the fate of individuals and nations will be decided not by automatons and electronic brains but by man's own intelligence. But you cannot manufacture it, you can only develop it by means of a world-wide, all-embracing process of education. Technical progress in the field of industry and commerce is becoming more and more a problem of education, for it confronts all branches of education with a categorical demand for closer contact with technology and industry which, naturally, should not be taken to mean the mechanization of education or of people. Education must always give first priority to the individual in all his facets, his mind, his will and his character, and this is equally true of education in relation to industry and commerce.

28

RENDER UNTO THE STATE WHAT BELONGS TO THE STATE

(Article in *Die Zeit* of November 21, 1957)

Any responsible politician or statesman must be prepared to do and say what he considers necessary without courting popularity. At the end of 1957 Erhard found himself bombarded with demands that threatened to undermine his policy. Some of these, such as more money for housing, roads, schools and hospitals, were justified. Defence and development also, of necessity, demanded higher expenditure. But other claims were more dubious: higher profits, more leisure and at the same time higher wages; higher consumption; less work, lower taxes and fewer duties; more for the individual, less for the community! Extravagance must inevitably put a brake on the nation's capacity to produce and expand, overstrain the economy and the state and so do moral and material harm to the community.

If I, as someone who is passionately opposed to the view that the state is an end in itself and should lead a life of its own regardless of the welfare of the people, defend the thesis, 'Render unto the state what belongs to the state,' then it is not without genuine misgivings, for I have a feeling that my desire to stimulate individual self-awareness and freedom of expression, with at the same time a sense of individual responsibility, has been in danger lately of being misunderstood.

We are running a grave risk of becoming bogged down in a morass of ultra-individualism. The reason is, quite simply, that we misconstrue the idea of freedom and would like to believe, out of sheer egoism, against our better judgment and indeed against our own conscience, that freedom implies the right to do or not to do whatever pleases the individual or the group, without regard to the community and the state. This I call misconstruing freedom.

If freedom cannot be fitted into a socio-economic or political system and so controlled by it, or if freedom knows no moral bonds, then it will inevitably degenerate into chaos, whereas, on the contrary, people who realize the value and meaning of freedom are fully aware of the responsibility it imposes on them; they are, therefore, never tempted to abuse it.

In the daily run of political discussion it might seem as if this warning was only relevant to the question of distributing the social product or the national income between the various so-called social partners or between all sectors of the national economy. But such a view-point, although one must take it seriously, is too materialistic. The question that arises here is not whether employers and labour, peasants, middle class and so on are receiving their proper share of the social product or of the national income; it is much more a question of making people understand and appreciate that each one of us and all of us together cannot hope to prosper unless we remain aware of our common destiny as a people, as a state, and are prepared to act accordingly.

The sense of fellowship which was so alive during periods of acute hardship becomes dormant as prosperity returns. In fact, I even wonder sometimes if I did right to make such an intensive effort to push forward Germany's economic recovery as quickly as possible. Naturally, this question is not to be taken too seriously. Given the choice, I would not hesitate to act again as I did before. And yet the mere suggestion of doubt clearly reflects a certain sense of disappointment at the behaviour particularly of organized groups in the country.

Does anyone still talk or think of what lies behind us, and of the national disaster we suffered? How many of us are prepared to take account of the fact that Germany's recovery began from rubble and ruins; that, as an outlawed nation, we had to win back very gradually the trust and friendship of other countries? How many of us even remember that today? We compare our living standards with those of the richest country in the world, the United States, and political visionaries imagine that we could rely on other countries to guarantee us our security and freedom without any sacrifice on our part.

At the heart of the present dispute in our midst is the question whether the demands of the trades unions exceed the increase in productivity, or whether a wage increase or reduction of working hours would mean a rise in prices. Seen in isolation, these questions may be entirely justified, but they also carry a disturbing undertone, for they seem to suggest that these are the main problems which a free society has to solve and that the only wise man is the man who gets the biggest share of the cake.

It seems to me high time, therefore, that this whole subject was discussed on a higher plane and that the following question was addressed to all, regardless of their partisan interests. Has not a people, which means, in effect, a state, obligations to fulfil which require the individual to make sacrifices? In periods of hardship it is taken for granted that any improvement and increase in the national output should be employed to raise living standards or stimulate production and productivity; I would even go so far as to say that, by and large, this is a sound principle, so long as people do not forget that there are also jobs to be done for the benefit and security of the community, for which individualistic or egoistic motives are not enough and which cannot, therefore, be approached in this way.

'Render unto the state what belongs to the state.' Surely this also means—that much and no more! But the opposite principle, whereby the fruits of any economic progress should be devoted to improving the individual's living standard or adding to his wealth, thus directly or indirectly denying the state the means it requires to pursue the higher interests of the state, is surely just as false and therefore to be condemned.

What I have just been saying has been clearly illustrated, during our recent period of development, by the demand for a wider and better education of young people in industry and in the educational stream itself, for promotion of the sciences and research. But a progressive nation which is enjoying a growing measure of prosperity also has many other general duties to perform, as, for example, in the field of public health or in stimulating a wider interest in works of art and in the arts as a whole. Then there is the incessant clamour for more and better roads; if traffic conditions become intolerable, the blame is simply laid on the state. Everyone protests if the house-building programme has to be cut down, and people naturally demand that, wherever possible, the social services should be still further improved.

But how many people stop to consider where the necessary funds come from and how the thousand-and-one demands are to be met! Let us never forget that freedom also has its price and that in this world of ours the blessings of peace cannot be had without sacrifice.

But on sober reflection we realize that, when it comes to distributing the national income, it can only be done once and that it is up to all of us to draw up a scale of values and objectives. 'All of us' means that each individual must bear his share of the responsibility. And, while I certainly take the view that human welfare should always have first priority, it is a principle that should not be allowed to degenerate into uninhibited, blind egoism.

'Less work', 'better living conditions', 'higher earnings', 'get rich quick', complain about taxes but demand more from the state —all these add up to a state of mental confusion and obscurantism, which, if carried to the extreme, would threaten the very foundations of our society. Instead of recognizing the enormous variety and urgency of the social and national problems confronting us and making a special effort to solve them, in order to free each and every one of us from material want, it often seems as if we prefer to ignore the ominous, even tragic, examples from other parts of the world and would rather make the childish and, at the same time, lamentable attempt to set up a new record in sinning against economic good sense.

This can only lead to disaster! Every German citizen must realize that those who flatter him and pretend to be defending his cause could, in fact, all too easily do irreparable harm to the future destiny of the German people.

The demands made on the state keep mounting; yet no one who derives any benefit from this financial expenditure is prepared to give it up. So the state is compelled to look round all the time for fresh sources of revenue. But where are these to be found if everyone is intent upon working less, thereby preventing a possible increase in the social product; if, in addition, the urge to consume more weakens the urge to save and capital formation lags behind the opportunities and necessities of investment?

I would feel reassured if I could see some guarantee that the German people, in looking after its own group interests, had at least decided to demand no more from the national economy than it was capable of providing. But even that would not solve the problem, because the state cannot afford, for the people's sake, to stop planning for the nation as a whole and for its future, regardless of how individual people may react. And because—to speak quite plainly—a nation would be sacrificing itself and condemning itself to oblivion if it allowed itself to be split up and exhausted by the atomization of group interests.

Is it really necessary to give any final warnings? The totalitarian powers have demonstrated all too clearly that the price of their rule is the suffering and hardship of their people. It is frightening to hear and see that this accursed doctrine has nevertheless great material, technical and scientific achievements to its credit. At such moments people in the Western world feel a certain uneasiness and many even accuse their democratic governments of lagging behind. But they still go on demanding everything for themselves and living only for the present.

Even although it is already rather late in the day, we must examine our hearts, our responsibilities, and our duties towards the German people and state. It is not as Minister of Economics and a member of the Federal Government that I utter the warning 'Render to the state the things that are the state's,' but as a citizen like any other, who feels in duty bound to hold a mirror up to the German people for their own sakes.

29

THE 'LIVING STANDARD'

(Article in *Die Zeit* of August 15, 1958)

While people in the Federal Republic are enjoying better and better material living conditions, the concept 'living standard' is coming more and more under public discussion. Frequently it is followed by a question-mark. It is pointed out that poverty and hardship have by no means been eliminated. But other critics seem to regard it as something almost entirely negative and 'materialistic'. The Communists have also 'discovered' it and set it up as the target for their plans and progaganda.

I do not know who coined the phrase 'living-standard fetish'. If he intended to discourage those who place too high a value on the material side of life, then his aim was praiseworthy and sound. I hope he realized that a synthesis had to be found, for in a free society the aim of all economic production can only be consumption.

No sensible person seriously disputes that any people with its future at heart must strike the correct balance between providing for the future and catering for the present generation. Not that this exhausts the problem. There remains the need to prevent certain classes of society from growing rich on the efforts of others.

This dilemma is not overcome by substituting 'public' or 'common ownership' for the private accumulation of wealth. The solution lies rather in a wider distribution of private property. But this is a process which cannot bear fruit from one day to the next. And yet no one will deny that, with rising productivity and a growing national income, the basis of private ownership is changing and expanding.

We are saving more and more, a hopeful sign that the material and ethical value of private capital is being increasingly appreciated. So one is justified in hoping that the predominantly technical concentration of productive capital can be offset by a deconcentration in the ownership of these means of production.

Particularly unhelpful in this respect are the frequent attempts to discredit an allegedly too rapid rate of investment. For the aim is to persuade the people that widespread consumption is being stifled by too high investments. If it were solely a question whether the various classes of our society are getting a fair share of a growing accumulation of wealth, then well-meaning people would still be able to find a reasonable answer, although with any income one would have to consider how much should be spent and how much saved. But there is no absolute criterion, so that no generally applicable decision is possible. Every man is the architect of his own fortune. We live by our personal freedom, and the less the state takes it upon itself to lead each single citizen by the hand or even to set itself up as his guardian, the more freedom he will enjoy. When the state becomes a 'benefactor' the people have to pay dearly; for no state can give its citizens more than it has already taken from them—and this takes no account of the cost of a social bureaucracy, which inevitably becomes an end in itself.

As a rule, therefore, nothing is more unsocial than the so-called 'Welfare State', which kills initiative and slows down individual achievement. It is a fraud which in the end—as many historical examples show—must be paid for with the curse of inflation, unless a policy of egalitarianism prevents the national economies from exploiting technical progress and thereby destroys their ability to compete. In that case the evil is, if anything, even greater.

A nation that wishes to be certain of its present and its future has, therefore, no other choice but to increase its creative energy and to realize that it must strike and keep the right balance not only between spending and saving but also between working hours and leisure. Other temptations are cheap and frivolous; they encourage a tendency to take things easy and their effect is all the more lamentable.

Part of the difference between totalitarian and democratic systems is that in every free society the citizens carry full responsibility for what they are and what they become—whether for good or for ill—whereas collectivism replaces freedom of decision by command and compulsion. Under a dictatorship the people are not allowed to create their own opportunities in life either by their industry or by their capacity to save; these are decided for them by the order of those in power, whose first principle it is, and will always be, to strengthen and extend their power. This power grows steadily as each free impulse is suppressed and a slavish dependence takes its place. But in the long run, totalitarian systems succumb to internal dissension and corruption unless they strive for expansion and a world revolution, which gives them a fresh motive for reinforcing the apparatus of power. From all this it is clear that the sole consolation of the subject peoples in their poverty and misery—namely, the 'paradise of tomorrow'—becomes increasingly unreal and less and less credible.

This, then, is the dilemma of totalitarian states; that, just as they cannot afford to relax their dogmas and revolutionary aims, so they also cannot afford to draw the bow too tight. It is a dilemma that is particularly apparent when a central totalitarian state like Soviet Russia also has to meet demands from satellite states. The salient feature of the period from Stalin to the present time with its constantly changing internal policy has been that a final and absolute decision between 'more (state) authority' and 'greater (personal) freedom' has obviously been impossible and will probably remain so.

But this antithesis also reflects the uneasiness of the free world, in so far as it is obliged, in the event of a conflict with the totalitarian powers or merely to prevent such a conflict, to have at its disposal the necessary defence forces and the armaments to go with them. And here the sociological problem arises in reverse. The question now is, not how much the state can provide in the way of living standards for the people, but how much the people is prepared to give the state in income and social product for the above purposes.

The cost must go on rising. By this I mean that in the Western democracies there is also a reciprocal action between the state and private incomes available—with the difference, however, that the alternative is no longer 'state authority' or 'personal freedom', but that a compromise must be found between the power of the state as an end in itself and the private interests or 'living standard' of the people. From a purely mathematical point of view a totalitarian system, the chief aim of which is political power and which forces the people to make material sacrifices, should be superior to any free system of government. But to believe this is to be a complete materialist.

We believe that we should pin our faith to the superiority of the free society. The achievements of the other system in certain limited sectors may alarm us, because it makes us wonder what will be in store for the Western world when backward countries with populations in the hundred millions, which are learning to adapt modern technical methods, become fully aware of their new-found energy and power. There is also the pressing question whether nations can simply by-pass intermediate stages of technical advancement, research and scientific discovery. Whether such dynamism is not, after all, subject to the laws of natural growth and organic evolution is something we cannot go into here. But one thing is certain: the desire of the Western peoples to go on improving their living standards at less and less cost to themselves is no answer to the problems confronting the world at large—at least so long as peace and freedom cannot be secured by universal disarmament and a relaxation of world tension.

The structure of a nation's economy reflects, amongst other things, the mental and moral attitude of its people and government. We may feel that the pace of our lives is being set for us, but it is equally true to say that our way of life and our awareness of life are exercising more and more pressure on the internal policy of the totalitarian states. There is a critical point at which sacrifices can no longer be exacted by force. And I am personally convinced that an attitude of mind which envisages a new and more equitable social order has a much greater appeal than the soulless ideology of naked power, which feeds people on crumbs and makes an idol of the state.

Soviet statistics give imposing figures of production increases in basic industries as well as in certain branches of capital goods production. The rates of growth of the national product are on the level of the most successful national economies in Western Europe and productive capacity is expanding rapidly throughout the country. Even if these facts cannot be checked, the progress made is undeniable. But what does all this mean in terms of people, of individuals?

The volume of the social product in totalitarian states is no indication of the material living standards of the people; in fact, the national economic figures are not even a pointer to the actual or potential increase in productivity. It is probable not only that in this system a growing social product is accompanied by a drop in living standards, but that the volume of the social product gives no indication as to the present or future living conditions of the individual. Where the meaning and aims of economic policy are being constantly and arbitrarily changed and falsified by those in power, the concept 'social product' has no relation either to time or to space.

Apart from this basic objection there is yet another, perhaps even more serious one : in a market economy with free prices and a free choice for the consumer the value of the social product, taking into account the consumption quota of the national economy, has certain important implications. The essential one, which guarantees our personal freedom and is the hallmark of a free society, is the endless variety and discrimination of our consumption. And in this field the difference between the achievements of East and West has become literally grotesque.

I am not referring to our practical experience in concluding a trade agreement, when we found that Soviet Russia had little to offer the Western consumer apart from certain raw materials and basic commodities of which there is an abundance elsewhere. Nor am I referring to our experiences in interzonal trade, though I would like to mention the observation made by visitors to the Soviet Union who were not hoodwinked by Potemkin villages and were unanimous in stating that it is the absence of small, everyday things that makes life there so dull. The powder compact, the cigarette lighter, the ornamental or fashionable touch—it is the lack of these that explains the discontent amongst the Russian people.

This gives added interest to the announcement by Herr Ulbricht, that the so-called German Democratic Republic aims to bring its living standard up to the level of the Federal Republic and even to exceed it within a few years. One can hardly suppose that the

'GDR' alone will be allowed to achieve this social paradise within the Soviet bloc (such exalted living standards are reserved for party officials, whatever their particular nationality may be). So this proclamation must apply to all the satellite states in the Soviet bloc.

Here, then, we have the two systems, the free and the collectivist societies, facing each other. The world is so sharply divided that the Eastern European rulers are incapable of understanding what is meant by a society of free men or what their living standard, that is, their whole way of life, really means. In the circumstances we in the West should certainly not assume with confidence that 'good living' has a value entirely of its own.

The 'value' of both systems cannot be measured either materially or quantitatively. For there is no doubt that the living standard of a people, translated into consumption of so many tons of raw materials, of iron and steel, of leather, chemicals or coal, tells us nothing about the enrichment of the human being.

The Western world and, in particular, the Federal Republic, accepts Herr Ulbricht's challenge without a qualm. Ulbricht has promised to raise the living standard of the Soviet Zone population above the material existence level of the free Germans in the West. Let him keep his promise! For it would mean that the governments of the Soviet bloc were prepared to relinquish some of their power and that even there the economic and social system would be exposed to liberal principles. It would mean the abandonment of the state's claim to absolute power.

Herr Ulbricht is deceiving himself and the world if he believes, and would have others believe, that everything depends on the quantitative production of goods. It may perhaps be technically possible to step up production, but how will he bring the right goods, in other words, the goods that are wanted by the people, to the people? That is precisely what every collectivist system has so far failed to do. We know from our own experience how easy it is with a market economy and a free choice for the consumer to supply 50 million people in Germany with the widest possible variety of goods, whereas it requires a considerable organization to supply a few hundred thousand soldiers, although their requirements are 'uniform'. . . .

Once again—we accept Herr Ulbricht's challenge. We welcome this kind of peaceful competition, because it harnesses the energy of nations to the promotion of international prosperity. We are even prepared to come off second best, if the result is to express a common will to employ human labour, whatever divisions may exist, to fulfil the desires of all those people who in a world of peace wish for a life of freedom!

30

THE DEVELOPMENT OF INDIA

(Speech to the Indian Council of World Affairs in New Delhi
on October 7, 1958)

*Amongst nearly 100 underdeveloped countries, in which about
two-thirds of the world's population live, the differences between
any one country and another and indeed within each country itself
are so marked that the national peculiarities can only be fully appreciated at first hand. Ludwig Erhard's five weeks' journey through
eight countries in South-East Asia and the Far East in the autumn
of 1958 left powerful impressions, which marked the beginning
of a new mental and economic approach to the problems of underdeveloped countries. Erhard's first stop on his long journey was in
New Delhi, where, as German Governor, he attended the annual
conference of the World Bank and International Monetary Fund.
Then, as guest of the Indian Government, Erhard got to know the
country and its people. In his speech to the Indian Council of
World Affairs he dealt with the possible lessons to be learned by
other countries from Germany's experiences in reconstruction.
Although there are certain factors common to all free political and
economic systems, which cannot be touched without doing serious
damage, nevertheless each country must go its own way, taking
its own special problems into account.*

It is an honour and a great pleasure for me to be allowed to
address such a distinguished gathering as the Council of World
Affairs on questions of vital importance to your country and mine.
The world is following with the closest interest and sympathy the
efforts of Prime Minister Nehru and his government to develop
the country's productive resources and to bring the people a greater
measure of prosperity and social security by increasing the
efficiency of human labour. This is a universal aspiration, but
experience and history have taught us that the solution does not

lie in a set formula, which can be generally applied, because there are psychological, sociological, historical and political imponderables, which must be taken into account and at the same time reconciled with the economic and financial realities. So the problems confronting each country are constantly changing.

I say this right at the beginning, because the success of Germany's reconstruction programme has led many people to imagine that I, who have carried the responsibility for our economic policy during the past ten years, had found the philosopher's stone and possessed a patent recipe to master any problem anywhere. The slogan 'German economic miracle' was invented. If I reject it, then it is simply because there was no miracle in Germany, but an economic policy based on liberal principles which set out to give meaning and purpose to human labour and to exploit the energy and devotion of a nation in the cause of human welfare. With the help of a currency reform which was as severe as it was unavoidable, our rigid state-controlled economy was converted into a system of a free social economy in which free price formation and free competition, unhampered by monopolies and power politics, were first in the list of priorities. If I attach the adjective 'social' to this system of a free market economy, it does not mean that capitalist methods were still being applied, however unobtrusively, but that we had definitely turned our backs on the old liberalism which, as you know, allowed the state to play only the part of night-watchman in the economy.

'Social Market Economy' means, therefore, that it is not merely the function but the duty of the state to set the economy certain political targets and to operate the whole machinery of economic policy in such a way that the free decisions of all those engaged in our economic life produce the desired effect. The Social Market Economy is based on the principles of freedom and order which, in my view, are inseparable if we are to have a harmonious society; for where you have freedom without a firmly-established order of things the result will probably be chaos, and where order exists without freedom it leads all to easily to brute force.

I believe that these views correspond fairly closely to the mental and moral attitude of your Prime Minister; for, while I would not presume to read that great mind, familiar as I am with his political achievements, I am nevertheless conscious of his longing—which is undoubtedly shared by the whole Indian people—to create a way of life for this country which will preserve its age-old culture, its religious and historical associations, but at the same time throw it open to modern civilization and technical advancement. When one considers the material and financial difficulties to be overcome, this is a stupendous task, which also presupposes a systematic process of education that must extend over generations. But, as we all know—and not least we in Europe—no statesman is given much time to realize his policy, for the peoples of the world are awakening and claiming their rights as they understand them.

When your Prime Minister calls it 'the paradox of our age' that, while science and technology have taught us how to control nature, we have had to pay for this by losing our soul, our moral substance and our personal sense of security as human beings, he is touching on a subject which affects all men of all races who still have the courage and the energy to think for themselves and who find it alarming that they should no longer be in control of the product of their own mind. I do not believe one can fairly regard this dilemma as a symptom or consequence of Western civilization, for, in the last resort, communism or totalitarianism, in so far as it operates on the same level of technical development and scientific discovery, is confronted by the same problem. The essential difference is that the older industrial countries are seeking solutions in harmony with the liberal systems in which they live, are trying, in other words—but so far without complete success—to reconcile the power they have acquired from their growing control of nature with the conception and realization of an individual way of life. In short, they are endeavouring to find a happy synthesis between power and freedom. If communism, on the other hand, refuses to recognize this alternative and believes it can eliminate it by suppressing the freedom of the individual by brute force, then this is certainly not a solution which either the Indian people or we in the Western democracies could accept.

And there is yet another, almost grotesque anomaly which must be mentioned here. Now that the peoples of the highly-developed industrial states are enjoying a high living standard, they are open to the taint of crass materialism, whereas the totalitarian states try

to make a virtue of the primitive conditions in which their peoples
are compelled to live, conditions which are allegedly evidence of
heroic self-sacrifice. But what is still worse is that this falsification
of values might well be accepted in other parts of the world. It is a
far cry from being accused of worshipping the 'living-standard
fetish' to aspiring to a modest standard of living; yet one thing
is clear, that one cannot set up standards of good and evil on a
purely material basis—unless those nations which have been
favoured by destiny and history are prepared to help others who
are lagging behind through no particular negligence or fault of
their own. Peoples striving for more prosperity, social security and
self-awareness can find little comfort in words like capitalism and
communism. I would even go so far as to say that those historical
precedents are likely to confuse rather than help those who are
seeking a human, personal solution.

Socialism, to many people in India, has the ethical connotation
of a kind of rule of life; in any case it has nothing in common with
the European brand of democratic socialism, which, as an economic system, will apparently lead by its own inherent logic to the
realization of a political aim. The mass-suggestion of Communist
slogans can, of course, acquire a motive force of its own, but this
force can, and indeed almost must, destroy everything. On the
other hand, a capitalism based on an excess of individuality conflicts no less sharply with the longing of peoples for a full life and
social security. Whatever one's personal view may be, no statesman
worth the name has ever been able to ignore these political and
sociological imponderables.

At this point I might speak once more about my own country
and the economic policy which I introduced. Communism, which
claims to embody pure marxism, rests on the belief that the
organic process of evolution will lead to a classless society. But we
know all too well that the reality in totalitarian states presents
quite a different picture. The so-called 'capitalist' countries, to
which the German Federal Republic traditionally belongs, certainly do not regard egalitarianism as an ideal, yet it is in precisely
those countries that the masses now enjoy such a high standard of
living. The social levels of the various layers of the population are
coming steadily closer together. Although it is not yet apparent in

individual cases, the old class-structure of capitalist convention can be said to have largely disappeared. I too was accused of having made the rich richer and the poor poorer by my economic policy. It was, admittedly, not possible to prevent social distinctions in the course of our economic recovery, and I have always declared that I did not possess powers of divine justice.

What and where is the key to a just distribution of the social product? Can anyone really believe that it lies in the struggle between collectivist power groups? The situation in my country after the capitulation was such that only one course of action was possible: to work in order to survive, and at the same time, through sacrifice and minimum consumption, to put enough of the proceeds of our national economic production on one side to restore Germany's competitive capacity as her productive capacity improved, so that, on this foundation, each individual could eventually and gradually improve his living conditions. Whereas communism, by harnessing human labour to the aggrandisement of the state and ultimately to the deification of the collective, can dispense with consumers, the so-called capitalist method of production—I prefer to call it the market economy—aims not merely at mass production but also at a corresponding mass purchasing power. Only the latter can safeguard the democratic world, geared as it is to technical progress, against severe crises. In this way capitalism, so much maligned throughout its history and yet constantly evolving becomes the motive force and the vehicle of social progress. How many millionaires there are in a country seems to me to be neither significant nor a barometer of the social conscience, so long as, in the same country, more and more people are enjoying more prosperity and social security.

I am also of the opinion that India's economic and social development cannot be modelled on that of any other country; for only the formative energy of this country itself and of its people can point the right way. But although economic planning in the sense of a conscious, clearly-defined purpose is essential, a nation's economy in its initial period of development takes shape not on the drawing-board but in the minds of men, and anyone who thinks he can read them in the abstract is bound to fail. This means that we must make the individual aware of the purpose and value of his work and effort and make it quite clear to him that greater effort will benefit him personally in his own daily life. He must be given the chance to develop as an individual and he must be rewarded for success.

It is for this reason that I applaud the aspiration and aim of the second Indian Five Year Plan to start the development of the country from the very bottom. Better cultivation methods in agriculture and a better supply of technical machinery for artisans and the minor industries should pave the way for a conscious and active interest in industry amongst the people themselves and for the emergence of private entrepreneurs, thus counterbalancing the specialized management of large concerns within the national economy. A people that wishes to preserve freedom of the individual cannot and must not act otherwise; for mammoth units of industrial production may serve to reduce the country's import requirements and improve the balance-of-payments position, but it can never, by its mere existence, guarantee an organic and harmonious development that also leaves room for the imponderable value of human life.

The objection can of course be raised that, in view of political and social phenomena previously referred to, the process of freeing people from hardship and poverty would last too long to make it politically successful. This is certainly true, and that is why the Western democracies are prepared to help your people not only for reasons of political expediency but also from a sense of moral responsibility and obligation. I would even maintain that giving and accepting help presuppose an equally high moral standard. Your Prime Minister is right when he says that to let things drift merely widens the gap in achievement, way of life and wealth between the countries and peoples of this world and gives rise to more and more unrest. Never before in history has it been so necessary for mankind to stand together, if the forces which have been unleashed are to be mastered.

In this context the question then arises almost automatically, whether the nations which are striving after economic expansion can simply leap over a century of technical development without breaking certain mental, spiritual and cultural links. As, however, there is no other way and as it would be unthinkable to perpetuate this gap, we can only recognize the danger and get together to do our best. Where action is dictated by sheer necessity, great courage, concentrated energy and a common effort are also required. The man who does not see the danger finds it easy to act. When, however, such a great man as your Prime Minister can survey the whole vast picture without allowing his insight and his knowledge to deter him, but is, on the contrary, fired by his responsibility, then it should be a happy omen for India that this great land and this people, to whom the world owes so much in the sphere of culture, will also master the problem of their living present, will overcome poverty and strengthen the foundations of their independent political life. The purpose of my visit was, and is, to capture something of this spirit and this energy, to feel for myself the longing and aspirations of men.

Practical co-operation would consist, in the first instance, in finding the appropriate means abroad to further the efforts of the Indian people. Above all, the industrial countries must be prepared, and in a position, to absorb in a steady flow the products of the developing countries. A stabilization of the world market would give protection, help and security to those countries in particular.

A country's economic life is not conducted in a purely economic sphere, much less in a vacuum. On the contrary, it is virtually impossible to separate the economic life of a people from its political destiny. And it is also inconceivable that these two fields of activity could be subject to different laws, in other words, to different human and moral standards. This is not the moment to try to demonstrate in detail why a democratic regime and a system of economic freedom must go together, whereas totalitarianism either presupposes or leads to the use of force. These parallels are logical and borne out by history.

I might, however, pose the much more fundamental question: which economic and social system produces the best results in terms of 'delivering the goods'. The capacity to build sputniks gives demonstrably no indication of the ability to provide people with what they need and want for everyday use. How, otherwise, could the German Federal Republic, for example, have managed to absorb an influx of ten million refugees and expellees and to cope with a population which today stands at over 50 million people? How could she have provided shelter, employment and wages for these poor people, who were condemned by injustice and brute force to become refugees and exiles in their own German homeland, if our free economic system with its high productive capacity had not laid the material foundations? We are in duty bound to feel for all refugees in this world and to take an active interest in their unhappy lot. And we, in particular, knowing the bitter sufferings our German brothers have endured, have a right to accuse. You can be quite sure—and this is a solemn declaration—that no one in my country, no statesman, no party and no group, has any intention of solving the burning problem of German re-unification by other than peaceful means. For we have been cured of the curse of our unhappy past, of the madness of worshipping force, and we know from our own tragic experience that what people throughout the world need above all is the blessing of peace.

We, too, believe in peaceful, friendly and neighbourly co-operation between all peoples, regardless of nation or race, irre-spective of their social systems and political ideas. But we cannot be expected to carry reunification to the point of abandoning 18 million Germans to an intolerable fate. Peaceful coexistence cannot and must not involve such humiliation. We Germans are also in deadly earnest when we say that we long for nothing more than that general disarmament and a relaxation of tension should lead to a lasting peace, allowing the nations to live side by side in an atmosphere free from threats; for we, in particular, living as we do on the very frontier of Communism, have nothing to gain and everything to lose by the cold war.

For me the ideals you are pursuing in your country have a strong personal appeal. If we are fated to live with the atom bomb, then we must do everything we can to avoid dying by the atom bomb. This means that the nations have a responsibility to settle their differences by peaceful means. What is happening today might even bring new hope! People are so constituted that they cannot live without hope. Even if it were necessary to believe in miracles in order to feel confident that this or that hope and longing would be fulfilled, people would still go on believing and they would be right to do so. Anyone who saw Germany reduced to ruins and untold misery could find no rational comfort or hope. And if the success of Germany's recovery is now a fact, it cannot be fully explained in rational terms.

Because I know that your government is firmly resolved to carry through the economic development and expansion of your country and because I can sense something of the perhaps still inarticulate longing of the Indian people for a better and more dignified way of life, I will venture, with my own experience as a German in mind, to urge you to show courage, hope and confidence. It may be that the saying, God helps those who help themselves, expresses an essentially Western thought; yet I believe that there is something of this in your attitude here in India—and, indeed, it must be so, if you are to succeed in your task of economic and social development. My best wishes go with you and the Indian people in your efforts to attain that goal.

31

IMPRESSIONS OF ASIA

(Broadcast on November 24, 1958)

The impressions Ludwig Erhard gathered on his Asian tour and the ideas he then formulated contributed to the establishment of a German policy for providing foreign aid for purposes of development. At the same time this broadcast was the prelude to an intensive campaign to create and promote amongst the German population the necessary understanding for the many problems of the developing countries:

I was happy to accept the invitation to report on my journey, which, as you know, took me through eight countries in South-East and East Asia. I cannot, of course, adopt the style of a travelogue, because, as a Minister of Economy, I am expected to draw practical conclusions in the sphere of politics and economics from what I have seen and experienced from my many personal impressions and reactions. Although each country naturally presents a different picture, I nevertheless feel it is permissible to look at the problems of the so-called 'developing countries' of South-East Asia as one complex whole, whereas the socio-political situation in the East Asian countries I visited is in many respects different. Let me add that, while in South-East Asia, I visited India, Burma, Thailand, South Vietnam, Ceylon and Pakistan; the countries I went to in East Asia were South Korea and Japan. I might also mention, incidentally, that this five-week journey was no pleasure jaunt; I was constantly on the move, including Sundays, from early morning until late at night.

At the very beginning of my tour I took part in the conference of the World Bank and the International Monetary Fund, which was concerned with international co-operation and better co-ordination of the widespread aid for the developing countries. The Indian Prime Minister Nehru in his speech of welcome presented the problems, as seen from the view-point of the underdeveloped countries, in very pregnant and perhaps even somewhat too detailed terms. Both in plenary session and in the many informal talks, the main question under discussion was whether a way could be found or a procedure devised of giving these countries not merely World Bank credits for economic and commercial purposes but also, in specific cases, funds for so-called infra-structural purposes on easy repayment terms. The Monroney Plan, which still needs to be examined in detail, provides for long-term credits of this kind against repayment not in transferable currency but in local currency; that is, in the currency of the particular country. Although such credits are open to much criticism, it must be admitted that projects in the fields of power and transport, for example, only pave the way for further economic development in countries that cannot carry through such projects with their own resources. It is, therefore, important to co-ordinate the commercial World Bank credits with softer infra-structure credits. Although this complex question has not yet been finally resolved, it was decided in principle that the World Bank should increase its authorized capital stock to provide further credit facilities for a more intensive programme. The discussions clearly centred largely round the demand that bilateral aid—whether as credits or gifts— should be raised to the multilateral level, in order not only to achieve better co-ordination but also to make it more effective. But this method also has the merit that development credits cannot then be regarded as a means of bringing influence to bear on the recipient.

Against this background of international co-operation countless talks were held with the heads of the various states, their Prime Ministers, heads of departments, planning and administrative officials, scientists, economists and representatives of almost every other section of the population. While I talk to you now, I can recall the extremely vivid and varied impressions I formed; these, because they were so varied, have lost none of their original impact and, in the last resort, have a great deal in common. Anyone who tried to comprehend the life of these peoples through Western eyes or to measure their habits and customs with a critical Western yard-stick, would either fail or despair. So I tried to bring home to my travelling companions that arrogance would be entirely out of place, that profit and loss were useless criteria by which to judge good or evil, and that we must make every possible effort to see things in their immediate context, against the background of the country and its people. This alone could entitle one morally to pass critical judgments, which, as I have learned, were always well received so long as an earnest desire to understand and help was also evident.

What I found particularly gratifying in my conversations with my foreign colleagues was that I was welcomed not so much as a German Minister who had, strictly speaking, no business to be concerning himself with other people's affairs, but rather as an expert who has been recognized in his own country and whose advice was eagerly sought. Again and again I was encouraged and even invited by the highest authorities in these states to express my views in public and moreover to voice criticism in order to make my visit as profitable as possible. I availed myself of this privilege as much as I could without giving offence, and I am pleased to be able to say that all my visits passed off in complete harmony.

But now to the problems themselves! If I begin by referring to the almost incredible poverty of the people in South-East Asia in particular, I am merely stating the obvious. To make the picture clearer, I might observe that the amount we regard as an average wage increase in normal circumstances, corresponds in those countries to the absolute total income of the most highly-paid. On the other hand, the difference in living costs is not the same. Thus, the staple food, rice, costs only slightly less there than here. The clothes people wear are surprisingly clean and neat, but housing conditions and domestic appliances are incredibly primitive. It is also possible to generalize about agricultural methods and implements, which can only be described as completely inadequate. At the same time one must recognize that, particularly in India, a laborious but on the whole successful effort is being made, by grouping village communities together in larger units and appointing expert managers, to demonstrate to the Indian peasant the advantages in using better seed, in rationalizing cultivation and altogether in taking technical advice to improve implements and irrigation. The peasants are also given instruction in sanitation and hygiene and in ways and means of improving their homes. The Indian Government's campaign to eradicate illiteracy is, in itself, a herculean task; to find school accommodation in over 500,000 villages for more than 100 million children and to prepare the corresponding number of teachers presents not only a financial problem but, even more serious, an almost insuperable administrative problem.

In the field of trade and industry conditions are much more varied. Although industry and private business in the Western sense are still only in their infancy, whereas many products show highly skilled workmanship and indicate that quite a well-developed artisan class exists, there are, particularly in India, a few large and medium-sized industrial concerns—one example is the Tata works at Jamshedpur—in private ownership. On the other hand, it is undeniable that industrial activity and national output are, on the whole, unsatisfactory and incapable of overcoming the mass poverty.

Let me take India as an example to illustrate what the problems are throughout South-East Asia. The people are in a state of unrest. India's political independence gave rise to a strong national awareness which is seeking an outlet and searching for solutions. Memories of the colonial period have left no resentment against Britain; on the contrary, the British are very popular, and I feel certain that from this point of view the Commonwealth is organically sound and firmly established. But the various peoples want to shake off poverty and share a higher standard of living; they want the gap between their way of life and that of the free world to become not wider but narrower. Whether the countries in question and their statesmen always adopt the correct standards and are aware of the actual possibilities is another question. But this urge for a better life is so strong that it is often a mere step from the wish to the demand that what these peoples cannot achieve from their own resources must be provided from outside in any form of aid or support. Here too the bow is perhaps being stretched almost to breaking-point, but we must be careful not to pass a moral judgment on what is a psychological and sociological phenomenon. One thing is certain: if the efforts being made to achieve higher labour productivity and higher output do not produce results soon, the gap between those countries and the Western industrial nations will grow steadily wider. If those peoples do not believe, cannot see and feel that material successes are being achieved, then out of despair will come the great danger that they will look to other systems and other principles, and that, without knowing where it is leading, they will accept a social and political change of course. I know that this is a daring statement to make, because the present situation certainly does not entirely warrant it. Moreover, in circumstances of this kind, one must not overlook personalities and the power they radiate. I am convinced that a man such as Nehru, for example, who has the confidence of the entire nation and in whom all their hopes rest, will lead the Indian people through the desert, until practical achievements have turned their longing into a firm faith. The political instability of other countries proves how different each structure is and how important it is that the political and social life of the country should be incorporated in its leading personalities.

We would be making it too easy for ourselves if we believed that people there simply do not work or do not even want to work and that therefore nothing can be done to help them. It may sometimes appear to be so on the surface, but this is not the real heart of the matter. At such a low and widespread level of poverty there is clearly little room for variation, and even an increased effort cannot produce an appreciably higher living standard. So for these nations the crucial question is how to bring home to the individual the real importance of his labour and to make him realize that more work means more wages and a better and freer life. I am almost tempted to say: the first step is the hardest. But if, to begin with, production can be rationalized on a more extensive scale and the output per man-day increased, so that the social product shows a steady upward trend which is reflected, gradually but appreciably, in improved living standards, then I feel reasonably sure that, once such a process gets under way, it will bring a fundamental change in the psychological approach to human labour and its importance. If people there do not work hard, it is not because they are lazy by nature but because they do not yet realize the purpose of human effort. There are, of course, great differences between the various peoples and races, but

I am not sure whether it was, so to speak, the will of God or historical and geographical circumstances that created these national and racial characteristics.

One must remember, incidentally, that throughout this whole area, with its 600 million people, anxious eyes are watching Red China across the frontier, where her communist economic experiment is given an even chance of success because the Chinese are regarded as intelligent, hard-working and capable of tremendous energy and dedication. If we start off from the premise that the unrest in Asia is due fundamentally to a titanic contest between two political systems, totalitarianism and democracy, or between a communist and a free society, then we must also take into account the human imponderables. In the eyes of the world the two main contestants in Asia are Red China and India. It seems to me that the outcome, the degree of success or failure, must influence and even decide the political fate of the adjoining states. When I broached this subject in the course of conversation with Prime Minister Nehru, he declined to think in terms of a contest or any kind of competition with China but emphasized that India was pursuing her own independent course; at the same time he was forced to admit that, in the final analysis, my conclusions were justified. It is also dangerous to imagine that religious ties or cultural traditions would provide an effective shield against intensive communist infiltration. This kind of inner resistance may be a vital factor in the behaviour of the individual, but it cannot immunize whole nations against collectivism.

If we are to move from the political to the economic sphere and gain a clear idea of the possibilities of economic development, we must begin by looking at the structure of these national economies. As I said earlier, much can certainly be done in the foreseeable future in agriculture by employing modern methods and better equipment—and this step should and must be taken. It is, after all, significant and depressing that those countries with 80% and more of their population engaged in agriculture should still be dependent on imports of foodstuffs. But the real problem—to improve social conditions and promote development, thus guaranteeing political security and stability—cannot be solved in the agrarian sector alone, because these national economies are based, though in varying degrees, on the single-crop system, so that their products are much too exposed to the whims and fluctuations of the world markets, which these countries themselves are not strong enough to influence. The same is true of the utilization or production of industrial raw materials. I have often heard people in those countries complaining bitterly that they had assumed they would become really free when they threw off the colonial system but had now learned that their dependence was merely one stage removed. And it is, in fact, true that all the foreign aid these countries have received over the past years, particularly from the United States, has not been enough to compensate for the losses they suffered through the drop in raw material prices.

In the circumstances, therefore, it is unrealistic to make to these countries recommendations which would either perpetuate or perhaps even increase the one-sidedness of their economies, particularly as practical experience and scientific knowledge have shown beyond doubt that, especially in our day and age, industrialization is the only way to achieve real social progress and a buoyant national economy. And perhaps the only irritant that still survives from the colonial era is the reproach made by these countries that they are looked upon and treated as mere markets and were prevented from embarking on any form of production other than agriculture and raw materials.

If there is any justification for such an accusation, then it is not just a reflection of the relationship between mother countries and their colonies but much more a symptom of the mental approach of advanced industrial states to underdeveloped countries overseas. During my tour, for example, I came across a German press report in which—and this in the year 1958!—the writer maintained that Professor Erhard's tour had aroused a certain scepticism in economic circles, for why should we throw good money after bad and go out of our way to reduce our export markets in that area. If statements of this kind seem to be inspired by an almost brutal egoism, a little reflection will show that it can become more or less the reverse and do inestimable damage to Germany's national economy, for nothing is more likely to lose us our markets in those countries than to leave them entirely to their fate. On the other hand, it does not take much imagination to realize what immense prospects would be opened up if these countries succeeded with the help of the Western world in converting 6–700 million people into more and more exacting consumers. Who could be so blind and so presumptuous as to believe that, if the whole of Asia with its immense and rapidly increasing population were to become communist, we and our children in Europe would be allowed to go on living in peace and security. I would be a most unworthy custodian of the destinies of the German people, if I did not look ahead and realize that the right or the wrong turning determines the future of those who come after us.

Recognize as one may the importance of increasing agricultural productivity in the countries of Asia, their only real solution lies in concentrating more and more on industrialization, and we should support, not hamper, them in this. Our advice to them should be, that it is no use building great steelworks or other mammoth concerns which may have a certain symbolic importance but are of doubtful value to the national economy, that, on the contrary, it would be much more profitable and imperative to develop and expand the existing trades and industries, thus creating more employment and spreading the nation's purchasing power. Time and again I stressed the fact that in these countries nothing is more important than to produce purchasing power. In well-regulated conditions, however, this can only happen by producing commodities. From this point of view it is highly desirable that foreign private capital—and I am addressing myself here to German industry—should be prepared to establish branches in those countries and not be afraid of the risks involved. A development programme which will carry these nations through the politically and psychologically lean period cannot be carried through on their own resources, for incomes are such as to permit very limited savings and the small-scale economic activity yields very little in the way of taxation. And revenue from customs duties or licences will become even smaller the more these countries have to cut back on imports to keep a steady balance of payments. So in plain terms the choice lies between leaving these countries to their fate and accepting the political consequences, or co-operating with them and convincing them that, quite apart from the common interests of the free world, we are not acting out of cynical egoism but from a sense of solidarity when we pool our resources to open up a brighter future for those countries which, through no fault of their own, have remained backward. We in the Western hemisphere may increase our productive power as much as we like, we may achieve still greater prosperity and accumulate even more wealth, but however much of this we choose to give to those underdeveloped countries either as grants or as alms will not solve the problem. These nations want to shape their own lives and it is up to us to give them the helping hand which will enable them to overcome their problems on their own responsibility and in accordance with their own ideas.

I know that mere preaching will not help and recommendations alone do not produce action in the Western camp. So the Federal Republic is prepared, in addition to the already existing Hermes guarantees for supply credits, to insure private capital investment in foreign countries against political risks. But this generous gesture also demands—and I made no secret of this in my talks with statesmen in the countries I visited—a similar attitude on the part of those countries which attach importance to German capital investment in their economies. Whether this security is given in the form of general legislation to meet third-party risks or by bilateral agreement seems of minor importance. Be that as it may, I found—somewhat to my surprise—that such problems were being discussed remarkably frankly and that people were, in principle, prepared to take the necessary steps. A magna charta of the sanctity of private property as an essential prerequisite for the solidarity of the Western world will never be achieved by international proclamation, but I am confident that a series of individual statements will have the effect of making this principle more and more widely understood. Only in certain isolated cases and only as the personal opinion of this or that individual did I hear the view expressed that, once a country has achieved independence, it should renounce foreign capital and rely on its own resources. Such views are basically emotional and as such can hardly carry much weight in practical politics. In this connection, I pointed out on many occasions, it would be nothing short of tragic if these countries, having achieved independence, were to become so besotted by nationalist delusions as to believe that they could withdraw into a kind of self-sufficient isolation. They would be preventing the development of their national economies for decades to come at the very moment when the highly-developed industrial states in the West had recognized the folly of the nationalist principle and were removing their national frontiers and joining together in a much larger community based upon greater freedom of movement. This latent danger, which in the long run would breed communism, will only be effectively overcome if we are frank and sincere in our efforts to help these nations satisfy their very understandable aspirations.

Now I know the objection is frequently made that growing industrialization in South-East Asia will have negative repercussions in this or that industrial state in the West—which naturally includes Germany. Far be it from me to deny that there will be repercussions, and yet I take the view that for our industrial and business enterprises to adapt themselves to this development before it is too late represents the lesser of two evils. When I read in the German press that every time I shook hands with the ambassador of a country I had visited and moved on to another it cost 100 million marks, I can only reply that this kind of speculation is completely misleading. And if the German textile industry was genuinely worried that my journey might result in larger imports of raw materials from India or Japan, then I have managed to allay their fears in the meantime. It was not questions of this kind that I discussed in my talks. At the same time I cannot and must not disguise the fact that my conviction of the need for more industrialization in these countries—not overnight but on a long-term basis—is bound to have an effect on the structure of German industry. It is also completely misleading to talk in this context of a dumping policy, which would sooner or later call for import restrictions, for if those countries cannot afford in the beginning at least to raise wages, it is not because they are pursuing an aggressive trade policy but because labour costs must be kept low. In the case of Japan, however, we can see how increased industrialization brings with it growing pressure for a rise in labour costs. Genuine economic development on an international basis would clearly be impossible if countries with high labour costs felt justified, due to varying wage levels, in setting up protective barriers. What would happen, for example, to trade between Europe and America if such principles were applied? In short, we, the European countries, must be prepared to leave the simple forms of industrial production to the underdeveloped countries and to concentrate ourselves on more highly-finished goods and on technical refinements. This will not be entirely an act of renunciation but will also be profitable, for let me remind you again what it would mean to the European national economies if 600 million consumers could be brought within the scope of the modern industrial economy.

So far I have been asking in terms of the material living conditions of these people. In view of their widespread poverty, I admit that it will not be easy to make these millions of people realize that an improved standard of living would mean not merely higher consumption but also the preservation of their spiritual and moral values. That is why Soviet propaganda finds fairly ready acceptance and is even, I believe, dangerously effective everywhere. During my journey I was given special treatment in this respect, for, if the first page of a local newspaper carried my photograph and a report on Germany's desire to help those countries, it was noticeable that four pages of the same newspaper carried articles, paid for by Soviet propaganda, extolling the achievements of the communist system with the most attractive pictures and urging readers to follow this example. To illustrate how shaky the ground is on which we are walking, let me tell you this story. At one university I had an opportunity of talking at some length to Professors of Economics, who asked whether it would be such a bad thing if their country surrendered to communism. They argued that their communism would be quite different from the Russian variety. It was not difficult to expose this illusion from practical and historical experience. In relation to the German refugee problem the view was expressed that such a development must have its reasons. They were prepared to admit that living conditions in West Germany were better from a material point of view than in the Soviet Zone, but then followed the breath-taking remark that I would surely not dare to suggest that people in the West can live in greater freedom than is possible under communism. If there is such blindness in intellectual circles, it is hardly surprising—and I said so quite bluntly—that Soviet propaganda should find its most fertile breeding ground amongst the broad masses of the people.

Of course, conditions vary from one country to another; this means that over and above what they have in common, which I have been trying to crystallize, there is a multi-coloured pattern of political and sociological activity. When people there talk of economic freedom, they naturally mean something different from the freedom that is characteristic of, for example, our German economic policy, and, when they talk of democracy, they are not thinking of the classic precedents of the past or present. In those restless, effervescent societies there are no fixed standards or formulae for what is good and what is worthless; the policy of a country is determined by individuals, who draw on their own personal ideas or political ideals.

Let me now summarize by saying that, from what I have seen and experienced, the vast populations of South-East and East Asia are basically in sympathy with the free world and can be won over to it. It would be more true to say that it is our duty to safeguard their freedom, for what is at stake here is not the material advantages or disadvantages to be gained or suffered from becoming partners of the free world but the fate of these countries themselves, not to mention our way of life and our future.

The Berlin problem has brought home to us how dependent we are on the confidence and friendship of the free world if the city is to be saved. Are we not all aware by now that, in the great world conflict for the freedom or enslavement of nations and people, those countries which will not accept slavery and which have higher values than the worship of power and the deification of the state must stand united?

32

GERMAN MARK FREELY CONVERTIBLE

(Broadcast on December 28, 1958)

*On December 28, 1958, a number of European countries an-
nounced that they had reverted to the free convertibility of their
currencies, which had been in abeyance since 1931, and on the
same date the European Currency Agreement came into force.
After intensive negotiation conducted behind closed doors, the
following countries decided to take this step: Belgium, the Federal
German Republic, Denmark, Finland, France, Great Britain, Eire,
Italy, Holland, Norway, Austria, Portugal, Sweden and Switzerland. Erhard, who had long been advocating a return to convertibility, issued a statement in which he welcomed the decision as an
event of historic importance:*

The fact that the main European currencies, in particular sterling,
the mark and the franc, have now become freely convertible, while
admittedly of little direct interest to the layman, is of very much
wider significance from the administrative point of view. The
occasion is of historic importance, and marks virtually a turning-
point in international economic relations. For too long the currencies of the world have been misused to subserve trade policies,
and these in their turn to correct the mistakes of a misguided
monetary policy. As a result, people and governments almost inevitably lost all sense of the value of a well-ordered system of
exchange, and awareness of responsibility in this direction
dwindled. The European Payments Union undoubtedly helped to
keep multilateral trading and clearing channels open, and the EEC
concept bears witness to an awareness of the need for the integration of closely related economic entities. And yet there has been
reason to fear that people might lose sight of the importance of
ensuring the all-embracing unity, that is to say the indivisibility, of
the firmly linked free world.

The narrower ties and obligations that characterize the Common Market will not be affected by the transition to convertibility embracing a larger area. At the same time, the far wider implications of convertibility are solid proof that the free world is in fact moving towards unfettered economic co-operation. There is thus no incompatibility of aims between the two groupings. All that is needed is to distinguish clearly between political aspirations on the one hand and concepts of an economic order on the other.

I myself for instance have always taken the line that the community of the Six represented in EEC could never arrive at a balance of payments within its own orbit, and that the idea of a currency union without surrender of sovereignty must remain illusory. The advent of convertibility disposes of such mistaken notions. Above all, it seems to me to be a tremendous step forward that countries conscious of belonging to a world-wide economy should now be prepared to act accordingly.

That I personally derive much satisfaction from this event is something I feel sure no one would wish to begrudge me. After all, I was one of the first European politicians to call for free convertibility of currencies in a world still labouring under injury, disruption and scepticism, and often enough I was laughed and sneered at for my pains. For eight years on end I went on making fresh efforts to bring a solution nearer. Now that the problem has been solved, no matter what fortunate conjunction of circumstances brought it about, I will always praise this day that has brought the world together in a spirit of free competition and given honest dealing its due reward. Of all the many possible forms which integration of the free world can take, free convertibility of currencies is the most fruitful. Through it we may yet be spared an unholy war between Common Market and Free Trade Association.

33

THE REINCORPORATION OF SAARLAND INTO THE FEDERAL REPUBLIC

(Broadcast on July 4, 1959)

Negotiations between the German and French governments led to agreement on the economic reincorporation of Saarland, following its political reincorporation into the Federal Republic on January 1, 1957. The date of July 4, 1959, was proclaimed Saarland's 'X Day', to be commemorated as making the first step towards German reunification.

You have just heard the official announcement of the economic reincorporation of Saarland into the Federal Republic. This notable event terminates the period of transition in which Saarland, politically already part of the Federal Republic, still remained economically part of France.

The people of Saarland and throughout the Federal Republic will be conscious of the full significance of Saarland's return to the German fold, for it means the ending, and I am sure it is a happy ending, to the long story of political wrangling and international haggling over the fate of this small territory on the Saar.

On this historic occasion I am also moved to give the German people of the Saar once more the assurance that their cares, their needs and their hopes are identical with ours. May I also say that I personally am deeply gratified at having been permitted to take part in effecting the economic reintegration of the Saar without friction as a first step towards the reunification of Germany. When I, as is only natural on this occasion, look back to the time of the currency reform in 1948 with its economic repercussions and the opportunity it gave Germany to regain a position in the world economy, and when I compare the situation then with our present economic and social situation, then I feel that the people of the Saar can indeed take heart at this auspicious turning-point in the affairs of Germany and face the future with confidence.

The German people in the Federal Republic and in the Saar have achieved great things in these last twelve years, in spite of all vicissitudes, inspired by the spirit of unity and of solidarity irrespective of all distinctions of class and standing. I therefore do not doubt for one moment that the economic reunification of the Saar with the rest of the Federal territory will take place without disturbance or tension of any kind.

From now on the new customs border will be the former frontier between France and the Saar; the German mark will be the official currency, and German law will apply in almost every sphere of life. For all this we have to thank the free decision taken by the German people of the Saar on their own future, for it was only on this basis that the Federal Government and the government of the Saar could pave the way, in close collaboration with the French Government, for economic reintegration. Here was democracy at work shaping a people's future.

At this point I would say, not only in the interests of truth but also in response to a sincerely felt need, that the economic reintegration of the Saar would not have been possible had not the participants—France, the Federal Republic and the Saar itself—tackled this task in a truly European spirit. The return of the Saar is a pledge of the *rapprochement* between Germany and France that forms, and will continue to form, an essential part of the foundation of any European integration. Both governments acted on the conviction that the peoples of Europe are no longer going to be kept separated by economic and national boundaries. In the events of these days we are witnessing an act of European unification.

I should also like to take this opportunity of thanking the government of the Saar cordially for their valuable co-operation in this historic achievement. Credit is due in particular to the former Minister-President, the late Dr Reinert, for his outstanding part in the difficult work of the preparatory stages. Not only is it a welcome duty devolving on me as a member of the Federal Government to express gratitude to him at this time, but I welcome no less the opportunity to express my high personal regard for a man of honest purpose and integrity.

R

I know very well that the thoughts of the people and business circles in the Saar are upon the months ahead, upon the link-up with the German market, in which hope mingles with a certain amount of anxiety. Consumers are looking forward to having access to German goods which they have so long had to do without, and which come nearest to meeting their needs in the matter of taste and custom, and to being able to buy them at very reasonable prices. And producers in the Saar are looking forward to many opportunities of supplying the German market. But alongside these positive expectations there are also misgivings—and this applies particularly to the processing industries—as to whether the German market will offer them the same sales and profit-making opportunities as they have had hitherto. And wage-earners are wondering what may happen to the real level of income and their standard of living.

In recent weeks all these questions have been the subject of heated controversy culminating in the Bundestag debates on the ratification of the Treaty for the economic reincorporation of Saarland into the Federal Republic.

The Saarland population opted for return to Germany for political reasons, or rather for reasons of sentiment. Opinions were divided only over questions of ways and means. As is usual in the discussion of the internal affairs of a nation, the issues in dispute were related exclusively to assessments of the economic and social situation.

Doubtless some of the wishes and expectations cherished by the workers and by the employers have remained outwardly unfulfilled, but this does not point to any lack of understanding on the part of those responsible for the decisions taken, whose one and only concern has been to do all they could, in the light of the experience gained in Germany, to strengthen the foundations of Saarland's economic existence. I am therefore convinced that there is no cause whatever for anxiety regarding the future development of Saarland. This new *Land* is being integrated into the German market at an extremely favourable moment, when employment is at a high level and prosperity is increasing. I know from experience how vigorously the people of the Saar have always cultivated the virtues of diligence, tenacity and good faith. The strength that comes from sources like these will prove itself all the more in the larger sphere of the Federal Republic. The Federal Government has never been one to let things drift, nor will it be in the future. On the contrary, it has initiated a great many measures designed to promote the health and development of the economy, many of them novel, and these will redound to the advantage of Saarland's economy and enable it to find its feet in the German market and participate in the steady process of growth now taking place throughout the Federal Republic.

Saarland will also benefit from the special provisions for the large-scale duty-free exchange of goods with France, while its unique position in this respect will also promote goodwill and co-operation between France and the Federal Republic. Every move in the direction of pulling down the barriers between states is welcome and can only be to the advantage of us all.

I have no hesitation in saying that the events we are now witnessing on the Saar constitute a step towards the unification of Europe. Even from the point of view of the larger issues affecting Europe as a whole, the reincorporation of Saarland into the Federal Republic has more than merely national significance; it is an act of mutual European understanding, and it strengthens the economic ties and the bonds of friendship between France and Germany. In this sense, Saarland has a mission to fulfil as a link between our peoples—and may it ever remain so. Germans in all parts of the Federal Republic look to the Saar with gratitude and joy in their hearts and wish Saarland well.

34

TRADE UNIONS IN A FREE SOCIETY

(Address to the Federal TU-Congress held in Stuttgart on
September 7, 1959)

*With the SPD deciding on a new party programme embodying
notable reforms, it was becoming clear that the leadership of the
large industrial trade unions was still unable to embrace the concept of the Social Market Economy. But in spite of all differences
between their respective approaches to vital questions of economic
policy, Erhard never broke off his open and direct discussions with
leading personalities in the trade union movement. In the following address, Ludwig Erhard once more expressed the conviction
that the trade unions, as well as the employers' federations, had an
important and essential part to play in a free economy and therefore carried great responsibility:*

Ten years ago I was with you when the German Trade Union
Federation was re-established, and I assured you on that occasion of
my best efforts to help you combat the troubles which beset us all
in those days; that we had the well-being of the working man
equally at heart. I believe we can today mutually claim—happily
for ourselves and for all our fellow-countrymen—that we have
indeed worked for this end, even though we have not always
agreed on the means. This too I said ten years ago and I repeat it
here today, although the situation does seem to me to have changed
considerably since then. Arguments there still are, and always will
be as long as men go in search of the truth, but all through these
years—and I also say this for myself personally—we have kept on
looking for opportunities for discussion, wanting to deal with the
problems that beset us, trying to see eye-to-eye. Sometimes with
more, sometimes with less success; but the will has been undeniable. For this I am sincerely grateful to you, particularly to the
members of the National Executive and the industrial unions, for

we are not here to represent individual interests; we are concerned not with ambitions, not with having the last word, but with working for one and the same end.

Meanwhile changes have taken place. The trade unions are solidly in favour of democracy, but this does not of course mean that they are equally in favour of any and every government; but does this really matter? What is important is that they should be on the side of a free democratic order, and bearers of true democratic responsibility, and this is the case today. The trade unions are so regarded and so recognized. In fact, I believe—and let us have the courage to admit it—that we have come to understand each other progressively better during these ten years, better maybe than we were willing to let others know. I think this needs saying.

And having said that we can claim that our united efforts have produced results, may I in all modesty add that the success of our economic policy was not the least of the factors which enabled the trade unions to do things on a wider scale and with greater success than would otherwise have been possible. Whatever you choose to call our system—Free Market Economy, Social Market Economy or any other name, and as far as I am concerned you may call it Capitalism if you like—let me say this: a free economy, so it has been said, is to trade unionism as water is to a fish. One cannot live without the other. There is some truth in this, I think, for it is only in a dynamically vital economy capable of free development and change in the course of its day-to-day life that trade unions really have a chance to achieve anything.

I do not know whether you are in possession of the key to a just order of society. I for my part lay no claim to possession of the secret. Yet that is what all the struggle is about—and it is to my mind a genuine struggle—with everyone in his own fashion and according to his lights trying to do what he believes best for everyone. One thing is quite certain: if you ever want the economy to set hard like concrete, then the days of the trade unions will be numbered. In an economy that has no earnings to show, that produces no profits, that loses the impulse to keep on creating anew, there would be no room for your work. That is why I believe— and I do not for a moment suggest that any of you would dispute it—that only in a free order of society will there be life in the trade

union camp. I have been told, and have also read in the newspapers, that there is arguing within your ranks. I congratulate you,
ladies and gentlemen. The same think happens elsewhere. No one
but the stupid or malicious would fail to rejoice in the fact that
you argue among yourselves. Argument is not a sign of weakness,
but of strength. I trust you appreciate what strength is, and so I
appeal to you to grant freedom of thought, to show tolerance. If
we look at what is happening in the East, and above all if we think
of our own tragic past, the truth is borne in on us that only in
freedom can man lead a life which is worthy of the name. In the
East—no trade unions there—we see how human dignity is
crushed, every trace of humanity stifled. One's mind is carried
back to the dismal conditions in the early days of the Industrial
Revolution, and one resolves never to forget what had to be overcome to enable us to lead a free life worthy of human beings.

As I see it, your task is one that recurs in every phase of democratic life. The individual does not of course have the power to
shape his own destiny; I would go further and say that today we
are ready to admit that not even nations are capable, in isolation,
of working out answers to our problems that will stand the test of
time.

Organizing there has to be, but naturally the institutionalizing
process has its dangers. To some extent human values are bound to
suffer; there is some loss of direct contact between people, social
intercourse loses some of its spontaneity, feelings of brotherhood
and solidarity are repressed. This happens in the trade union
movement, it happens in all democratic institutions. Where the art
comes in—and, I would have you know, it is an art whose sphere
is the 'possible', in other words it is the art of politics—is in reconciling the inherent remoteness of the machinery with the inborn
human yearning for warmth and directness in human relations.

The perfectionist Welfare State could also, in my opinion, become a threat to the trade union movement. This implies no
criticism of our social achievements in these last ten years. We had
a plain duty here. But I believe there is a limit. Once people feel
that everything is looked after to perfection, and there is no room
for improvements of any kind, I cannot imagine what there would
be for trade unions to do. If everything were regulated and

managed by the state, and no wish remained unfulfilled, the trade union movement would simply die.

If we possessed the philosopher's stone and knew exactly how to achieve a truly just distribution of wealth—which is of course impossible and belongs to the realm of illusion—the result would be a petrified or utterly sterile kind of millennium. I cannot imagine that any human being would be happy in such conditions. No, we must wrestle with each other and we must have the courage to face this fact and at the same time to see in each other not opponents, still less enemies, but partners working for one and the same end.

There is another matter I would like to raise. At the heart of all our problems lies the question of how to combine, or reconcile, what is socially desirable with what is economically feasible. And there is invariably a point at which you cause pain if you touch this question. Now, generally speaking, you and I have always managed to get over our differences and come to understand each other. What I now want to ask you to consider is whether, precisely in view of our present prosperity, we should not perhaps drop the subject of shorter working hours, at least for the time being. I risk saying this to you because I am certain we now have it in our power to increase our social product, and therefore to improve our living standard, to such an extent that we should simply be throwing away chances if we even thought about doing less work.

The statistics show that there is at present no noticeable inclination to work overtime. Although the total employment figure has again gone up considerably and is half a million higher than last year's, the total number of hours worked has gone down. On a monthly average, German industry is receiving a volume of orders which exceeds its productive capacity by 12%. This means that 'cushioning' surplus orders build up, with all the unhealthy consequences that follow from this state of things.

Do not, I beg you, misunderstand me. Of course I am just as keen as you are to see that people have more freedom, more leisure, more opportunity to sit back and think, so far as this can be made possible by technological progress, higher productivity and greater efficiency. This goes without saying. What I am asking you to consider is a problem of the moment. It would be a pity, I feel, from your point of view as well, and from the point of view of those you represent, if we deliberately checked the further growth of prosperity or failed to make the best use of it, merely for the sake of pursuing a traditional aim which could perfectly well be taken up again tomorrow with renewed vigour. Let us look at how things are going and just ask ourselves whether today is or is not the right time to risk calling a halt.

One more point: solidarity is the key-note of trade unionism, and I am delighted to hear it sounded so clearly by you. You have done a great deal in giving aid to the poor and destitute, and that brings us to the question of the developing countries. If we are out to do less work, and I am not thinking only of wage- and salary-earners, then I think we should turn over in our minds whether we ought not rather to keep up the effort for the time being and devote the extra earnings and profits gained in this way to assisting these needy peoples. This would surely be solidarity in the truest and widest sense. There will be opportunities I am sure for me to take this matter up with your delegates and others who may be interested.

The temptation to go on speaking to you is strong, especially since I am acquainted with all your propositions, but this would not be seemly in an address of welcome. However, all the matters included in your deliberations here will certainly be discussed between us in due course, since your concerns are the concerns of all of us and of the Government. The points you raise are points for the Government to consider.

After working together for ten years, let us at the conclusion of this meeting reaffirm the wish and the will to continue working together to find solutions to our problems. We shall presumably never see completely eye-to-eye, just as you probably are not all in complete agreement with each other on all matters. But let us be honest with each other and with ourselves and always have the courage to speak our minds. I leave you to your deliberations in this spirit, and wish you success in your efforts on behalf of workers everywhere.

35

'WHAT DOES DISARMAMENT MEAN ECONOMICALLY?'

(From an interview with the *Politisch-Sozialen Korrespondenz*
of November 15, 1959)

*In the year 1959 when the ideal of world disarmament was upper-
most in international politics and there seemed a fair chance that it
might become a reality, the view was put out by various interested
parties—in marked contrast to the exaggerated fear, some years
before, that rearmament would upset the economic structure—that
disarmament would permanently weaken the industrial economy
of the West. And spokesmen behind the Iron Curtain stated fairly
bluntly that, in pressing for disarmament, Communism was
pursuing this aim.*

Question: Are there any economic drawbacks to general, controlled disarmament? According to an old argument, which the
Communists have recently revived, the 'capitalist' countries could
not do without the stimulus of the armaments industry and have
good reason to fear that effective disarmament would upset their
economic life and their whole industrial system. For that reason,
it is said, they are opposed to disarmament. What is your view?

Answer: Whether this or that disarmament plan is feasible or
not is something I would rather not discuss here. In any case, the
free world will have to be careful not to get caught up in a web of
illusions in its attempts to achieve a relaxation of tension. For then
it would lose its freedom of action. The end result would be not
general disarmament but a tilting of the armament scales to one
side. For that reason, so long as the propagandist's shop window
does not offer the necessary guarantees of control and inspection,
all disarmament proposals must be scrutinized with great care and
caution. But we will never turn down any truly sincere and

practicable proposal in which disarmament is put forward as a first step towards genuine relaxation.

In reply to your question concerning the Communist assertion of alleged economic drawbacks to a general disarmament, I can only say quite simply: On the contrary! The Western world would welcome nothing more than to shift production from armaments to capital and consumer goods, which would add to the welfare of mankind. General controlled disarmament would undoubtedly have a very positive and beneficial effect on the economic growth of our nations and would bring a further improvement in their living standards, to say nothing of the spiritual relief of the German people at seeing the problem nearest their hearts—the security of Berlin, reunification and lasting peace—finally resolved.

In many countries a production switch from defence weapons to increased manufacture of goods for the civilian market may create difficulties, but economically and technically these can easily be overcome. One has only to look at the aircraft industry, shipbuilding and the electrical industries to realize how closely linked military and civilian production are. The same is incidentally true of research and development.

The idea that in the course of disarmament there might be a temporary fall in demand springs from a mechanistic turn of mind, for, apart from the fact that any such phenomenon could be offset by a corresponding tax reduction, there is no lack of opportunities for expanding production in any country. It would be too much to hope that, with the disappearance of military expenditure, the burden of taxation will be quickly and appreciably reduced. Many other desirable targets which in every country have had to be shelved in order to satisfy defence requirements would be pursued in place of defence programmes, above all social welfare. Moreover, as I have already said, the industrial countries of the West are committed to increasing their aid to the underdeveloped countries. In the event of a general disarmament a not inconsiderable part of their present defence expenditure could be diverted for this purpose, thereby benefiting the world as a whole.

There will, therefore, be no lack of demand for the funds and means of production which are released. Besides, at the present stage of our economic development there is considerably more anxiety over the failure of supplies to keep pace with growing demand than there is over a possible surplus of productive capacity following a reduction in defence expenditure. The Communist claim that general disarmament would knock the bottom out of the healthy economic situation of the 'capitalist' world and that the crisis which they have been prophesying for so long would finally come is no more than a pipe-dream. It has become more and more remote from reality during the past few years, when economic co-operation within the free world has made great progress, making it easier to avoid recessions.

36

WE ARE NO LONGER LIVING IN METTERNICH'S DAY

(Article in *Die Zeit* of December 25, 1959)

Erhard has often appealed for a fresh approach to politics and for greater cohesion. He repeated his appeal in several newspaper articles in the winter of 1959, of which the following appeared in Die Zeit *on December 25, 1959:*

It follows as a matter of course that, in so far as any dualism is conceivable between politics and economics, the relationship between the two in a changing political world and with a simultaneous process of socio-political expansion must also be constantly changing. The idea that a country's economy operates, as it were, in a sphere of its own, far removed from politics, and that, on the other hand, 'policy' should merely be taken to mean anything that concerns the relations between one country and another, is a concept that belongs to the last century and is no longer in keeping with the requirements of our day and age. Not that the importance of foreign policy should be in any way underrated. But not everything that links or divides nations is properly speaking 'foreign policy'. While political results or decisions undoubtedly impinge on the economy, it is equally true to say that politics is influenced by economic factors.

By defining a given phenomenon as a political or economic question, one cannot do justice to the complexity of national life, in which mutual associations, not priorities, are of first importance. The modern tendency is for every national decision to have repercussions beyond the national boundaries, so that no effective socio-political solutions are now conceivable within narrow national limits, and the more this trend increases, the clearer it becomes that the character and substance of foreign policy is virtually indefinable and that a new political style is needed to mould international relations. Foreign policy as practised in Metternich's day, before the invention of the steam engine or even in the mercantile system, is not an adequate standard for the present day. Where national frontiers are little more than constitutional lines of demarcation and in human terms are of little more than symbolic significance, it is not possible to regard everything that concerns the relationship of one country with others as foreign policy.

Economics now plays a major part in international relations and to a large extent friendship between nations depends upon the fact that their prosperity and social security are products of a free exchange of goods and the movement of capital. What is really essential to the performance of these functions is not technical arrangements such as the drawing-up of an international railway timetable; the crucial problem is a political one which is of increasing importance for the friendly or unfriendly relations between the nations. Nor does departmental authority matter here. What does matter is the attitude of mind and its relevance to contemporary questions. To take an example, if Saharan oil is being discussed in relation to the power supplies of the Common Market, there is not the slightest doubt that this is a question of economic as well as of foreign policy; but it is only the two together that constitute 'policy'.

It is becoming increasingly clear that a country's internal economic and socio-political system determines its relations with other countries. We know all too well from our own experience that contrasting social systems create irreconcilable differences. Friendship or enmity between nations today is not based only on foreign political agreements or disagreements but is usually, though in varying degrees, the expression and emanation of a whole complex of problems which are primarily economic and socio-political in character.

It was certainly true of the last century that if not the sole, at least the predominant, influence in international relations—more often than not motivated by dynastic interests—was foreign policy. In the meantime, however, the people of all nations have come so much closer in countless ways, and at the same time the urge for mutual understanding and co-operation on a supranational plane has become so pronounced, that there is hardly a sphere of human activity in which national isolation is possible. The various forms of economic and political integration and the many institutions which have been set up on a world basis are a constant reminder to us how the shape and, above all, the spirit of international relations have changed. Political alliances, as they existed up to the beginning of this century, are things of the past, although, in view of the threat to the free world, defence communities of vital importance naturally still exist. But they no longer stand by themselves; they are merged into supranational and international associations, the main purpose of which is to increase economic and social welfare. Who would deny, for example, that the nature and extent of the economic relations between the countries of Europe also condition their political relationship! The co-operation between the highly-developed industrial countries in providing fruitful and effective aid to the so-called underdeveloped countries reflects very clearly a lively sense of common responsibility and obligation. And here we have yet another illustration that, while this problem undoubtedly has its political facets, the economic, social and humanitarian idea is uppermost.

Even the relations between the countries of the free and the Communist worlds or the tension between democratic and totalitarian systems cannot in any conservative sense be interpreted in purely political terms. It is significant that the Soviet Union, without prejudice to its political aims, has recently made economic and trade policy a part of its over-all strategy. Krushchev has not only declared in unmistakable terms that the Soviet bloc feels strong enough to increase her production sufficiently in seven years to reach a Western standard of living. He has also expressed his personal conviction that 'capitalism' is incapable of a comparable effort and is condemned to extinction. What is important here is not whether this statement was made in earnest or what credit one can attach to it—the significant feature of it seems to be the change in Soviet tactics, and the inclusion of new weapons in their armoury.

The fact that the Western world—apart from occasional statements by individual statesmen or politicians—has not yet given any definite answer to this challenge gives me an uneasy feeling that a foreign policy which operates for the most part on a traditional and conservative pattern of thought is no longer suited to the present day and its problems. I am convinced that what is needed to meet the threat to our social and economic freedom is not only unanimity of approach but also concerted action to achieve the highest possible concentration of all the productive forces in the free world.

So to my conclusion, that economics or economic policy cannot lead an existence of its own on the fringe of foreign policy. Economic and trade policy, however divided departmental responsibilities may be, are by their very nature an organic whole. The cardinal principles that decide the fate of nations operate both internally and externally and the two cannot be separated.

37

HARMONY BY 'HARMONIZATION'

(Article in *Frankfurter Allgemeine Zeitung* of December 31, 1959)

Much of a politician's work consists in warding off opponents and proposals, frequently well-meant, by actual or ostensible friends—ideas which do not fit in with the politician's own political aims or with the system he is striving to create. From 1945 onwards Ludwig Erhard was compelled to devote a considerable part of his time to combating socialistic ideas of a planned economy. He fought equally hard to establish the spiritual foundations of Germany's economic policy. Only at infrequent intervals did discussions on these questions break out in public:

A politician concerned with economic policy must be constantly on his guard that anything he says is not distorted and that the economic forgers do not bamboozle him. A new idea or thought has hardly been born before soulless rationalists are tossing it about with the result that what finally emerges is a parody of the original and more often than not the direct opposite. During the past few years, when the search was going on for nothing more nor less than a New Order, which, for all its imperfections, nevertheless deserves to be described as free and social, what views have we not heard of the real definition of 'Order'! There has been talk, for example, of a new 'style' of economic policy, which I apparently had to evolve, of an 'active' industrial policy to which I had to devote much of my time. Goodness knows what else was to be 'put in order'! By the word 'order' some understood 'cartels', others 'syndicalism', some 'market controls', others state-intervention in general. There was almost complete confusion.

We are experiencing a similar confusion today with the word 'harmony', which is being bandied about almost daily by people who make it abundantly clear that they do not know what 'harmony' really means. Used in the socio-political sense, 'harmony' presupposes a closely-knit system based upon a free and balanced economy and having as its focal point social justice and a fair distribution of interests in the social and economic life of the nation. The verb 'to harmonize' and the slogan 'harmonization' which derives from it have fundamentally very little in common with harmony.

What is really going on? It seems to me that the chief culprit is a kind of 'social mechanic' whose feverish activities are both spurious and dangerous and who is concerned not with gaining knowledge but with 'constructing' the world in his own image. As he is incapable of appreciating the immensely complex process of co-operation by free individuals because of the mental darkness in which he lives, he needs as simple a recipe as possible, an economic and social mechanism with which he can tinker at will. He has more confidence in organizations and institutions than in the compensatory function of competition in society, or than in free price controls and currency regulation. He believes that a state machine with powerful administrative bodies would offer greater security and that the kind of integration we are trying out in Europe must be accompanied by a higher degree of organized intervention and administrative action.

Perhaps it is fear of the incalculable, of something quite unforeseeable happening on the road to European integration, that explains why so many of these 'social mechanics' are constantly appealing for 'harmonization'. Does this mean 'harmony' by way of 'harmonization'? This is what many understand by the so-called 'equal starting conditions'. Some take it to mean the collaboration of national cartels or their 'integration' in supranational organizations. Others believe that equal tax and social burdens must be the prerequisite of free competition, and uniformity of wages and working conditions follows inevitably. The number of things that should be 'harmonized' is legion! Fortunately the Almightly imposed limits on the folly of egalitarianism when he endowed people with different talents and even with widely divergent interests in work, to say nothing of the varieties of climate and fertility. God, it seems, knew nothing about 'harmonization'.

It is a degradation of science to expect it to prove such 'nonsense'. It is high time this particular form of mental observation

S

was laughed out of court and the whole mischievous farce disposed of. For precisely the opposite is the case: it is the varying factors of environment, production, labour and costs that make an exchange of goods and services between national economies possible. If it were true that national economies willing to integrate could only succeed in doing so if they had the same social standard to begin with, then the results would be disastrous; this would ensure that the strong had absolute power, while the weak would be condemned to extinction. The free convertibility of currencies as a typical form of rational integration has never given rise to the illusion that the countries associated with this system had the same social standards or that they must 'harmonize' with one another. The misconceived word 'harmonization' must mean that national economies, joined together in a common effort, must accept the worst economic, financial and monetary blunders committed by any one partner as binding upon all, instead of accepting a corporate obligation to eradicate such weaknesses. As long as the individual nations in, for example, the European Economic Community retain their sovereignty, the peoples will have to shape or endure their own fate; they will live better or worse than their neighbours, and they will also have different ideals. If by the end of this process there has been a considerable amount of assimilation or even structural change within the various states, 'Gleichschaltung' in Europe will still be inconceivable.

So what are we left with as possible forms of 'harmonization'? A free system which alone can guarantee the expansion of productive capacity, both in goods and in labour, will only tolerate a national 'policy of harmonization' if it stimulates those sectors of the economy which are capable of development, but certainly not if competitive capacity is reduced by a national process of assimilation. Institutions such as a Capital Investment Bank or a 'Mutual Aid' body can only be fully effective in our society if it is associated with private initiative, which should always take precedence. The state has to guarantee and protect the liberal system; it is not its function to lend official support to the establishment of what is alleged to be harmony in all fields.

'Harmony' as a socio-political phenomenon always embraces all fields of human activity. But those who talk of 'harmonization' want to 'create order' in one sector at a time. The 'harmonization' managers make a socio-political jigsaw puzzle out of it and fail to realize that they are atomizing life. One must keep on warning those devotees of order, who think of nothing but subjecting isolated sectors to mechanical rules, that they are grossly underrating the value of an all-embracing order of things.

Remaining on the plane of national or international politics, we also have to consider whether it is right for us to neglect the whole in order to 'integrate' or 'harmonize' isolated sectors of our political life on the basis of departmental requirements. If applied to the European Economic Community this would mean that, in addition to the Ministerial Council responsible, the Ministers of Justice, of Finance, of Transport and so on would be trying to realize their own particular conceptions of harmonization. Now I have too much respect for the expert to reject such a proposition out of hand; but I cannot help feeling that a misconceived departmental confidence, possibly allied to vanity and jealousy, might lead to disintegration rather than cohesion. To take an example, the technical side of a tax system could certainly be 'harmonized', but not the level of taxation. The same is true of transport questions and so on. May we never, at all events, be in the situation of having the component parts in our hands without the spiritual factor that links them together.

I do not subscribe to the mystical belief that he to whom God gives office is also endowed with understanding. What I mean is that, particularly in our time when fateful decisions have to be made, lack of specialized knowledge or scientific expertise cannot be taken as a criterion by which to judge the ability of a politician. To shape the future one must be able to see the present in its full context, in terms of its dynamic forces and its development trends, and one must know how to exploit these. The 'urge to organize and harmonize', on the other hand, leads almost certainly to disaster.

38

THIRTY YEARS OF ECONOMIC POLICY
1929-1959

(Article in *Via Aperta*, No. 12, December 1959-January 1960)

Despite the continuous upwards trend of the economy since the currency reform and despite years of full employment, the German people have not forgotten the horrors of unemployment. Time and again the Federal Minister of Economics is asked if there might not be a repetition of the economic crisis of thirty years before. Professor Erhard has never treated such questions lightly. He bases his firm belief that trade cycles are not inevitable not merely on improved methods of economic policy but above all on his confidence in the stabilizing effect of a liberal economic system and the growing interdependence of national economies. In this article he warns of the dangers that may arise from a misguided desire for security and from group-egoism; he underlines the special responsibilities which fall upon individual nations as their economic and monetary systems become interwoven with those of other countries:

In October 1929 the entire world was profoundly shaken by the collapse of the New York Stock Market which will go down in history as 'Black Friday', and the dramatic economic crisis that followed swept round the globe like a tornado. It is not my purpose here to try to analyse the causes of such a disastrous chain reaction, which crippled national economies and destroyed international unity. It might be useful, however, to pinpoint a few outstanding features which help to explain the profound changes which have taken place in economic and trade policy during the past thirty years. We are not concerned here with apportioning praise or blame but solely with reaching an objective assessment on the basis of which we can pursue and, at the same time, guarantee a policy of stability.

It is common knowledge that the main cause of the crisis in Germany and many other European countries was the fact that they had taken out large, short-term foreign loans, especially in the United States, and had invested the money almost entirely in long-term and largely unproductive projects. As a result the countries in question could no longer meet their international obligations and a process of international disintegration set in over a wide front which inevitably brought with it atomization of the world economy and isolation of national economies. Individual currencies collapsed and with them the international currency system as a whole. This meant that the bonds which held the world most closely together were broken and all kinds of economic, financial and monetary experiments on a national scale became possible. The world economic crisis, in short, resulted not from a too close interlocking of national economies but from a too tenuous relationship between them, which, furthermore, was based on false premises. Symptoms were eradicated but no attempt was made to get at the root of the evil; a system was created and accepted which was more apparent than real and which was technically just workable, because no one had the vision and the courage to produce liberal and organic solutions. An all-embracing, evenly-balanced national and international system, which would have been most appropriate and most consistent, was abandoned in favour of an intricate network of devices, which were more or less unconnected and merely exposed the underlying chaos. This marked the beginning of currency controls, which led to a loss of freedom and a loss of ethics and turned what still remained of genuine foreign trade into a playground for discriminatory practices and the debasement on a national level of real values and achievements. As planned economy ideas gained ground creative initiative was stifled and a feeling of frustration and helplessness engendered an atmosphere of profound resignation. To keep down increasing unemployment by means of a deflationary policy was bound to prove a costly mistake, draining any blood industry still had left.

The vicious circle was complete. A national economy such as that of Germany, which had been given an artificial blood-transfusion and was tied to a severely shrunken world market, was no longer in a position, for reasons already stated, to keep its manpower adequately employed. A steadily dwindling number of workers in employment had to support a steadily increasing number of unemployed. As the national income dropped the national product dropped with it, endangering and even destroying the very foundations of large sectors of the national economies. The effort to satisfy the understandable desire of entrepreneurs to get at least a proportionate share of the shrinking national product and to meet as equitably as possible over the whole range of the national economies or even of any one sector of industry the steadily decreasing demand, which resulted from the drop in national incomes, led to a heightening of nationalist feelings and to an industrial policy which was based on the crazy idea that the evils could be cured by adapting, which in this case meant reducing, production to the level of the demand. In fact, this only made the situation worse, for every drop in production brought a fresh drop in income, more unemployment, increased costs and reduced turnover. When, due to inaction by the various governments and the collapse of the world economy, currencies had dropped so much in value and there was no longer any semblance of order, then it must be admitted that integrity on the part of the entrepreneurs was no longer enough in itself to rectify, much less to rescue, the situation. But this does not alter the fact that the course adopted at the time, namely of trying to find the remedy in cartels, was the most futile of all.

The ideas of a liberal economy, free competition and free price formation, of honest money and international plain dealing were so far removed from the minds of nations and above all of responsible statesmen in those tragic times, that one has a sense of complete unreality when one looks back on them today. But we learned from those tragic events—and we shall not forget the lesson—what it means when individual countries and economies shape their national lives according to the same basic principles and on the same basic pattern, and how important it is—whatever the particular context may be—to lay down economic and social rules that are universally applied.

It would, of course, be both wrong and dangerous to conclude from this that there must be a so-called harmonization of costs and burdens between nations in order to make way for international competition. Any attempt at a levelling-out in the economic and social fields could only introduce a new element of disruption into the economy, for one cannot simply reverse the process of cause and effect.

I do not propose to analyse the most tragic period, from an economic point of view, in Germany's history. I will pass instead to the present, posing the question that interests every citizen in this or any other country, namely, whether we are today immune against a possible recurrence of that political, economic and social disaster. The question can be answered with a flat 'Yes', although this should not be taken to mean that, apart from all sorts of possible political upheavals, our social development might not also be endangered by economic changes. The dangers have merely changed their character. There can be no doubt that we are better equipped today to deal with trade cycles and economic policy in general, and that we have learned from bitter experience. Contrary to many pessimistic forecasts, world economic relations grew closer and closer after the second world war and have today reached a pitch of intensity which makes us aware not only of our bonds but also of our dependence. National currencies over a wide area have again become stabilized and, with the return of convertibility at the end of 1958, were also internationally regulated. Wartime and immediate post-war economic practices in the form of state controls and rationing, price fixing and price cartels have either been completely eliminated or are in the process of disappearing and there is a growing awareness of the blessings of freedom.

On the other hand there is an alarming tendency to try to develop social security in every conceivable form and with a marked collectivist trend. There is no denying that this is hardly likely to encourage initiative or to develop personality and that, if such thinking becomes general, it may cast a deceptive cloak over the essential relationship between outlay and return, productivity and income. This is the surprising phenomenon of our time, that, as increased prosperity has brought improved social security, and as the uniformity of a steady economic upwards trend, which carries no risks with it, has laid the ghost of social hardship, so the cry for more and more collective security grows steadily louder. There may be several explanations for this, in particular those bearing on the tragic political experiences of the past, but nevertheless they do not touch the real heart of the problem, because no state and no national economy can distribute more in the way of social gifts than is earned by the people. Against political disasters in particular there is no social security. This was brought home to us after Germany's collapse, and that is why, in the course of a successful reconstruction programme, we set about making reparations in various forms and creating social justice.

A second problem is in what form international co-operation will develop in the future, both in the political and in the economic sphere. It is clear that the fusion of nation states into one unit must also compel national economies to unite, but the more pressing question, particularly with reference to the Common Market, is whether economic integration must also lead to a political fusion. In a protectionist world I would unhesitatingly answer 'Yes', but a world system, which is tending more and more towards liberalism and freedom of exchange, does not automatically and of necessity mean political consolidation. The aims of the European Economic Community will always presuppose a conscious political will. A better distribution of economic forces within larger economic areas undoubtedly provides better opportunities for an effective trade policy, but it would be foolish to ignore the fact that, particularly in the gestation period of this new entity, a preferential system must create tensions between it and the rest of the world which do not further the cause of a uniform or universal world economy. In the years to come, before this problem is solved, fateful decisions will have to be made.

I cannot help feeling that, for all our good intentions, we are becoming bogged down in attempts to organize and harmonize everything and are thereby not merely losing all feeling for what is really organic and harmonious but are also finding it more and more difficult to achieve. The technical age in which we live doubtless encourages a mechanistic view of our social and political life, and for that reason we must never lose sight of this mortal danger. We believe implicitly in the blessings of freedom, yet we follow paths in our social and political life which lead to a mechanistic—collectivist—way of thinking, and eventually place freedom itself in jeopardy. There are undoubtedly conflicting forces at work which, on the one hand, serve more and more as buttresses of freedom but which, on the other hand, help to undermine it. That is what I was trying to bring out when I referred to the inestimable advantages of a world-wide merging of national economies on the basis of identical, liberal principles but at the same time felt bound to voice my anxiety that new preferential systems might, by their sheer accumulated weight, produce a new brand of international group-egoism.

Let us also not forget that rapid technical developments together with the discoveries of modern natural science must influence the structure, shape and size of industry and that, in consequence, the politicians will be confronted with the urgent problem of how best to avoid the danger of a too great concentration of the means of production in too few hands, in other words, how to safeguard the principles of a Social Market Economy, satisfy the need for a property-owning society, and provide for a large and independent middle class. Personally I believe that 'there is room in this world for all', but such a belief will not always be enough to allay the anxieties of a broad middle-class section of society. On the other hand we can neither aim to create a classless society merely to satisfy a misguided conception of justice, nor can we regard it in these modern times as a practical proposition to revert to the economic ideas of the past and attempt to impose a static system on our dynamic society. The strongest guarantee of a liberal economic and social system is the will of the individual to preserve his personal freedom and not to allow his way of life to become regimented and collectivized.

It is one of the basic principles of the Social Market Economy that the state has an overriding obligation to prevent the abuse of economic power. This is also implicit in the German 'Law against Restrictions on Competition', which is based on the principle that anyone wishing to be free should not possess power, but this also means that anyone possessing power loses part of his freedom. So a close watch must be kept to see that competition in industry is guaranteed and that it is safeguarded against abuses or interference by power-blocks. At the same time, both history and logic show what a crass error it is to believe that a detailed 'control' of industry by the state or by official bodies would cure or prevent the disease, or even to indulge in the illusion that state-owned enterprises, by their very nature, are entirely free from sin. Nothing is more likely to lead to an abuse of power than concentration of power in the hands of a collective. A mere glance at the totalitarian states and their collective economic system is enough to prove this, but there are also countries in the free world whose past sins confirm the justice of my thesis.

A world economic crisis, like the one that broke upon us like a cloud-burst thirty years ago, will certainly not happen again, and it is just as unthinkable that we should have the sort of economic fluctuations in the future that could produce the social distress we experienced in the past. The misunderstood Keynes doctrine is just as much out of date now as the early liberal conception which forbade the intervention of the state in things economic. What means it employs to intervene depends on the pattern of causes and the motives which go to make up a trade cycle and which are by no means always material factors. The accusation frequently levelled against me that my efforts at 'spiritual massage' have nothing to do with market economy is based on *laissez-faire* ideas and takes no account of the fact that trade cycles are conditioned by human behaviour. The factors that influence this behaviour are relatively unimportant. The real danger—and I cannot say this too often—comes from the social planners and romantics, who believe that the complex life of a nation can be reduced to a blue-print, who see the intricate process of free co-operation in purely mechanical terms or who start out with romantic ideas of a social system in which man, as God created him, is a mere abstraction.

It is an insidious poison that is infecting human society and depriving it of its immunity against the deadly germs of collectivism. This is equally true of the political, economic and social spheres of our national life. If therefore, we want to preserve our way of life and our freedom, we must be on our guard and arrest those first symptoms, which, unfortunately, have already left their mark.

39

ECONOMIC POLICY AS A COMPONENT OF SOCIAL POLICY

(Speech to the CDU Federal Congress in Karlsruhe
on April 28, 1960)

*At the very beginning of his career as a political economist, Ludwig
Erhard realized that there was a close connection between economic
and social developments and that they influenced one
another. For that reason he regards it as the aim of economic
policy to do more than just keep the economy sound and give it
impetus. In this policy statement he speaks of the duties incumbent
upon the individual and society:*

Any statement of economic policy, if it is to further the dynamic
expansion of our national and social life, must be constantly under
review in order to link past, present and future together in one
smooth and unbroken harmony. This means that the guiding
principles of economic policy not only leave their mark on society
but are also shaped and altered by it. The echo that economic
policy finds in the minds of a nation will resound all the more if
that policy succeeds not merely in fulfilling its more immediate
aims but also in giving a convincing answer to contemporary
spiritual problems. This does not, of course, mean that it should
adapt itself to every passing whim, romantic dream or unrealistic
demand of this or that group. Truth is not so variable that it
can, like fashion, respond to any and every mood, any more
than the laws of logic can be dissociated from their inherent
necessity.

Ever since the days of the currency reform the policy of the
Social Market Economy has revolved round the central idea of
combining personal freedom, growing prosperity and social
security within the framework of a free, competitive economy and

of bringing nations together by means of a policy of universal plain-dealing.

Who still remembers today the bottomless despair we once felt and have since shaken off? Elementary supply and production problems, unemployment, refugees, the need to restore an efficient commodity and capital market, to create fresh confidence in our new currency and to make the Federal Republic part of a renascent world economy—these were the practical problems which had to be solved if we were not to become a prey to shortages, want and hardship. Today even the opponents of the Social Market Economy no longer deny that it succeeded to an astonishing extent in providing our people once again with a soundly-based livelihood. The CDU/CSU has no need to feel ashamed of the fruits of its policy. This is something that the faint-hearted, even in our own ranks, might bear in mind when they are beset by resentment, disquiet or uncertainty.

It is not in our nature to allow pleasure or pride in work well done to degenerate into vain complacency or even to give rise to the belief that our work is done. But we are not prepared to accept criticism at any price from those who, lacking imagination and original ideas, steal the patent of the Social Market Economy and try to sell this second-hand product as if it were their own. This in itself should dispel quite a few doubts about the rightness of our economic policy, for it means that our political opponents cannot make any headway in the country today unless they renounce their old traditions and ideologies and resign themselves to the sort of liberal system we are advocating.

I do not want to be misunderstood, still less to evade the mental awareness, and above all the self-awareness, which is enjoined upon us by our consciences and by our responsibilities to the German people. That is the purpose of this congress, to ask and to answer questions.

While we have no sympathy with the debased views of those whose cynical egoism leaves no room for social considerations, we are also vehemently opposed to those destructive elements that revel in their enjoyment of material gain and adopt a heartless, snobbish attitude towards what they mockingly refer to as the 'economic miracle' or the 'children of the economic miracle'. They give the people stones instead of bread. We are, on the other hand, ready to welcome anyone who takes life seriously and who, even if he finds much to criticize, is anxious to find something better, to experiment and to help.

I hope you will not take it amiss, however, if I say that I find many criticisms and many judgments highly contradictory. When there were acute shortages and conditions were at their worst I kept hearing people say that a free market economy was no way to solve our problems, and when I contradicted them the reply I usually got was hate and scorn; now we are told that the liberal economic principle is only really equipped to deal with shortages, whereas prosperity and abundance call for quite different principles. 'Common sense becomes nonsense, charity a plague.'

No, what we must do is carry our inner convictions to the logical conclusion and remain true to our ideas. During the past twelve years questions of supply and employment have been uppermost, particularly in relation to an industrial state which is functioning in a confined area, but there have been many indications, such as the increase in personal savings, that the Social Market Economy, as it develops further, will succeed in mastering the problems created by the rise in incomes and property.

No truly sincere person can deny, after the experiences of the past twelve years, that anything we have not so far achieved is in process of achievement, and that any further progress we make in the economic field will, in the first instance, benefit the broad mass of the people. To take only one example, the total of private incomes available for consumption and saving rose by 122% between 1950 and 1958. The net incomes of self-employed have increased by 71%, while the earnings of the mass of the people have gone up by 142%. In making these comparisons, however, we must bear in mind that invisible profits are not included and that the numbers of employed persons increased between 1949 and 1959 from 13.6 millions to 20.1 millions. But this in itself seems to me to be not the least of the achievements of our German economic policy, and it is also worth pointing out that the obvious success of a free economic and social system in Germany has produced a more and more pronounced trend towards market economy methods in other parts of the free world. One can, indeed, say that the basic pattern, which Alfred Müller-Armack and Wilhelm Röpke were largely instrumental in creating, has so far proved itself as to be generally accepted today as the prototype of a world-wide system of free trading.

What then is lacking? Why is it that, for all the achievements and the almost grandiose triumphs of the Social Market Economy, people are still not entirely content and society is not entirely satisfied? How is one to explain the fact that, despite security of employment and growing production in a steadily expanding economy, people are still not satisfied? The prevailing and all too obvious unrest in our democratic society is alarming. When times were bad it was barely noticeable, whereas today it is quite apparent and, as an endemic weakness of any free society, seems hard to counteract. Where perfectly understandable differences of opinion emerge they meet head-on in an atmosphere overcharged with emotion, and we have not found any routine method of keeping such clashes within bounds. If storms blow up through lack of proportion and restraint we are certainly justified in recalling all that has already been achieved and, where it seems advisable, in making an ethical appeal. I quite realize that such appeals are limited in their effect, and yet I am confident that one can appeal to people's consciences and ask them to reflect on the true values of life.

This raises the question whether the unrest and excitablity of the general public do not have their roots in the deeper recesses of their consciousness, which can only mean in the still unsolved problems of a free society. I do not believe for one moment that our achievements are being deliberately and maliciously misunderstood. Material living standards have so obviously improved that simple denial is not possible. But that is precisely why it is so surprising that these material improvements should have produced on every side an almost irrational, negative reaction.

On closer reflection we may come to the conclusion that, where a democratic society such as ours has undergone tremendous industrial expansion and has been shaken to its foundations, a special effort is needed to evolve a social policy which will encourage a new approach to life in keeping with the times. Probably all that is needed in many cases is a conscious reappraisal of the bonds that still exist between the individual and his environment, 'his' world. Let us not overlook the fact, however, that industrialization, the development of our transport system, the loosening of traditional bonds with the home or the job, and a loss of independence have all had a serious, adverse effect on our society. Our form of society has been described figuratively as a 'classless society'. This concept, which has undergone a considerable historical change, can be taken to indicate not merely that the rise of the working class led to a process of deproletarization which is still going on, but also that the property-owning and professional layers of society have become fluid and that, throughout the whole range of modern consumer goods right up to the motor-car, the television set and all gadgets designed to lighten the burden of housework, a highly desirable trend, the market for consumer goods is widening, with the result that class privileges are disappearing and will continue to disappear. In this 'classless society' the great problem is one not of class but of the individual, the average man, who feels that he is subordinate to the community and therefore has a sense of insecurity. The problem of how and where he finds his rightful place in professional and social life is undoubtedly much more difficult to solve than it was in *dirigiste* systems. There is also the fact that trade cycles, market fluctuations and changes in production appear to involve him in mechanical processes which are impersonal and leave him dissatisfied because he finds it hard to understand how these forces work. The more such uncertainty leads to a vague feeling of anxiety, the less surprising it is that people escape from their sense of isolation by forming groups and organizations, which in their turn give public expression, in amplified form, to the individual's inner disquiet.

A process such as this naturally not only produces effects which heighten the danger both of atomizing and of collectivising life, but also intensifies the desire of the individual for some kind of bond in which he can find warmth and security. The more intimate communities of the family and the church are thus supplemented by social groups of people with common interests in the form of clubs or other associations. I would even go so far as to say that human nature needs some kind of personal com-

pensation, of spiritual balance, some way of reconciling the purely
practical requirements of one's daily work, which condition one's
relationship with society as a whole, with the desire for peace and
security in mental and spiritual associations. It is asking too much
of the Social Market Economy to expect it to break down the
visible social manifestations of our present-day life and recreate
them on an idealistic basis. But it does have an obligation to live up
to the precepts of a Christian social policy and to implement them
in a better society.

Seen in terms of economic policy, the problem is one of working
towards a humanization of our environment in all spheres of life
but particularly in the economic sphere.

If this is not to remain a mere phrase we must translate our
general purpose into specific principles to be actively incorporated
in our economic and social policy. Alfred Müller-Armack has ideas
on this subject which we have developed together and which will
soon be the subject of a more detailed report. To avoid any misunderstanding, let me say that we have no intention of renouncing
the prevailing principles of the Social Market Economy. Life does
not progress by fits and starts, any more than economic and social
developments can be reduced to a series of acts; they must always
be seen as a continuing process. The Social Market Economy has
been regarded by its spiritual founders, ever since its inception, as
one coherent economic policy. But, in view of the standard of
productivity we have achieved in our industry today, of the steadily
improving position of our national income, and of the hopeful
prospects of spreading ownership, more and more can be done in
the future to give concrete expression to that coherent policy in
broad social terms. Although it would be a mistake to consider
this problem solely from the ethical view-point, nevertheless one
should not underestimate the importance and the advisability of
ethical values even in the economic sphere. But to imbue our social
system with moral content would be a fruitless task if concrete
ways and means could not also be found to create a society of free
people. So the Social Market Economy did not prove itself merely
by virtue of the idea it represents but essentially because its aim is
to combine the practical methods of economic policy with the ideal
of social security in economic freedom.

In the spiritually unsettled conditions of the so-called 'classless society' it will, therefore, be necessary to build in social stabilizers which are designed to counteract the modern trend towards isolation of the individual and to give him the consciousness, and indeed the objective assurance, that he is living in a unified and coherent society. It is fairly clear that to the average man that is less easy to understand than a *dirigiste* principle, but this does not seem to me a valid criterion. From a political view-point, the problem is to overcome the suspicions aroused by a free market economy and to realize that a purely intellectual solution is no longer adequate to meet the problems of our modern society. The flow of its technical expansion and sociological transformation is so rapid and so powerful that it becomes increasingly difficult to take our bearings on the river bank behind us, unless we also study the currents themselves.

Of course the policy of the Social Market Economy has come to stay. I would even emphasize that we and the Western world as a whole have every justification for claiming the birthright to a far better economic policy, which is based on the principle that industry must, first and foremost, serve man, and which, in view of the sharpening competition with the collectivist world, must not be sacrificed or betrayed. A collectivist-totalitarian economic system, which in the final analysis serves only to glorify and increase the power of the state, can achieve great success in the easily controllable field of the basic industries but it will always remain incapable of serving man, in other words of providing the rich abundance of goods which gives the individual consumer a free choice and which enriches and beautifies his life. We would be contemplating the worst of all possible solutions if we were pre-pared to accept primitive leanings towards and ideas of a policy that aimed at egalitarianism, regardless of whether or not it stems from ignorance of social and economic conditions, while in the Soviet-dominated world forces might be at work to make people conscious, however slowly, of their God-given rights.

The latter would be a blessing, but a reconciliation in midstream would be a calamity.

It follows from all this that, in the future development of the Social Market Economy, problems of social policy will rank

T

equally with economic problems. The need for our economic system to develop further in this direction has been recognized for years by those intimately concerned with this problem. But it is a problem that must be tackled in its entirety. Efforts to create new forms of property undoubtedly deserve every support, but they are limited in their scope in that they make only a material contribution towards solving the problems of different income and property-owning groups in society. The attempt to interpret our social problems purely and simply in terms of the industrial 'middle class' suffers from the same limitation. Important as it is to keep a balance between the various forms of industrial enterprise, we must strive in our social policy not merely to safeguard the existence of independent units at present in being, but perhaps still more to encourage a spread of independence, otherwise we shall find ourselves the prisoners of a backward-looking ideology. From the view-point of social policy, the attaining of independence in whatever shape or form must, in fact, take priority over mere survival. This does not mean that our entire attention should not be directed to considering whether present legislation covering, for example, taxation or industrial companies does not unwittingly favour enterprises of a certain kind or size and thereby militate against others.

A social policy which aims to be more than just an ideology and to be realistic and progressive must have as its basis the actual conditions of our economic environment, and this means developing aims which also do justice to the large industrial organizations that have kept pace with modern technology. However clear our purpose might be, we would be frittering away our energy in a purely *pro forma* struggle against concentration of power if we were not prepared to admit that the large industrial units in our economy have achieved a great deal and can rightly claim to have made a major contribution to the general growth of prosperity. It is not the large concern as such but the unbridled lust for power that tends to produce the sort of concentration which is harmful to our national economy and socially undesirable and to which we are therefore opposed. So it is our intention to restrict, and indeed to suppress, all restrictive or monopolistic control of markets by introducing further legislation to protect competition and by pursuing an appropriate taxation policy. But wherever the market is influenced by a lowering of prices and society benefits, then we should acknowledge that such an influence is indispensable. This implies, of course, that even large concerns must recognize that they too have social obligations, especially as they can do much to expand the independent, self-supporting sector of industry. To take only one example, they can leave certain functions and services to independent suppliers. The more liberal our economic system becomes the more importance will accrue to the larger industrial concerns, but this certainly does not mean that intermediate enterprises must go to the wall. Let us also never forget, when we are thinking of our social policy for the future, that we are not alone in the world and that competition will, in fact, increase, from which it follows that our aims must conform to what is actually possible. As no one, either in our personal or our national life, can give more than he has, we would be gambling not only with our future as a nation but also with our social security if we demanded more of the national economy than it is capable of producing to meet its world commitments.

Several attempts have been made, particularly during the last few years, to benefit certain sectors of our society by adjusting taxes. It seems to me, however, that such a social policy, which confines itself to technical measures, is not sufficient to meet the psychological situation we are confronted with. The social blueprint we have to develop must do more than just prescribe certain individual measures to be taken; it must open up a complete vista of social policy, the aims of which can command the moral support of the mass of the people. What this means can best be imagined if we think of the appalling developments in East Germany, where free peasants are enslaved and the independent artisan is deprived of his livelihood.

No one would now deny that the Social Market Economy has provided this kind of comprehensive blue-print, more particularly during the period when our economic policy was undergoing a complete transformation. But today we have a new responsibility, namely to evolve a social policy for the future which will supplement and also perpetuate the functions of the Social Market Economy. As I have said time and again, the focal point of our

economy is the individual. It is now up to us to translate this incontrovertible general principle into concrete terms, and in so
doing we will find the the economic basis established by the Social
Market Economy can serve as the foundation for a continuing process of development.

Although social policy and economic policy must be regarded as
not so much coexisting as cohabiting, nevertheless there is bound
to be a certain shift of emphasis in that social policy embraces a
wider field in which not only the resources of the Federation, the
Länder and the Provinces are involved but all private concerns,
associations, organizations and enterprises should also participate.
This does not mean that we should now make an all-out effort to
forget, on principle, the lessons we have learned and break new
ground at any price. In many cases it will simply be a question
of reinforcing developments which are already under way, of in-
corporating what we have learned and seen in one coherent scale
of values, and of making the individual the conscious purpose and
objective of our social policy.

There is no doubt, for example, that modern industrial development requires more specialized production in every department,
whether technical or administrative, whether in business, education or in professional training. This almost structural growth of
education and training compels us to invest more and more in
intellectual capital, in order to make it easier for young people
who are trying to find their true place in society to embark on a
professional career and gain advancement. Apart from the
material, utilitarian effect achieved, the main sociological value
lies in making this advancement so apparent that the individual's
fear of not being able to find his way in this mass-society is overcome.

No less important is our responsibility to encourage independence. Here it is not enough simply to think of a 'middle-class'
policy, however strongly we may defend it. Independence in a free
society cannot be confined to specific groups, and it is equally
wrong to try to secure existing positions by measures which are
likely to debase or even destroy a genuine competitive impulse. The
process by which men of the most varied professions become independent is not something that can be institutionalized, nor can

we hope to start at every point in exactly the same conditions. In view of the many forms of assistance already being given to the professions, partly by limiting competition, and also in view of the difficulty of entry by means of examination and so on, an effort should be made to offer those who want to be self-supporting certain inducements which will encourage them to accept the risks involved. A policy with this in view would increase the element of competition and would not cut across the basic principles of our market economy. In so far as economic independence rests upon genuine achievement it is a social asset which should be maintained and expanded. In this connection we should consider whether existing legislation does not unwittingly create incentives on the one hand and disincentives on the other.

By and large, of course, the problem of economic independence will be confined to small and medium-sized concerns and to the professions. But it seems to me to be just as important to give the formally dependent employees and workers in heavy industry enough freedom of action to enable them to play their part in a free society. This process must be further developed and expanded from the beginnings that have already been made and every opportunity within the industries themselves must be explored of so organizing the work of both employees and manual labour that groups can be formed and responsibilities allotted which gave the individual a sense of relative but nonetheless growing independence. There is a great opportunity here to create a new and genuine middle class in a more modern sense of the word. The state will provide the initial stimulus but will also be in a position to lend practical assistance. What has hitherto been largely dependent on private initiative should, after an experimental period, become an integral part of our social policy. And let us not forget that full employment provides a particularly sound material basis on which to bring such ideas to fruition!

While, therefore, the individual and society can only be reconciled if each person is given the opportunity to find his niche in society by providing him with suitable training and scope, any such policy is incomplete unless an effort is also made to allay people's fears, justified or unjustified, of the machinery of a free economy against which they feel more or less helpless. Most important in this respect is to maintain a stable currency, a factor of increasing sociological importance. When a private citizen earns enough to acquire capital he must be free of anxiety about what he has acquired. If even hard-currency countries could not hold out entirely against the perhaps slight but nevertheless perceptible trend towards devaluation, this imposes on a country's economic policy the responsibility to resist such a softening-up process still more firmly in the future. And it must be taken as a hopeful sign that such an undisputed expert as the President of the International Monetary Fund should have spoken of a new era in which the world must learn to live without price inflation, and added that those who are the first to learn will profit most from the future.

But we can only be certain of succeeding if the entire German people in all groups and classes can be made to realize that the Notenbank and the Government cannot master this alone and that people must exercise self-discipline. When, for example, the SPD in their programme claim that there is an obligation on the Government to produce a national budget but stress at the same time that the social partners are under no obligation of any kind, they are taking up a clear stand against any positive social policy.

To arrive at the right proportions of national investment, private consumption and state expenditure, taking account of net exports and savings, requires more than just a mathematical calculation. There is no absolute long-term recipe; the only solution is for all the component elements of a social system to work together consciously and responsibly to achieve the objectives which the nation is capable of pursuing. It cannot be said too clearly that a monetary and economic policy which concerns itself solely with repairing the damage caused by irresponsible behaviour will never be satisfactory. The logical consequence of this is not for the state to influence investment or wage levels but for it to make the industrial community realize how these factors are interrelated and so induce them to behave accordingly. Anyone who feels that there are hidden strains and stresses here which are intractable is giving a false meaning to the idea of freedom and is closing his eyes to the fateful question on which our future will largely depend.

This also raises indirectly the problem of trade cycles or the working man's fear of crisis. The fact that the expansion of the national economy as a whole, which has been going on for twelve years, shows signs of slackening in individual sectors can be taken as symptomatic of a liberal system and not least of a free consumer market. The free entrepreneur must be prepared to accept such shifts and adjustments as part of his function, just as workers of all categories must feel quite certain that they are not being helplessly exposed to some impersonal market manoeuvre. Perhaps the best indication that this is not so is the fact that such fluctuations are accompanied by an increase of labour productivity and that an economic policy geared to expansion will strengthen and stabilize the social and personal situation of the employed. Moreover, production switches of this kind will become necessary as part of the international division of labour at which we are aiming, and they also have a salutary and beneficial effect.

Germany's initiative in proposing that a supranational trade policy should be worked out by the Atlantic powers met with general approval. Just as we have elevated the competitive system as envisaged by our friend Franz Bohm so to speak to the level of official policy, so trade policy should also become a recognized feature of our social policy. Considerable work will no doubt have to be done on the public and on the individual to make it clear that the free societies of the West have the means to defend themselves against the recurrence of crisis which every Communist since Lenin has been hoping would undermine the democratic states. The economic and social developments of the past twelve years have already shown, however, that the spectre of unemployment has been effectively and finally banished.

What we are striving for is a social policy inspired by the determination to create a clear and coherent mental image of the sort of environment in which the individual can live in freedom and security. This implies a better over-all view of every sphere of our national life. Whereas in the early period, when we were rebuilding our economy, sheer necessity forced us to concentrate on material problems, as we look to the future we shall give more attention—without neglecting the material side—to improving and, indeed, humanizing our environment. And we are not prepared to hand over the responsibility for developing our economic and social system to a party which has only just begun to grasp what we planned and fought so hard to implement twelve years ago in the teeth of their resistance.

So much importance attaches to working conditions in our factories that we must make an intensive effort to improve them. Until now issues concerning the factory laws have bulked largest. To mention only a few examples, questions of accident prevention, of health, of air pollution, and so on, are increasingly important where severe nervous strain is involved and where demands are made. They point to something like Alexander Rüstow's *Vitalpolitik,* a policy which looks beyond the economic to man as a vital unit. We cannot safeguard this unity of the human environment solely through the family, important as this question is. Modern man is compelled to live in a much wider environment, of which his job forms an integral part. Future legislation must embody the basic assumption that more exacting standards will have to be applied than were in force at a time when the factory was regarded as primarily a mechanical workshop. Yet another indication that the Social Market Economy is on the right lines is the fact that in so many of its principles the production target, even where the internal organization of the factory is concerned, is closely related to the sociological aims.

I am becoming more and more convinced that the problem of social environment must now be tackled in as concrete terms as possible and with the accent on the human element. During the past decade, when our industry and our communications were undergoing enormous development, we released two forces which were answerable, as it were, only to the logic of their own expansion and which did lasting damage to the natural form of life. Despite prolonged scientific and practical experiments, we have not yet succeeded—apart from a few lucky exceptions—in producing even the rudiments of a real solution of our accommodation problem. Romantic visions such as the dispersal of industrial areas have merely served to bring genuine plans for a better utilization of space into disrepute.

The scientists who represent these views believe that the less the need is felt for active state intervention in industry, the more it should concern itself with the specific, concrete problems of environment. The best example of this is the competitive system as a framework, erected by the state, within which a free society can function. In a very interesting analysis which was recently made of the sociological aspects of our urban development it was clearly shown that, while city-dwellers enjoy city life, they avoid the city centres on the grounds that they no longer offer the facilities for orderly public life. Hence the drift into the suburbs and the country by people who are not seeking the beauties of nature but are natural town-dwellers deprived of the kind of life they want to live. The result is a senseless, nerve-wracking human shuttle-service, which makes people restless and excitable, despite the fact that they are enjoying greater prosperity.

This raises problems which should not be dealt with on a casual, hand-to-mouth basis. What we must do is plan urban and rural areas on an ambitious, functional scale. The classification of our towns and cities into commercial and administrative centres, places of education and culture, residential districts and communication-points is something that cannot be left entirely to local authorities but calls for a collective effort which will have to be backed by central funds. And, in view of the dynamic technical forces at our disposal, it is naturally out of the question that we should embark upon a meaningful transformation of our environment with no more in mind than a static reconstruction programme. If we are to introduce harmony and balance into the life of our cities, then it seems to me important that, in planning them, we should provide as much space for people in their natural role of pedestrians as for mechanized transport.

To anyone who appreciates the importance of those facets of our free society which I have outlined must come the conviction that the economic policy of tomorrow will not only have to continue performing its present tasks but will also acquire new ones. Everything points to the fact that the present rate of development of our production will increase still further and that, as a result, the present divergence of views between those who favour the traditional and those who favour a more modern approach to the planning of environment will become even more marked, particularly with the rapid technical advances in industrial production. Social policy, too, will be compelled not merely to continue performing its present functions but also to take account of the change in the over-all situation, for with growing expansion more and more people and even larger categories of people are earning the sort of livelihood that should make them more self-reliant. This means that cases where help is genuinely needed can be treated more generously and more humanely.

But modern social policy in the free world must not be merely inward-looking. Our economic and social life is largely dependent on the world-wide ramifications of our economy, and in consequence our internal national structure can only be properly judged and effectively moulded if we are constantly aware of the implications of our economic dependence on the outside world. Seen in this light, European integration at all levels and in all forms acquires an almost prophetic significance. As you know, we are striving at this very moment to find a solution which will guarantee that the European countries are treated as one and without discrimination, which will foster friendship without having to damage friendship. A short time ago I pointed out how important it is that, within the widest possible context of the free world, our country itself should derive from its economic environment the degree of security necessary to preclude any damage to our society.

There is another problem, that of aid to underdeveloped countries, which is of paramount importance but which I can only touch upon here. In those countries and continents the really urgent problem is one of supply. The general public throughout the world is becoming more and more anxious and ready to help. What is needed is to devise ways and means whereby the underdeveloped countries can increase their own output by methods which are applicable to them. But it seems to me particularly important to organize the aid from outside in such a way that it becomes a co-operative effort and does not provide yet another excuse to divide up the world into spheres of interest and influence.

I have tried to show how the functions of the Social Market Economy in a free society go far beyond what has in fact been achieved. In view of the fact that personal savings are widespread and on the increase and that our industry can meet at least a considerable proportion of its own production and investment needs, to that extent the state should be relieved of the many subsidies to private industry, which still represent a substantial financial burden. Given this appreciable relief and bearing in mind also that economic expansion provides the state with additional resources, the public services should be reorganized and expanded, both quantitatively and qualitatively, along the lines I have already suggested. For the public services play a major part in shaping the environment in which, quite apart from our domestic and professional routine, we lead much of our lives.

To sum up, we know today that the development of our public services has not kept pace with the growth of industrial production. The means required to plan our environment are treated as residual items in our budget surpluses; they receive no serious consideration because group interests are not prepared to support them.

The fact that, in spite of the growing volume and variety of consumer goods, people are still unsettled can be taken as an indication that material prosperity loses its savour if the life of the individual does not fit organically into an environment which both the individual and society find congenial.

Of course, a mere quantitative increase in the funds set aside for public services is not enough. What is needed is a qualitative reorientation in the direction I have suggested, which will follow a detailed blue-print and will give a new urgency to the search for new standards in planning the structure of our society.

It will be our party's responsibility to present this blue-print to people so clearly and so incisively that it will not merely appeal to their heads but also stir their emotions and become a goal worth striving for. To fill the vacuum of which we are all conscious is the real purpose to be achieved by the integration of our society. Just as the Social Market Economy was only feasible on the basis of common values and convictions, so our need today is for an idealistic realism which will bind all groups of society together in a common will.

Any liberal system must proceed from the assumption that freedom is one and indivisible and that elementary human freedom in all spheres of life must go hand in hand with political, religious, economic and spiritual freedom. The strategy of collectivist thinking has always been to split up this most essential and most universal of human values as a means of making inroads into the free system itself. So that system can only be made secure if we bring home to the German people that their social and economic life, in all its manifestations and ramifications, is the outward expression of an inner will and a spiritual fulfilment. When our economic and social policy is seen in this light it will be in a position to make a vital contribution to the cause of peace and will thereby satisfy the desire of our people to share in one all-embracing way of life.

40

THE FAINT-HEARTED WILL GO UNDER

(Article in *Bonner Informationen aus erster Hand* of July 8, 1960)

Increasing pressure was brought to bear on the Federal Republic to make a higher material contribution to the development of the backward countries. The size of the contribution which we could afford to make for this purpose was a question that dominated not only international conferences but also public discussions in general. As many problems, including domestic ones, still remained to be solved, 'development aid' was not, and still is not, universally popular. But something that is really essential cannot be weighed up in terms of popularity. In this article Ludwig Erhard addresses himself primarily to parliamentarians and publicists:

For years the foreign policy of the free West towards the Communist states was like a single-track railway. It was determined solely by external circumstances. All practical or even speculative attempts to find a completely new point of departure came to nothing in face of the glaring clarity of Moscow's aims. The West's ability to manoeuvre in the field of foreign policy was restricted to blocking each Soviet forward thrust as soon as it was made.

In the meantime the hollowness of Moscow's coexistence phraseology has become so obvious that in the Federal Republic even the Social Democratic Opposition, which at one time favoured all kinds of foreign political experiments, has produced an election slogan for 1961 which barely disguises the fact that it has taken shelter behind the same objective views held by the Federal Government, against which it has been fighting for eleven years.

But it is the abiding tragedy of the Social Democrats that their moments of truth always come too late. Those who cry out today for a 'joint' foreign policy and take this to mean simply a readiness to march more or less in step along the same foreign political road as we have been pursuing for twelve years, they themselves are lagging far behind. It has become almost a commonplace to remark upon the almost breathtaking speed with which major international developments are becoming detached from the dualism of the sole remaining military giants, the USA and the USSR.

Every African country that achieves its independence, that gains a seat and a vote in the world parliament of the United Nations, that takes its place in the Concert of Nations; every Asiatic country that is faced with the alternative of improving the lot of its rapidly increasing population either by following the totalitarian examples set by Moscow and Peking or by modelling themselves, as circumstances permit, on the natural and more effective Western patterns—all these new, emergent forces have given the concept of external power a new meaning. These nations wield power simply because they represent the majority of the world's population, and, whichever direction they choose to take, they will eventually help to change the face of the modern world. They are world powers of crucial importance.

But these countries do not form a solid bloc. Most of them are just embarking on the first stage of development of their new-found nationalism. And for that very reason their entry with full and equal rights into the realm of world politics marks the beginning of an epoch in which the distribution of power will be in a constant state of flux. One possibility, which many must have believed had been relegated to the past, now looms up again, namely, of conducting foreign policy strategically to realize major, carefully planned conceptions and employing day-to-day tactics in their proper role of a flexible means to an end. But great conceptions are not plucked out of the air. They must be developed and then pursued. Twelve years ago we developed our European conception and since then we have followed it through unwaveringly in the face of adversity and at considerable material sacrifice to its final realization. The same is basically true of our future policy, which, on the present European basis, should lead to a working partnership with the emergent countries of Asia, Africa and South America.

As is the case in Europe and in the Atlantic Defence Community, this policy of aid for development will be strongly in-fluenced by initial economic achievements and financial moves. And there are further efforts we shall have to make, for we have not the slightest reason to assume that the military measures in defence of our freedom will, in the foreseeable future, take second place behind the new politico-economic efforts to maintain and develop our way of life.

At this point financial considerations come into play and what has so far been largely a theoretical discussion develops all kinds of practical implications. There is the question whether in a modern industrial society the parliamentary form of government, with the steadily-increasing burdens it has to carry, can take vigorous enough action.

Those who do not believe that our four years' parliamentary mandate imposes an obligation to act to the best of our ability, that it is merely an interval between two elections, will confine themselves, out of expediency, to activities which promise actual or apparent popularity. Those who are given to thinking first and foremost of election tactics will begin, in the middle of the four-year cycle at the latest, to make generous promises rather than to ask for special sacrifices, even though these may be in the best interest of the entire people.

But, as far as the Federal Parliament and Government are con-cerned, there is, on the whole, room for some confidence. After all, we recognized the need for national defence and accepted the material consequences of it at a time when it seemed far from popular and when our economic situation was nothing like so sound as it is today. Without shrinking from unpopularity we used enormous amounts of money from our taxation revenue to press on with our country's reconstruction, and with the same end in view we decided to forgo a substantial amount of revenue from taxation in certain sectors, although it would have been better vote-catching tactics to adopt quite a different fiscal policy. We shall have to act with the same resolution and insight if we are to achieve a sufficient increase in our output to enable us to help the people of Asia, Africa and Latin America in their development, and so enable them to help themselves in close partnership with the free countries of the West.

We shall have to consider whether we should continue to distribute billions of marks of the taxpayer's money each year in state subsidies, now that our economic situation has vastly improved and many of these subsidies are no longer absolutely necessary—agriculture, which is facing particularly acute problems in all industrial states, is a notable exception. We shall have to look round for possible ways of offering tax concessions—such as the methods we adopted for the reconstruction of our own country—in order to make it easier for private industry to make a start in under-developed countries, an objective which would profit our own industry as much as the host countries themselves.

We shall have to guarantee specialists who wish to take employment in the developing countries—how many there are will depend on the effectiveness of our development aid—the appropriate financial and professional inducements. We shall have to interest young people more than we have done in taking a stake and sounding out the great possibilities in these countries. And after that we shall have to decide whether the additional expenditure and the drain on our revenue can be covered by growing economic strength alone or whether we must accept certain additional burdens.

Of one thing we can be absolutely certain: anyone who is prepared to shirk necessary sacrifices in order to court immediate popularity is violating the most vital principle of parliamentary democracy. Moreover, the electorate will surely catch him out and condemn him when today's omissions lead to serious setbacks tomorrow and place our security, the survival of our free society and our welfare in jeopardy.

41

THOUGHTS ON THE DEVELOPMENT OF AFRICA

(Address to the German Africa-Society in Bonn on October 21, 1960)

Development aid, to be effective, requires something more than a readiness and capacity on the part of the donor countries to supply material and personnel. It is just as important that the developing countries themselves should weigh up their own potentialities. In a successful partnership, therefore, the donor countries must be prepared to provide the developing countries with advice and practical assistance, based on their own experience and on their knowledge of what is economically relevant, possible and necessary, even at the risk of finding now and then that their conclusions are unwelcome. In this connection, the Federal Republic, whose rapid rehabilitation has been closely watched by the developing countries, has a special responsibility, not least to its own taxpayers.

The President of the Bundestag, at whose instigation this meeting was arranged, gave me my subject and at the same time warned me that I must promise no more than the Government can carry out. I shall stick to this! But let me first say a few words on the meaning of the terms 'development aid' and 'developing countries'.

It has frequently been my experience that they can lead to misunderstandings through being used in a 'grading' and, in the worst case, a 'down-grading' sense. There is, of course, more than one type of 'developing country', a phrase which covers countless different forms and endless variations. Perhaps I can best sum up the situation, that is, be most objective, if I say that I myself still regard Germany as a 'developing country', for any nation that is striving for something better is in process of developing.

After these preliminary remarks I can turn now to my real subject and pose the question which we are asking almost daily. How can we best come to grips with the problem of development aid, what are the possible solutions offered to us, and what are the most fruitful means of achieving, both for the giver and for the receiver, the maximum usefulness—I prefer to say the most successful results—not only in material and financial but also in spiritual terms?

One is tempted to believe that we should be able to press forward from the first stages of a development, which by our technical standards may seem primitive, immediately to the latest forms of modern technology, from automation to the use of atomic power. I believe this would be a mistake. I do not mean that you should pass through all the stages we have passed through in 120 years of industrialization, much less than you should allow the same time to elapse. That, of course, would be a bad prescription. The truth surely lies somewhere in the middle. There is no doubt —and we ourselves are dimly aware of it when we think of the dread possibility that our modern knowledge of the natural sciences might run out—that revolutionary changes threaten to throw us spiritually off balance. It is not only the mind but still more the heart and soul of man that are overstrained when he jumps more or less from nothing into the modern technical age, even assuming that it can be controlled.

It is also dangerous to believe—and this is on roughly the same plane—that success can only be guaranteed by building symbolically large mammoth concerns. I would be the last to deny that in the right place, these too can serve their purpose, as, for example, when it is thought necessary to instil in this or that nation a firm belief that a fresh beginning will succeed. But, by and large, it seems to me much more appropriate to launch a development programme on the broadest possible basis, comprising not only the exploitation of material wealth such as mineral resources and improving agricultural productivity, but also the establishment and development of an indigenous industrial economy. I am firmly convinced that the desire of peoples to progress from poverty and hardship to prosperity and social security can no longer be satisfied merely by improving agricultural methods and exploiting natural wealth, but that industrialization is indispensable. There may be people in Europe who are critical or sceptical of such a view, who may even condemn it if they believe, quite wrongly, that a growth of industrialization in other countries must reduce our own chances. The problem of development aid raises many questions, not all of which are material ones, and it also must not be regarded as primarily a political problem; it must, in fact, be construed as a problem of humanity, in the best sense of the word, as imposing a moral obligation, if the aid we offer is to be accepted with trust or, indeed, accepted at all.

Apart, however, from any question of interpretation, the problem before us is how to induce people to take certain forms of action which are indispensable if a country is to pass through a process of development that alone can produce the desired economic and social effect? It has been said—I hear it everywhere—that the Federal Republic has so far done too little in this direction. It is naturally difficult to apply any objective standards to what is possible or necessary, but one thing I would like to say—and I mention it not as an excuse but so that the conduct of our country and our people may be better understood. Faced with the complete collapse of our political, economic and social life, with extreme hardship and the necessity to rebuild modern technical equipment, faced with the disintegration of our state and social system and the elimination of German capital, our first task was to re-establish and reconstruct the foundations of our own national existence. This has nothing to do with egoism, for only a sound national economy and a prosperous people can afford to offer development assistance. Today, having fought our way back—although we have not yet completed the journey—and reached a point where our material and financial prospects are steadily improving, you can be sure that the problem of development aid will meet with more and more sympathy in our country, not only from the Government and the Parliament but also, I believe, from the people themselves, thanks to their sense of responsibility. And this problem will be with us more and more as time passes.

This meeting takes place at a moment—you may think it a 'coincidence'—when we in the Federal Republic are seriously considering how we can build up a development fund which, to begin with, will establish a basis for effective investment and at the same time will ensure that this fund is not suddenly exhausted but can be renewed from fresh sources. I am in a position to reveal to you and, above all, to my German friends that this fund will almost certainly be on a bigger scale than we had dared hope or assume. If Germany is being criticized today throughout the world for her high balance-of-payments surpluses, because they are a disruptive factor not only here at home but also in those countries in which positive trends take a negative turn, we propose to answer this not entirely justified accusation by trying to reduce our surpluses by exporting more capital and thereby also giving substantial assistance to the developing countries.

I am firmly convinced that, from every point of view, we are starting on a new phase, not only as regards our moral position, not only in relation to the world political situation, but also in terms of present material resources—and I hope it will be a fruitful phase for all and that it may contribute further to understanding and reconciliation between the nations.

And now I pose the question again. What is the best way? It is certainly true to say that the model of a free social economy—known here in Germany as Social Market Economy—is not one that can be slavishly followed by or imposed on other countries, and that even the principles underlying it cannot be applied unreservedly in the developing countries. Certain modifications will always have to be made to fit in with local circumstances. But these modifications must not be so far-reaching as to destroy the essence of a liberal system. When development plans were first mooted many were convinced that industrialization of developing countries must of necessity be based on a state-controlled economy, because, in the absence of sufficient private capital, the state alone with its managerial resources was in a position to promote and carry through a programme of economic development. Here and there this may be the case, and I am the last person to wish to throw out the baby with the bath water; in principle I take the view that what has to be done in the infrastructural field is primarily the duty of the state and that aid given for such purposes should naturally not be given on a commercial basis or on private business terms. On the contrary the full facts of such a situation must be taken into account and long-term credits offered on terms which are appropriate to each individual project and to its potential yield.

I would say yet again that we should use every ounce of imagination we possess to work out new forms of co-operation between entrepreneurs who have sufficient drive, enterprise and sense of responsibility to branch out in the developing countries and who are at the same time prepared to work together with the peoples and the people in question, in order to pass on the 'know-how' in the most direct way. For whatever is provided in the way of, for example, technical aid, the building of schools and training establishments, all this is certainly important and generally valuable. This should certainly not be underrated, but I would like to believe that it is at least as valuable if the people in those developing countries can themselves play a direct and active part in the work of development with an awareness of what consequences it can have for them in their daily lives, and if they can feel that they are partly responsible for increasing their productive capacity. Here, too, there is more than one form of model, for, apart from state aid in the shape of state loans for infrastructural purposes, and apart from credits or credit guarantees, such as, for example, have been customary for the employment of large investment funds for export purposes, private industry must also be prepared in future to branch out more into development areas.

The Federal Government is prepared to encourage this kind of private initiative and also to reduce the risks, although they are inseparable from any genuine enterprise and should not be entirely offloaded on to the state. We will only win the confidence which is essential as a basis for genuine co-operation, if it is apparent to all that we are willing to help and are also prepared to be humanitarian as well as venturesome in our actions, not only within the safe boundaries of the National State but throughout the whole of the free world. If we succeed—and this applies to Germany as well as to many other countries—in winning the confidence of the nations and the people in these developing areas, who have become conscious of their independence and their responsibilities, and in working together with them, if necessary in quite new, still untried forms, then we shall have found the starting-point for truly effective development aid.

Much has been said of the political issues, and it must be admitted that there is one aspect of any development aid programme that stretches beyond the humanitarian and the commercial. It is repeatedly said today that the colonial age is over. I hope the African peoples who have gained their independence are conscious of the fact that there is no worse form of colonialism than the communist-totalitarian kind of imperialism.

Here I would like to say something that applies not only to Germany and all other free countries but also to every developing country in Africa, because it touches on the very core of any community and society of free men : freedom is such a precious possession that it must be defended daily and earned daily. I maintain that the very people who are most aware of the value and blessing of freedom sometimes feel almost afraid of the responsibility that freedom places upon them. 'Freedom and responsibility' are inseparable, which also means that 'freedom and order' are inseparable, for freedom without order is always in danger of degenerating into chaos, while order without freedom may become mere brute force. For that reason it is important to find a synthesis of order and freedom. It is my heartfelt hope that the African countries and peoples, who have found self-awareness and a consciousness of their responsibility to themselves and to their freedom, are also mindful of their obligation to maintain order, so that they may be sure of a happy future based on this indivisible unity.

I believe that the Federal Republic will be in a position before very long—I am thinking now not in terms of years but of months —to start concrete negotiations with the developing countries of Africa and to consider with them in what orders of magnitude and for what purposes we, in partnership with them, can contribute to the solution of their problems. Perhaps not all dreams will be realized, but you can be sure that the Federal Government —and, indeed, the German people—is more willing and more consciously willing than ever before to walk side by side with you on the road that leads out of the colonial era into independence, away from poverty and hardship into a finer and better future, in which the great gift of freedom and the rewards of a conscious determination to shape your own destiny beckon you on.

I hope that any such co-operation will not be confined to examining projects in detail and giving priority to technical questions such as finance. All that naturally is part of any business, if I may put it like that. But we should also put our heads together and consider how best—which means not only in the fixed form of five- and seven-year plans—we can harness the brains, hearts and souls of men to a worthwhile goal, how we can awaken their energies and help to arouse their initiative, which so far has been dormant and perhaps could not be anything but dormant. For believe me—what we can give you and what, apart from capital, is required from us in technical know-how, is not in itself enough. I believe that, because we feel there is a bond between you and us, we can give something more, namely, our knowledge of all the social, economic and socio-political problems that must be solved in the course of an economic development programme. We know the dangers, we know the obstacles that have to be overcome, and we also know how easily a nation can blunder. We regard development aid as a task complete and coherent in itself. It is a whole that cannot be divided up into individual sectors. A truly productive co-operative effort can only grow out of a sense of partnership, out of an awareness of what one can or will give, the other take. That is the right starting-point for joint action. So it is from this basic principle that we shall begin.

It is my fondest wish and the wish of us all that you may find in the consciousness of your independence the strength and the taste for responsibility that will enable you to make the most of your freedom, not only for the well-being of your peoples but also as a step towards a happier coexistence, a closer co-operation and understanding between the nations and the continents.

May the work that you are beginning in a spirit of fraternity and humanity serve to promote the indissoluble unity of free men in a free world.

42

THE ATLANTIC COMMUNITY

(Article in *Die Zeit* of November 16, 1960)

While economic interchange after the end of the war covered only very small areas in West Germany and economic policy could only be applied to a Land area and later to the Occupation Zones, the Basic Law of 1949 brought the whole of the Federal Republic within its scope. The first steps towards collaboration in the OEEC were followed by the partial integration of the iron and steel economies of the Six countries, the European Economic Community and the European Atomic Community. Economic links with the USA and Canada become closer and closer. In the North Atlantic Treaty Organization, which the Federal Republic joined in 1955, the military basis for the defence of the Atlantic area was set up. The unity of this alliance is essential to counter the growing pressure from the Soviet bloc. In this article Ludwig Erhard comes out in favour of close economic co-operation within the Atlantic family of nations.

It may be that those who first spoke of an 'Atlantic Community' that would also cover the economic sphere of international relations were anxious to evade the issue of a European integration. The dispute, which has now become almost a part of history, as to whether there should be a *rapprochement* or even a reconciliation between the 'Six' (EEC) and the 'Seven' (EFTA), frequently came to a dead stop in political discussion when it was suggested that any such solution would not serve the interests of the USA and Canada but would lead to still further discrimination against these two allies of ours.

Seen from a purely static point of view, this might well be one result, but it seems to me that, without prejudice to the unity of the 'Six', an economic merger of all the free nations of Europe would offer the national economies of the United States and Canada better prospects than a division that would run directly counter to political instincts and requirements. Besides, I believe I am justified in thinking that both the business world in the United States and economic circles in the EEC and EFTA countries desire a more far-reaching solution, each one considering it to be in his own interests, and have little time for political manoeuvring.

The threats to the free world by repeated attempts at intimidation have made it abundantly clear that only the broadest possible community with a resolute determination to defend itself is adequate to safeguard our peace and freedom, and that any idea of Europe as a third force—however great the defence effort that even such a Europe would have to make—cannot stand up to sober examination.

It is an incontestable fact that only an 'Atlantic Community' such as we have in the NATO defence alliance—or, more precisely, such as we are developing and must develop—is adequate for the defence of 'our' world. This alliance alone gives us protection against aggression, at a time when constant modernization and adaptation are called for. So a sober assessment of our position gives life and meaning to the concept of an 'Atlantic Community.'

But what is the situation as regards economic co-operation, which, in the final analysis, is also vital to the social life of the nations? Is it conceivable that the free peoples, knowing that their interdependence is a matter of life or death and that they must stand or fall together, would go their separate economic ways and adopt forms of integration within EEC and EFTA which, in the last resort, do not draw together but pull apart? Does anyone really believe that the life of nations can be organized in separate compartments, each governed by its own standards and ideas?

I for one am certain that the process of history has an inner logic of its own which will shatter such illusions, and we must therefore guard from the beginning against dangerous misjudgments. In other words, we should not allow national sentiment or resentment to stand in the way of compromise solutions which will turn out in the end to be unavoidable.

Those forces and bodies of opinion who have resisted an economic agreement between all the free countries of Europe may, for the moment, find some vindication of their resistance in the attitude of the United States. But the assumption that an agreement between EEC and EFTA would lead to further trade discrimination against the United States is no longer valid, for, as I have already said, it is being increasingly realized in America that a divided Western Europe would not serve the global political interest of the United States.

Apart from the fact that any economic expansion in Europe is bound to lead to a growth of liberalism in foreign policy, it is as well to realize that the American investments in the EEC and EFTA countries as well as the growth of mutual investments within the two groups are not due to any market pressures but purely and simply to the fact that private industry is anxious to avoid discrimination in areas that become increasingly isolated. Here there is a danger of bad investments, for which, in view of our joint responsibility to divert surplus funds to development aid, there is simply no justification.

If, in addition to this, individual countries are not prepared to relinquish their national sovereignty, with the result that a new European-type constitution may not emerge from EEC, this will reduce the obstacles in the way of a European economic solution. We must, therefore, pursue a 'Realpolitik' which should teach us the following—we must on no account do anything that might lead to clashes of interests in the free area of the Old World. This prospect is all the more sinister at a time when I can, I think, detect signs that the highly industrialized countries of Europe on the one hand and the United States and Canada on the other are beginning to come to terms.

If, as I hope, some mutually agreeable formula can be worked out between EEC and EFTA, then it will certainly not be the last in a sequence of cures for the Atlantic area. From a historical point of view, the desired conciliation within Europe can only, in my view, be the beginning of a continuous process of coalescence that must embrace all the civilized nations of the Western world. We can see for ourselves how the national economies of Europe are growing every day more conscious of their increasing strength and their successful efforts to create bigger markets, and furthermore, how modern technology and the applied knowledge of the natural sciences are making a vital contribution to narrowing the gap between American and European production. But this simply means that the national economies of Europe will produce more and more under American conditions and cost rates, and that, in consequence, the obstacles to an integration of the American and European economies are disappearing. And that, I am convinced, will be the reality of tomorrow.

43

ECONOMIC POLICY AND PUBLIC OPINION

(Broadcast on November 28, 1960, following a public opinion
poll organized by Bavarian Radio on the economic views of
the West German population)

*As early as the 1920's at the beginning of his economic career
Ludwig Erhard had become involved in market and public opinion
research. Later, as Federal Minister of Economics, he made full
use of it in all branches of his work. What interests him is not so
much the quantitative results achieved by these investigations as
the human ideas and motives behind the statistics. In the long
term no democratic government can pursue a policy which does
not have the backing of public opinion, but, as Erhard points out, it
also cannot afford to become the slave of the public:*

The Bavarian Radio has performed a great service by the initiative
it has taken in organizing a large-scale public opinion poll to
ascertain the views of people not only in Bavaria but throughout
the whole of the Federal Republic on questions concerning our
everyday economic life, our economic system and our economic
policy. I also welcome this poll because, as a politician and Minister
of Economics, I can no longer do without scientifically cor-
roborated data, without a picture based on expert evidence of what
the public is thinking about the important questions of the day.

I had already become intensely interested in market and public
opinion research long before it had ever occurred to me that I
might one day become a Minister in our state, and I can still
remember very clearly the first experiments we conducted in this
field in Nürnberg in the twenties.

But what fascinate me particularly about the Bavarian Radio
investigation, apart from its obvious thoroughness, are certain
results which it has produced.

Naturally any Minister of Economics must be pleased to learn that around 88% of the adult population describe the economic situation as very good, good or satisfactory, while another 82% say the same of their own position. Only a minute percentage believe that a change in the present economic policy is advisable or necessary.

But this gives only a very superficial impression of what struck me about this poll. It is not unlike an exciting account of a journey through an interesting country with even more interesting people. Almost every statistic has a bearing on some function, which I as Minister of Economics am called upon to perform.

What is one to say, for example, when one learns from the poll that nearly half the adult population of Germany does not know what a pound of margarine or butter or any other daily consumer commodity costs? Does that not show how indifferent we are to the prices we pay? Or does it merely prove the comparative un-importance of such expenditure to the average citizen? Do these and other replies to questions put in this enquiry bear out the con-tention that the consumers really do not know their way about the markets, that they can all too easily fall victim to sharp practices in business, and that they are still inclined to think the most expensive goods must be the best bargain, without even trying to put their theory to the test?

We must naturally be careful not to draw any false conclusions, for we know from many other replies to questions how price-conscious public opinion is. There are indications that, during the past twelve years of market economy, the consumers have learned a great deal. They are no longer so uninformed or inexperienced in the workings of a free market as they were, to my knowledge, twelve years ago. The consumer is becoming more and more conscious of the possibilities and, if he makes proper use of them, of the power open to him as a purchaser.

But the research conducted by the Bavarian Radio has also brought home to me very clearly that we in Germany still have a great effort to make if we are to increase our knowledge of econ-omic questions. Although I myself and my Ministry have been at great pains in the last twelve years to spread this knowledge, there are still great gaps to be filled. To a large extent this can only be explained by the complexity of many of these questions themselves, but much of it is also due to shortcomings in our school curricula.

The Minister of Economics, still more so as Federal Minister, has no responsibility for the education in the primary and secondary schools. I think this is a problem which can only be solved in close collaboration with the Land authorities, within whose competence it falls. How can we set about interesting young people more in the basic problems of our economy and of day-to-day economics? The last thing I would suggest is that we should live economics, but I must admit I am rather alarmed when I see how little the young people on leaving school, and indeed adults too, understand of these things, even in the most general terms, although their personal lives and the life of the nation are profoundly influenced and directed by economics. I am not being sarcastic when I say that this may be the explanation why everyone regards himself as an expert in economic questions. I do believe, however, that there is a very worthwhile function to be performed here by the Land Ministers of Culture, by competent organizations and by the appropriate Federal authorities in friendly co-operation.

But now to another side of this enquiry that particularly interested me. One of the questions asked was what appliances and household machines were used. From this we learn that, for example, 70% of all households own a vacuum cleaner, about 50% a refrigerator, 40% a camera, 20% a typewriter, 28% a television set and 22% a record player. Another question asked was what new articles were likely to be bought in the next six months. Refrigerators, washing-machines and television sets were at the top of the list.

All very interesting and important questions, but I cannot help pointing out that the initiators of this enquiry—whether they are in Bavarian Radio or in my Ministry—were guilty of one omission. Both lists failed to include what, in my view, is one of the most important household appliances, the automatic dish-washing machine. I feel sure that our womenfolk, and particularly those who have jobs and those who have children, would welcome the chance to be relieved, at least in part, of a chore which is one of the most disagreeable in any household, namely, of washing-up and drying.

It is hard to understand why, with such outstanding technical achievements in shipbuilding, electronics and engineering, not to mention other fields, we still have not managed to produce a dishwashing machine for the average household, which would lighten the burden for our housewives. Perhaps the reason is that the men who are responsible for these technical improvements have too little practical experience in the house and therefore too little understanding of household problems! In America, for example, where things are different, the men have, in this respect at least, 'seen the light'.

These are only a few examples from a wealth of information. In conclusion, I would like to say—and this also makes one think—that, despite a strong vote in favour of our market economy, which surprised even me, it is clear from the dissentient voices that in some people's minds the influence or even the power of the state is overrated, while others are strongly in favour of it. If I may employ a metaphor, I would say that, while the principle of experimenting in freedom is accepted, most people regard economic experiment as a dangerous game and would like to be sure that there is a net below to catch them if they fall.

I understand this desire for security only too well, but I also realize that it is still not generally appreciated that a liberal system with a forward-looking and dynamic economy is the best form of security not only for the individual but also for the advancement of public social services.

44

STRATEGY AND TACTICS IN ECONOMIC
POLICY

(Article in *Frankfurter Allgemeine Zeittung* of December 3, 1960)

It is not only the 'art of war' that has always been interested in these concepts. Economic policy in particular also has its long-term and short-term aims, its 'operational' decisions and directions for the solution of day-to-day questions. Whether a decision was 'right' or 'wrong', however, sometimes does not become apparent for years after and frequently in a sector of economic and social life which seemed quite unaffected. If the art of economic policy is not easy to master, then it is because, in our society, it has to do with free men and parliaments freely elected by them, whose reactions and resolutions are public and only in exceptional cases can be foreseen with certainty. It is an art that calls for an unceasing scrutiny of what it achieves or fails to achieve in the light of its political aims.

Although these two concepts are not exactly contradictory, much less irreconcilable, in their application, although strategy does not preclude, and may even demand, the necessity or advisability to make a tactical approach in line with the facts of the situation, there is nevertheless a difference of approach, both mental and moral, implicit in the customary interpretation of these terms which I think it is important to clarify. As used of economic policy, 'strategy' means recognizing and applying irrefutable, scientifically verified principles, which must not be exposed to passing influences but should serve as an objective criterion for the constant reappraisal of our political conduct. In this context, therefore, strategy means keeping to a broad line of policy; strategy thinks in systems and established conceptions or order; strategy is so deeply rooted in knowledge and the conscious will that it transcends day-to-day events and leaves its imprint on the attitude of mind. So strategy comprises the aim and the substance of a policy. Tactics, on the other hand, should rather be defined as a mode of action. Seen in this way, the justification and value of tactics lie in giving expression to the principles which lend a deeper purpose to the changing events of the day. Mere tactics is rightly despised if it is 'devoid of character or principle' and sets out only to exploit the present, without enquiring into the whole or into the future.

I have shown often enough that I personally do not object to the use of tactical manoeuvres as an instrument of economic policy, for, particularly in this field, the necessity arises almost daily and even hourly to adapt policy not only to structural changes in society but also to the psychological reactions of people in industry. I have repeatedly found, for example, that people accused me of inconsistency when I attached different values to the same phenomena, such as savings, investments and consumption, in the light of new data and of the economic situation as a whole, although I always had the same ultimate end in view. Similarly the motives for what has been called my 'spiritual massage' have sometimes been misconstrued. Psychological reactions are amongst the tools of any responsible politician's trade, whether he is operating on a large or a limited scale. My attitude of mind is, however, always determined in the last resort by factors that are real and fundamental, whereas the very dubious aim of the ultra-pragmatists (a special breed of men) is to achieve a preconceived and permanent purpose by means of tactical flexibility. In my view these pure economic tacticians are finally caught up in their own web, for anyone who thinks only in terms of day-to-day tactics must sooner or later lose direction and become a mere tool in the hands of group interests, which he thought he could guide and control.

Present economic developments provide an almost classic example of what strategy and tactics mean. Whereas the whole of my economic policy is designed to maintain the present boom conditions, by allowing our technical capacity and labour resources full freedom, and for this very reason to correct as promptly as possible any faults that may develop, tacticians and interested parties are foolish and sometimes almost childish enough to try to

x

deny the existence of a boom by pointing to weakness in the national economy, with the sole object of exploiting to the full a situation that offers them certain momentary advantages, regardless of what the future may bring. The chaotic conditions in the labour market are hushed up, the fact that delivery dates are falling behind is said to be a misleading sign of unevenly distributed orders, indications that prices are rising are made light of, increased building costs, we are told, are merely an error of statistics, and the permanent balance-of-payments surpluses are explained away as being to some extent normal. In fact, to hear day in day out, as I do, from all kinds of people with vested interests that all is for the best and in some quarters even that anxiety about the boom is justified, is almost to doubt one's own sanity. As I do not, I hope it will be appreciated that to me there is nothing more dangerous than this deliberate policy of tactical manoeuvre, which is too transparent to be taken seriously by someone whose duty it is to treat the national economy as a complete whole. Heaven help the German people if a mere tactician or pragmatist should one day gain control of the German economy and set out on the path of least resistance or aim to please everyone. For this would mean in practice that the sheer volume of noise made by organized groups would be the deciding factor and that might would triumph over right. On the other hand, the unorganized consumers and particularly the housewives, who cannot be blinded by figures but take a realistic view of life, or all those who have put their life-savings in securities, would have to pay for the sins of a false economic policy that violates the basic law of internal economic stability.

The tactical policy of allowing each group to reap special benefits and of accepting as a criterion of justice that each man should think only of himself must in the end become a national curse, for such a gross error leaves no room whatsoever for a national economic policy, that is, for a deliberate long-term effort to secure the welfare of all.

At the moment there is a great deal of talk in the Federal Republic of a boom programme which on the one hand confirms the need for active intervention in economic affairs but at the same time is designed to prevent any arrangements being made that might interfere with the special interests of private industry. I do not want to be misunderstood. I acknowledge with gratitude, for example, that German industry is prepared to underwrite a $1\frac{1}{2}$ milliard loan to provide funds for development aid and at the same time produce a certain damping-down effect on the economy. But, when I consider the imbalance of demand and supply in our national economy, I am not entirely satisfied that this sacrifice will be sufficient to prevent further tension.

At present two factors in particular are influencing the economic situation in Germany. In the first place an inevitable result of the balance-of-payments surpluses has been to reduce the supply of commodities to the German market, and secondly the German level of prices, which by international standards is still relatively low, makes it possible to increase wages and prices in excess of the increase in productivity. To adopt this solution one must be prepared to take the social and economic consequences, which could be disastrous. On the other hand, to resist any such dangerous trend—and this I regard as my duty—one must reject the principle of mere tactical manoeuvre and be guided by strategic considerations, in other words, by a responsible, forward-looking economic policy.

I have no hesitation in prophesying that any attempt to cure complaints in our national economy, which are international, not national, in origin, by means of tactical tricks and devices is doomed from the start. I also fully realize that attempts, however laudable in principle, to persuade the entrepreneur to practice price restraint despite surplus purchasing power, and efforts being made in this direction by large concerns, are merely designed to show that the modern system of a market economy—our Social Market Economy—is collapsing. Prices, we are told, should not be determined by the market but only by costs, and if the cartels can to all intents and purposes guarantee price stability, they virtually become charitable institutions. Let no one imagine that I am taken in by such tactics and would not be prepared to fight once more for a free economy.

In saying this, I make no accusations. I am merely explaining that tactical means can be employed for the most questionable motives. I am convinced that it is an essential part of our education and our responsibility as citizens to bear in mind, both in questions of detail and over-all, that tactics is devoid of moral sense and that no policy can be morally justified which does not rest on firm and sincere principles. A statesman in any branch of public life must naturally master the art of tactics, but he will only earn confidence if he can convince people that his actions are based on deeper knowledge and an informed will. The Social Democrats recently provided a classic example of how not to achieve this. They have thrown overboard virtually all basic principles (except those of the government party) and thereby made tactics the very substance of politics. Strategy as a fundamental attitude of mind takes precedence in politics over tactics and modes of action. Fruitful action can only be achieved—and herein lies the mastery—by combining an overriding strategy with subsequent tactics in one united whole.

45

WHAT WILL BECOME OF EUROPE?

(Article in *Handelsblatt* of December 23-24, 1960)

Discussion on the most desirable form of unity for Europe reached a new peak in the autumn of 1960. At that time a report by Erhard appeared in a number of German daily papers entitled: '6 + 7 + 5 = 1!' Erhard pursued his campaign in numerous speeches and articles:

Although we have good reason to congratulate ourselves on the economic progress made in 1960 and, despite many temporary anxieties, can look ahead with confidence, the European problem still remains unsolved in spite of the storm signals of class-war aggression from the East. I am referring here not to NATO's problems, to the organization and arming of the defence forces, although these also are no small problems, but to the economic co-operation of the free nations of our ancient continent.

Starting from the integration of the Six in the framework of the Common Market, a highly praiseworthy and sober move was made back to the foundations of the Treaty, i.e. to its economic objectives, and if not a stop at least a brake has been put on political speculation. This clear definition of duties clears the way for realistic decisions, and one is no longer branded as a 'bad European' if one rejects the highly subjective fantasies of those who will only think in terms of the Six. Although it has become abundantly clear in the meantime that, without prejudice to the proper application of the Treaty and to the solidarity of the Six, this integration of Little Europe, particularly in its political implications, is not sufficient to solve either the European problem as a whole or that of the Atlantic Community, I would like to point out once more that no such limitations were envisaged when the Rome Treaties were born. In fact, a formal and officially inspired announcement was made by the then President of the European

Commission that a widespread European free trade zone would be set up as a defence against destructive influences and any disturbances created by them. The responsible statesmen in the EEC countries have accepted the principle of a multilateral association with regard to their economic relations with the other free countries of Europe, and the EEC Council of Ministers passed resolutions to the same effect. Every citizen has a right to know what has come of these good intentions and he will want to know what has stood, or is still standing, in the way of their realization.

The year 1960, as far as integration of the Six is concerned, began in a rush with a shortening of conversion periods and a simultaneous drop in tariffs as the first step towards a common tariff. Lest this should lead to a drawing apart of EEC and EFTA, the deadline of July 1, 1960, was postponed until January 1, 1961, not least at my instigation, in order to give time for the EEC and EFTA countries to negotiate a *rapprochement*.

I would not say that this period was wasted, for there were conversations between responsible European statesmen, between the Federal Chancellor and the British Prime Minister, for example, and between Mr Macmillan and the Italian Prime Minister, in which at least the political will was expressed to avoid a division of Europe. Unfortunately, these political conversations were not followed up by similar exchanges between Ministers with both political responsibility and economic expertise. So the political declaration of intentions has remained more or less in skeleton form, without really coming to life.

The European Commission's activities and pronouncements did not give the impression, much less arouse confidence, that it was seriously interested in a multilateral solution. In fact, it even declared that it regarded this course as either inopportune or impossible. Naturally this attitude brought corresponding reactions in the EFTA camp and the prospects of successfully bridging the gulf would be even more remote today if we could not feel confident that political, economic and human reason will compel the two economic groups in Europe to come together and eventually to work together.

I would like to ask what became of the European Commission's Liaison Committee which was set up to enquire into possible ways

of achieving an understanding. It lies forgotten in some pile of
dusty archives, having never really seen the light of day. And what
has become of the 20% drop in tariffs? The European Commission
offered, in the course of the GATT negotiations, to consolidate the
tariffs of the Six, which were due to come into force on January 1,
1961, without the 20% cut, and it also offered to continue negotiations on a basis of mutual concessions. This was not what we in
Germany at least had understood by integration. What is happening has nothing in common with the liberal foreign policy that
was promised, and the attitude adopted towards third countries in
GATT is even likely to have unfortunate repercussions throughout
the world. Moreover, the German consumer must feel cheated
when on January 1, 1961, the tariffs between the Federal Republic
and third countries, instead of being lowered, are appreciably
increased. This is not the fault of the Commission, but it does show
its structural defects.

Before the system of differential tariffs has had time to take
effect, an increasing number of reports have been coming in from
German industry that business with the EFTA countries has not
only become much more difficult but that in certain sectors
practically no orders can now be placed. The foreign businessmen
point out that they are now having to concentrate on building up
contracts within their own area, particularly as a further increase
in differential tariffs suggests, from a purely commercial point of
view, that a regrouping is called for. What I feared in the beginning is now about to happen—the two parts of Europe are drawing away from one another, even ideologically, new group
interests are emerging, and new organizations are going out of
their way to hasten the process.

The foreign trade figures of the European countries for the year
1960 will bear out what I have said, and, unless events take a
decisive turn, I can foresee almost a kind of revolution in international economic relations in 1961. It is simply not true to say,
as the 'Little Europeans' do repeatedly in their defence, that a
deliberate move to bring EEC and EFTA together would be the
end of the Common Market, and it is also not true that this step
would mean greater discrimination against the United States. This
is a purely academic argument that takes no account of the signs

of the times, of the need for all forces in the free world to combine in a multilateral system and of the power that would emerge from it. There are many indications of a change of heart in the United States on this problem, which gives one reason to hope that the concept of an 'Atlantic Community' can embrace more effectively the spheres of trade and economic policy. There is certainly food for thought for the politicians of all nations in the fact that commercial people throughout the world all share the same desire for a better and more rapid *rapprochement*. The nations themselves—meaning here consumers—are if anything even more strongly in favour.

There is no longer any point in beating about the bush and looking for temporary or unreal remedies which in modern times have an almost spectral air. When I hear, for example, that dissatisfied business partners are to be offered long-term bilateral agreements as a cure for their ills, but, in reality, as a means of evading the only sensible solution which is multilateral, then an enlightened political economist in the second half of the 20th century feels like clutching his head in despair at such a relapse into 19th-century thinking and the revival of economic machinery from the early period of world trade, and asking openly and publicly, how long this quack medicine is to go on. I am speaking now not merely for myself but, I am happy to say, also with the whole of German industry solidly behind me.

In conclusion, let me say once again in all seriousness, that we cannot hope to master the political problems, to remove the cares and threats that lie over the whole of Europe and more particularly our own country, so long as we worship the mad doctrine that, while we must stand together politically and militarily, we can go our separate economic and social ways.

46

FOREIGN POLICY BEGINS AT HOME

(Article in *Aussenpolitik* of January 1961)

The world conflict between East and West became in the post-Stalin period more and more a political struggle with ideological aims and economic weapons. The great politically neutral development areas of Africa, Asia and Latin America became a major battlefield in this cold war. Development aid acquired a significance far beyond economic and humanitarian considerations. In many cases it became a means of influencing the foreign and domestic policies of the receiving countries. Furthermore, this conflict is also a pretext for employing other means, mainly propagandist, in order to implant in the developing countries either the totalitarian doctrines of the Soviets or the liberal ideas of the West. This fact makes it imperative to look at the internal economic and social system of the free world, including the Federal Republic, with reference to its effect on the rest of the world. Seen in this context, it forms part of foreign policy. In this article Ludwig Erhard considers the relationship between the domestic system and its effect on foreign policy:

In many respects 1960 was one of the crucial years of our century. I do not propose to go into the unusual developments that took place inside the Soviet bloc nor into the reasons why Red China today pursues an independent policy. Nor do I want to discuss European politics, Berlin, the German question, or the problem of strengthening the Western alliance, making it indivisible and extending the unity of this alliance to economic co-operation by the Atlantic States. From not only a historical but also a topical point of view the outstanding feature of 1960 seems to me to have been the new-found independence of numerous states in the African continent. With this as a starting-point, but also taking account of the fact that in other parts of the world the states of the post-colonial epoch are acquiring more and more influence in world politics, it seems to me appropriate to ask what relationship exists between our domestic system and the internal and external policies of these states. The question is, therefore, how far Germany's reconstruction programme and her type of economy can serve as an example for one or other of these countries to follow. If our answer is in the affirmative, whether wholly or in part, then we must be prepared to draw certain conclusions.

In this restless world, in which we can no longer find security in ourselves, the politician is like a chess player who is suddenly confronted, halfway through the tournament, with a board which has 100 squares instead of 64 and an extra dozen unknown figures. The rules of the game remain unchanged, but, in order to win the game, the player must be fully cognizant of the new conditions under which he is playing and must adjust his game accordingly.

We know that the future can no longer be determined by the policies of the great Powers—the United States, the Soviet Union, and the free states of Europe—alone. The countries of Asia and Africa will have a decisive influence on the course of world politics in the future. This means that we must redouble our efforts to strengthen the bonds of working partnership with these states. We have no political ambitions in these areas except to help preserve for these nations the freedom to choose their own political and economic institutions. In other words, our aim is to place our advice and our experience at the disposal of these states. The same is fundamentally true for the countries of Asia, Africa and South America as for the industrial states of Europe and America: 'Good management is sound policy'. This sentence should not, however, be taken to mean that the best recipe for Asia, Africa and Latin America is necessarily to copy West European civilization. There is no such thing as one model which can be applied equally to all countries.

A common characteristic of young states is 'first-generation government', and this compulsion to 'govern in the first generation' often leads to a policy of trying to make rapid and visible progress at all costs and therefore looking round for ready-made patterns of economic and political development. The governments of quite a few of these young states are faced at the very beginning of their economic and political development with a choice between the Eastern and Western examples. So we must offer the leaders of the young and old states of Asia and Africa even more opportunities than before of getting to know the human, technical and political ingredients of a free constitution and a liberal economy, so that they can appreciate the profound contrast between East and West. But it is not merely a question of 'understanding'; equally important is the ability to test modern methods of development for their applicability to the home territory and to convert them to the territory's special requirements. On the other hand, it is equally important that German technicians, economists, teachers, in fact suitable men of all categories, should go out and, with their knowledge and example, help the young peoples to find their way. Upon this will largely depend whether development aid as a whole is successful.

In the highly-developed industrialized states present-day requirements and international changes in outlook in recent years make it imperative to have political leaders whose minds are attuned to reality; who are, therefore, qualified to represent their liberal forms of government, and who can set an example to those states which are seeking solutions to their problems. Success in this struggle for the minds of men will come in the end to those who in their own spheres of responsibility are dedicated to social forms and systems which radiate inner strength. Even an adversely biased observer, whether from Asia, Africa or Latin America, will be forced to admit that the projected image and the tangible reality are fundamentally the same.

Lest there should be any misunderstanding, what I am asking is not that we should go forth as demagogic missionaries to preach our system of government. What is really required is that the free states of the West should achieve a harmony of well-being and humane living in society, which we ourselves have need of and which makes a simple and convincing appeal to others. A comprehensive domestic policy of this kind speaks for itself and makes an effective contribution to foreign policy. To achieve such a purpose the responsible politician must exercise an unusually high degree of imagination and resolution.

The time has passed when we could pursue a social policy, a

trade and economic policy which took no account of how each individual measure might change our image in the outside world or how the outside world might react. We are face to face with our adversary in an open arena, playing not a part which we have chosen for ourselves in order to make a good impression but a part allotted to us by nature.

We, that is all free and prosperous nations, must set an example in the future that will convince half the world that ours is the right way. In other words, we must win a spiritual battle knowing that, if we lose, the light of freedom will be extinguished throughout the entire world. And in this struggle we must remain true, even in our domestic policy, to the vow we took at the outset, to resist every attack upon our liberal, anti-totalitarian social system, whether it appeals to selfish, short-term interests or occurs in the normal run of our economic life.

This is a necessity which has not just arisen now, but we have become so splendidly practical—and at the same time so incredibly short-sighted—that in the minds of too many people long-term planning has been abandoned in favour of mere tactical expediency.

What kind of response four years ago could any politician—I could say quite a few things on this score—who underlined the need for a working partnership with the developing countries have expected? At best an uncomprehending shake of the head. What reaction could he have hoped for two years ago if he insisted that development aid must amount to something more, and something different than merely exporting commodities? What reply did he get a year ago, or even a few months ago, when he pointed out that development aid, a political and economic necessity, called for appreciable sacrifices all round?

In the meantime 'development aid' has become—unfortunately, in my view—one of the fashionable subjects of discussion. Everyone feels called upon to talk about it. And people have finally been forced to realize, not least by pressures from outside, that sacrifices will have to be made. Yet even now people would consider it unrealistic to insist that the tasks immediately before us, such as the maintenance of the Social Market Economy or closer co-operation between the countries of free Europe, must be approached with due consideration for the indirect effect our actions will have on the Asiatic, African and Latin American development programmes. Our daily actions must be strictly in accordance with the principles we stand for, because the future of the world depends largely upon the extent to which our established institutions make an impact on the peoples of Asia, Africa and Latin America and serve as examples to them.

For this reason any compromise with state-controlled economic methods should be avoided. We can no longer command confidence if, on the one hand, we champion individualism and human dignity, personal initiative and a free economy, and, on the other, supply equipment and personnel to help promote state capitalism and collectivism and, in consequence, a loss of human freedom in the developing countries. The extent to which state initiative and state regulations are unavoidable in the early stages of development is something only the developing countries themselves can decide, but we should certainly not foster such a process against our better judgment, especially as it frequently arises from a too favourable assessment of collectivist principles.

We shall win if by our actions we gain the confidence of the developing countries and the newly-independent peoples. But this not only means that those working out there must inspire trust— whether they are skilled workers, diplomats, technicians or businessmen; it also means that our German firms and public bodies must give sound advice, that great efforts must be made to paint a true picture of conditions here in Germany so that these nations may be won over by our example and will be proof against the false values of Communism. If we remain true to ourselves in our own sphere of activity, we can face up to the Communist East with the inestimable advantage of inner truth on our side.

47

AN INTERIM STATEMENT ON EUROPE

(Speech to the 'Gesellschaft für Auswärtige Politik' and the
Austrian 'Industrielle Vereinigung' in Vienna on
February 8, 1961)

*On the eve of a visit by the Federal Chancellor Adenauer to the
French President De Gaulle, Ludwig Erhard addressed a gathering in Vienna of leading personalities from the political, scientific
and economic life of Austria. The speech was made a few weeks
before his aim to revalue the mark was achieved. As on so many
similar occasions, Erhard reviewed the entire economic situation
of the Federal Republic and the questions arising from closer
economic co-operation in Europe and throughout the world:*

My subject is a very wide one. It is not confined to the relations
between EEC and EFTA, although there are problems here which
I do not propose to pass over. I want to speak about economic and
trade policy, and you can be sure that I see the problem not only
in a national context but also as a world problem carrying world-
wide obligations.

I do not think we need go on discussing economic systems, for
there is practically no dogmatic dispute any longer as to the
desirability or value of economic forms. When we in Germany
speak of 'Social Market Economy' we do not mean a liberal
economy based on the doctrines of the English Manchester school;
in fact, I do not even mean what is known as 'neo-liberalism'. No,
the Social Market Economy—and I claim no copyright on the idea
—sets out to achieve something different and something more. Of
course, it too aims, through the medium of competition which is
inseparable from any successful and liberal economic system, to
achieve a synthesis of personal freedom and social security.

The concept 'Social Market Economy' still requires a certain
amount of explanation, but first I should like in this brief digres-

sion to make clear what is really at the heart of the Social Market Economy. Moreover, I believe that, while our economic principles may differ from yours in certain respects, they are not diametrically opposed.

When we came forward in 1948 with a new economic philosophy we had no literature to fall back on, for the competitive principle as the principal objective of the neo-liberal school is not an adequate exposition of what we have, if not yet fully achieved, been trying to achieve with the Social Market Economy. By contrast there was, for example, the socialist doctrine which filled volumes and had, therefore, a substantial literature to fall back on, one which created such a stir in schools of political economy. We were, so to speak, breaking new ground with a concept that was by no means divorced from the past but set out to create not only a new economic system but also a new socio-political image, or at least tried to move in that direction.

The question which is the most successful economic system has surely been answered; indeed, it is not even dependent upon any particular national conditions. For who would have dared hope, after such an unprecedented collapse—and I am thinking not merely of my own country but also of the dislocation and pernicious isolation of Europe's national economies and their attachment to false ideologies—that it would be possible to rebuild a world out of spiritual and material ruins, a world far from perfect—perfection we shall never achieve—but in which productive capacity has expanded, prosperity and social security increased, to an astonishing degree, while the free world has become more or less reunited again with a feeling of solidarity and a conviction that no single country, whether large or small, can today shape its own destiny. This was only possible by productive co-operation between all concerned and by acknowledging the same ideals, however much party-political views may differ. This is as true of the Federal Republic as it is of Austria. There has never yet been a time in which such a dynamic development of human and material productive capacity was successfully accomplished as following this devastating and disastrous war, following this unprecedented collapse.

I can still distinctly remember how, at the beginning of 1948, before the German currency reform, when I was made responsible for Germany's economic policy, no one had a clear idea by what law we should proceed, for we were all prisoners of the times rather than of any ideology. No law has since been applied. It was thought that only a state-controlled planned economy could clear up this appalling confusion, remedy the bitter hardships of the population and restore hope and even prosperity.

At that time, whenever we met under the auspices of the OEEC or anywhere else in Europe, we racked our brains to find the right principles to apply, to try and devise suitable economic and socio-political machinery. All that is in the past. The productive power, welfare and social security which we have all achieved in the last twelve years are so unique in our history that the economic system of a free economy is accepted today as an inviolable and binding principle.

What we understand by 'Social Market Economy' and what is also finding its way, often in modified form, into the economic policy of other countries, is certainly no panacea. It also has no roots in an ideological past but simply sets out to diagnose our present and future problems, as far as this is possible, and then to proceed to create a system in which personal freedom and social security are merged into one.

It would be easy to demonstrate by means of statistics what has become of our German economy, but it is not my intention to brandish progress figures. I am concerned with something more, namely to keep us up with the present, as far as anyone can, and to take appropriate steps so that people who, in spite of our progress, are still fundamentally restless can regain their own peace of mind and their inner security, and can rid themselves of the haunting fear that they might become the helpless tools of an inscrutable, mysterious and in the end perhaps destructive power.

This economic form, this economic philosophy, is not so easy to understand as a planned economy, which anyone can grasp. Even the simplest mind can form some idea of the latter and, therefore, believes, in view of the many problems, the rapid technical advances and the complexity of our economy, that the modern age demands planning of our social and political life and that this is our only salvation. What is remarkable, of course, is that, although the planned economy is so easy to understand, it never works in practice, whereas the immensely complex market economy, which is not so easy to understand, clearly helps people to satisfy their desires and ambitions. I am naturally not prepared to resign and am therefore not in a position to make way for such simple and simplified ideas. It is not so difficult, even when people do not understand, to arouse their confidence—not least from their own direct experience—that the market economy is, after all, the right system and is practically taken for granted.

If I speak of my own country—where, as you know, elections are impending—then I must say that the least controversial issue between the various parties is economic policy, with the possible exception of social policy. This I regard as a great advance, that the free world as a coherent unit is no longer divided over ideological problems but is unanimous in its acceptance of liberal principles.

The question still remains, however—and it is all too relevant—why it is that, in spite of growing prosperity and social security, in spite of the steady rise in national and personal incomes, people should still feel a certain uneasiness or restlessness, and why they lack inner satisfaction and contentment, although their material existence has undoubtedly progressed from dire poverty to quite a high standard of prosperity with much happier material prospects.

This question must be answered, for, if we cannot answer it, we may draw the wrong conclusion, that we can give people happiness simply by steadily increasing production, by greater prosperity, by higher incomes and by further collective social security. But I think we are mature enough today to realize that what we have so far achieved and the far greater achievements we are undoubtedly capable of in the future are not in themselves enough to make people and nations feel that they are living in a harmonious, well-balanced society or to create an atmosphere in which they feel happy and secure. If at one time socialism was presented as the logical consequence of a natural development, and the classless society as the end-product of this process, then I can only say that we are out to create another kind of 'classless society'. In the final analysis we have, in fact, a special type of 'classless society', for the social discrepancies and tensions, which formerly led to outbursts of hate, no longer exist today. I do not mean that there are no

Y

further differences in our social life to give offence. But anyone with eyes to see and a heart to feel things as they are will be forced to recognize that the ways of life of people from the most diverse layers of society are becoming increasingly alike. One's estimate of people and society does not vary fundamentally because one man has a larger car or a better television set than another. People's demands, their consumption, have become more homogeneous! Let us hope this does not lead to uniformity. There is no longer a fashion or style that bears the imprint of a ruling class or is displayed by it. The outer forms of life are becoming more and more alike. And the mental attitudes of the various classes and groups have become so similar, that, although for the moment this is perhaps only comparative, we are on the road to a 'classless society'.

I am not saying that this is in any sense an absolute value, for that could be taken to mean that equality as such is a value. Nor do I mean it in the sense that differences of rank and class should continue to act as guiding principles. What really matters is to arrive at a closer understanding between the mental attitudes of people, between their sides, their degrees of awareness of the value of human freedom and the real meaning of security, that is, independence from all forms of collectivism.

Heaven forbid that we should ever seek a remedy in uniform consumption or in blind adoration of only one ideal or one principle. That would be disastrous! Society, the life's blood of a people, demands that they argue; everything depends, however, on what mental and moral plane the argument is conducted.

One of the effects of modern technology is that mass-produced goods are more or less uniform, so that a certain uniformity of consumption is bound to result. But that is only one side! We are making a special effort in the Federal Republic to check the concentration of economic power and to pursue a deliberate middle-class policy, the purpose of which is to preserve the viability and vitality of those independent and dependent sectors of industry, together with the urge to acquire greater independence.

Of course, modern technology demands certain amalgamations and concentrations of the means of production, but this does not apply to the same extent throughout industry as a whole. Where economic and technical requirements lead to a concentration of

the means of production and—in socio-political terms—to a concentration of economic power, we make every possible effort to
counteract this concentration of productive capital by a deconcentration of ownership of the means of production.

This is something that cannot, of course, be accomplished from
one day to the next. There is no cornucopia from which property
and wealth can be distributed at will, and it would be an unsound
principle to lay hands on private property in order to remedy
apparent defects in the social system. The development we set in
train must—and let us make no mistake about this—ensure that in
the future there is a fairer distribution of the national income and
the social product, and with regard to property we must see to it
that we do not have, on the one hand, a mass of people without
property and entirely dependent on collective security, and, on the
other, relatively few in whose hands the economic wealth of the
nation is concentrated and accumulated.

One may perhaps hold different views as to the causes, but the
important thing is to make a start and go forward with resolution.
Whether we in Germany decide to tackle the problem by distributing federally-owned productive capital in the form of 'people's
shares'—as was the case with the Volkswagen works—or whether
we resort to 'product-sharing', in order to ensure that capital also
gradually accumulates in the hands of people who are not self-
supporting or self-employed—all this is certainly not the final
answer. But you will, I hope, appreciate that there is a serious socio-
political effort being made to move on from a traditional economic
and social system to more modern conceptions of human society.

Anyone who has been as long in office as I have and has lived
through all kinds of phases—from the grimmest disaster any
economy ever had to suffer to the situation as it is today—has lost
all his illusions. Everything we take on and start has a hard core
of political realism and should be judged in that light. In 1948 I
was told: Your first task must be a just distribution of the social
product. My answer was: If I had to confine myself to a just
management of poverty I would never have accepted office. My
whole endeavour is to eradicate poverty. I know better than anyone
that the standards adopted were not always or everywhere those of
divine justice. But who commands such wisdom? My opponents

have certainly no monopoly of it, and you cannot plane wood without producing sawdust. That is what happened in the Federal Republic.

So if you ask me whether in the space of the last twelve years the social product was fairly distributed, there is more than one reply. By strictly moral standards I would say: No! By the standards of reality and of the tasks which had to be performed in the interests of all, I would answer: Yes!

For this poor, prostrate Germany, with its worn, outdated equipment weakened still further by dismantling, with 50% of its houses destroyed, this divided Germany, weighed down by a mortgage—or so it seemed to begin with—of 12 million refugees, its public institutions in ruins, a Germany in which a chaotic currency situation bred immorality, which was cut off and even despised by the world economy, and utterly friendless, had to start by putting its own house in order. We were not even in a position to establish any sort of priorities; we had to make a start everywhere, in every hole and corner.

We had to give people back their belief in the value of work, we had to consolidate the German economy and make it productive so that it could regain a secure position in a free world economy. All this had to be taken in hand and successfully carried through. Otherwise how would it have been possible not only to absorb the 12 million unemployed who had come over to us but also to create another seven and a half million jobs and, in addition, to make our economy so viable that Germany could once again hold her head up in the world economy.

When you also consider that the currency reform wiped out 49% of our liquid capital resources, then it was all too clear and understandable, after the criminal destruction wrought in those dark years of our recent history, that people should think first of their own survival and that there could be no question of accumulating capital from savings. But we needed capital, so by means of self-financing we built up private wealth, which is viewed now, in retrospect and from a political view-point, with a very jaundiced eye. I am even prepared to join in the criticisms, though not in the sense that I admit to having made a mistake but to the extent that I realize this phase must be brought to a halt. We now have to see to it that those who apparently did not fare so well can have a bigger share in our future progress but that they also carry their share of the responsibility for economic policy. The sharing of responsibility seems to me to be one of the impulses that is most essential to a modern economy and society. It is, after all, not the state that is primarily responsible for the direct action of the individual. It is not its task alone to care for the well-being of the people. Its responsibility lies in passing legislation which creates a sound system of government, thereby providing the framework for a purposeful and productive society. In a modern industrial economy this by no means implies that the state itself must or should play any direct part in the economy. We have acted on this assumption in the Federal Republic.

In 'developing countries' the situation may be somewhat different. I am far from suggesting that the Social Market Economy, such as we are practising and trying to develop further in Germany, is a panacea. Yet I am glad that this example has been followed and that even in the developing countries the idea is gradually losing ground that the only valid principle for these areas is to expand and develop production by means of a modified form of state capitalism or state socialism. There, too, it is gradually being realized that the right way is to arouse people's imagination and to instil in the broad mass of the population an awareness of the value of work—not merely in the ideal but still more in the material sense.

I always had grave doubts when we built ultra-modern steelmills in the developing countries. I often felt that these were not really steelmills but national monuments designed to kindle faith in these peoples without, however, achieving the economic and social effects that these developing countries need. What they require above all is widespread employment to increase consumer power and raise the people out of poverty and want.

The state has no direct responsibility to cater for the well-being of the people by intervening directly in the economic sphere. Naturally we have federally-owned enterprises and we do our best to stimulate healthy competition between them and private industry. But we also intend to transfer ownership of these means of production to the people on as broad a basis as possible by issuing 'people's shares', which will be the first step towards private ownership of production.

But it is not the duty of the entrepreneur alone to see to it that a national economy becomes increasingly productive. The entrepreneur certainly has a tremendous task to perform. I have complete confidence in private initiative and believe that it has more power that any other force to produce the maximum results from any given resources. But until we can persuade the wage-earner that the destiny, the future and the security of the entire nation depend largely upon his playing an active part in our economic life and sharing the responsibility for the maintenance and improvement of our productivity, we shall not be able to overcome our internal division and the party-political differences or indeed the whole concept of class-warfare which is still very much with us.

It is easy to say, the worker would be only too happy to save, if he could only earn enough. This is a relative question. In other words, it is not possible to make an absolute statement as to the size of income a man must have in order to put something away and take the first step towards private ownership. But what does a moment of time matter if we know for certain that we are in the process of making rapid and tremendous progress, particularly in the social sphere. It is essential that, on every level of the population, every single citizen should realize that he cannot simply abuse the 'capitalists' and hold the state entirely responsible for his social position, but that it is also up to him to help shape his own future and that of us all. The ordinary citizen must know that on his own conduct and mental outlook depends whether the national economy, of which he is a part, can continue to compete in world markets, or, in other words, whether a growing measure of inner harmony can be achieved in our social system. If I can bring the worker to realize that he only has a right to criticize the social system or the state's economic policy if he himself is prepared to lend a hand in moulding and developing the social system, then much will have been achieved. If the worker realizes that by saving he is making an important contribution to his own future security, then many differences that exist at present between the social partners will become less sharp. Then a better understanding will follow.

We are pleased that, starting from nothing, we have managed not only to make considerable economic progress through our Social Market Economy but also to strengthen the foundations of our social system and increase our social services to an extent that seemed impossible only a few years ago. This principle of social policy will certainly remain unaltered, but I do not believe that this alone provides the security which gives people a sense of true inner freedom and an awareness of their value to society and their personal dignity. This can only come with the feeling, or still more the conviction, that they are not dependent on the grace and favour of some collective but can behave and move about as free citizens. The phrase 'even a cat may look at a king' can also be applied to a democracy, even though the relationship of ruler to ruled is different. In my view this is a goal which is worth striving for.

Why is it then, we must ask, that, in spite of immense improvements in our social and material conditions, the man in the street is restless, that there is an undeniable sense of uneasiness. One might almost say that the more social security is offered through collective channels, the steadier the upward trend of our economy and the more people are protected against crises, the greater their unrest and almost incomprehensible feeling of insecurity. We have given up thinking in liberalist terms of regular trade cycles which in a period of about seven years go through the whole gamut of upward swing, boom, recession and crisis. For twelve years now our national economy has been moving steadily and continuously upwards. This proves that today we are better able to control the mechanism of international trade or that new economic and social principles have come into force. Despite all that, however, despite increased security, higher incomes and the knowledge that we are no longer threatened by crises, the cry for security grows louder. This, I am convinced, is not a cry for more collective social security by means of state or public institutions but a longing for personal security, for privacy, a desire for a sense of well-being in human society. Anyone who closes his eyes to this phenomenon is making a grave mistake. The state can, by pursuing a sound policy, increase the national income, raise personal incomes and improve investments, but this is not enough to make people happy.

There is surely something wrong here! This is not something

for which a government, whatever its politics, can be blamed. This is not a phenomenon with which a so-called capitalist government here or a socialist government there is confronted, but simply a sign of the times.

In the 'closed economy' that was taught to us at university there can be no insecurity. Here we have a self-contained group at work, which has its ears so close to the ground that it can have no illusions. There is no question of demand and supply. One glance in the larder is enough to show each one just what and how much can be consumed. The 'inspection of the granary' provided a kind of security. In the mediaeval feudal state people regarded the hierarchical system as an inviolable, divinely-ordained social principle. Then came a spiritual revolution which gave people a consciousness of freedom, and a sociological process began which for the past 170 years has been reshaping the world and our environment, bringing with it tremendous advances and achievements but also tensions, which not only emerged within individual states but also manifested themselves in military clashes between these states.

I believe that the widespread uncertainty today is largely due to the fact that the ordinary man cannot fully understand what is happening around him. We launch sputniks into space, but the effect upon us is bewildering rather than reassuring. Hearts and minds are disturbed. Every day modern technology is posing new questions and we must answer them. We do so more or less successfully and skilfully. But can anyone explain the underlying purpose linking these political, economic and social developments which have such a disturbing effect on people. The ordinary man does not really know what to make of this whole business. Where can he find peace and happiness? It may be, of course, that this unrest is a blessing in disguise. It may be the reason why people are taking refuge more and more in spheres of daily life which they can comprehend—in the family, in the society of their friends, in the club, or, on a higher plane, in religion. Wherever it is, they are seeking refuge, protection and salvation from something they can no longer grasp, at least intellectually. And it is here, I believe, in understanding and guiding the mental and spiritual energies of the people that the major challenge lies today.

Fleeing from reality is not the way to salvation. We must face up to it that, whatever the individual's occupation or private life may be, we have a duty to help him live with his environment and regain a sense of belonging to a whole. It is not enough for the individual to believe that, when he has finished his day's work, he can turn his back on the world. This may give him a temporary sense of relief but it is no permanent help to him. In the relations between employer and employee, in the planning of our towns, which offer no real peace of mind or even harmony to the eye, in regulating our economy, traffic and so on, we must either re-establish or re-create the bond between people and their environment. It must start in the factory, in the occupational field, and spread throughout all branches of human activity, whatever they may be. That is why I believe that the economic policy of the future must become more and more closely bound up with a conscious social policy. We have already shown what economic policy can achieve. But we have not yet demonstrated that more wealth brings more happiness. We are coming to realize that something more is needed, and it is up to us, regardless of our political views, to accomplish it, if we value our freedom. That is the problem of our time, and we must solve it.

This brings me, incidentally, to another problem, that of international coexistence. To American eyes life in Europe may appear somewhat puzzling. But if we here in Europe are to count for anything in the world of the future, then we must preserve the infinite variety and colour in the lives of the nations in this old continent. Any tendency towards egalitarianism breaks down, indeed any move towards it would be a sin.

We must settle with our past and, in spite of it, we must build a future. This is a task, however, that cannot be achieved through the paragraphs or clauses of a treaty, but is one which demands an act of will and the maximum of mutual understanding and sympathy. The Chairman said earlier that Austria's industry remains loyal to the EFTA treaties, and in that connection I would like to say quite categorically that I would be the last to suggest that contractual obligations should not be fulfilled, and not merely to the letter. But that is only the beginning. Is there anything in writing to show that this is the ultimate as far as the peoples of

Europe are concerned and that we have no further obligations? I will never tire of issuing the same warning, that the free nations of Europe, or those that remain free, must have a sense of spiritual unity and must be prepared to carry it to its ultimate conclusion.

It is simply inconceivable that, at a time when our freedom and security depend upon our all standing together, we nevertheless follow paths that diverge in the economic and social spheres of the nations. This is contrary to all reason and common sense. For that reason I think that both historical necessity and economic reason are on our side, that is with the community of people and nations that satisfy this need. It is sound common sense—and people know it—that one must not diminish the importance of Europe or undermine its spiritual unity by dividing it. It would be particularly disastrous—and no one has more right to say this than someone from Germany—if we once again committed the criminal folly of placing the economic strength and social security which we are striving for, and which are undoubtedly of the highest value, on the same level as political power. They are two entirely separate spheres of national life. Heaven help us if we reach the point of attaching more value to something simply because it is bigger, and less value to something that is less mighty and not so big. We must never allow values of this kind to invade our political and moral life again. Precisely because the EFTA group comprises countries and free people that are not among the big and the mighty, it is important that we should lose no time in reconciling differences.

There is no such thing as a patent solution which will dispose of all problems from one day to the next and satisfy all those involved. But let no one tell me that these problems cannot be solved. Why, when the Rome Treaty and the EFTA agreement were signed, was the solemn assurance given that each group was prepared to reach a settlement with its European partners as soon as possible, if nothing concrete was envisaged? This is not a question of economic possibilities but only one of political will, and this will must be there from the beginning. I, for my part, have always remained true to myself, and, if there is any question of having paid lip-service, I leave it to others to beat their breasts.

Ladies and gentlemen! You will appreciate that, on the eve of the discussions the German Federal Chancellor is to have with the

French President, I cannot make any detailed policy statements. But my views, which are sufficiently well known, remain unaltered. I shall always be in favour of a *rapprochement* and the removal of all discrimination inside free Europe. I almost shudder to think what might happen if no understanding were reached. Until now the situation has not taken a dramatic turn, for the lowering of tariffs within the two economic areas has only just begun. The damage has not yet become fully apparent. But no one will ever convince me that the developments set in motion by the Common Market will only bring material changes in trade. A new attitude of mind is being created. The inherent logic of two separate economic units must lead to a widening of the gap between them; new group interests emerge and naturally contrasts also arise—and all this in the heart of Europe which must stand together if it is to have a happy future, if it is to preserve its security and freedom. This is a trend which must on no account be allowed to continue. And it is my firm conviction that it will not continue. I admit that Germany's position in the world economy does not permit her the luxury of isolation, but I believe that a country like Austria is still less able to afford it.

Any economy that imagines it can solve its problems by self-confinement, whether by stifling or restricting competition, by cartel-like agreements or the like, is acting contrary to the spirit of the times and damaging itself. I wish I could say that German industry has as yet fully realized this but I hope that there are also men among you who are prepared to uphold these principles, even in the face of much resistance. For if we abandon them, we also give up all moral right to defend ourselves seriously and with good reason against the isolation of national economies. It is only the principle of freedom at home that entitles us, with a clear conscience, to demand freedom outside and, so to speak, 'document' the homogeneity of the free world.

On the other hand, I do not regard even an agreement between EEC and EFTA as the final solution. I admit that the concept 'Atlantic Community' still cannot be fully and exhaustively explained. As seen from Germany, the Atlantic Community undoubtedly finds expression in the NATO alliance. But in my view the essence of the Atlantic Community is not adequately expressed in terms of a defence community. For this world of ours cannot be defended with arms alone, but only by virtue of our mental outlook and our spiritual resolve to preserve our free way of life.

I do not want to emphasize any specific points or suggest any order of precedence, but for me the Atlantic Community also has a very real economic purpose. This may seem a trifle far-fetched, for in addition to, and with a wider scope than, the OEEC, we now have an OECD, which, as the first Atlantic body, is more loosely knit than was the OEEC. But it will certainly not remain so. In the meantime, what was achieved in the OEEC can, for the time being, bear imitation! It marked an enormous step forward and one that could not have been taken without the spiritual bonds that exist between the peoples of Europe. The OECD, as I said, is not so closely knit, but I venture to believe, nevertheless, that we shall also manage to remove the many sources of tension on this level which are plaguing Europe today and creating doubts in our minds as to whether the paths we have so far taken were necessarily the right ones.

Added to the sense of insecurity and uneasiness there is also the nagging question whether everything we have realized in the socio-economic sphere during the past twelve years will be of lasting value, whether there is any real point in saving and in accumulating property and wealth, or whether the value of what we have saved might not be undermined by inflationary trends. We have a tremendous task before us here which we have not yet completely mastered.

When we realize, for example, that in the Federal Republic during the past twelve years prices have risen by 'only' about 18 to 20% and that even so we are in a better position than most other countries where prices have risen by 30, 40, 50% and more, we have little real reason to congratulate ourselves. We must engender a feeling, indeed a genuine awareness, of common responsibility. That is what I meant when I said that everyone shares in the responsibility for the fate of the national economy, that is for the shaping of our future by means of a positive economic policy. We must give people a feeling of assurance that, both as regards trade cycles and monetary policies, nothing dramatic can happen—but this assurance must be more than credible, it must be true.

We in Germany have put forward proposals designed to damp down and stabilize trade fluctuations on a supranational basis, in order to protect us on the one hand against recessions and on the other to prevent an over-inflation, of which there are already signs in your country and mine, and which would damage the economy in a different way. This is a problem that can no longer be solved on a purely national basis.

The fact, for example, that Germany has large balance-of-payments surpluses is not, despite what many Americans believe, a sign of particular wealth, any more than America's balance-of-payments deficits were symptoms of poverty or want. Any such contention would be nonsense. But if I have spoken about Germany's balance-of-payments surpluses in this way, it is not because I want to present Germany as a poor country and invite sympathy for her. All I was aiming to do was to illustrate the confused and even prejudiced state of people's minds. The international evil of fluctuations in the balance of payments arises from the fact that the present system of currency exchange is simply inadequate. There can be no effective system so long as different national economic policies and differences of approach lead, as they have done over the past ten years, to entirely different price movements in each country, while rates of exchange have remained fixed. That is why surpluses and deficits are no longer symptoms of wealth or poverty but result from mere miscalculations and also, to some extent, reflect the domestic situation.

Why should we not—or will we not—take up this problem, which is becoming more and more of an international bone of contention, and reach some international agreement on it, possibly on the OECD level? If we have reached the stage of agreement on economic principles—and this is certainly true—we should have the strength and the insight to tackle those problems, which are occupying the minds of the international public and indirectly contributing to the widespread unrest. This, again, we cannot do as separate economic units but only in a world system.

At one time the prevailing view in Europe was that we 'poor wretches' simply could not be compared with rich America. We gazed spellbound at this country with its enormous productive capacity and immeasurable prosperity, its high wages and high standard of living. America represented, so to speak, the acme of all values. This view undoubtedly still persists, though somewhat modified, but there have also been certain fundamental changes. We no longer have the impression that we in Europe are lying beyond help and beyond hope on a deserted battlefield. We are also applying the most modern technical devices and we shall, I hope— let me emphasize, I hope—bring our standard of living nearer and nearer to that of the Americans. Whether this will take a long or a short space of time seeems to me to be relatively unimportant; the process is under way. In our fast-moving age this development will probably go forward more quickly than we can foresee today. So, apart from economic, moral and political necessities, we are moving steadily in the direction of closer co-operation between the Atlantic peoples, towards an Atlantic Community. We must, therefore, strive to overcome our differences and not become embroiled in a policy of discrimination, which will lead to a widening of the gulf between economic groupings that are not yet completely isolated. If we are guided by this idea, then we can look forward from tomorrow to a community that will embrace the free world. The benefits of a liberal economic policy and of a social system based on freedom derive from the fact that each people can pursue its own way of life and, at the same time, share in the blessings of the wider community, assuming that the peoples are bound together by freedom and common traditions.

I am known in my country to be an optimist. This does not mean that I have not sometimes been disappointed, as, for example, in the case of EFTA and EEC. But nothing can really shake my confidence, for it is rooted not in a superficial study of day-to-day problems but in the profound conviction that the free world is indissolubly bound up together and that men in their hearts want to achieve a harmony between their daily lives and the world about them—whether on a national or on a world basis. Let me conclude by expressing the hope that this harmony may come about some time in the future.

48

WHAT YOUNG PEOPLE SHOULD KNOW

(A letter to the Upper Sixth Form of the Martin-Butzer-Gymnasium in Dierdorf/Westerwald on March 1, 1961)

The Federal Minister of Economics receives many letters and messages daily from all sections of the population. Frequently they convey hints and suggestions, sometimes personal problems, and quite a number seek advice. This letter to the Sixth Form of a grammar school contains ideas which Ludwig Erhard is anxious to communicate to young people:

In your letter you ask me the following question:

'What part do political forces play in shaping the lives of young people, should this be considered in a wider context, and is the prevailing attitude one of indifference to sharing in political life or of a move towards it?'

The phrasing of your question does not make it any easier for me. It is an invitation to theorize, which is not my strong point and which would be of no help to you. As you, however, express the laudable intention to help those entering professional life to find their way and to clarify their minds and have appealed to me because of my experience of politics and people, I would like to say a few brief words on this subject.

For the process of the education you complete with your school certificate examination and for the educational facilities now open to you you have to thank a number and a variety of political actions in which the whole nation was involved. This simple reminder will not make any particular impression on you, but it is very much to the point. Moreover, the fact that you have expressed yourselves so frankly and freely and can raise the question of indifference to politics may be taken as a point in favour of the importance of political forces in the sense of your question.

343

The most obvious evidence in support of it, however, is the growth of prosperity by which youth is also profiting. To describe as an economic miracle the raising of our standard of living to that of other industrial countries by dint of conscious policy and hard work following the collapse of our economy is something that can be left to prodigal children. That prosperity has its blemishes is well known, and that it does not bring satisfaction is an old story. Herodotus would find plenty of examples today to confirm his dry remark: 'When people are well off, they can never have enough!' This much should be clear. Prosperity is a basis but not a pattern for the future. It is even more difficult to preserve it than to acquire it. So we are faced with the difficult task of mastering it mentally. We must discipline our demands increase the demands on ourselves, and modify those on the com munity as embodied in the economy and the state. The fact that young people in this technical civilization of ours sometimes kick over the traces and often show a marked indifference is due essentially to boredom with the struggle for material well-being and to a demand for something more from life than shorter working hours and higher wages, less risk and more profit, to say nothing of state welfare services from the cradle to the grave. For the first step a young person who is looking for spiritual values and personality takes towards playing an active and effective part in politics is to go to the heart of things and draw practical conclusions. Everyone for himself and in his own way; the wider context you ask about will then appear of itself. But anyone who believes that a high standard of living is enough to set against political Communism is nearer to its doctrine than he realizes or intends.

Ours is not a rich country. Ideas to the contrary which lead, both at home and abroad, to many an excessive demand being made upon us, rest upon a false equation of income and wealth. We have, it is true, a relatively high income but out of this we must repair fortunes and carry heavy post-war burdens, as distinct from countries that suffered less from the war.

Now a word on a key problem that especially affects our young people, because it helps to decide their future.

The population of the earth, which has increased by leaps and bounds in the last hundred years, continues to grow at a bewilder ing pace. Experts forecast that by the turn of the century, that is within forty years, it will have doubled. This produces changes of gravity and supply requirements of the highest political and economic importance. By contrast with Asia's vast masses, the population of divided Europe is increasing only slightly. The greater part of the world's population is vegetating in hunger and poverty. This hunger, beneath which there is a great deal of suppressed energy, is now becoming politically active—and activated. The peoples of Africa are pressing forward with growing self-awareness towards technical civilization, often with inadequate means and by tortuous routes. Everyone who is thinking of the future will have to face up sooner or later to these facts which I have merely outlined here. They are of supreme importance. To the very serious question of what means we, a small country, possess to hold our own in such a situation, there is only one answer: creative energy and will to work; to be on the alert and to press on towards a united Germany and a unified Europe. Here the relationship between a nation's destiny and its politics becomes clear.

The most immediate task, however, is to help those nations which are striving to develop their resources to help themselves by giving them adequate and continuing aid. This is not just philanthropy, it is an urgent political necessity. This development aid will cost a great deal and over a long period. But more important than money and goods are the services rendered willingly by well-trained, disciplined men from all trades and professions.

I have indicated here, to use your own words, the wider framework for active participation in politics as a means of influencing the lives of young people. As you see, this old earth presents greater and more interesting, certainly more important, challenges than the moon.

As regards indifference to political affairs, it is an attitude that is possible in a free society, just like arguing or fundamentally opposing. It has the fatal effect, where it gains the upper hand, of facilitating the emergence of dictatorial powers which exploit indifference in order to dispose of it later in their own way. For thinking people candid, positive criticism is still the most salutary method of expressing disagreement with the artist or dissatisfaction with the politician.

z

So much for politics. As you also refer to my experience of people, I would like to give you a few ideas to ponder over.

That the allocation of time is a deliberate act of the will that takes place 'in the head' is something that even people who have not studied philosophy are beginning to understand. The shorter the working hours, the longer the leisure hours (which is not always the same as 'free time'), and the more horse-power is exhausted in faster travelling, the less time people have. In fact, the only people who have time are those who take it or make it. The person who makes time for learning or working, who is, so to speak, mentally a pedestrian, manages not only to get through a lot of work but also to have leisure, that rare commodity, and has no need to have his free time organized.

The growth of automation, as part of the general process of mechanization—mankind's answer to its own growing numbers, as Rathenau so admirably put it—is necessary in the full sense of the word. You cannot avoid it, but this does not mean you should be afraid of it. Machines are made by men and operated by them, and men determine how much and what they produce. It is in men's hands, or more precisely in their heads, to adapt the machine, its output and its product, to human requirements. Remove the word 'perforce' from your vocabulary; it has, in any case, become rather archaic. 'There is nothing either good or bad, but thinking makes it so!' Hamlet's words apply particularly to atomic power. The fear it inspires gives us grounds for hope that it will be put to good use.

Finally I would like to impress upon you the importance of improving your knowledge of languages. It gives you a broader vision and self-assurance and furthers the cause of understanding in a world that is striving for unity despite all the conflicts and clashes of doctrines and interests.

My young friends! No matter what profession you take up, the future holds out many opportunities for good work and active participation in political life. Make the most of them! I wish you luck in your school certificate examination, the first and easiest test of your lives.

With friendly greetings,   Yours,

LUDWIG ERHARD

49

THE REVALUATION OF THE D-MARK

(Broadcast on March 6, 1961)

The conflict which had arisen from growing payments surpluses and, at the same time, continuing trade crises reached a point in February 1961 where a revaluation of the D-Mark became inevitable. The Notenbank had tried in vain to control the boom by making credit dearer and scarcer. An increase in the supply of money from outside almost entirely nullified the intended effect of the credit policy on trade and prices. From the autumn of 1960 onwards, when the pressure of foreign currency was so great that the Federal Bank began to adjust its policy once more to the balance of payments, it cut more and more across our trade requirements. The decision to alter the exchange rate became unavoidable when it was clear that the parity of the world's main currencies would remain unaffected. Moreover, there was no longer any likelihood of multilateral action being taken to correct currency disparities. And finally, such prospects as there had been in the autumn of a more stable trade situation had come to nothing. Regulation of foreign exchange was suggested, but such a step was incompatible with the position of the D-Mark as a convertible currency. Another suggestion, which had been put forward on several occasions abroad, namely, to raise the level of costs and prices in Germany, was unacceptable to the Federal Government. In the interest of price stability, therefore, the only course open to the Government was to alter the exchange rate. By so doing, it also recognized its share of the responsibility for ensuring that international trade and payments continued undisturbed.

Following yesterday's press conference, at which the Government's revaluation of the D-Mark was fully discussed, the object of this broadcast is to explain to the German people why this decision was reached and what the consequences are likely to be.

It is undeniable that revaluation will make our exports rather more difficult and more expensive but that, while some branches will be affected more than others, the reduction in our exports will be temporary. On the other hand, the reduced cost of our imports will doubtless exercise a certain pressure on Germany's price level but this will also contribute to greater stability. So, as regards both imports and exports, competition will become livelier not only in the Federal Republic but also on third markets.

I hope and expect that this new situation will also give rise to a more cautious attitude in the social partners, because higher costs can no longer be absorbed automatically in higher prices and every mistake made will almost certainly affect both employers and employed. In this same context one must expect a slackening of the hectic activity on the labour market and, in spite of full employment, it will be possible to achieve a more effective balance between the supply of labour and the demand. The industrial entrepreneur, who, I can readily appreciate, is dissatisfied and even worried, would hardly accuse me of being prepared to damage the German economy either thoughtlessly or still less intentionally, for precisely the opposite is the case. It is just because I am anxious to ensure a steady and sound upwards trend that I aim, by revaluation, to re-establish the firm foundations on which a meaningful and active trade policy can be pursued. Moreover, I have too great a respect for the achievements and initiative of the German entrepreneur to believe that certain temporary difficulties could seriously damage the German economy.

The entrepreneur is once more being put to the test, with the eyes of the whole nation upon him, and I am confident that he will pass it. Let us not forget that the Federal Bank had an insoluble dilemma on its hands, being faced with the mutually exclusive issues of, on the one hand, Germany's internal trade crisis and, on the other, the balance-of-payments surpluses. It was no longer in a position to influence, much less control, the boom in Germany. At the same time, there could be no question of reintroducing control of foreign currency without abandoning free convertibility. So, unless the Government was prepared simply to do nothing, it had to recognize the necessity for, and have the courage to introduce, revaluation, otherwise it would be failing to carry out its responsibilities to the German people.

Although I am pleased this step has been taken, I can assure you that my advice was only given after I had considered all its implications for the future. When a step, which I already realized years ago was becoming increasingly inevitable, is dismissed by the opposition as a short circuit on the part of the Federal Government, such an interpretation cannot be taken seriously by any thinking person. For myself I can only laugh at such childish statements. I hope the German people will recognize that repeated statements by the Federal Government to the effect that the continuing stability of our money, protection of savings and an extension of private ownership are fundamental to its policy, were made in all seriousness and were acted upon.

Nominal savings in the Federal Republic have risen to 136 milliard D-Marks. This means that if, for example, rising prices were to bring a 3% drop in value, those with savings would be subjected, willy-nilly, to a loss of four milliard D-Marks. Any policy that allowed such a thing to happen would not promote but undermine the urge to save as the first step towards private ownership. But savings also provide a secure basis for economic progress and the productivity of our national output. This fact may even be appreciated by those who felt confident that there would be no revaluation and reproached the Federal Government.

In this connection it should also be remembered that the widespread belief last autumn in a levelling-out of the boom and a general stabilization no longer applies to our trade situation, that the uncertainty people felt about the monetary policy of the American Government after the Presidential election has now passed, and that any change of monetary policy on a multilateral basis is out of the question. Moreover, the events of the summer and autumn of 1960 showed all too clearly how dangerous it is to discuss the question of revaluation openly and at a politically responsible level. That is why the Federal Government took such pains, in conjunction with the Notenbank, to keep their plan of action secret. I am convinced that the entire German people not only understands but approves this attitude.

Suggestions in today's press that the revaluation of the D-Mark was the result of American influence or even pressure are disproved by suggestions frequently made in the same newspapers that the Federal Government took this step in order to escape international pressure for payments to be made to meet the balance-of-payments surpluses. Both interpretations are completely and utterly devoid of foundation! As the honour of friendly governments is being called in question, I feel in duty bound to deny these imputations most emphatically. And equally emphatically I would like to repeat the statement I made yesterday that the Federal Government, in taking this step, has not for one moment considered going back on assurances given in negotiations or weakening in its determination to play its full part with other nations in preserving the peace and security of the world.

We can take satisfaction in the knowledge that opinion abroad is almost unanimous in welcoming the German step as an essential contribution to the stabilization of international monetary policy, which will help to correct the imbalance in international payments that is poisoning even the political atmosphere. No one maintains that revaluation is a panacea that will cure all our economic, social and financial ills. But it does provide the basis for a coherent, active trade policy.

The German people can look ahead to the future with more confidence than before. I hope it will not allow itself to be misled by the all too transparent and dishonest machinations of the Opposition, which are designed to spread unrest and to present the government in a false light as untrustworthy and under pressure from abroad. This same Opposition, which has been trying particularly hard recently to make the German people believe that the Federal Government had made price agreements with industry and was, in consequence, powerless to take any effective action that would benefit the German people, has now been confronted, before the German people and the public of many other nations, with the revaluation of the D-Mark. This clear, forthright answer is no more than they deserved! I am certain, however, that the German people, regardless of party or profession, is firmly convinced that it can trust the Federal Government.

You may be wondering what the revaluation will amount to, what exactly the adjustment of our currency parity will be, and whether the figure quoted, 4.76%, is correct. This, of course, is something that no computer can prove. But a close study of our national economy since last autumn and a comparison of the purchasing power of various international currencies justify the assumption that the new parity will produce a better balance.

Let me give yet another reason why the Federal Government decided as it did: Germany's supply of credit from the influx of foreign money and from credits abroad was particularly favourable to heavy industry, whereas lesser concerns were not in a position to exploit these opportunities. Revaluation put a stop to this injustice.

To sum up, I can tell you tonight that, judging by the many views expressed by all sections and classes of the German people, the overwhelming majority welcome the Federal Government's action and are grateful to it for its courageous decision.

50

SOCIAL ORDER CREATES PROSPERITY AND SECURITY

(Speech at the CDU Federal Party Congress in Cologne on April 26, 1961)

In his speech to the CDU Party Congress in Cologne Erhard continues to develop ideas he had expressed in his speech on social policy at the Karlsruhe Party Congress in 1960 and—with the Federal elections of 1961 also in mind—relates them to contemporary problems:

After twelve years in power the Christian Democratic Union in common with its sister-party, the Christian Social Union, is today making a progress report to the German people in preparation for the elections to the fourth German Bundestag. Despite the tremendous success it has achieved and despite the years of fruitful work, during which our country and those Germans who live in freedom have emerged from a chaos that engulfed every walk of life, the party is without pride or arrogance but is conscious of the good fortune that attended its work.

Concerned as we are about the future of our people and about historical truth, we will naturally continue to deal unmercifully with those Opposition forces which for more than twelve years have sought to undermine our laborious efforts to rebuild our country politically, economically and socially. Nor shall we be fulfilling our obligations to the German people if we stand idly by while the Opposition, with a somewhat belated flash of insight, promises that it will make an even better job of what we managed to achieve from almost hopeless beginnings. This political confidence trick is, of course, so primitive and so transparent, that it would not convince even the simplest of minds. But, as promises are easy to make and cost nothing, whereas their realization is a hard and arduous business, it should not be forgotten that the Social Democratic Party has quite simply opposed everything that contributed to the prosperity and social security of the German people and that, above all, won back the political confidence of the free nations. We know from within the ranks of the SPD itself that the Godesberg Programme was inspired largely by tactical considerations. The German people would be endangering its future and would have only itself to blame if it did not remain constantly on the alert, for what we are witnessing in the SPD is not genuine political insight but a tactical move, behind which the old illusions and fallacies are as alive as ever.

We know from experience that you cannot place any confidence in someone who, after prolonged and bitter hostility towards those in positions of responsibility, takes five, eight or ten years to realize the errors of his own ways. For a nation, delays of this kind can be fatal.

We in the Christian Democratic Union have no need to keep on giving fresh assurances on the pretext that we are clarifying our views; we have no recantations to make; we have no use for six-monthly revisions of neatly formulated party programmes which are designed to reassure the party rank and file and at the same time present an attractive image to the outside world. The CDU is sufficiently above-board and alive to measure up to the dynamic events of our time and their political consequences, but in the final analysis its decisions are inspired not by tactical opportunism but by its Christian, humanitarian liberalism. We have no need to woo the electorate with high-sounding promises, for the average German has only to look back over the past fifteen years to realize how much he has gained by the government policy laid down by the Union and what he can expect from the Union in good times or bad, for this policy is the very stuff of life, is fully realized action.

And yet we do not expect to be given a blank cheque for the future. We are aware that in such troubled times the German people have the right to know what provision has been made for the morrow and what kind of policy will decide their future. On the other hand, it is more difficult today than at any previous time to interpret human life, political life or even economic life in terms of figures. It is more than ever necessary that we should combine a sober sense of reality with imagination and intuition, if we are to find security in this world. Our domestic and our foreign policy now and in the future is one, not of drifting aimlessly, but of taking a stand, holding our ground and working together with other countries for peace, freedom, prosperity and security.

The term 'social order', therefore, when taken as a major premise, must be given the widest possible interpretation. It does not only cover social legislation in the narrow sense, nor does it confine itself to the methods, processes and objectives of economic policy; it is not bounded by domestic administrative measures; it means more than just budgetary, financial and monetary order. It is not limited to the problems of housing, refugees or other such questions. Social order means the all-embracing development of our time, in which all facts of human and social life are caught up. Social order is the ground on which we stand and move, in fact the very air we breathe; social order is the bridge that links today and tomorrow. It alone provides the security we must have to trust in the future.

Our Christian way of thinking not only makes it impossible for us to accept the materialistic concept of history, which argues that man and society are merely products of their environment, but requires us to shape this environment as part of our responsibility towards God and mankind. Thus the Union has nothing in common with those who believe that the sole function of social policy is to solve the material problems of life. I hope the Socialist Opposition will understand what I mean and not produce in reply the old hackneyed phrases about the unfair distribution of the national income and the national wealth. For no German government since the Reich was founded—including the Socialist-led government of the Weimar period—and scarcely any other Socialist government in the free world, has managed to produce out of so much misery the benefits for the great mass of the people and the social progress that we, the Christian Democrats, can claim to have achieved as a government and a party. We know the value and the importance of the material in human existence and we do not feel any special sense of virtue or claim that we have dispensed divine justice. We did not merely talk, we acted, but, if we are challenged by the Opposition, then it will give us genuine pleasure to lay once more before the German people, in print, on records and on tape-recordings, all the statements of the SPD which clearly reflect their attitude towards and their opinion of our policy over the past twelve years. And we would leave the German people to judge how such consistent error could produce the moral right to decide the fate of Germany.

How impressive the achievement of the German people itself appears beside the blatant attempts of Social Democratic officials to keep a bland smile on the face of the marxist Adam! We at this Party Congress are here to pay tribute to that achievement. We owe a debt of gratitude to the workers in the towns and in the country who, nearly sixteen years ago, when the fighting ended, began rebuilding Germany with their bare hands. If Germany's reconstruction was a glorious feat it was largely the feat of the German worker. Let us be grateful to him. The Union is a People's Party and the worker also has his place and his home in it; he belongs to us and we belong to him.

We also thank the employees and officials who worked to serve the whole and who, by their self-discipline in difficult times, helped to reorganize the social life of our nation.

But above all, I believe, we have to thank the women, without whom our great work would not have succeeded. We have to thank them for their contribution as mothers and housewives and also in the professions. It must be recorded for posterity that, in the great tragedy of our people, the spirit and work of our women shone like stars in the darkness. It was they who saw to it that our families, the keystones of our social structure, remained united, and by so doing they created the foundations on which we were able to build. This quiet, untiring devotion is not recorded in any statistics, because happiness cannot be expressed in figures.

We thank those of our fellow-citizens who, by their work in agriculture, helped us to weather our most serious emergencies and to begin the work of reconstruction successfully. German agriculture has a great future and its future will be all the more assured as agriculture sees itself as a part of the whole.

On this day of retrospect we must also not forget those who have found a home here in the Federal Republic, the refugees and the expellees. They have contributed in their millions to the success of our reconstruction and the internal consolidation of our national life. What may have seemed at first to be a social and economic burden became a blessing, for it welded us together as one people. I know that many still have their worries, their unfulfilled wishes and longings; I know that countless people have suffered untold hardship. They can always be sure of our active help.

We have to thank those people who held key positions and contributed directly to our reconstruction: the entrepreneurs, the merchants and the engineers, members of the learned professions, teachers and doctors; the journalists, the administrators, and those who often worked unseen yet contributed nonetheless as inventors and thinkers to the creation of this new Germany. The last of these in particular had—and still have—a great part to play in our rehabilitation by opening up new avenues and fresh horizons.

Countless men and women in our country go on working quietly and conscientiously, without making any great demands; their work bears lasting fruit yet the public knows nothing of them. They live by the principle that deeds are better than words. We have to thank them. Perhaps their quiet, unassuming examples should be more widely followed. I mention only two groups out of this great host of people: the nursing sisters in their tireless work of charity and the old people who so often do their stint faithfully. They should know how much affection and respect they command.

We greet the young people of Germany to whom the future belongs. It is right that they should know the importance of youth but they must not believe that youth in itself is a qualification. Our youth of today, like no generation before it, has the whole world at its feet. When in our history have there ever been such opportunities for young people to develop, to employ their education and energy not merely for their own personal advancement but also to play a responsible part in public affairs, whether at home or abroad, a case in point being the developing countries in various part of the world!

While the Social Democrats are still wrestling with their marxist doctrines, with grouses and grievances among themselves, we are thinking of the future. I leave it to the Social Democrats to explain how rigid adherence to the marxist philosophy of economics and history by well-known and powerful trade union leaders from within their own ranks can be reconciled with the profession of liberal doctrines by the party leadership itself. How the old comrades will come to terms with those whom the party hopes to win over from the bourgeois camp by making a seductive yet hardly convincing appeal to their liberal feeling is the SPD's own affair. The Social Democrats have still not realized that day by day they are sloughing, that the socialist panacea of yesterday is no more than an unsubstantial ghost today, that our youth is not interested in the language of class warfare, and that the term 'proletariat' reeks of mothballs.

Precisely because we had to overcome unprecedented material hardship and were able, in what is in the historical sense a short period, to make the transition from dire poverty of growing prosperity, do we seek to know the purpose and value of material wealth in human life. I would not want it to be thought that we are not aware of the humble circumstances in which many people live and the material hardship that many families are still suffering. One cannot state every individual case; one can only speak in general terms of a social phenomenon. Given this limitation, I think I can say that we now find ourselves in a position where it is justifiable to maintain that we are at the beginning of a new phase of our social and economic life. If one cannot put one's finger on any one day as marking the change, one can on reflection distinguish between the events of the past twelve years and the tasks that lie before us. It is not Germany's destiny that has changed the world but rather political developments in the world at large that are drawing us into their orbit and challenging us to employ our energies and our capabilities to shape our own destiny and thereby play our part in the defence of freedom.

If we believe we have reached a milestone in our social development at which we should take stock and look both back and forward, then this certainly does not mean that we can afford to renounce the methods and principles of the Social Market Economy. What we must do is determine whether our standard of values should not be somewhat adjusted; whether we are not looking farther ahead, as indeed we must, than when we were surrounded by ruins.

On the whole we are today justified in talking of the prosperity of our people, but we must try in future to interpret this as meaning more than just the possession of material things. Prosperity creates the basis and the prerequisite for man's liberation from dependence on the state and for his enjoyment of the spiritual and cultural riches of the world. It is our duty to implement a policy which enables us to adapt our environment, both in town and in the country, at the work-benches and in the homes, to the requirements of a modern, free society.

We are proud and happy that we have been able to achieve so much for our people particularly in the social sphere. Let me give just a few figures: the total expenditure on social security in the Federal Republic has risen from 10 to over 35 milliard marks, while expenditure in the Federal Budget alone has gone up from 4 to 12 milliards, pensions insurance as a whole from $2\frac{1}{2}$ to 16 milliards, payments in kind and cash for sickness benefits from 1·7 to over 8 milliards. These are not merely the fruits of a successful social policy but also proof of a socially-conscious economic policy, for which our party will gladly answer to its own conscience and to the German people.

This substantial progress reflects an increase in the gross national product from 97 milliards in 1950 to 276 milliards in 1960, and an increase in the national income from 74.5 to 212 milliards in the same period. In those ten years an average of 60% of the gross national product went to private consumers, while investments varied from 22 to 25%. This relatively high figure is accounted for by the great efforts and outlay on the part of private industry and public authorities on Germany's reconstruction. So the Federal Republic need fear no comparison with any other country either as regards economic development or social advancement.

I must emphasize at this point that our reconstruction programme was not confined to material things but also included large-scale investments in the cultural sphere. Many people who have benefited by this are not fully aware of it. Apart from transport, the biggest investment of public funds has been in the cultural field.

Although, even in terms of real purchasing power, the standard of living in this country has doubled, we, as Christian Democrats cannot afford to overlook the fact that people have not become correspondingly more content. One can hardly expect that a still further improvement in the over-all standard of living will bring with it the same degree of personal happiness. We all know the law of diminishing returns, but this would be a highly superficial way to explain something that is rooted in the souls and the minds of men. Here we are dealing with a complex mixture of profound human emotions and conscious ideological factors.

I do not agree with those who place a purely negative interpretation on the malaise or even discontent of the average person and dismiss it as lack of sensitivity or ingratitude. I am much more inclined to regard it as, to a large extent, a sign of self-awareness, perhaps even of disenchantment, the result of persons asking themselves whether the whole purpose of human labour and indeed of life as such is to seek material enjoyment and to be a mere consumer. The cross-fire comes from those who are engrossed in party-political opposition and who, in order to justify their own existence, arbitrarily foment unrest and discontent of a different kind, setting out to persuade the organized groups in our society that, in spite of the steady increase in their standard of living, they always come off worse and must step up their claims. None are so guilty as those who foster the illusion that a nation can consume more than it produces, let us say 120% of the national product; can have today what is not earned until tomorrow. The individual's self-possession is constantly being undermined by external influences which threaten to stifle his conscience and his sense of responsibility. The result is mental confusion and a sense of unrest. In the final analysis, it is a struggle between the individual and the collective, between responsibility and the lust for power. I would be the last person to preach renunciation and self-denial, but I do want people to realize that, in addition to the things each one of us can and should enjoy, there are common tasks for us to perform as a community, as a people, as a state, and that welfare means providing not just for the present but also for tomorrow and the day after tomorrow, for our future.

If we can assume that we shall be able to continue for another twelve years in raising the living standard of our people without any serious crises, then it is not only those who adopt a material view of history who will wonder how such a development is likely to change our view of life and our way of living it. It is thoughts of this kind that bring home to us how inadequate our lives would be if our sole purpose were to redouble material consumption.

But let us for the moment keep our feet firmly on the ground and cope with the work we are called upon to do here and now. If the Party Congress that was held before the Federal elections of 1957 took as its slogan 'Prosperity for all' and declared itself further for individual ownership, this was not intended to be a Four Year Plan on the Communist pattern but was a statement of our intention to pursue a course that would free the individual by making private ownership available to more and more people. No one can seriously deny that we have already passed the initial stage and are also courageous enough to strike out on new and, some might say, even revolutionary paths. There is, of course, no cornucopia from which private ownership flows, but it seems to us only fair that we should not merely promote the accumulation of private wealth on a productivity basis as a means of building up our economy but should also give more incentive to the broad mass of wage earners to benefit by private ownership.

The idea of People's Shares did not, of course, originate with the Opposition; it is an expression of our political intent to offset the inevitable concentration of productive capital by a deconcentration of property, and in future, when trading licences are being allocated or new shares issued, to try, even with private shareholding companies, to create openings for small-scale investment by the general public. We are anxious to encourage private saving in every shape and form, but we categorically reject the Socialist method of expropriation as a means of subjecting private industry to the expansionist ambitions of mass collectives, which must eventually dominate it.

The Social Democrats propose to skim off 'surplus profits' without even suggesting what sort of standards they would apply, or indicating where this process would begin and where it would end; without considering whether 'surplus profit' might not be a symptom of a purely temporary improvement in trade, whether the result of genuine productive enterprise or of the exploitation and even misuse of economic power. The opportunities for arbitrary action are endless and in the long run our democratic system would go to the wall. Apart from accepting our programme and our ideas and giving them a slight socialist bias, the Opposition has thought of nothing new; it can never entirely break away from its marxist past.

The social policy of the CDU/CSU is not designed to produce results that are merely popular election slogans but is based upon a long-term yet practicable programme with a definite end in view. Even prosperity and private ownership are not ultimate and absolute values, but they help the average citizen to achieve that inner enrichment which comes from self-awareness and a sense of human dignity. We would have wasted our lives and certainly failed to meet our obligations to God and our fellow-men, if, at the end of our days, all that could be said of us was that we had lived well and amassed property. Knowing this, we cannot simply sit with folded hands and forget that we have political obligations to fulfil in this world.

Just as we have managed to surmount many obstacles and remedy many mistakes in our national affairs, just as we have shaken off sectarian and feudalistic ideas, just as the concept of 'class rule' only persists today as an ideological caricature of the past and the concept 'proletariat' has become meaningless, so, too, relations between peoples have changed for the better. The sham values of the past, which set nation against nation in the interests of decadent nationalism and narrow-minded protectionism and which almost destroyed our planet, have given way to the knowledge that what really binds or divides states, peoples and individuals is the firm resolve to live in freedom according to the laws of God, or to be prepared, if not compelled, to bow to the yoke of a collective or totalitarian authority.

Far be it from us to accuse our party-political opponents of holding undemocratic beliefs, but no one can accuse us of being deceitful or malevolent if, on the basis of the Opposition's attitude for more than twelve years, we still do not feel confident that it has entirely abandoned the marxist ideal of society as the cradle of collectivism and communism. And if we have declared political war on the Opposition, we have done so in the sure knowledge that we are creating the outward guarantees for the defence of our

AA

nation's freedom. The fact that we do not worship power but believe in the strength of the human spirit means that our first and immediate responsibility lies in the limited, tangible sphere of the Federal Republic itself.

Such harmony as has been achieved within the free world and its close-knit democratic system has its roots—leaving aside the activities of many supranational organizations—in the more limited spheres of governments and parliaments with their executive and legislative powers. That this thesis by no means excludes the closest possible collaboration is clear from our efforts to pursue a commercial, economic and monetary policy within the various national economies, consistent with supranational obligations and with our common tasks and objectives.

In revaluing the D-Mark, for example, it was clearly our purpose not merely to keep the purchasing power of our national currency stable and to protect savers against loss but also to show solidarity with our partners in the free world in accordance with our supranational obligations. It is clear, on the other hand, that no country can by itself solve monetary crises of a multilateral kind. So the Union through the Federal Government will urge, today and after the elections, that the new Atlantic organization, the OECD, should not merely deal with the specific problems of development aid but should go beyond that and grapple with the task of co-ordinating more closely the economic problems I have mentioned. This talk of co-ordination is the real cause of our balance-of-payments problems. In fact, the plans and machinery for closer integration are still lagging far behind what has in practice been achieved.

Let me make a few more observations with regard to recent events following the currency revaluation. One has heard people in the most diverse quarters say that an improvement in the balance of trade and payments and a certain pressure on the German price level, which were the object of the exercise, would not result at all. This obvious contradiction could only have been put forward by interested parties, for it is not only contrary to economic good sense but it is not even good arithmetic. No expert could expect the desired effect to be achieved overnight. It had to happen gradually but surely, as part of the normal commercial process. I myself made it clear, when I first defended revaluation, that this would not cure all our ills. But what is one to say when a political measure of paramount importance to the nation brings the response from well-known trade union leaders that they are not prepared to take any account of this action and will therefore continue to press claims previously made? Such statements reveal the mortal danger inherent in regarding a state and its economy not as a common responsibility but something distinct from certain collective bodies, whose sole aim it is to pursue their own ends. The Minister of Economics is to be denied the right to enlighten people. But when, in 1960, the growth of productivity per man in industry dropped from 9.1% in the first quarter to 3.6% in the fourth, and per hour of work from 11.3% to 6.8%, whereas during the same period the increase in wages per hour rose from 5.9% to 13.6%, then it is my duty, particularly after the revaluation, to issue a warning.

It is phenomena of this kind that reveal the defects still present in our competitive system, defects which we must eradicate in the near future. True, the idea that the state should be responsible for protecting competition has gained ground in parliament, and the German people has, by and large, come to recognize, that the basic and most important element in the Social Market Economy is free competition. If, on the other hand, no further progress could be made during this parliamentary session with the complex questions of second-hand price fixing, of price recommendations, of market domination by certain enterprises and of industrial concentration, this was due not to lack of courage in our party to grasp these nettles but solely to the need for more practical experience and precise information on which to base a judgment. At all events, the cries of despair that were uttered when the relevant legislation was passed have been entirely unjustified. This does not mean that we should underrate the activities of the pro-cartel group, whose aim it is to undermine our competitive system by introducing restrictive practices legislation.

The European Economic Community will have to take a stand on this same subject and must leave no doubt that it is committed to a liberal economic system, for abandonment of free competition would sooner or later turn the Community into a rigid, centrally controlled organization. And in the same area you cannot have two different approaches to competition working side by side and on an equal footing.

We know, of course, that there are various theories as to the function of competition. The Union has made its position unmistakably clear in its political programme, of which free competition is the keystone. That is why any attempt to undermine this policy must fail. One has to be blind not to see the intimate connection between personal, economic and political freedom. Those who, like our party, are ready to protect, and to go on protecting, freedom of enterprise as an indispensable part of any market economy against all criticism and opposition, are also entitled to expect the entrepreneur to realize that his freedom requires the courage to face up to competition with all its opportunities and risks.

This is not the place to probe more deeply into this question, although it is one of crucial importance to our social system; but when, as one of the objections to the Cartel Law, it is argued that concentration is an unavoidable process which must be accepted, then we disagree. Not that we are iconoclasts, who are allergic to progress and do not realize that modern technology makes large industrial units in certain branches inevitable. But we are not prepared to sit idly by and watch the growing trend towards more and more concentration in the shape of recognizable or, in some cases, invisible cartels, and more particularly as the company and tax laws are no longer consistent with the present economic situation but give unfair advantages and privileges, which cannot be reconciled with our social commitments. And this raises the problem of *Organschaft* and *Schachtelprivileg,** which require careful review.

---

* The terms *Organschaft* and *Schachtelprivileg* are virtually untranslatable as single words and have therefore been left in their German form. *Organschaft* is the position of a subsidiary company which in its finance, organization, and trade activity, has been integrated into a parent company to such an extent that to outside parties it appears to act as a mere organ of the parent company. Trade Tax is assessed on the parent company alone in this case, but Corporation Tax can only be treated in this way if the tax authorities recognize a profit and loss transfer agreement between the two companies. *Schachtelprivileg* is an 'intercorporated privilege' with regard to intercorporate dividends payable between parent and subsidiary companies.

It is completely misleading to argue that competition must be restricted in order to protect the middle class against the power of the big concerns, when one's real object is to find some spurious moral excuse to oppose the Cartel Law. Here and there the beguiling voices of entrepreneurs, who are still wedded to the cartel-ridden economic system of a past era, may fall on willing ears, but nothing can alter the fact that this era, this spirit of a bygone age, is doomed. The independent small or medium-sized firm is by no means at the mercy of the big concern, so long as the little man can be sure of starting off in competition on an equal footing. Besides the arguments that give the big concern a natural advantage, there are not a few on the other side in favour of the advantages enjoyed by small and medium-sized firms in a dynamic economy which calls for constant adjustment and adaptation. There is also the fact that, as the output of quality manufacture grows and production becomes more varied, there is less and less room for the cartel, so that the alleged advantage, namely the chance to get a higher price through a cartel than on the free market, is only available on the fringes of industry. But this makes a mockery of equal competition within the industry itself and, at the same time, penalizes the consumer. It is no accident, for example, that the handicrafts and manual trades are wholeheartedly in support of the Social Market Economy.

As far as future development is concerned, the security of our industrial 'middle class' lies not in associating with cartels but, on the contrary, in the continuance of a liberal social system, in the conscious desire of ordinary people to give expression to their individuality and personality in their everyday lives. Only if we were prepared to let our souls and spirits become stereotyped and to pursue the path of uniformity and mass-production would the big concern get the better of our middle-class industry. The more each individual insists on leading his life according to his own ideas and desires, the more firmly will the middle class become rooted in our social system. This is just one aspect of the power of freedom to shape the lives of people and nations.

One might approach this problem from the bleak view-point of the rationalist and consider in purely mathematical terms which social principle or economic system is 'cheaper', in other words, which one guarantees the consumer the maximum of material goods. Were it possible to calculate units of consumption, we might well come to the conclusion that the maximum effect could only be produced by a national economy based on highly rationalized mammoth concerns with a very high degree of automation. But this would simply not make sense, and what might appear to be of benefit to society would prove a disaster; we need only look eastwards at the totalitarian economic systems behind the Iron Curtain to realize the consequences of such materialistic realism. Life becomes pointless, barren, shallow and grey, and the men and women who vegetate in such a world are no longer in the image of God but are mere ciphers in a soulless machine.

Freedom has its economic price, but comparison shows an enormous profit to the free society, which is constantly giving a fresh impetus to life and allows people to develop freely as God's creatures.

An essential component of society as we see it is the free peasant with his own farm. Reckoned in marks and pfennigs, it would doubtless be cheaper for us to import agricultural produce, but as in this instance, for reasons dictated by nature and beyond our control, free competition is impossible; to apply the rational principle here would mean the end of the German peasant. If we in the Union do not even pose the question whether we wish to maintain a healthy peasant community, because the answer, for political, sociological and biological reasons, is self-evident; if, in other words, our decision on this point is unambiguous and final, then we must be prepared to implement our decision in, for example, our marketing regulations or in the 'Green Plan'. It is unrealistic to support such legislation for political reasons but to shy away from the consequences. If one also considers that the growth of productivity in German agriculture can compare favourably with that of the industrial sector and that the structure of our agriculture is showing visible signs of continuing improvement, then this is further evidence of the wisdom of the Union's agrarian policy. Here again the cheapest source of food supplies does not mean the rational or social optimum, for agriculture, as an integral part of the economy, must be seen and judged as part of the whole.

Although we stand by the Social Market Economy, which has

succeeded in freeing the German people from poverty and hardship, we know all too well that, quite apart from the agricultural marketing regulations, there are still traces of the economic planner's mentality in our economy. This applies particularly to the considerable number of official restrictions still in force, especially in the field of transport. Here again we recognize the special circumstances that made legislation necessary, for the Federal Railways, a big concern, has to compete with a large number of predominantly medium-sized firms in road transport and inland waterways. But, while it may be necessary to draw up certain rules governing competition in this sector, this should not prevent us from ridding our transport system, as we have done in other branches of industry, of too many official regulations. As we see it, a better distribution of traffic between the various modes of transport would be achieved by healthy competition than by official regulations. That is why tariffs should be relaxed to leave room for price competition. In this field, too, competition will prove to be a better yard-stick than any officials, and without damaging the transport firms.

The Common Market is also forcing us to make speedy decisions in this sector. Even at this early stage one can say with certainty that in this wider area transport will not be subject to as many official regulations as is the case today, so no better service could be rendered to transport firms in the Federal Republic than to steer them in this direction and to pass legislation as soon as possible which will take account of the future.

If we review all the individual sectors of our national economy, we are forced to realize that wherever there is free competition with prices regulating supply and demand the market works smoothly and there is an effortless flow of consumer goods. At the same time, the market is never in danger of becoming artificial as a result of central directives and thereby attracting the wrong kind of investment. On the other hand, wherever the rudiments of a planned or controlled economy are still present, we always have friction and disturbances to reckon with which call for further controls and so perpetuate the planned economy. Surely this should give us courage to move forward with determination on the road of the Social Market Economy!

If this progress report is to be complete, the Opposition might well be asked whether the large cities under Socialist administration build only hospitals and schools with their surplus funds or whether these too are not spent on general building work which should have been postponed in the interest of the whole and to maintain price stability. There is no more flagrant example of the Opposition's lack of imagination and vision than its habit of searching like a bloodhound for superficial defects, without itself being able to offer anything more constructive than torrents of abuse.

It is, of course, our wish and our hope, after all we have experienced since 1948, that the principles of the Social Market Economy may also serve as a guide for international economic cooperation between the free peoples of Europe and the world. One of the most surprising developments after the appalling war which had forced almost every nation into the strait-jacket of planned economy was the fact that not the least of the factors that contributed to the establishment of a world-wide liberal system was Germany's economic policy. Although we are still far from our goal, it is already clear that we are on the right road, for it is worth noting that, for example, within the European Economic Community there was never any question of choosing between a market and a planned economy; a liberal system was adopted automatically as the one most suited to our times. We are not claiming any patent rights, but no one can deny that, through our economic and social policy, we rendered a service to the spirit of freedom.

My views on the problems of European integration are well known, and I am happy to see that solutions are being worked out as a result of which the union of the Six will mark the beginning not of an isolationist movement but of a *rapprochement* between the freedom-loving peoples and states of Europe.

There is a growing awareness that the free part of Europe cannot afford to be weak, either in the economic or the military sphere, if it is to hold out more or less indefinitely against the forces that threaten it. As the realization is also growing that we must form a closely-knit community, there is reason to hope that an 'Atlantic Community' may become a genuine political reality. We for our part have made contributions, which have been generally acknow-

ledged, towards the evolution of a Free World approach to problems that would transcend considerations of national policy or
national economy or even regional conceptions. The NATO
alliance, which is designed for our defence, must find its counterpart in the economic field, otherwise purely national interests or a
combination of such interests in inter-state relations will triumph
over the consciousness of a common destiny.

The most characteristic feature of the times in which we live is
the division of the world; from it we on our side have come to
recognize the common destiny of the Atlantic peoples without,
however, having achieved sufficient maturity to transcend our
national egoism, in other words, to work for the good of the whole
even within our national boundaries. We must interpret and carry
out our national responsibilities in a way that does not separate but
unites peoples in their political and social lives. That is the outstanding problem of our age; that is our gravest obligation.

We are aware of it when we recognize the claims made upon us
for development aid. We would not have needed the shock
administered by our balance-of-payments position to rouse our consciences. Four years ago I issued a warning and stressed the value
and importance of a German contribution, and indeed of a German sacrifice, in this direction. It is impossible here even to outline
the almost endless problems involved. But I would like to express
my satisfaction at the complete agreement that has been reached
between the departments concerned, and also my conviction that
what we are contributing in the way of development aid outside
our borders will also redound to our benefit inside them. Here
again figures cannot tell the full story. I am glad to see that the
German people itself has recognized the importance of this task.
We must know that the most valuable things in life are those with
the right motives.

It may be that some people suspect me of seeing only the
philanthropic side, so let me be a little more concrete for a
moment. What we can give naturally depends on what we can
produce. However misleading it may be to regard trade surpluses
and balance-of-payments surpluses as a measure of a country's
capacity to give aid, it is nevertheless understandable that Germany's favourable position in international payments should have

given rise to a request for increased German aid. Germany's exports have risen over the past ten years from 8 to 48 milliard marks, while our imports have increased from about 11 to 43 milliards. As a result of this almost incredible development, our gold and foreign currency reserves rose to over 32 milliard marks.

How our problems have changed! Whereas our position today as a creditor nation threatens to become almost a disturbing element in the world economy and we are anxious, in the interests of world solidarity, to strike a balance, the leading SPD spokesman on economic affairs maintained in 1951 that, as our balance-of-payments deficit had reached 475 million D-Marks, we would have to declare ourselves bankrupt. He predicted that if we continued with our liberal policy we would sink even deeper into the mire. So there you have the Opposition trying to teach sound economic policy.

In view of Germany's high productivity and competitive capacity, as reflected in the figures I quoted, the recent revaluation of our currency can never seriously reduce, much less endanger, our foreign trade. We fully realize the paramount importance of the Federal Republic's economic interdependence with the rest of the world and we must learn to think, economically as well as politically, not just in terms of our national responsibility and capacity but in terms of the world as a whole.

Our party has good reason to be proud of its achievements and of the work done by its members, and it is happy to think that it has led a defeated Germany back on to the right road. But salvaton on this scale can only have enduring effects if it produces gratitude and humility and the determination never again to worship false gods. The German people must know that the Christian Democratic Union will never permit a policy that re-opens the door to destructive forces. Our tragic past is a constant reminder! It is, of course, our duty, together with our friends and partners, to be strong in defence of our freedom and our very existence, but it is no contradiction to say, in the same breath, that we want to banish the worship of power from our land for ever.

We want to base our way of life on those values which enable us to live as God's creatures and as citizens of a free society. Anyone who believes that we can adopt any other standards in formulating our policy is paving the way for those very forces that proved our undoing once before.

Although the age of the class war is obviously behind us, we must not delude ourselves into believing that there are not still forces at work in our society—and not in Germany alone—which threaten our accepted values and our system. Workers and employers are no longer on opposing sides; we no longer have 'poor' versus 'rich', 'weak' versus 'strong', or 'hand' versus 'head', but there is a danger that a new form of feudalism might emerge which would not fit into the old 'right or left' formula but would cut clean across society. We are faced with claims which we are not supposed to discuss, or rejection of which by those responsible to the community as a whole is condemned as unwarranted interference or even as aggression. I would like to make it absolutely clear that the Christian Democratic and Christian Socialist Union is opposed to any form of new feudalism, wherever it may arise. Every individual and every group, whatever his or its beliefs, has the right to be heard, but within the parliamentary democratic system of our state only the constitutionally appointed bodies can decide.

Who are the people who oppose the system we want to set up? Are we ourselves the culprits through lack of consistency and perseverance in fulfilling the task our age and the situation of the German people have set us?

Because the word 'tough' has a special meaning for us in view of the tough times behind us, I prefer to say that we must be courageous enough to combat the spirit of disruption which wants to drag everything down, which is concerned not to give people inner peace and security but to keep them in a constant state of confusion and to exploit human anxiety for political ends. It is around this problem that our battle with the Opposition partly revolves. If they are adopting a more conciliatory tone today, it is because they have not the courage of their convictions, because they dare not issue a challenge for fear of the response it would arouse.

The SPD need have no fear; we have no intention of lapsing into the jargon they employed when they felt sure of victory and when their party leader said: 'The slogan "Social Market Economy" is nothing but a lie à la blood and soil. I ask the non-valeurs of the

CDU: how long do you propose to go on swindling us?' And a leading spokesman of the Opposition said after a local Government victory: 'When I see the CDU benches in the Bundestag, I always think: Ah, you poor devils, you are merely political corpses on leave.' I myself was faced with a challenge in an election campaign that almost brought tears to my eyes. 'You are no longer the great show-piece of the CDU,' I was told. 'Your day is past! Today you —that is me—with your economic policy are shooting into your own ranks'—that is you, my friends.

Then followed the Federal elections in 1953 and 1957, and we await with confidence the result of the 1961 election. The Social Democrats may talk as much as they like; it is we, the CDU/CSU, who have to give an account of ourselves to the German people, to the free world, and eventually to history.

We feel committed to a system in which the German people in the Federal Republic, allied with the free world, seeks friendship with all peoples and, by its conduct, strengthens the consciousness and power of the political, military and economic unity of the Atlantic Community.

Our aim is the reunification of our people in one German state in peace and freedom.

We recognize free Europe as one unit and are prepared to do all in our power to deepen and strengthen co-operation with the United States and all other countries in the free world.

I hope the German people will never forget that our freedom is indivisible. We want to develop the social system in the Federal Republic to the point where the finest qualities of our people can blossom in freedom and our cultural and spiritual life can flourish.

We want the German people to feel that it is a society of free men, in which there is no room left for class-struggle and envy. We must see to it that group interests are subordinated to the interest of the whole.

When the work of reconstruction is complete, we shall pursue our economic and social policy, our financial and monetary policy in a way that will best serve the dignity of man, the security of the family, the freedom of society and the stability of our state.

The social security of our country will continue to depend upon our economic growth. We are not afraid of trade cycles, but we must be sure that we have them under control. We want to awaken and strengthen in all strata of society the consciousness that ownership brings freedom but that ownership also implies saving. We want to ensure that every citizen can acquire property.

Above all we want work to be properly rewarded.

We shall do everything in our power, together with our friends, to improve economic and social conditions in the underdeveloped countries of Asia, Africa and Latin America to the point where these countries can continue to live in freedom, both internally and externally; we shall give them our help in co-operative partnership. We now see growing up in Germany a new generation which will realize more and more, not only that there are almost unlimited openings for them in their own country but also that the world at large offers them more opportunities than ever before. The attitude they adopt will play a crucial role in maintaining freedom in the world.

Modern technical progress must serve not merely to increase productivity but also to help the man at the work-bench to be something more than just a unit of manpower. It must contribute, with other means, to the humanization of labour. It is one of our great responsibilities to see that, even in a modern industrial society, the smaller and the medium-sized independent firms have enough security to work and prosper.

We want to fortify those who not only make demands of the state but are also prepared to give to the community. We want to encourage those to whom service and good-neighbourliness still mean something and who know the difference between 'earning' in terms of achievement and 'earning' in terms of the wage packet.

Let me say in conclusion that in our policy we must never forget what lies behind us and that our actions are rooted in Christian principles and customs: let the other party programmes promise what they may, we shall continue to let our actions speak for us.

So we embark with courage and confidence upon the 1961 Federal election campaign. Forward, friends! To work!

ʃ1

FREEDOM AND RESPONSIBILITY

(Address to the 9th Federal Congress of the Evang. Arbeitskreis
of the CDU in Hamburg on June 2, 1961)

*Ludwig Erhard speaks of the Christian's responsibility in the
economic world and of an economic system in which freedom and
responsibility can become realities. At the same time he replies to
those who, from a theological view-point, sometimes question the
validity of Germany's reconstruction. How does one set limits to
group influences, and what compass will point the right direction
to take in order to avoid harming the individual, the family and
the nation in a growing economy which brings increasing prosperity to the individual? But we must also be on the lookout for,
and exploit, the opportunities which a dynamically expanding
economy provides for strengthening the foundations of our society
and for the promotion of other than economic tasks in the field of
training and education. These are questions which, if correctly
answered, can have a more decisive influence on our future than
the solution of many a pressing day-to-day problem. Seen in this
light, modern German economic policy must be actively and simultaneously engaged in several fields: its primary task is in the economic field but it has also become an important instrument of social
policy.*

'Freedom and responsibility', as concepts, are open to different
interpretations. If it is the freedom I mean and you mean, the
freedom everyone understands, then it can almost amount to chaos,
to something so undisciplined that it cannot be fitted into any
system. In fact, however, we all tend to understand something
positive by the concept of freedom. Responsibility, on the other
hand, is not quite so simple. Many people regard it as an unwelcome adjunct of freedom, one which takes something away
from it. If an interpretation is adopted which implies that freedom

is promised but might be restricted for political, social and religious reasons, the way is not then immediately opened to arbitrary abuses —but where does one draw the line?

I could pursue the subject from a historical point of view. It would undoubtedly be easy to prove that, wherever nations failed to achieve the right balance between freedom and responsibility, disaster lay round the corner. Perhaps, too, in recent history a rather false note crept into our conception of freedom, in that one always spoke of 'freedom from . . .' as, for example, freedom from hunger, freedom from want, but never 'freedom for . . .'. But I believe that the real heart of the matter does in fact lie in the proposition 'freedom for something', for it appeals directly to the individual and highlights the commitments of good neighbour-liness, duty, human dignity and other high values.

When I speak of responsibility here, I mean not merely respon-sibility for the sort of specific action or decision that arises every day, but responsibility for our actions and attitudes in general, in other words, our responsibility to our conscience, our responsibility to God and to men.

So freedom must not degenerate into a form of idolatry without responsibility, without commitment and without roots. The re-lationship between freedom and responsibility implies a system of some kind. I would almost have preferred to talk about freedom and order, for to me responsibility belongs to the concept of order, a conventional concept of order, because it is only if freedom is limited by responsibility in an orderly system that we find the right Christian and socio-political basis for such values. There is no doubt that freedom by itself, without order, threatens to become chaos, just as order, if it is only an outer frame, a mere form, can degenerate all too easily into brute force. It is with and around these values, to which, of course, the concept of right also belongs, that we have to move.

Freedom is certainly a right! Freedom tastes sweet, while re-sponsibility has for many people a somewhat bitter after-taste. If one were to take a political illustration, perhaps from the Weimar and pre-Nazi period, then one might say that the tragedy of that period lay in the lack of courage to take responsibility and a mis-interpretation of the concept of freedom, not merely of personal but also of democratic freedom. One of the chief lessons we have learned from our whole history is that freedom cannot be divided at will. It is a mistake to think that one can retain one's own freedom while all around a sense of the value of freedom is lacking, whether it be in the nation at large or in the narrower or wider social spheres in which one lives. The individual may retain his sense of freedom before his own conscience, but his links with the world around him and with himself must snap if freedom is divided between what the individual feels in his heart and the concepts of order and institutions he sees around him.

Communism has already been mentioned at this meeting, and it is clear that the Christian is called upon to declare himself on the side of freedom, but a freedom that also appeals to our sense of responsibility and does not carry the seeds of chaos in itself. There is no evading this. It may be necessary to make compromises in everyday politics, but we cannot compromise with our own conscience.

I have frequently said jokingly in the German Federal Parliament: I know that I sometimes sin. But at least I know when I sin; I can answer for it to my conscience and that proves that my conscience is still awake. The man who knows what is right can also sin. But, from a socio-political view-point, we must pose the question where the borderline lies, in other words, how often and how far a society and a community can sin against the principle of freedom and responsibility without endangering the existence of the whole, of the community, the people and the nation.

Freedom has its price; it is not given to us. Where there is no real sense of duty, no sense of honesty, integrity or humanity, freedom will and must deteriorate. In relation to the developing countries—it has become quite the fashion to discuss them—this means: What kind of freedom will we help these nations to introduce? Is it to be merely freedom from hunger and want, or do we have another freedom in mind? I think the problems overlap here. Freedom from hunger and want is not the only one; we also have the task of guiding these countries through various stages of thought, knowledge and understanding of the world around them to the point where they can reflect seriously on forms of communion and co-operation amongst themselves and also with us. We know, of course, from our own experience, how closely the concept of freedom is bound up with the danger of its misuse. Wherever an attempt is made to extort freedom, freedom of decision and freedom of the will, by force, without regard to the freedom of one's neighbour, the very foundations of freedom are undermined.

And now let me say a few words about the problems of social economy. All forms of economic compulsion, even though they may sometimes be successful, are fundamentally immoral, because they destroy what is of supreme importance to us; living man and his conscience. I am always careful to avoid making such absolute statements because I would hate to appear self-righteous. We too are by no means averse to claiming more rights than duties, but at least one thing is certain, that we do not shirk the crucial socio-economic and political problem : How much freedom, how much responsibility, how much order are embodied in our social institutions? I do not propose to draw up a complete list, but if you follow the course of history from slavery to the corporate state, then feudalism, from there to capitalism and then to marxism and communism, you will realize that, when all is said and done, we have acquired a delicate sense of the inner value of these forms of society, and, if we look closer, the valences—positive and negative —always correspond to the relative proportions of freedom and responsibility.

And here a study of history yields a particularly valuable result. Of all these periods the Middle Ages was the one in which people were yoked to a hierarchical system based upon an ultimate, other-worldly value. In this society social inequalities and injustices were accepted, because other and higher values were predominant. They were not material nor were they even of this world. The concepts of right and freedom were not based on any standards of this world but implied a future beyond it, an after-life. Social forms of this kind cannot be constructed; it would be foolish and wrong to assume that we could ever resuscitate the heyday of the Middle Ages or that the principles underlying it could ever be binding upon us again. It is enough if we draw the moral from it, namely, that our life and all that we accomplish here cannot have absolute value.

BB

We must beware of those who prophesy that our life and, above all, our social and political life will be governed by certain natural laws against which we are completely powerless. As you know, Marx tried to demonstrate that we would pass through an apparently inevitable process of development, at the end of which the expropriators would be expropriated, the means of production socialized, and a classless society would emerge, which would bring eternal happiness.

This is not the place to go into the marxist doctrine in detail or expose its many errors. I would just like to emphasize one thing: the historical materialists believed that the things of this world must develop according to certain laws and that it was pointless to put up any resistance. Here one can draw a striking parallel with Mr Khrushchev, when he announces to the world with great conviction—subjectively speaking: 'Capitalism is dead', whatever it may or may not do. The evolution of history is such that communism is its ultimate end. Karl Marx, at least, employed rather more intellectual reasoning to try to prove his case. The marxist predictions of the evolution of the classless society have turned out quite differently from what socialism once prophesied. And the same will be true of Khrushchev's prophesies. I also speak, though in jest, of the 'classless society' we have achieved. What I mean is that bitter class-distinctions have disappeared from our society, because the various ways of life are becoming more and more alike, because everyone derives more or less the same degree of satisfaction from life, because our desires and our ideas are becoming more akin.

I would like to mention another example that has aroused some controversy in the last eighteen months: the process of concentration in industry. As you know, the 'Verein für Sozial-Politik' discussed this subject at its Congress in Kissingen. A famous scholar, who on many occasions has passed (mis)judgments on German conditions, said something like this: Do not go on opposing this concentration! It is all prescribed; it is part of a technical process that is irrevocable. We can only go along with it, but to oppose it is pointless. His attack is, of course, directed against the 'Ordo-liberals', of which I am one. They take the view that there is no economic process the nature and direction of which cannot be controlled by us. Where would we finish up if we no longer felt confident that we could consciously change our environment? There may be trends in this or that direction, but one cannot simply say that concentration of industry is inevitable and must lead to a dangerous change in the pattern of ownership. The number of employed, it is argued, will go on increasing and, however well they may live, however many of them acquire 'People's shares' and become part-owners of the national means of production, the process of concentration with all its social and political consequences will continue regardless. But that is exactly where I completely disagree. We can and shall direct the structural development of our economy in such a way that it has the same intrinsic values as our whole national policy. We are not against size as such. But we are determined that freedom should be matched by responsibility. For that reason we are pursuing a structural policy which will be reflected in an amendment to the Cartel Law.

This brings me to one of the crucial problems of our time. Who carries the real responsibility and who is responsible to whom? Naturally the Christian reply is: Let every man carry respon- sibility, and in fact each man is responsible to his conscience, his fellow-men and finally to God. But when I, for example, have the pleasure of holding discussions with representatives of various groups, I seldom feel that they are aware of this responsibility; on the contrary, I hear talk of nothing but a unilateral responsibility to the interests they are representing. In such cases, if the concept 'responsibility' is not turned upside-down, it is at least so devalued and falsified that one can only speak of rank misuse.

I have nothing to say against representing interests. This is entirely legitimate, but only up to a certain point. Officials, organi- zations and representatives of group interests must recognize that they have to fit into a whole and that you cannot balance the accounts if every man believes that he can ride roughshod over other people's feelings and interests and use such power as he has to take what he can get at any given moment.

I am all for competition, but I do not mean by this employing strong-arm methods to acquire for oneself and one's group what can only be obtained by force. This is the real purpose of our Cartel

Law, to see that any over-concentration of power is held in check and that competition is conducted within the bounds of human decency. What is one to think, for example, if, when a measure like the revaluation of our currency is introduced, the man who is freely elected by the people to carry the over-all responsibility is told that it does not really concern individual groups. Then we are half-way to anarchy. Yet the currency revaluation was something that concerned the whole German people. So there is cause for anxiety today when the concept of responsibility is given a very one-sided interpretation to satisfy certain group interests, whereas responsibility to the nation as a whole is not nearly so apparent.

Herr Blumenfeld is certainly right, and no one has said it more often than I have, when he points out that it would be a sad business if economic policy were to be regarded as merely the manipulation of a machine which enables the national economy more and more to increase productivity, in other words to keep raising the national income and with it personal incomes, to provide better and more varied material standards of living and pile up one consumer commodity on another. At the end of the day we would have to ask ourselves if that was really all? The question still needs to be asked, and I have the impression that many more people are asking it today than we imagine. I believe that today our workers and employees in particular, that is people who, as consumers, are still by no means fully satisfied, are asking this same question more and more often. They say to themselves: 'Now we've managed it again; we have a television set and we have a car too; that gives us social status'. After all, these are all outward signs of prosperity, but let us not forget that, as soon as one demand has been satisfied, the manufacturer is getting ready to produce something new to attract people. Are we to go on like this to the end of our days? Is it not a rather sad business? The man who asks that sort of question is right; I am of the same opinion.

In a modern society with a dynamically expanding economic policy a rise in income and an improvement in consumption are, so to speak, the by-products of labour. This is a process that cannot be prevented, unless a crisis breaks. So, if we continue to pursue a successful economic policy, we will be able to, and in fact must, improve the material living standards of the German people; for without growing production, and barring inflation, the national and personal incomes cannot increase. But, without this process, the means whereby the community can perform more responsible tasks are also lacking. It is a chain reaction from which no modern economy can escape. The one is bound up with the other. This does not indicate, however, what use we as individuals make of it, and whether we are interested only in material or also in intellectual, cultural and spiritual things. These too must be earned; they too cost money.

Here, in a sense, my hand is forced and tied at the same time. Unless we are prepared to gamble with Germany's position in world politics and our freedom, we must realize that the strengthening of our defences can only be achieved on a strictly material basis, by producing goods. There is always something aggressive, something destructive about naked power. If power is constantly met with power, then one day such a clash may plunge the world once more into disaster. I believe that power and strength are not the same. Power is directed outwards, strength is a personal quality, an inner preparedness, a determination to be prepared both spiritually and materially. Naked power cannot triumph over strength. Power alone pitted against power can all too easily lead to disaster.

There are already signs of a reconciliation within our society. If we increase prosperity and the individual can lead a better and better life, then sooner or later there will come a point of satiation. Then the law of diminishing returns begins to operate. Incentives become blunted and with each further effort the sense of satisfaction it brings, the inner contentment, becomes relatively smaller, till the point is reached where the wave breaks, where the expenditure of material resources, of human industry, of bodily and mental strength is no longer worth it. In this way we come nearer to the moment—not, of course, statistically predictable—at which the individual says to himself: 'This cannot be the real purpose of living.' And then we must be ready and in a position to give him an answer. Therein lies, in my view, our Christian duty.

We should have the courage to speak out. Is it not the case that many things have not turned out as we would have wished them to and as we could have reconciled with our conscience and our understanding, simply because we did not have the courage to speak out but chose instead to capitulate? Capitulation will never save the world or save humanity.

We must stand firm and we must have the courage of our convictions in the face of calumny. We must bear witness to life, as is our Christian duty.

Yes, that is our task.

52

ENGLAND IS PART OF EUROPE

(Speech at the opening of negotiations on Britain's entry into
the European Economic Community in the Salle des Horloges
of the Quai d'Orsay, Paris, on October 10, 1961)

*It had been a long road that led to the turning-point in the history
of European unity, when negotiations began with Britain on her
entry into the European Economic Community. Ludwig Erhard
had been trying for years by every means in his power to create a
greater Europe. When he made this speech he was President of
the Council of Ministers of the EEC. In welcoming this meeting
in the Salle des Horloges at the Quai d'Orsay, he felt a certain
degree of personal satisfaction:*

It is a great honour for me and gives me particular pleasure to
preside over this memorable session today. First, I would like to
thank you, my esteemed French colleague, Monsieur Couve de
Murville, very warmly for the friendly words of greeting which
you, as host, addressed to us. We are particularly grateful to you
for putting this illustrious place at our disposal for these discussions. Within these walls many decisions have been reached before
which pointed the way to a new system in Europe and in the free
world as a whole. And I think I can say in a spirit of realism that
we are entering today upon one of the most significant phases,
perhaps even a decisive one, of Europe's postwar history. It is a
source of particular pleasure to me and should be an encouragement to us all, that we are agreed upon the principles and
aims of our work, for such unity creates the sort of spiritual
atmosphere in which we will and must conduct the negotiations
before us.

We recognize that the years behind us, despite many disappoint-
ments and misunderstandings, were by no means wasted. Any one

of you, if he were in my place today, would express the same views and convictions, for we all welcome the courageous decision of the British Government to enter into negotiations for the entry of the United Kingdom into the Common Market. I also regard it as a happy coincidence, which at the same time should be a warning to us all, that the fresh start we are making, on the same spot where our first attempt to reach an understanding failed, should lead on this occasion to a sound and happy solution. What three years ago could be rated a failure would do serious damage to Europe today. I know that I speak not only for all present here but for all the peoples of the free world when I say that we must be fired by the determination to bring our negotiations to a happy conclusion, to a political triumph for free Europe. This is no mere formal assertion, for during the past few years we have made considerable progress along the road to unity and the acceptance of the bonds that are common to us all. So not only is there a greater realization of the need for closer co-operation but quite a number of misunderstandings which stood in the way of it have been removed. We are, therefore, not approaching the new task before us entirely unprepared.

We welcome the British step firstly for political reasons. The present world political situation calls more than ever before for a united Europe, for if we were in need of one final lesson, the events of this summer have taught us it. That all countries of free Europe—not all of which are represented here—should join together is a simple question of self-preservation. True, Europe has hardly ever achieved political unity in the past, but it has always been dominated by the idea of freedom, which has coloured its whole history from its ancient and Christian beginnings up to the present time. It is in this same spirit that we are defending the cause of the entire free world by working for European integration, for our aim is not merely to serve our national or regional interests. We are also conscious of our links with the Atlantic community of free peoples. But how could such a Europe come into being and endure without the full and active participation of Great Britain? That every economic consideration speaks in favour of such a union seems to me hardly worth mentioning, much less underlining.

I beg you, however, not to interpret this statement as a mere personal observation, for I also speak here with the full support of all present member countries of the EEC. The EEC made known—not only in the preamble but also in an article of the Treaty itself—its intention to work towards the harmonious development of world trade, the gradual removal of restrictions in international commerce and the lowering of customs barriers. The resolution I am referring to—it is Article 110 of the EEC Treaty—is the guiding principle for the negotiations we are about to begin. But, apart from the political and economic aspects, I would like to emphasize the cultural ties that bind our countries together and the need for collaboration in this field, for education, research and art are more than just beautiful gifts. The wealth, morality and dignity of Europe rest on its common civilization, the defence of which is more urgent today than ever before. But this is unthinkable without the participation of a country like Great Britain, to whom Europe owes so much in all spheres of national and personal life. The fact that we can record this measure of agreement in our political, economic and cultural aims gives us the necessary basis, and should be a guarantee, for the success of our common efforts. I do not deny, of course, that there are considerable obstacles to be overcome, but we shall remove them in the consciousness of our common bonds and of the needs and interests of our countries in all vital questions.

Let me say again in conclusion how happy I am I have been privileged, by the grace of the standing orders, to preside over our meeting today, and let me also express my profound personal satisfaction that we are about to make this new, decisive and, I hope, propitious beginning.

53

BERLIN AND OURSELVES

(Speech at the opening of the 12th German Industrial Exhibition
in Berlin on October 14, 1961)

*The attack on the freedom of Berlin and its lines of communica-
tion with the free part of Germany awakened a new spirit of
resistance, not merely in Western Germany. In the world at large
Berlin became a symbol of the determination to resist force. But
before August 13 the Berlin situation had already subjected the
solidarity of the Western Powers, and indeed of the entire non-
Communist world, to a tremendous test. The German people's
refusal to abandon Berlin had resulted over a period of years in
growing material aid. For the economy of the Federal Republic
the decision to do everything possible for Berlin was not solely
based on economic considerations. As early as 1950—and every
year since—the great Berlin Industrial Exhibition was started. It
became traditional for the Federal Minister of Economics to open
it each year on the Funkturm exhibition ground. In his speech in
1961 he dealt with the consequences, as he saw them, of the events
of August 13.*

I officiated at the baptism of the first German Industrial Exhibition. I have come to the 12th German Industrial Exhibition in
Berlin, so to speak, as godparent. I must confess that, while my
confidence is unshaken, I am filled with a sort of melancholy at
the thought that during this whole period we have not made any
progress, that, after twelve years, we are still not in a position to
give Berlin and its people a final guarantee of a secure life. Perhaps
in the years to come we shall have to adopt a somewhat different
approach to these exhibitions, for, as has been pointed out today,
one purpose of the Industrial Exhibition, which is to show some
300,000 visitors from the East Zone each year what a free and
dignified human life means, can no longer be fulfilled. I agree

entirely with your Governing Mayor that, quite apart from the self-evident duty to give the people of Berlin economic and social security, the German economy, and in particular German industry, must do everything it can to strengthen the faith of the population in their city. The Federal Government will also play its part. But we must also give more attention to the idea of Berlin as a 'cultural centre'. When I think of the overcrowded German high schools, of the universities in which there are barely enough seats for the students and in which regular tutorial work has become impossible, then I cannot help feeling that, if we here together create the necessary facilities, we could help to bring out the character of Berlin in yet another way. If we employ all the means at our disposal to offer students from all parts of the free world a course of studies here, of genuine, practical studies with teachers whose relationship with the students is a personal one, then these young people will see the tragic reality of life in Berlin, and that, I believe, will be valuable in itself. For this wall through the heart of Berlin is designed not to prevent West Berliners from crossing over there but, on the contrary, to imprison our brothers and sisters on the other side and so make it impossible for them to see that there is another and a free world. They must not be allowed to breathe the air of freedom or see the light of freedom.

One can say with justification, that the co-operative effort of the West finds perhaps its most visible expression in Berlin and, in fact, that the Berlin situation has done much to confirm and strengthen the solidarity of the Western free world. There is no doubt that the blockade of 1948 not only captured the attention of the whole world but profoundly alarmed people everywhere. And it is surely no coincidence, although the sequence of cause and effect cannot be definitely proven, that the increased speed at which NATO, the Western defence alliance, was set up was not entirely divorced from such considerations.

I am putting historical data side by side here without trying to prove that there is any immediate cause and effect. And yet I believe in such motive forces. One thing at least Berlin did for the free world out of the sufferings and anxieties the people of this city have endured. It has become a beacon of freedom and has remained so to the present day. No other point in the world has illustrated so visibly what is really at stake, what the moral and spiritual, economic, political and social conflict of our times really amounts to on a world level. This is visibly demonstrated here in Berlin and finds its symbolic expression in the Freedom Bell. For that reason I am particularly happy to meet my esteemed friend of many years' standing, General Lucius D. Clay, again here, for in that crucial period when Germany's future was at stake and her present was still indeterminate, when, in fact, we could not even guess what the future had in store for us, he championed our cause and helped to save this city.

The acts of inhumanity that are perpetrated on this shameless border before our very eyes are undoubtedly designed to intimidate and demoralize people, to undermine and destroy order. But I put the question: Have they not achieved the opposite effect? Have they not exposed the defects and weakness of this inhuman system before the entire world? If you have nothing to conceal, you have no need to lock yourself away and make yourself invisible —but we know, without drawing on our imagination, what inner strains and stresses this system has to cope with.

The world cannot be ruled by force and no human system of government can be maintained indefinitely by compulsion. This may offer little consolation to those who think only in terms of the immediate present, but, if we look at the position from a historical view-point, we are justified in feeling confident that our combined efforts can save this world of ours. And above all I would like to say yet again, although it needs no emphasizing, that the Federal Republic together with its Western friends will defend Berlin to the last and is prepared to make any sacrifice, however great, for Berlin.

The latest events in Berlin since August 13 have undoubtedly helped to shatter any illusions that may still have persisted in the Western world. The Russians are squeezing the last dregs of peace-dreams and gullibility out of people and make it abundantly clear that only if one goes into negotiations with them backed by strength and firmness of purpose can one hope to hold one's ground. It is perhaps not altogether appropriate at this moment of tension to point out that, in terms of the philosophy of history, the power-policy of the totalitarian states is the force that strives after evil but eventually, and in spite of itself, leads to good results. For it is certain—and here I come back to what I said at the beginning—that the unity of the Western world in every imaginable and practical form ranging from social, economic and political activities to questions of security and freedom would not have been so firmly based or so purposeful, if we did not know what is at stake and what we have to defend. The will to supranational co-operation has also been clearly outlined by the previous speaker, President Berg. I believe this deserves to be hailed as a new phenomenon of our time.

When I think back to previous crises, like the one in the thirties, which were not essentially political yet shook the world to its foundations, and compare them with the present economic situation in Germany and in Berlin, then it seems clear to me what a profound transformation has taken place. If what has happened today had happened 30 years ago, we would have had an endless succession of black Fridays. Admittedly, even today our economic and social life is shaken but its foundations remain undisturbed. I think it is worth considering why this should be so, for the spiritual and intellectual structure of our lives has not changed so drastically in the past 30 years. It seems clear, then, that our environment must have undergone some major change. And when I think of the crises of the thirties this is obviously true; my generation had first-hand experience of it.

What did we do at the time? It was thought that the cure for a ruined economy lay in national isolationism, in reverting to protectionist restrictions and in looking after one's own immediate interests. But this was exactly the opposite of what was really needed. Today we are experiencing violent political shocks which would undoubtedly also have a tragic effect on our economic and social life if in the meantime we had not acquired greater insight and taken the opposite road. We have broken free from narrow national boundaries and entered into a close association with other national economies in order to work out a joint future. Perhaps you can realize how much satisfaction I in particular derive from this, having so often been accused of being a bad European because I have never believed that the European Economic Community is a sort of philosopher's stone or the ultimate solution, although I have always supported it as a major step forward towards wider communities. Now suddenly new factors are emerging from European integration, and I am certain that the clock can no longer be turned back. The start of discussions with Great Britain last week and other negotiations due to begin with Denmark—Ireland has also expressed a wish for talks and other European countries are about to reach decisions—are milestones on the road that will lead from what is today free Europe to a spiritual, economic and social unity and, eventually, to a common political will. Here we really see the motive force, of which I spoke earlier, at work. Herein lies the irony, that precisely those who set out to destroy Europe and to whom freedom is anathema, have provided the stimulus needed to remove the last remaining barriers and inhibitions. In other words, they have been instrumental in persuading the individual nations and countries to lay the ghosts of their own history, to forget their differences and concentrate on what they have in common.

I have no doubt that the political will to master the problems of our time will enable us to clear many hurdles which we were unable to surmount during past years by purely technical discussions. I am even convinced that the behaviour of the Russians and the events here on the border in Berlin have also made an impact on the developing countries. They will come to realize what it could mean to be caught in the embrace of the tentacles of this barren power. Then they will recognize that it would also be fatal to them. But this awakens once again in us the confidence that brute force has no intrinsic value, with which one can win over people. Force can only be used to oppress, but oppression generates a counter-force and this we can feel in Berlin. At the risk of being over-bold, I would even say that I believe—here one can perhaps not speak of countries but only of people—there are people within the Soviet bloc itself to whom Berlin still represents a gateway of hope and faith, even if the gate has been barred! So visible has this wretched business become that it has become an issue of humanity, appealing to the deepest longing that is in us. We will not and shall not be forced to our knees. We know what we have to defend, we know what is at stake. We are grateful to the people of all nations and to the governments for having identified themselves with our aims. We ourselves are under an obligation to make every possible effort to consult them, just as they have accepted the obligation to stand by us and act in concert with us. Serious discussion must now take precedence over mere fantasies and conjectures which can only lead to misunderstandings.

It may sometimes sound as if we Germans are too self-important, as if we are demanding that the rest of the world should concern itself only with German questions. That is not the case. But it is nevertheless a fact that our present and our future have become a focal point of interest for the entire world. And when we speak here of freedom, when we urge that the ideals of the free world must be preserved, the 'German' element is not intended to be the dominant one. We would think and act in exactly the same way if the fate of any other free country were in jeopardy, and I think the world public will become increasingly aware that it is not we who will not leave the world in peace, who are constantly thrusting our own interests forward. No, it is not like that! We are simply destined to be a target of aggression, of totalitarian power-politics. And that being so, as this conflict is being fought out on German soil, as Berlin has become a channel and symbol of this great East-West conflict, we are fully entitled, and with a clear conscience, to testify to it. In this connection I would like to say to my fellow-citizens again that, at a time when everything is at stake, when we must be prepared to defend our future, our lives, our freedom, I am sometimes filled with shame when I hear demands for higher wages, more consumer goods, more leisure and less work. As if these were things one could even mention at present without blushing!

I do not propose to discuss this in detail, but I would like to say one thing. We can only hope to succeed in our stand and our common fight for freedom if we are able to maintain economic and social stability in our country. This is not just a task for the 'social partners'; in our day the maintenance of economic and social stability is a prerequisite for the most vital political decisions. The more we realize this and act accordingly, the more certain we can be of carrying our nation through present dangers and finding the permanent way of life our German people is seeking. We shall live and work together with our friends in peace and freedom, in so far as this is possible, and we will not be afraid of the forces that threaten us. When Western co-operation has become so close that the community acquires shape and substance, then even two divided worlds can coexist without danger. During the past few days I glanced through the historical atlas from my schooldays. How the map of the world has changed in the last thousand years! Nothing seems to be built for eternity. Perhaps we should react to many developments a bit more coolly and with more self-possession and not assume that complete solutions can be found to every kind of problem in one fell swoop, with one negotiation or in one brief discussion. This will not be the case; moreover such illusions are dangerous. But amongst the crucial questions of the moment, on which our stand is clear, unmistakable and unshakeable, are the freedom of Berlin and its indissoluble links with the Federal Republic.

I hope that the 1961 Berlin International Exhibition, even in these changed circumstances, may nevertheless prove an auspicious occasion and may confirm the people of Berlin in the knowledge that we belong and stand together. The ultimate purpose of any human labour must surely be to add to human welfare, but human labour must also strive to fulfil those communal duties which earn us our place as a people and a nation in the community of nations. With this in mind I declare the 12th German Industrial Exhibition in Berlin open.

54

HAVE WE LEARNED ANYTHING FROM RECENT HISTORY?

(Article in *Die Zeit* of December 15, 1961)

Ludwig Erhard is constantly grappling with this question. Is there such a thing as an order of precedence within the various sectors of policy as a whole? What purpose is served by political and economic successes? Of what value are the great military defence efforts if people have no faith in their future? The realization that our system, based on freedom and responsibility, is superior and the will to make it stronger and more complete imply an awareness of the past and an obligation towards the future.

If naked power and brutal force of arms appear to decide the fate of humanity today and if foreign policy merely aims to avert the horror of war, then we must ask ourselves if we have not omitted something or taken a false turning that has confronted us with such a dangerous alternative. Are we not to blame if the totalitarian forces and powers, which have trampled human dignity underfoot and exalted force both at home and abroad to an absolute principle of politics, also forced us, the free world of the West, to submit to the same law?

The Soviet rulers, right up to Khrushchev, have realized with diabolical consistency that the moral values of a liberal-democratic system require free nations to use the human and material forces of production for the peaceful purposes of social welfare. The totalitarian world, on the other hand, can set all human considerations to one side and employ a much greater proportion of their potential energy to strengthen and even deify the state. No one can deny that this inhuman, brutal philosophy compels us to make corresponding defence efforts if we are not to be faced with that final alternative—war or peace.

CC 393

One thing disturbs me about this whole situation, namely, that while we employ opposite symbols, we follow or become caught up in the same lines of thought, instead of breaking out of the magic ring and going over to the attack at a point where the East is vulnerable. For the principle of individualism as accepted in the West only appears to be inferior to the dynamic will and expansive power of the totalitarian states; we do, after all, know that there are also internal tensions and conflicts in the Eastern camp.

Despite the far-reaching political and social effects of these ideological conflicts, they have made little or no impression on the foreign policy of the Western world. It admits that the freedom-loving peoples are shamefully exploited in monstrous Ten or Twelve Year Plans and gives no answer to the forcefully-presented communist thesis, that socialism is destined by force of history to replace capitalism. The citizens of the free world hear this challenge, but their governments do not make it clear to them that the spectre of capitalist society, which the Soviets denounce, has long since passed into history, and, in fact, that the historical reality of the free world has already provided a satisfactory answer to totalitarian socialism.

Our present-day social system with its liberal communal and social structure is clearly superior, not only in its potential and its economic efficiency but also in its inner strength, to the barren and sterile mechanism of the communist system. Why do we not say so every day? Why do we not bring such decisive political facts to bear on world-wide disputes? Why have we not learned to make the most of our resources?

This is not an indictment but an expression of concern that the foreign policy of the Western countries has not yet registered these vital facts. In this connection, we politicians of the Old World must take hope from a figure and personality such as President Kennedy, who is completely dedicated to the ideals of the free world but is also sufficiently unorthodox to spice its foreign political principles and maxims with new ideas and values, for it is high time we realized that policy is the expression of an all-embracing combined effort by the community as a whole and that there can be no such thing as 'policy per se'.

We need a form of Western integration that does not merely

express itself in isolated and adjoining fields, amounting to little more than a continuation of conventional national policy with improved international co-operation. What we really need is the integration of our various concepts of political, economic and social life as a basis for our liberal Western way of life.

In a speech I made at the rededication of the old synagogue in Worms I tried to explain how much direct practical importance and influence such a global view can have :

'The nations have awakened and are taking up new positions in order to reorganize their lives. Strong forces throughout the world are pressing more and more for the abolition of non-democratic and collectivist forms of government. The so-called realist may regard such ideas as wishful thinking, but more dangerous than having the courage to look ahead and think ahead is refusing to recognize forces and movements which are in a position to mould the world of tomorrow. In my view a timely appreciation of political, economic and social processes, a correct assessment of them and their incorporation in the lives of communities is an essential prerequisite of well-regulated individual conduct. Anyone who is incapable of such appreciation, who lives merely from one day to the next, runs the risk of losing himself and everything else. The same is true of nations.

'How differently the tragic fourth and fifth decades of our century would have turned out, how the destinies of nations would have been changed, if, around 1930, we had realized something of those latent forces—and, at the same time, of the indissoluble links between politics, economy and society ! The fact that such knowledge and imagination was absent from our mental world enabled criminal elements to let loose an inferno of terror.'

Does this not also apply to the present day? Have we really learned all the lessons and drawn all the morals we need from history to prevent another and possibly even more terrible calamity? Have we yet realized that, when one considers the means which are necessary to keep the peace, in spite of continuous political tension, the arsenal and machinery of conservative foreign policy inherited from another, I might almost say defunct, world of national states with its balance of powers and spheres of influence are no longer adequate as tools or weapons?

cc*

Foreign policy, we are told every day, should be our destiny. I would agree if the entire destiny of a people is meant, a destiny that embraces all spheres and is moulded into one coherent whole. But I strongly disagree with the view that would lead us to believe that a foreign policy, divorced from all forms of popular activity and personal life, could by itself have value and purpose and eventually be successful.

55

FRESH OPENINGS FOR EUROPEAN AND ATLANTIC CO-OPERATION

(Speech at the Commercial College, St Gallen, on January 15, 1962)

Early in 1962 Ludwig Erhard visited the United States. He discussed questions of European and Atlantic policy and of development aid with the American President. One of the principle subjects dealt with in his talks with John F. Kennedy and members of the American Government was United States plans for a new trade policy which aim to stimulate world trade and closer economic co-operation amongst the countries of the Atlantic Group by applying the principle of mutual tariff reductions. The Federal Minister of Economics had already put forward proposals of this kind some time before. Speaking to a gathering of leading personalities from American industry in New York, he recommended that the American President's new plans should be supported. A few days later, when he received an Honorary Doctorate at the St Gallen Commercial College, he returned to the same theme.

I have been asked to talk about European integration, Atlantic co-operation and an Atlantic Community. I am aware that these concepts can be variously interpreted. Let me say at once that I am not thinking primarily of institutional or constitutional forms but of the substance of the matter, namely, the question how we can best organize co-operation in order to achieve maximum efficiency in the political, economic, social and personal spheres. Naturally quite a number of different forms and methods could be adopted; I shall deal with them in this address. But one thing at least has become clear—whether we regret it or welcome it—European integration is a development that will have a decisive influence on our future. We must realize—quite apart from any personal assess-

397

ment, whether positive or negative—that this process of growing integration—growing even beyond the bounds of Europe—is a historical reality, a fact which we must all come to terms with. And it should not be forgotten—it is, indeed, to be welcomed—that the threat to the free world, in whatever forms or places it manifested itself, has clearly led to a consolidation and a greater awareness of the free world. The power that worked for evil has done good.

As you know, various suggestions have been made in recent times as to how a stronger sense of European, and lately of Atlantic, solidarity might enable us to accomplish what is necessary for our protection and betterment. If I ask whether only great and powerful states can be expected to overcome the threat that hangs over us all, then the latest development in the Atlantic area might be taken to mean that we should concentrate rather more on finding the right way for us to follow together. We have been discussing European integration and its problems for some considerable time past. We made a successful attempt to organize a common defence, and, while I include this on the list of technical questions, I recognize that vital political considerations were also involved. We tried it in purely practical terms, in organizational and institutional forms, but I do not think that we covered the 'whole', that we solved the really essential problems on which the future of us all depends.

I would like to draw one conclusion, to begin with, from what I have been saying. It seems to me that the time is past when nations and still more perhaps their governments can cling to the illusion that human existence can be split up into spheres of activity which are merely linked together for convenience, as if here exclusively questions of defence were involved and there questions of foreign policy or economic progress, social security or welfare, or anything else one can think of. I believe these categories are dead and gone!

The more we feel threatened from outside, the more we realize that our lives—and with them our policies—are an indivisible whole. The destinies of peoples cannot be divided and sub-divided, and the tasks confronting us every day can only be properly understood in the widest context and can only be performed with this understanding. It is my firm conviction that we have reached a turning-point which forces us to work out a new mental approach. This applies just as much to the scientific sphere as to our daily lives and to political life; in fact, it applies to everything around us that goes to make up our daily routine. This awakens in us a new vitality. We become conscious of the eternal values of the past, seeing them with new eyes, and we feel the urge to produce something new. Politics no longer seems a metier for specialists or for those who are called to it by chance. We see in politics today an all-embracing purpose that concerns everyone, that determines our future and that directly affects all spheres of life, all expressions of life, all thinking and feeling. We have indeed entered a new era, and it is now our far from simple responsibility to make this new present and future happy.

After these preliminary remarks I come now to Europe! I have spoken on this subject on many occasions and even incurred the suspicion of being a 'bad European' because I was not satisfied with the simple answer that Europe is what understanding between the nations permits her to be at any given moment. That Europe, seen in this way, cannot be regarded today as a mere geographical entity hardly needs mentioning. So what is Europe? When we consider whence we come and what binds us together at this present moment, we understand by Europe a spiritual and moral entity.

But, if this is so, then we must ask where the frontiers of this Europe lie. They cannot be mere political boundaries that emerge almost accidentally from the events of the day. So there is something almost sinister in the idea that it could and should be possible, within what we today call free Europe, for the member states to split up into two groups. Here we have the problem of EEC and EFTA, which we have been discussing for so long. You know that I have frequently been misunderstood when I declared, despite opposition both in my own country and in the countries of the Six, that it seemed to me impossible, in view of the obligations of free Europe as a whole and of the common danger, for the continent to divide. One cannot argue on the basis that the life of these European nations in its various spheres must be regulated by certain organizations or institutions in varying degrees. One must be prepared and do everything possible to bridge the differences. I do not propose to outline the history of the formation of the EEC or the EFTA; we are all familiar with it. We can all derive pleasure from the fact that the idea of an unshakable and indissoluble unity has sunk its roots deeper and deeper. It is—if I may be allowed to repeat myself—impossible to call upon the free peoples of Europe to stand together to the last in defence of their lives and to agree in questions of policy on joint action and common reactions, yet at the same time to assume that everything concerned with their economic, social and personal existence, which affects almost everyone every day, should be separated or even divided up. This is a conception that I have always resisted and fought against. We should feel happy that we have survived this interregnum, this critical period for Europe, or at least we should have reason to hope that a happy outcome is possible.

I feel certain that treatises will be written one day which attempt to explain what idea, what occurrences, what intellectual stimuli were responsible for the sudden lowering of barriers and greater freedom of thought. In particular, investigation should be made into the reason why Great Britain decided to open negotiations with the object of entering the EEC, and why the neutral countries, Sweden, Switzerland and Austria, about which I will say more later, have proposed negotiations for associate membership. What has been happening? Some believe that the undertow produced by the progress of EEC has become so strong that European countries on the fringe cannot help joining it, although the exponents of this view are not always champions of a greater Europe. I am one of many who are convinced that most of the credit belongs to those who insisted that the door should be left ajar. This view is based on the realization that the European Economic Community is not a panacea but a step towards a European, or, as we can now say, an Atlantic solution. But let everyone claim the credit for himself; perhaps there is a grain of truth in all the various view-points. The essential thing is that the development of Europe is moving forward. For that reason I am unreservedly in favour of European integration, which means an expansion of Europe. For the same reason I said 'Yes' to the EEC, because I realized that a grouping of this kind would mark the beginning of a forward movement that could not be halted, and that any beginning which is likely to free us Germans and other nations as well from the nationalist clichés of the past must be welcomed and supported. But not the least of the reasons for my attitude is the experience that we are being presented today not with one but with a variety of forms of integration.

As you know, I have just returned from the United States where I had long discussions with the American President himself and his leading advisers. It was clear from these discussions that the idea of Atlantic collaboration is gaining ground and becoming more and more concrete. At least the Atlantic idea has given birth to a conscious will, although the United States have stated distinctly that their world-political commitments will not enable them to relinquish any of their sovereign rights. These world-wide commitments make it impossible for the United States to abandon the most-favoured-nation principle. She is, therefore, not prepared to join a preferential system, but she would be ready to do everything in her power, by adopting a policy of extreme liberalization—the word 'extreme' is mine—to try to undo any harm that might result from a system of preferences. I believe that the American attitude could help towards a solution of many still unresolved problems in Europe. In any case it is clear that the United States of America attaches the greatest importance, and, in fact, regards it as one of the prerequisites of a new trade policy, to Britain's joining the Common Market. That will mark a new phase in Europe's progress and it will certainly not be the last. If, as is to be expected, Britain, Denmark and perhaps Norway enter the Common Market as full members and the three neutral states become associate members, a strong force will be created in Europe.

This greater Europe, loosely linked with the rest of the world, will be free from any suspicion that it is a prisoner of its own past, that the grouping together of some countries will lead to discrimination against the other free countries of Europe and to invidious comparison with them. I am profoundly convinced that, the wider the area, the more likely we are to get rid of tension, which in a confined space has so much more effect and is so much more noticeable. It has been said of the European Economic Community that its foundation was a really great achievement, an act of liberation. It provided, we are told, the historical and political proof that France and Germany were no longer 'hereditary enemies', in that both nations had come together in mutual trust and friendship. Every sensible person, particularly in Germany, naturally welcomes this reconciliation with all his heart. Today it is so much a fact of life that any alternative suggestion would be dismissed with a shake of the head. This shows how the world-political situation has changed. But, without wishing in any way to disparage the important part played by the EEC, I would like to say that such a one-sided interpretation cannot be the whole truth. Otherwise one would be equally justified in asking—and the question has been posed often enough—whether Great Britain is perhaps still the great 'divider' of Europe. This is another 19th-century ghost which must be laid. We are really doing a disservice to the cause of European understanding if we do not get all our weights and measures right. And we are still thinking in past clichés if we can find no better values and no clearer ideas for the future than those that are still being invoked as relatively simple explanations of much that is happening.

I put it to you—what is it that is drawing us closer together? Is it perhaps the task, the by no means unimportant task, of defending our way of life, our freedom and our security, or is it the realization that we must go forward together if we are to build a united political front that will be proof against the constant threats by the totalitarian world? Is it perhaps merely an expedient move to join forces economically in the interests of maximum efficiency? Is it technical progress that forces us, perhaps even against our wills, to transcend our narrow state boundaries, because they have outlived their economic and military usefulness? No, I believe that all of this still does not provide the full explanation. The pure politician may shake his head at this. I, however, am convinced that what we need is a fusion of the intellectual, spiritual and moral forces of the free world, because our main task in Europe is to turn it into a living and conscious force. Europe, it is true, has become a force in the world as a result of progressive integration in the economic field alone, and when I was in the United States I had the distinct feeling that people there look upon us today through quite different eyes. We are no longer the so-called junior partner, in whom one takes a kindly interest, but, and this will be even more the case if Britain joins EEC and we can work out further positive forms of co-operation, we have become a genuine and fully-fledged partner. All credit is due to the United States for making no reservations. They know too well that precisely this development seems best designed to unite the various forces of the free world and make them a dynamic element in the shaping of policy. I would like to believe that the United States is even destined to play the leading role in this mental and moral reformation. Not that anyone would suggest a system based on superiors and subordinates, but there is still too much diversity, too little shape in Europe for any European country to assume the role that naturally falls to America as a world power. The United States has the historical task and also the responsibility of gathering together the forces of the free world and herself setting an example.

It is my conviction that the United States—and I am thinking in particular of the American President—has drawn the right conclusions from the historical premises, in other words, has learned especially from the more recent political developments that we are all required to take action. I also felt that people in America were increasingly concerned about the direction in which Europe might develop if bridges were not built between the continents. The same concern was also felt here. But all this was only feasible if bridges could be built inside Europe.

America's new trade policy—that is, its reorientation—is an extremely bold one. It means no more and no less than a request by the American President to Congress for powers to reduce tariffs by up to 50%. Naturally he expects us in Europe to respond accordingly. If 90% of the free world's trade is between the North American and the European continents, then a sudden trend towards liberalization should sweep aside many of the barriers and inhibitions that still exist between individual states. One thing is certain: if this vision, which is backed by a strong political will, were to become reality, the shadow of the preferential system, which in my view is outdated, would become appreciably shorter and less dark. But the powers the American President has asked for go still further. He is prepared to abolish altogether customs tariffs on specific commodities in which the trade between the two continents amounts to 80% or more. This is almost too good to be true! If the countries of the free world were capable of such an approach and acted accordingly one might almost feel inclined to regard preferential systems as designed to do evil—the satisfaction of selfish interests—but destined, nevertheless, to do good—the abolition of protectionism.

The trade policy of the United States has become unmistakably dynamic. The question we are asking ourselves in Europe is how high one can rate our chances of success. I cannot, of course, answer this question; I would not have the presumption to try to work out the pros and cons in percentages. But I have the impression that in Washington, in government circles, there is a general feeling of optimism. On the other hand it is only natural that in business circles, as is usually the case in other countries, the mood is one of caution. But it is my experience that there are times when the businessman's hand must be forced for his own good. If we go on discriminating against one another by means of preferential systems and setting up quotas and other restrictions, then we shall never achieve the ideal of a world-wide, world-free trade. The decisive and the right step undoubtedly lies in the direction of comprehensive and consistent liberalization.

Now, if I apply what I have just said to the European Economic Community, the position is as follows: if the 'European Economic Community' were a state with a constitution of its own or at least the visible signs of one, then no one could object to the policy of the EEC, for it is taken for granted, that in two states different conditions prevail, both internally and externally. But the European Economic Community is only in the process of acquiring a political identity and what form it will eventually take is something no one can yet tell you with complete certainty. Even if one considers what the various groups in the member countries envisage as the eventual political constitution of the European Economic Community, one finds a very wide divergence of opinions. I say this without wishing to criticize or pass judgment, but merely to try to get to the heart of the matter, which I am obliged to do here today, for so many variations are possible, from the loosest form of international institutions to a federation or, beyond that, to a tightly-knit federal state. No clear picture has emerged as yet. The situation may change one day. But what, for example, about association with the African territories, which are certainly not prepared to become members of a European bloc? This means the emergence of a new preferential system. That is why I believe that the transition period, that is, the next six or eight years, when all kinds of difficulties must arise, will be perhaps the most difficult.

We already know from experience that, regardless of continents, individual countries are coming to us and explaining why and how they feel that the European Economic Community is discriminating against them. We shall be constantly handing out sops and making amends. For this reason we should aim to keep on expanding the framework of the EEC and at the same time to achieve a greater degree of formal clarity inside the organization. This will lead to much less friction in the development of our relations with other continents, by which I mean, for example, Latin America or South-East Asia.

In the negotiations between the European Economic Community and Sweden, Switzerland and Austria on the same issue of associate membership the question will inevitably be asked by our neutral friends, what commitments are involved. They will probably point out that the Treaty gives no indication and that no one so far has been able to give a final definition of what, in fact, the concrete political implications are.

I do not wish to be misunderstood. Naturally the European Economic Community has political implications. There is no doubt about this. A movement that aims to merge spheres of human activity on a supranational plane cannot fail to have a political effect. But, precisely because of this, the states, like any ordinary citizen when he signs a contract, will want to know what they are signing and what obligations they are entering into. One cannot just evade this prosaic question, and the finest rhetoric and the boldest political visions do not help. Every country in free Europe and outside it is interested in getting an answer as soon as possible. I also have the impression that the responsible political circles in Europe are fully aware of it, so I hope that the answer will be such as to lead, through the associate-membership negotia-

406 *The Economics of Success*

tions, to the closest possible bonds between the neutral countries
and the European Economic Community.

This Europe of ours has a character of its own. I have just come
from the United States; I feel at home there and the outlook of the
American people is very close to mine. I sense a kinship of spirit,
and yet there is no denying that, in the final analysis, the
Americans cannot understand us and we must accept this fact.
There are, of course, differences between Texas and California and
Virginia, but they are not so deeply rooted in their history and in
the evolution of the American people as is the case in Europe. We
are burdened with a thousand years of history and with a countless
variety of pronounced characteristics that play a significant part in
our daily lives. And so we are afflicted, burdened or blessed with
very special sets of values.

When I think of the neutral countries—as you know, I have
always sympathized with their problems—then the political status
of these small countries presents a European problem of the first
importance. For that reason I broached this subject in the United
States, because, unless it is more fully understood than at present—
something for which the Americans are not to blame—it will
remain unsolved.

The Belgian Foreign Minister, Henri Spaak, is certainly wrong,
however, when he says that neutrality is a barrier to co-operation.
Perhaps he did not put it quite so strongly, but it certainly sounded
very negative. Association is, as you know, amongst the provisions
of the Rome Treaty, although Article 238 does not lay down in
detail what form it should take, what conditions it involves and,
therefore, to what extent it can become effective. It is not the 'if'
but the 'how' that remains open. It has been a source of particular
satisfaction to me in the six months in which I had the honour to
be President of the Council of Ministers of the European Economic
Community—without my having earned it, I may add—that Great
Britain and Denmark applied for membership and the neutral
countries applied for associate membership. In my personal view,
we, that is, both the three neutral countries and the present members of the Community with, I hope, the full understanding of
the United States, must do everything in our power to make the
economic bonds as close as possible. It has been said that those

who are not prepared to accept the full political obligations cannot expect to enjoy all the economic advantages. We are not making a trade deal here between specific spheres. To me the 'evolution' of Europe seems much too important for us to think in materialistic terms of profit and loss. We know from our European history that the neutrality of Switzerland plays an important part in Europe's affairs. We need only remember the world-wide symbol of the Red Cross! No, to be neutral is neither a crime nor something to be ashamed of and cannot therefore be penalized. Quite another question, and one that neither you nor I can answer today, is whether, at a future stage in the development of free Europe, when its destiny is more clearly predictable, the time might not come for these questions to be carefully re-examined.

So the question whether the neutral states, despite close economic links with the EEC, can lead their own lives indefinitely outside it, is not at all an easy one to answer. I for one would not venture to give an answer. But I am all the more convinced of the importance of liberalizing our policy and uniting the intellectual and spiritual resources of our nations to enable us to overcome many hardships and to clarify people's minds. It is undeniable that a sound economic development presupposes stable political conditions, but it is no less certain that political strength cannot endure indefinitely without a sound economic position and that, in consequence, any attempt to separate them cannot be reconciled with the responsibilities and trends of our time. The modern and yet old-fashioned approach to 'Politics and Economics' can no longer be dealt with in terms of 'either . . . or' but at best on the 'both . . . and' principle. To recognize the indivisible is, in my view, essential if we are to do justice to our day and age, which, as I said at the beginning, can no longer be thought of in watertight compartments.

If I speak of power and strength in the political sphere and refer to them as political values, I interpret this in the widest sense. Political power and political strength can also have its roots in human reactions and in the human soul itself. It must not always be interpreted as 'power-politics'. Power and strength have their roots in inner firmness and are the expression of a conscious conviction. Your Excellency was right in describing my attitude to this question as an expression of my being. I know all too well that our world, constantly threatened as it is, has particular need of a consciousness of power and strength in the most real sense. But I do not want it to be confused with the negative idea of power, which, in my opinion, is always barren, dangerous, brutal and, in the last resort, even stupid. It is not for nothing that this kind of power is always associated with the danger of its abuse. In our German Cartel Law, for example, there are several passages on the abuse of economic power.

Much more menacing, of course, as we know to our cost, is the abuse of political and military power. And at this very moment we are experiencing once again how power and force attempt to create fear. How can we possibly meet this threat, if the only remedy we can think of is to pit force against force. The outcome would probably be extremely dangerous. I believe, on the other hand, that a consciousness of strength and positive power, which must naturally have a solid basis of reality, is most likely to defeat naked power.

In this connection I would like to draw your attention to something rather remarkable. The challenge that is issued to us, the free world, daily consists not merely of a threat of war; no, it also comprises an attack on our liberal system of society, in other words, on our freedom as such. With unparalleled cynicism we are told that the free economy has outlived its time. We are branded as tired old men, who are practically incapable of whipping up any spiritual vitality! But what, in fact, is the so-called capitalism of today? If we look back to its beginnings and compare them with the present, only then do we fully realize how much malicious dogmatism there is behind the slanderous charges made against us. We all know that present-day capitalism has nothing in common with its early manifestations. So it is particularly tragic that we continue to employ the same outward symbols and are satisfied with rational explanations, almost if as we were justifying ourselves. We listen to statements that 'capitalism' is a system of exploitation but say nothing or, if we do speak out, cannot muster the necessary powers of persuasion! We talk of freedom, but we must be clear in our own minds that to many nations, to many millions of people, freedom does not mean the same as it does to you and me. The word 'democracy' also has quite a different meaning for the undernourished peoples of the world from the meaning we give to a democratic system. If we persist in meeting the Soviet challenge by referring to 'our' freedom and 'our' democracy, then I fear it will not be enough.

It has been my experience in many countries and continents that these coins are well worn, and that is why I said on another occasion: I am firmly convinced that we must evolve a new type of ideology, or philosophy if you like. I would almost go so far as to say that it should be an article of faith which brings home to us and others the all-embracing values of our free world and makes us believe in them. Us, above all! For I have the impression so often that, like rabbits mesmerized by a snake, we can no longer find our own answer to the challenge. The good is worth something, and —as I have said before—it is also a good thing for people to have enough. But satiety as an attitude of mind could be the downfall of the free peoples. I do not believe that it is enough to meet the Soviet challenge with statistics showing how many cars, refrigerators, televisions sets etc. are produced by us. The challenge must be taken up on the mental and spiritual plane. It is from there that we must draw our strength, the strength above all to feel secure within ourselves. We must come to realize that we are on safe ground and that, as the community of free peoples—I am not thinking now of forms of integration—we can wield great power. Not only power of arms in our defence, however important that may be, not only economic power and technical achievement, not only the power of greater prosperity and social security, but the power one derives from knowing that our values must be defended, must not be allowed to go under, if this world is to be worth living in.

The Marshall Plan was of vital importance to the nations that lay prostrate, not so much for the material and financial aid it provided but for the moral strength it gave us, and with it the certain knowledge that we had not been abandoned by the rest of the world. The morals, the ethics, in other words the solidarity, of the free peoples was the spark that, in my view, set Europe free. And now, on a wider plane, America may be called upon again to help us Europeans to make good mistakes we have made and disentangle ourselves from awkward dilemmas. To help us with a generous, liberal policy or, far beyond that, by awakening a new vitality, a new faith and confidence, which will lead us eventually to join forces in a greater, common whole. When I think that the sort of bold vision which the American President sees before him might tomorrow become our reality, then I also know that there are many who hold back and say that this is too much at one time and one must move forward more cautiously. As you know, I am not one for caution; I take the view that one must strike out boldly if one wants to achieve anything really decisive. In my varied experience as Minister of Economics I have learned that, for example, it is very much easier politically to reduce all trade and industrial tariffs by 45%—in a two-stage operation—than it is to reduce tariffs on five commodities by 5%. That is the way things are. Yet this is encouraging, for it means that one can appeal to nations and people on big things. One must not bother them too much with trivialities and with the minor everyday details. I would be glad if the example of Germany's reconstruction were to give the hesitant more courage. At one time we had an antiquated and worn-out technical apparatus and were hardly able to compete, and yet we opened up our frontiers. The currency reform of 1948 involved us in the most severe sacrifices. As I have just said, we carried through a two-fold reduction of German tariffs by altogether 45%, unilaterally and without asking for anything in return; in the past year, as you know, we have revalued our currency, again unilaterally, in order to subject German industry to the strong pressure of competition and stimulate it to use its resources and increase its output to the maximum. If, in so doing, we also perform an act of international solidarity, so much the better. At all events, I think we have no reason to feel weary as we look ahead; on the contrary, we must be alert, because we know what is at stake.

Any association with the Common Market will tend to intensify the competitive situation in the countries concerned. But is that really a drawback or a bad thing? We can only move forward if we measure our strength against that of others and if we stimulate each other to hold our own in the world. After all, we are not in the position of a communist-totalitarian state, which is at liberty to deal with its economic and social problems as it thinks fit. We cannot say, now only armaments matter or power production or any other specific sector of the economy. We must carry out all tasks at the same time, from defence and other political responsibilities to increased productive power and finally to social security and the preservation of peace and freedom as the supreme objective of our policy. The same is true of the new system in Europe. In the lives of free nations you cannot suddenly switch targets as you think fit. But if policy embraces all walks of life, then, in order to succeed, it must have the entire resources of the nation at its disposal. If one considers Europe's efforts to integrate—perhaps we will talk of the Atlantic Community earlier than we think today—not merely from the technical point of view but as a historical process based upon human volition, then those who are open-minded and alert know that we are entering a new era.

Now let me summarize. What use can we make and what can we learn from all that we are experiencing from the tasks and obligations ahead of us? If we regard the last war as a turning-point in recent history, we also realize that it was only the beginning, for it was the solidarity of the free world that saved Europe from collapse. Without this spiritual and moral perception, Europe would have gone under—including even Switzerland, which was spared the worst of the tragedy. In fact, but for this development there would have been no European Economic Community. But without the European Economic Community no bridge to an Atlantic Economic Community could be built, and but for its swift and strong recovery the free world could not have mustered the material strength to defend its own life.

We can only go forward. There is no development backwards. To recognize the signs of the times means to realize that, just as our development progresses from the past up to the present, so the morrow will confront us once again with new forms of life and new tasks. What we do today will determine what we become tomorrow. Belonging as we do to a peace-loving, free world, we shall man our defences if called upon to safeguard freedom, the rights of man and peace. But we should go over to the attack wherever our spiritual heritage is threatened, wherever it is necessary to oppose the barrenness of communist-collectivist totalitarian ideas with the dynamic force of our world values and to press these values home. I have the greatest respect for school books but we need something more than book learning here. For these are not problems to be discussed as part of a curriculum but a continuous, conscious experience that calls for equally conscious action. I feel most profoundly that we are called upon either to endure the future or to concentrate all our energies on moulding it. We must set against the spiritual sterility of totalitarianism the dynamic power of our way of life with its traditional values, its religion, its ethics and its justice. It is imperative that we stand together. We are on trial and may God help us to emerge from it at peace with ourselves and with history.